Greenhill Books

# GO TO YOUR GOD
# LIKE A SOLDIER

# GO TO YOUR GOD LIKE A SOLDIER

## The British Soldier Fighting for Empire, 1837–1902

## IAN KNIGHT

*When you're wounded and left on Afghanistan's plains,*
*An' the women come out to cut up what remains,*
*Jest roll to your rifle an' blow out your brains,*
*An' go to your Gawd like a soldier.*

From 'The Young British Soldier' by Rudyard Kipling

Greenhill Books, London
Stackpole Books, Pennsylvania

Greenhill Books

*Dedicated to the memory of Sergeant 1313 Thomas Cooper, 1/24th Regiment, who went to his God like a soldier, and lies somewhere beneath the whispering grass at the foot of mount Isandlwana*

First published 1996 by
Greenhill Books, Lionel Leventhal Ltd,
Park House, 1 Russell Gardens, London
NW11 9NN
and
Stackpole Books, 5067 Ritter Road,
Mechanicsburg, PA 17055, USA

*British Library Cataloguing in Publication
Data*
Knight, Ian, 1956–
Go to your God like a soldier: the British
soldier fighting for empire, 1837–1902
1. Great Britain. Army – History, 19th
century – 19th century
2. Great Britain – History, Military –
19th century
3. Great Britain – Colonies – Defences
I. Title
355.3'52'0941
ISBN 1-85367-237-8

*Library of Congress Cataloging in
Publication Data*
Knight, Ian, 1956–
Go to your God like a soldier : the British
soldier fighting for empire, 1837–1902 /
by Ian Knight
264p. 27cm.
Includes bibliographical references and
index
ISBN 1-85367-237-8
1. Great Britain – History, Military –
19th century
2. Great Britain. Colonies – History –
19th century
3. Great Britain – History – Victoria,
1837–1901
I. Title
DA68.K585   1996
355'.033541–dc20

Edited by Ian Heath.

Produced by DAG Publications Ltd.
Designed by David Gibbons.
Layout by Anthony A. Evans.

Printed and bound in Great Britain by
The Bath Press, Avon.

*Overleaf: 'All that was left of them': a typically dramatic Caton Woodville painting of the last stand of the 17th Lancers at Modderfontein, South Africa, September 1901. (National Army Museum)*

# CONTENTS

# INTRODUCTION AND ACKNOWLEDGEMENTS

For sixty years, the greater part of the nineteenth century, the British Empire dominated the world. The extent of its possessions was enormous; it controlled territory in every continent in the world, and in India alone it was directly or indirectly responsible for the administration of 400 million people, whilst its economic and political power shaped events far beyond its immediate control. Such an empire could never, of course, have been won and held without at least the tacit support of the people over whom it held sway, and the fabric of empire was further tied together by a complex web of visionaries, administrators, traders, bureaucrats and missionaries, men and women of very different backgrounds, and often of different motives, who nonetheless drove the Empire forward and held it together. Yet the advent of Empire was seldom welcomed with open arms, and in the forefront of all of them, often quite literally, yet usually unappreciated, misused and despised, was the British soldier. Born in an industrial slum or, for much of the time, in an impoverished Irish village, he was always there at the sharp end, required to stand his ground, often in a bright red coat and absurd head-dress, in the sweltering heat of the Indian plains or the claustrophobic damp green half-light of the West African rain forest, keeping an exotic and terrifying array of enemies at bay with inadequate weapons which he probably scarcely knew how to use.

And stand his ground he so often did, doggedly, brutally, sometimes with rather too much liquor in his veins, accepting the often idiotic commands of an officer class which was as alien to him as his enemy, putting up with floggings, bad food, poor water, and as often as not dying, not even in the excitement of battle, but of any one of a hundred half-understood and unspeakably foul diseases. It was expected that he could be relied upon to go where he was sent and do what he was told, and at the end receive precious little thanks from an ungrateful nation at large who thought him nothing but a drunken reprobate, beyond redemption. Yet without the British soldier, above all, the Empire could never have grown as it did, nor ever hoped to be secure, for ultimately all the efforts of the administrators, traders and, so often, even the missionary, rested on his lash-scarred shoulders. The faults of the British army during the Victorian era are obvious enough. It was undoubtedly conservative – as most armies probably are – class-ridden, and slow to recognise flaws which seem glaringly obvious with hindsight. It is easy to look at the list of famous defeats and disasters – Chillianwallah, Balaclava, Isandlwana, Maiwand, Majuba, Spioenkop – and see traces of an ingrained stupidity, of an almost stubborn inability to learn from past mistakes and adapt to changing times. Certainly, there are stupid men in all walks of life; perhaps in an institution affected by patronage in the way that the Victorian army was, they achieve greater prominence than they might elsewhere. Nevertheless, whoever said that whilst other professions can find ways to live with their mistakes, the soldier's are laid out in gory detail for all the world to see, had a point. The Victorian army was perhaps hide-bound, slow to change, and prone to making mistakes on a grand scale; yet it was clearly not just these things, because in the final analysis, it was extremely successful. It was required to fight in an extraordinary variety of difficult environments, against foes with widely different military traditions about whom it usually knew nothing when conflict began. Yet it's experience over the Victorian period was unparalleled, far greater than any other army in the world at that time. For all its errors, for all its Isandlwanas and Spioenkops, the Victorian army had an almost unbroken record of losing the odd battle, but winning the war. Indeed, only one campaign – the 1881 Transvaal War – can be said to have been a total failure, a succession of battles, each one a defeat, ending in a peace which abandoned British political considerations.

My original intention was to write a book for the general reader which sought to explain how a conservative organisation like the British army rose to the challenge of colonial campaigning. It soon became obvious that it was not possible to divorce colonial campaigning from conventional warfare, since the Crimean War, in particular, had a profound impact on the development of the army thereafter. Nor was it possible to look at individual battles or campaigns in isolation, without something of their political context, or without something of the way of life of the individual soldier who took part in them. What prompted men to enlist in the army of 1837, which from today's viewpoint seems a distinctly unattractive institution? What did they do with their time, what did they eat, were they trained to fight, and if so what was the tactical theory of the time?

What did they think about their job and the cause they fought for, and what was life on campaign, and the terrible crucible of battle itself, like for them? Many works of far greater scholarship than this one have looked in detail at aspects of these questions, but it seemed to me there was much to be learned by putting the answers side by side, to form something of a whole. Of course, to tackle every aspect of Victorian military experience of life in detail would require many volumes, so it has been necessary to adopt some arbitrary parameters; I have concerned myself throughout with the experience of the full-time professional regular British soldier; I have not considered the role of the East India Company – although its contribution to the conquest and retention of India is glaringly obvious – nor of the militia and volunteer formations, nor even the colonial or auxiliary forces, which played such a prominent part in the battles I've described. For the same reason, a number of minor campaigns, which involved only small numbers of regular troops (for example the Mashona Rebellion in Rhodesia/Zimbabwe in 1896-7), have not been described.

I should also say that throughout this book I have tried to use modern spellings for the names of places where battles and incidents have occurred. This is partly for the sake of consistency with modern maps, and partly out of a personal preference to see names spelt according to modern orthographic conventions, rather than – as they so often were – spelt phonetically by outsiders who had little understanding of their meaning. This is common enough in the Chinese context – Beijing for Peking, and so on – but I hope readers will forgive me using Satlej rather than Sutlej, Spioenkop rather than Spion Kop, Mafikeng rather than Mafeking, Asante rather than Ashanti – and so on. I hope I will be forgiven, too, any occasions where through error I have fallen short of my own pretensions in this regard. For similar reasons, I have referred to the series of campaigns against the Xhosa people of southern Africa by

their modern name, the Cape Frontier Wars, rather than the name by which they have been known until recently in Britain – the Kaffir Wars. It may surprise some British readers, for whom the term kaffir has no connotations beyond the obvious (an old term for the Xhosa), that the word is extremely offensive in the South African context.

My interest in the Victorian soldier has grown out of a deeper interest in the British military involvement in southern Africa, particularly the Anglo-Zulu War, which has preoccupied me for more than twenty years. It is difficult to pick apart the strands of obligation, since I've learned much about the British soldier from those who have taught me about the Zulu War; I have thanked many individuals by name elsewhere, and won't embarrass them again this time – they know who they are. For this project, however, I must single out for thanks Lieutenant-Colonel Ian Bennett, who has been unfailingly generous with advice and information, and has given me many invaluable insights into military life. My thanks are due, too, to Michael Barthorp, whose correspondence over the years has been quite invaluable, and upon whose work in the field of Victorian military dress in the field I have relied heavily in my résumé of the same. I have benefited, too, from more than twenty years' association with the Victorian Military Society, though it would be impossible to mention all the individuals who have helped me or influenced me. Colonel Peter Walton, Vice-President of the VMS, was most generous with his advice, and allowed me access to the collections of the National Army Museum's Ogilby Trust. On a personal level, my thanks are due to my Zulu War colleague Ian Castle, for his suggestions and advice; to Keith Reeves, who has allowed me free access to his library and his lifetime's knowledge as a collector of militaria; and to Rai England, for his magnificent collection of Victorian newspapers. Without access to Bryan Maggs' quite extraordinary photographic collection, this book could not have been illustrated, and certainly not with so many unusual images. Mr Bill Kirkby allowed me access to the letters of his forebear, Donald MacDonald of the 21st, which struck me as typical of the experience of many ordinary Victorian soldiers. I have been in touch with many regimental museums whilst writing this book, and all have been unfailingly helpful; it seems invidious to single out any in particular, but the Royal Engineers Museum in Chatham, the School of Infantry Weapons Collection, and the Royal Archive at Windsor merit special thanks. In South Africa, Graham Dominy of the Natal Museum has always been most helpful in searching out material in regional conflicts, as have the staff of the Killie Campbell Library in Durban. Finally, this book could not have been written without the patience and understanding of my wife Carolyn, who has learned rather more of the adventures and eccentricities of the Victorian soldier than perhaps she might have liked, and will, no doubt, be relieved to see him continue his march, over the hills and far away.

# PRINCIPAL BRITISH CAMPAIGNS, 1837–1902

| | |
|---|---|
| 1836–8 | First Carlist War (Spain). |
| 1837–8 | Canadian Rebellion. |
| 1838–42 | First Afghan War. |
| 1839–40 | Campaign in Aden. |
| 1839–42 | First China War. |
| 1840–1 | Syrian Expedition. |
| 1842 | Occupation of Port Natal (South Africa). |
| 1843 | Conquest of Sind (India). |
| 1843 | Gwalior Campaign (India). |
| 1843–5 | First Sikh War (India). |
| 1845–7 | First Maori War (New Zealand). |
| 1845 | Expedition against Voortrekkers (South Africa) |
| 1848 | Expedition against Voortrekkers (South Africa). |
| 1846–7 | Seventh Cape Frontier War ('War of the Axe' – South Africa). |
| 1848–9 | Second Sikh War (India). |
| 1850–3 | Eighth Cape Frontier War (including BaSotholand campaign, 1851–2; South Africa). |
| 1851–3 | Second Burma War. |
| 1854–6 | Crimean War. |
| 1856–7 | Persian War (Iran). |
| 1857–9 | Indian Mutiny. |
| 1857–60 | Second China War. |
| 1858 | Sittana expedition (North West Frontier). |
| 1860–1 | Second Maori War (New Zealand). |
| 1861 | Sikkim expedition (India). |
| 1863–4 | Ambela and Shabkadr expeditions (North-West Frontier). |
| 1863–6 | Third Maori War (New Zealand). |
| 1864 | Japan expedition. |
| 1865–6 | Bhutan expedition (India). |
| 1865–6 | Aden expedition. |
| 1866 | Fenian Raids (Canada). |
| 1867–8 | Abyssinian War. |
| 1867–8 | Black Mountain expedition (North-West Frontier). |
| 1870 | Red River expedition (Canada). |
| 1873–4 | Asante expedition (West Africa). |

| | |
|---|---|
| 1875–6 | Perak expedition (Malaya). |
| 1877–8 | Jowakhi expedition (North-West Frontier). |
| 1877–8 | Ninth Cape Frontier War/First Sekhukhune expedition (South Africa). |
| 1878–80 | Second Afghan War. |
| 1879 | Zulu War. |
| 1879 | Second Sekhukhune expedition. |
| 1881 | Transvaal War ('First Boer War' – South Africa). |
| 1882 | Egyptian War. |
| 1884 | Bechuanaland expedition. |
| 1884–5 | Sudan campaign (Gordon Relief Expedition, Suakin campaign, defence of Egyptian frontier). |
| 1885–9 | Third Burma War. |
| 1888 | Suakin operations (Sudan). |
| 1888 | Sikkim expedition (India). |
| 1888 | Hazara and Black Mountain expeditions (North-West Frontier). |
| 1888 | Dinuzulu rebellion, Zululand (South Africa). |
| 1889–90 | Chin-Looshai expedition (India). |
| 1889–92 | Burmese expeditions. |
| 1891 | Samara and Hazara expeditions (North-West Frontier). |
| 1891 | Manipur expedition (India). |
| 1893 | Kachin hills expedition (India). |
| 1893 | Ndebele (Matabele) War (Zimbabwe). |
| 1895 | Chitral campaign (North-West Frontier). |
| 1896 | Asante expedition (West Africa). |
| 1896–7 | Ndebele/Mashona revolt (Zimbabwe). |
| 1896–8 | Reconquest of the Sudan. |
| 1897–8 | Pathan revolt (North-West Frontier). |
| 1899–1902 | Second Boer War (South Africa). |
| 1900 | Boxer rebellion/Third China War. |

# 1
## 'THINK OF YOUR DUTY'
## The British Army, 1837–1902

'My Dear Brother,
　　　　Ship Street Barracks, Dublin, 1st
　　　　　　　　Septr. 1878

'In case you may think that something has happened to me I write this to inform you that I enlisted in the above Regiment on the 3rd of July last in Dublin. I took steamer from Greenock on the Saturday and listed in Dublin on the Monday following.

I may say that I like the soldiering life very well, and I feel my health much more improved since I joined them. I can assure you that I feel very much ashamed in writing to you, but there was always an inward thought struck me that I should do so. I wish you to let my poor mother

know about it privately and I would like it to be private and not to let anyone know about it except our own family.

The Captain and the Colour Sergeant of my Company has taken great interest in me and I hope that whenever I am dismissed drill that I shall get to be Corporal and gradually getting up by degrees afterwards.

I do not wish to write you too fully at present as I am afraid you shall never write when you hear what I have done, but I can tell you that I am much more happier now than I think I have ever been. It is a very strict life and you must think of your duty when you are on duty. In cases of exceeding drunkenness you are Confined to Cells, or what we

*The march of Empire; an unidentified infantry battalion (the black belts suggest Rifles) in India in the 1890s. (Bryan Maggs)*

call in Civilian life imprisonment. I may say however, that I have not been guilty of anything of the kind, and hope never to be so.

My Dear Brother you might write me a note, or even send me a weekly paper, it would always service you in my memory. If you write I shall give you full particulars of barrack life. As regards leaving Campbell's shop I may inform you that most of them fellows working there had a great inclination to drink at nights and I was of course always in their [company], for which reason I thought it better to get out of the place altogether.'

My dear love to Hannah and all the children, No. 1636 Pte. Donald MacDonald, 2/21st Royal Scots Fusiliers.

It is possible to argue that, when Private MacDonald wrote this apologetic letter home to his brother in 1878, the well-being of the British public owed a good deal to the efforts of men like him. Britain, at that time, was undoubtedly the greatest military and economic power in the world; large blocks of the map, across all five continents, were painted Imperial red. The Empire had been framed by lines of trade which had fed the process of industrialisation at home, and financed the growing prosperity of the middle classes. Red was, perhaps, an appropriate colour, and not merely because it was associated with the military prowess of the red-coat – very little of the Empire had, after all, been acquired by purely peaceful means. The soil of Britain's overseas territories was figuratively stained with the blood of both the original inhabitants who had died defending them, and of the ordinary British soldier who was always in 'at the sharp end' of expansionism. There was, the Zulu King Cetshwayo kaMpande noted after he had failed to prevent British incursion into his territory in 1879, a distinct pattern of Colonial penetration: 'first comes the trader', he recalled, 'then the missionary: then the red soldier'.

Yet, for all this, the British public held its army in no great esteem for

most of the nineteenth century. Private MacDonald realised it: 'I am afraid', he wrote, 'you will not write to me when you hear what I have done'. Although in his case that fear was unfounded – his brother replied to his letter, and we shall hear more of Private MacDonald's adventures later on – it was true that the civilian population regarded army life with contempt. The army traditionally drew its rank and file from the very lowest levels of society, the unskilled labouring classes, for whom long periods of unemployment, without any form of social welfare to alleviate the horrors of penury, were a fact of life. For such men the future offered little but the prospect of physical exhaustion, the workhouse, and a premature death. Nevertheless, even in such circumstances 'going for a soldier' was considered a disgrace on a par with being sent to gaol. Private MacDonald's careful – if not entirely convincing – reassurance that his colleagues in civilian life had been worse drunkards than his comrades in the ranks suggests one of the reasons why; it was popularly held, in the Duke of Wellington's memorable phrase, that the army was 'composed of the scum of the earth ... fellows who have enlisted for drink – that is the plain fact.'

## Wellington's Legacy
The Iron Duke himself, of course, had done nothing to dispel this image. Despite the fact that his years of active campaigning had ended with Napoleon's defeat at Waterloo in June 1815, Wellington bestrode the British military scene like the proverbial colossus for the next forty years. His achievements in his day had been quite stunning, and in their immediate aftermath his experience made his opinions unassailable. By nature stern, traditionalist and conservative, he became if anything more reactionary in his old age, at a time when his personal influence was greater than ever. By turn Prime Minister and Commander-in-Chief – a post which he held during the Victorian era, from 1842 to 1852 – he was the establishment personified, the grand old man of

military affairs, who stated quite baldly that he was against any reform of the army on the grounds that a system which had worked well in the past would do so again, and should not be interfered with. As a result the British army still found itself waging war in a Napoleonic fashion more than half a century after Bonaparte's defeat. It was not until after Wellington's death, and the highly publicised shambles in the Crimea, that any real process of reform began, and even then haphazardly and at a stumbling pace, always two steps forward and one back.

It was partly because of this stunted growth at the beginning of her reign that the changes in Queen Victoria's time were, in the end, so spectacular. In 1837, when the young Queen came to the throne, the army was still recognisably the same institution which had defeated Napoleon. It was entirely dominated by the Duke, and by a clique of officers who had served under him in the Peninsula or at Waterloo. They trusted to their reputations to see off the challenge of new ideas, and until the middle of the century they were faced only with minor campaigns which did not unduly test them. Weapons, uniforms and tactical theory were all based on those that had smashed Boney: foot-soldiers still wore red coats, and were trained to fight in dense formations – column, line or square – blasting away at the enemy with muskets that made a great deal of smoke and noise, but were scarcely accurate beyond a hundred yards' range. Yet by the time the Queen Empress died in January 1901 they had been replaced by a recognisably modern army, which fought in drab khaki uniforms, using breech-loading magazine rifles, quick-firing artillery and machine guns, and employing open fire-and-movement tactics. Indeed, in 1901 the army was heavily engaged against an enemy whose tactics Mao Tse-tung and the great military theorists of the twentieth century would instantly recognise: the Boer farmers of South Africa were a guerrilla army, masters of the hit-and-run tactic, flexible, independent groups who 'swam like fish in the sea' of civilian complicity, and who were ultimately only defeated by the destruction of that civilian support base in an all-too-modern programme of forced removals. That such profound changes occurred within the reign of a single monarch is surely unique.

The extent of this change was dictated by the army's almost continuous campaign experience, which was predominantly colonial in nature. Between 1837 and 1901 the army fought no war in Europe, and only one war in a recognisably European style – and that was waged not on the continent, against the French, but in the Russian Crimea, with France as an ally. Indeed, in the aftermath of Napoleon's defeat, Britain felt confident enough to stand aloof from European affairs for decades. Successive governments dismissed the idea of any direct intervention in Europe's troubles, and despite occasional invasion scares, military conflict with a European power was never a real possibility. Had it been, the Navy, rather than the Army, was widely regarded as the first line of defence; Britain was, after all, an island, and her undeniable strength as a maritime power did more than just protect the highways of Empire. Nor, in any case, were any European powers in a position to mount a threat to Britain's position world-wide, at least until France began to broaden its own imperial horizons late in the century, and a freshly united Germany began to yearn for its 'place in the sun'. Yet the Pax Britannica and 'the Long Peace', were only relevant concepts within a European context, for the British army was almost constantly at war during Queen Victoria's reign, and the nature of this fighting deeply affected its understanding of its own role. The British army did not exist in a vacuum, and theorists were aware of the implications of events in the wider world; to some extent both the American Civil War (1861–5) and the Franco-Prussian War of 1870 were scrutinised for appropriate military lessons by the more imaginative of the British military establishment. Yet in practical terms, the experience of the army in the field was very different from these large-scale, industrialised conflicts, being shaped instead by a constant round of small-scale colonial campaigning.

The British army had been deployed in small parcels across the Empire since the Seven Years War (1756–63). The long succession of European wars, the various manifestations of a lasting imperial rivalry with France, had ended by the time Victoria came to the throne, and had left Britain with a jumble of overseas possessions which had grown almost by chance. In the late eighteenth century Britain had defeated France in North America, only to lose much of her territory there to her own colonists, though she still held Canada – despite the resentment of much of the French-speaking population. Through the agency of the government-licensed East India Company Britain had, by 1837, extended her influence over much of the Indian sub-continent. Small trading enclaves on the west coast of Africa, which had once flourished exporting slaves to the Caribbean, had left a residue of British responsibilities, even though slavery had been abandoned in 1833. The very tip of Africa, the Cape of Good Hope, had been seized from the Dutch in 1806, to prevent the French from threatening the long sea-route to India. The administration of many of these possessions was a pragmatic business, which the home government acknowledged was often best left to men of resource and initiative on the spot. As a result, it was not always possible to control colonial affairs too closely, since a wilful, aggressive, or ambitious local representative had plenty of leeway to pursue his own agenda. In volatile frontier situations the arrival of the British had inevitably upset the local balance of power, and the boundaries of British influence often crept forward, driven by local imperatives, and without any broader international strategy. Such adventurism was common in the 1840s and 1850s, and this gulf between government policy and local realities could still be exploited well into the second half of the century, as Sir Henry Bartle Frere, the High Commissioner at the Cape, demonstrated when forcing a confrontation with the Zulus in 1879.

Under conditions like these, the British army found itself fighting a kaleidoscope of different peoples, each with their own military traditions and practises, and in a variety of hostile environments. Tommy Atkins was required to battle mixed-race rebels in the Canadian winter; the Asante (Ashanti) in the rain-forests of West Africa; Boers, Xhosa, Zulus and BaSotho in the veld of southern Africa; Mahdists in the Sudan; Egyptians; rebellious sepoys in India, Afghans on the North-West Frontier; Burmese, Chinese and Maoris; not to mention the Russian Bear himself. For an institution which might be characterised as fundamentally conservative and unimaginative, this encouraged a remarkable degree of flexibility. British troops were almost always fighting on enemy soil, in a country about which they knew little, and which was usually marked by extremes of terrain and climate which were decidedly unfamiliar. The army usually had to seek out its enemy – who were of course entirely at ease in their own territory – before they could give battle, and reaching the enemy was therefore often a feat in itself. To sustain themselves in the field, the troops had to take with them all their equipment, tents and supplies, and they became adept at finding inventive solutions to problems of transport and supply. When confrontations did at last take place, the tactics necessary to defeat one group were seldom appropriate to another. The extended firing lines used to good effect in the Ninth Cape Frontier War (1877–8) proved disastrous against the Zulus in 1879, whilst the skills needed to overcome the Maoris' sophisticated earthwork defences were very different from those required to face down Mahdist shock-charges in the Sudan. Indeed, the British experience across the

*Left: Symbols of British might in a far-off land; artillery parked at the foot of Burmese statues, Second Burma War, 1853. (National Army Museum)*

*Right: The Victorian army as an aid to the civil power at home: the 45th Regiment suppressing 'Mad Thom's' insurrection, Bossenden Wood, Kent, 31 May 1838. (National Army Museum)*

period suggested that, if anything, lessons learned in one campaign were almost never appropriate in the next, and campaigning tended to follow a predictable pattern. The British would begin a campaign with too few men and knowing little of its enemy's strengths, and, in pursuing inappropriate tactics, would invariably suffer an initial defeat A painful period of readjustment then followed, which allowed them to maximise their greatest assets – their superior weapon technology and discipline – and bring about a final victory.

If this experience produced a readiness to improvise on a small scale, it nonetheless presented wider problems. The Victorian era encouraged the army to think of campaigning in terms of short, sharp expeditions, waged with the minimum necessary troops. Insufficient attention was therefore paid to the possibility of mounting a major war, with the wholesale mobilisation of men and supporting services which that entailed. There was almost no attempt to create the integrated network of trained Staff officers needed to ensure that a large army, controlled by a number of senior officers, could function together smoothly and efficiently. The short-

comings of this approach were woefully exposed in the Crimean campaign, but despite the obvious lessons – and the willingness of a number of influential officers to listen to them – the situation had only marginally improved by the time of the Anglo-Boer War (1899–1902).

## The Army at Home and Overseas

Not that the army was only employed in campaigns of overseas conquest during the Victorian era. It was also required at home, both to guard against the unlikely event of foreign invasion, and to support the civilian authorities in times of severe public disturbance. Given the enormous social changes that took place in British society between 1837 and 1901, and the frequent social unrest that resulted, this role could never be discounted. A threat of violence always attended mass rallies like those of the Chartists in the 1840s, whilst disputes over harsh industrial conditions occasionally led to incendiarism and rioting. Although the Militia had been created during the Napoleonic wars specifically for the purpose of local defence, it was considered too close to the community from which it was drawn to be employed during riots, and its role was therefore limited to countering

the threat of overseas invasion. Instead, the role of maintaining civil authority fell to the regular army, which over the period found itself deployed in such varied locations as a wood in Kent (the bizarre 'battle of Bossenden Wood', 1838), Trafalgar Square, and the cities of the industrial Midlands. No less important was the large garrison maintained in Ireland throughout the nineteenth century, where Fenian unrest, stimulated by the economic hardship unleashed by the potato famines of the 1840s, was a permanent threat. Nevertheless, the Duke of Wellington's opinion, that an army which was seen too often on home soil was not only a threat to civil liberties, but also too conspicuous an expense, led to a policy of official neglect. Home garrisons were scattered across the country, out of sight and out of mind, in crowded, inadequate and crumbling barracks, and successive governments did little to address the hardships this entailed. In the colonies, by contrast, it was necessary to maintain a more obvious presence. The one disadvantage of securing imperial possessions by force was that they often had to be maintained by implied military threat; the Great Mutiny in India in 1857 proved that even the most apparently successful colony might suddenly erupt into violence under the right circumstances. Even where European settlement was at such a level that it dominated indigenous groups – in Canada, for example, or Australia – the settler community might itself be a source of unrest if it included a significant element whose origins and political allegiances lay outside Britain. Furthermore, most

colonial possessions produced frontier zones, where a melting pot of different cultures, often stirred by economic rivalry, frequently led to clashes. Nor could a direct challenge to British possessions by an imperial rival be ruled out. Throughout the nineteenth century Britain was acutely suspicious of Tsarist Russia in particular. Russia's lasting desire – to open a free passage to the Mediterranean via the Black Sea – manifested itself in a persistent attempt to displace Turkish influence in the Balkans. This was the main cause of the Crimean War, whilst the supposed threat to British India – which was only separated from Russian central Asia by Afghanistan – led to endemic conflict on the Raj's North-West Frontier.

The scale of Britain's military commitment was impressive. In 1846, a total of seventy-seven infantry battalions were on overseas postings, twenty-three of them in India, and just thirty-five at home – and the Empire had not then reached its zenith. For the most part, then, any man enlisting in the ranks could expect to spend much of his period of service overseas, often in an environment which would strike him initially as exotic and fantastic. A life spent in rural poverty or an urban slum would scarcely prepare him for the stifling heat of the Indian plains, and the strange sights he would experience there. The lot of garrisoning the Empire fell largely to the infantry, who could be posted in piecemeal battalions according to need. Guards regiments, who had been founded as the monarchy's personal bodyguard, were always based at home, and only rarely sent overseas as part of a specific expeditionary force. Although regular cavalry sometimes saw overseas service, there was a general belief that their garrison role could better be performed by locally-raised irregular or volunteer horsemen. Until the Indian Mutiny, the Royal Artillery never served in India, its role being performed instead by the East India Company's troops. The Royal Engineers, however, whose expertise made them an essential part of any military activity, were posted in small detachments almost everywhere in the world. For many, particularly in the early Victorian period, an overseas posting could last for years, perhaps even for the entire period of his enlistment. In the Seven Years War it was not unknown for overseas garrisons to be largely forgotten by the government, who resented the cost of maintaining them once the immediate dangers of hostility had passed; they were left to survive as best they could, eroded by disease and desertion, until some new crisis brought their plight to someone's attention. The situation was not that bad in the 1830s, but even so, the early Victorian infantryman could expect to serve an average of ten or twelve years overseas, or nearly twenty if he were sent to India.

### Life in the Victorian Army

Most overseas service would have been uncomfortable, to say the least: a life of crushing discipline and routine, and even more crushing boredom. Colonial barracks were often decaying and unhygienic; men were cooped up in cramped and stifling conditions for most of their time, and often only let out for monotonous parade-ground square-bashing, or to seek oblivion in cheap alcohol in a canteen run by private contractors, under government license, on the premises. Little was understood of the need for good ventilation or clean water; in the tropics barracks were often airless, and sewerage facilities were minimal; even in Britain it was common, until at least the 1850s, for a wooden urine tub to stand open for use in a barrack room overnight. Such tubs were only lightly rinsed in the morning, and were then sometimes used for other duties, including storing rations. Since soldiers often blocked up barrack doors or windows to keep out draughts, the smell from the urine tub, liberally mixed with body odour, was often quite literally enough to make strong men faint, and was a major contributory factor to respiratory diseases, such as tuberculosis. Wherever possible, the government economised by putting off repairs until barrack buildings were virtually in a state of collapse, with the result that many permanently were. Outbreaks of contagious diseases such as cholera and typhoid were common, whilst men in hot countries were exposed to a variety of deadly diseases – malaria, dysentery, yellow fever – which medical science scarcely understood and had few cures for. In some stations, such as the West Coast of Africa – the so-called 'White Man's Grave' – mortality rates were consistently and shockingly high.

As a result, desertion was a perennial problem. For men who had enlisted to escape the drudgery and hopelessness of life at home, the colonies sometimes offered a tempting alternative, with the army paying the shipping fee. It was particularly rife in Canada, where the proximity of the American border offered easy access to a new life, and to a lesser extent in Australia and South Africa. In the latter, for example, the annexation of the Transvaal in 1877 had led to a British garrison being scattered about the country in small pockets. Campaigns against the Zulus and Bapedi had offered some prospect of excitement, but once they were over the troops settled down to a soul-destroying routine. Few were housed in permanent barracks, food was poor, duties were mundane, and there was little to alleviate the numbing boredom of the featureless veld. By contrast, the spate of minor campaigns had leeched volunteers out of settler society, and there was a steady and none-too-choosy market for white workers. The story is told of one officer, out riding, who stopped at a newly-established blacksmith's shop to have a shoe replaced on his horse, only to find that the blacksmith was one of his own men who had absconded a few weeks earlier. For many, the diamond fields at Kimberley held an irresistible lure, whilst others slipped away to join volunteer forces in the hope of seeing some action; it was not unusual, indeed, for former deserters to return to their regiments when these set off for active service. In 1880 as many as 260 men deserted from a total of 3000 in the Transvaal, 70 of them in one month alone, and each desertion was considered to cost the Government £200. Those who remained in the ranks had an unenviable reputation for hard drinking and brawling on those occasions when they were unleashed in town – yet these were the same men who had fought well against the Zulus, and would do so again when the Transvaal revolt broke out in December 1880.

## Recruitment

Throughout the Victorian era the army was dependent not on conscription but on voluntary service, which, however – despite changes in recruiting methods and attempts to improve the ordinary soldier's lot – seldom proved sufficient to compensate for natural wastage. All in all it seems scarcely surprising that army life held little attraction, even at a time when civilian life could be equally grim. In theory, civilian society should have proved a fertile recruiting ground, since unemployment amongst unskilled labourers – for whom lack of work meant starvation and degradation – remained high throughout the century. Yet so strong was resistance to the idea of enlisting that only a small proportion of such men ever did. Nevertheless, unemployment was undoubtedly the greatest single factor which prompted men to enlist: as many as 90% of soldiers had been out of work and hungry when they joined up. Of the rest, a few enlisted for the prospect of travel and adventure; many more to escape bad marriages, family quarrels or other indiscretions in their private lives; and some were criminals or drunkards. Indeed, the Duke of Wellington had not been far wrong when he stressed the role of drink in a recruit's priorities, at least until the 1870s. Recruiting Sergeants regularly frequented pubs and taverns, and seduced the unwary to 'take the Queen's shilling' – a literal payment which was a legally binding contract – by seducing them with free booze and exaggerated tales of the delights of army life. As often as not, therefore, men were drunk when they enlisted, though they had some slim chance of escaping the consequences if they sobered up in time. After taking the shilling, they were taken before a Magistrate to attest, and could change their minds at this stage if they could find a £1 escape fee, wryly known as 'Smart Money'. They were then taken to a doctor and given a cursory medical examination, before being taken to their regiments. Many simply took any opportunity to desert before it was too late, and no doubt congratulated themselves on having cheated the Queen out of her shilling.

Not that the army took just anyone. In theory, it was particular in its requirements, since it preferred men of good character and good physical condition. In the Seven Years War it was not unknown for the feeble, diseased and decrepit to be enlisted, simply to keep numbers up, but the Victorian army never sank to such depths. Until 1871, the minimum age for adult enlistment was seventeen – it changed to eighteen that year – and the maximum was twenty-five. The minimum height preferred was generally 5 ft 6 ins (1.67 m) for the Infantry, and an inch or two taller for the Cavalry, Guards and Artillery, all of whom required greater physical stature. In practice, however, the height requirement was frequently changed when recruits were in short supply, and often dropped to 5 ft 3 ins (1.6 m), whilst there was nothing to prevent men lying about their age. Recruits from rural areas were generally considered more wholesome, since they were likely to be fitter than their slum counterparts, and to take to the disciplined life more easily. Nevertheless, there was a marked demographic change in the composition of the rank and file over the period, reflecting changes in agricultural practice and a shift of population to the towns.

Even by the 1830s there were less rural recruits than there had been a generation before, and by the 1890s they constituted only about a quarter of the army's ranks. There was a change, too, in the national mix within the army; in the 1830s it was predominantly non-English, with over half the rank and file being from Ireland. (It is one of the ironies of Irish history that the army which helped maintain English supremacy in Ireland was predominantly composed of Irishmen.) This began to

*Right: Going for a soldier: a recruiting sergeant and his catch at the time of the Crimean War. (Rai England Collection)*

*Below: After taking the Queen's shilling, recruits were given a medical examination; this engraving from the 1860s leaves no doubt as to the social origins of most recruits. (Rai England Collection)*

change with the potato famines of the mid-century. Although, in the short term, many young Irishmen sought an escape from hunger by enlistment, this brought the army only temporary benefit, because in the long run the collapse of Irish agriculture led to a wholesale exodus from the land, mainly through emigration, particularly to America. By the 1870s the Irish peasantry was simply not the recruiting pool it had once been, and by the end of the century only about 13% of men in the ranks were Irish, a figure which roughly reflected their proportion within the population at large. Similarly, the social conditions that had facilitated the raising of Scottish regiments late in the eighteenth century had altered significantly by the middle of the nineteenth, and in particular the decision to replace tenants with sheep had weakened traditional clan loyalties to the laird, and recruitment suffered as a result. The proportion of Scots in the ranks, although it had never been as high as that of the Irish, also declined steadily across the Victorian period.

Until the first steps were taken to re-introduce a programme of short service in the 1840s ('limited service' had existed for a while during the Napoleonic Wars) – which was, in any case, largely undermined by Wellington's opposition – soldiers enlisted for a remarkably long time; twenty-one years in the infantry and twenty-four in the cavalry. To some extent this was part of its appeal; it meant at the very least twenty-one years of regular food and shelter. Given the extent to which the hardships of their service aged them, however, and the generally lower rates of life expectancy in the nineteenth century, such service meant in effect that men signed up for life. At the end of their time most could expect to be worn out if not actually injured, and, being untrained in anything but the profession of arms, they were unfit for most types of civilian employment. Although most received a minimal pension from the army, it was scarcely sufficient to live on, and was, in any case, refused to those who were invalided out, unless they had actually been wounded in action. The spectacle of the old soldier, reduced to begging on the streets, was commonplace for much of the century, rather to the embarrassment of the government, who realised that it was not an aid to recruitment. Rather than improve the soldiers' lot, however, the government preferred to claim back its uniform when a soldier left the ranks, in the hopes that if he became a beggar, he would not at least be one in uniform.

## 'All for a Shilling a Day'

Even where the lure of regular food and pay had drawn many into the army, they were likely to be disappointed. The soldier's pay was fixed at a traditional rate of a shilling (5p) a day for infantry – slightly more for the cavalry, reflecting the greater expense of training man and horse – which changed scarcely at all across the Victorian period, and which, even at a time of low inflation, was still significantly below a comparable civilian rate. Unlike his civilian counterpart, however, the soldier was at least immune to the vagaries of seasonal employment and market economics. From this shilling, however, the cost of almost everything he used in army life was deducted. In 1837, as much as half of it would be 'stopped' before he received it, to cover the cost of his food, and from the rest he was required to pay for such barrack services as tailoring, laundering, and the barber. If he was sick, the cost of his medical treatment was deducted, and when his unit was transferred he was expected to contribute towards the cost of repairing any damage that had occurred to the barracks during his regiment's occupancy. His uniform and clothing was regularly – but not frequently – replaced, but if any was lost or damaged between issues, the individual soldier had to pay to have it replaced or repaired. Military regulations specified that stoppages could not account for his entire pay, and that each man was to receive at least a penny (0.42p) a day; few early Victorian soldiers would have received much more than that. With this he had to buy any extra groceries he needed – if they were available – and pay for tobacco and recreational activities. Until the 1860s few of these were available, beyond large quantities of mercifully cheap alcohol. Although successive governments in the second half of the century sought to improve the soldier's pay, there was a marked reluctance to change the basic rate. Stoppages for food were discontinued in the 1860s, and extra allowances introduced, but even by the 1890s the level of the remaining deductions remained consistent, amounting by that time to nearly a quarter of the total. For a lucky few, there were limited opportunities to augment basic pay, notably by taking work as an officer's servant, a job that had to be fitted in around ordinary duties, but which was paid for by the officer at a set rate. In addition, men with particular skills – carpenters, cobblers, tailors – were able to earn a few extra pence by providing services for the regiment. Nonetheless, throughout the Victorian period the pay of the ordinary soldier remained poor.

Similarly, the greatest attraction of army food was that it was regular. Like pay, the basic ration remained largely the same throughout the nineteenth century. Soldiers were entitled to a mug of coffee and a pound of bread for breakfast, and three-quarters of a pound of meat for a midday meal. In the first half of the century cooking facilities were minimal and trained cooks unknown, and the meat – usually beef or mutton – was simply boiled or stewed until tender enough to eat. Sometimes, at home, it was augmented with potatoes, and overseas soldiers often sought to add variety by purchasing local vegetables. In some garrisons, however, it was common for the troops to live for long periods on barrels of meat preserved in salt, which, in the absence of refrigeration, at least kept it from decay, but which was neither palatable nor healthy.

## Army Wives

For most of the period, the army was an exclusively male preserve. It preferred to enlist unmarried men, who brought with them few emotional entanglements, and provided no extra cost or administrative headaches. Indeed, recruits could be refused enlistment if they admitted to being married, and enlisted men needed the permission of their commanding officer before they could marry. This was often refused, since on the whole wives and families were regarded as an encumbrance. Only a very small proportion of wives were allowed to live in the barracks, officially 'on the strength' as it was known, and therefore receiving half-rations from the army. Wives could earn a few extra pence by washing the men's clothes or by tending the sick, but generally they were regarded as an inconvenience, and there were few enough concessions made to their presence before the 1860s. The army possessed no barracks with married quarters, and wives were expected to share accommodation with the men, a curtain made from a blanket providing their only privacy. Although it was generally held that the presence of women in a barrack had a steadying influence on the men, curbing the worst excesses of drunkenness and foul language, only six wives per hundred soldiers were allowed to accompany a regiment on overseas service. These were chosen by ballot; although some colonels turned a blind eye and allowed a number of wives to accompany their men unofficially, the fate of those left behind was grim. The government accepted no responsibility for their welfare, and it was left to their husbands to try to save and send home some of their pay. This almost always meant unremitting hardship, for as well as protracted separation from their loved ones, the women had to keep themselves. Some soldiers took advantage of overseas service to abandon their wives, and many were forced by economic hardship to live either on the parish, or to resort to prostitution.

For unmarried men there were, of course, no acceptable ways of expressing their sexuality, and they either had to resort to prostitutes, or to repress their urges in heavy bouts of drinking. Prostitution was an inevitable consequence of single-sex garrison life, and the authorities reacted to it with varying degrees of pragmatism. In India, indeed, the principle garrison town boasted a number of official 'regimental brothels'. The chief concern was not the soldier's morality – in the first half of the century it was taken for granted in any case that all were irredeemably depraved – but venereal disease. In the years before antibiotics, gonorrhoea and particularly syphilis were incurable and ultimately disabling diseases; in the 1860s, during a particular scare about the army's moral condition, it was estimated that as many as a third of the home-based rank and file were infected. Treatment of the disease was minimal, and the authorities tried to restrict prostitution around garrisons rather than change the soldiers' pattern of behaviour. The problem of prostitution was inextricably bound up with that of drunkenness, since prostitutes also frequented the places where soldiers' sought escape in alcohol. Drunkenness was a perennial problem amongst not just the rank and file, and the army never really succeeded in containing it throughout the nineteenth century. Indeed, for much of that time it made no attempt to, as most barracks had a canteen where civilian contractors, operating under official license, supplied cheap beer by the quart and astonishing quantities of potent spirits, notably rum and brandy. This was despite the fact that drunkenness itself was a military crime, and it was recognised that it led to other transgressions such as desertion, insubordination, dereliction of duty, and brawling. Nevertheless, until the 1860s alternative off-duty recreational facilities were considered an unnecessary expense, and large numbers of soldiers regularly sought to escape the boredom of their routine by drinking themselves into oblivion.

## Crime and Punishment

Punishment for indiscipline, whether induced by alcohol or anything else, was severe, at least until after the Crimean war, though there had been some softening of the worst aspects of the Wellingtonian regime. Flogging had been an almost universal punishment in Napoleonic times, when the various levels of court-martial had practically unlimited powers to dictate the number of lashes. The miscreant was stripped to the waist, and strapped with his arms above his head to a triangle of poles, originally made from spontoons – sergeants' pikes – tied together. The lash was then laid on with a 'cat o'nine tails', a whip with nine knotted strings. Punishment was usually a public affair, carried out with the entire regiment formed in a hollow square, so as to witness it as a deterrent; a senior officer counted the lashes whilst a military doctor looked on, and drummers played to drown out the screams. The whole business was a gory one, since the lash stripped off skin after just a few blows, and tore and lacerated the flesh, often to the bone. Sentences of 500 lashes were not uncommon in Wellington's army, and men often died as a result. Men watching in the ranks sometimes fainted at the sight. After the punishment was inflicted, the man was cut loose and his wounds washed with salt water; this served as a crude antiseptic, but did little to ease the pain. Flogging was such a conspicuous and barbaric symbol of the worst aspects of the army regime that it was one of the few areas of military life that attracted the attention of civilian reformers, who were otherwise hardly interested in the common soldier's lot. By the time of Queen Victoria's accession the number of strokes permitted had been reduced to a maximum of fifty. In 1867 it was restricted to serious crimes such as mutiny, and within a few years it was outlawed for troops on home service, but retained as a field punishment. It was not abolished entirely until 1881, following publicity over the number of instances in the Zulu War. Its direct replacement was Field

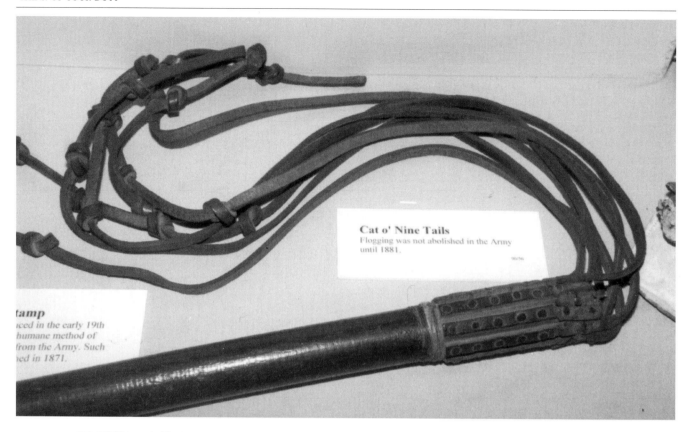

Cat o' Nine Tails
Flogging was not abolished in the Army until 1881.

...tamp
...ced in the early 19th
...humane method of
...from the Army. Such
...ed in 1871.

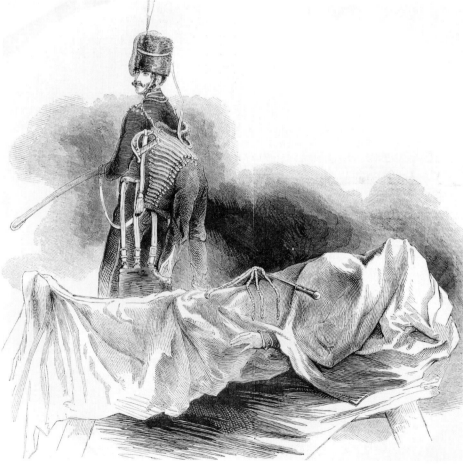

*Above: The Cat, the symbol of army punishment until its abolition in 1881. (Devon and Dorset Military Museum)*

*Left: 'Before and After'; a macabre comment on the over-zealousness of army punishment, published in 1846 alongside a report on the death of Private Frederick White of the 7th Hussars. Twenty-seven-year-old Private White was sentenced to 150 lashes for striking a sergeant; the punishment was administered by two farriers, and after 100 strokes the 'cats' were changed for new ones. During the course of the punishment several men fainted. White walked to the hospital after the punishment was completed, and later complained of pains in the chest, but was not attended by the Medical Officer until the following day, when he was found to be dead. (Rai England Collection).*

*Right: A stamping tool for tattooing deserters. (Devon and Dorset Military Museum)*

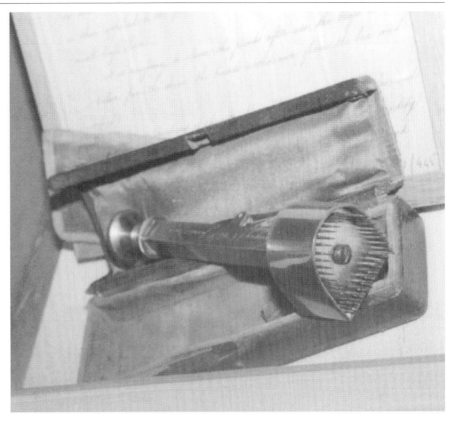

Punishment No. 1, in which a man was tied to the wheel of a gun carriage for a specified period. Gradually, however, corporal punishment gave way to an increasing reliance on custodial sentences, army prisons having been first built in the 1840s. Other, almost mediaeval forms of punishment were also phased out as the century wore on; the practise of tattooing deserters under the arm with the letter D, by using an iron tool with pins attached to the head, was only discontinued in 1871.

## The Officer Class

Much depended on the attitude of individual commanding officers. Many had inherited Wellington's belief that the army would only perform when flogged to it, but the tradition of humanitarianism had its roots in the attitudes of Napoleonic commanders like Sir John Moore, who were deeply influenced by the ideas of the Enlightenment. The two schools of thought had an almost philosophical difference of outlook; for the traditionalists, it was anathema to encourage men in the ranks to think for themselves, since this bordered on sedition. They believed that the army worked best when the soldiers reacted to orders instinctively, and performed manoeuvres on the battlefield like automatons. A growing liberalism in society at large steadily undermined this view, which was eroded still further by improvements in military technology which rendered close formations impractical. Others had a more paternalistic outlook, believing that by educating their men, by weaning them away from drink, and encouraging individual initiative, they would produce more motivated and self-reliant soldiers. The old school was somewhat discredited by events in the Crimea, and a growing acceptance among the elite of the principals of *noblesse oblige*, that rank and the right to rule carried with it responsibilities, which came to dominate the outlook of the officer class in the late Victorian era.

Nevertheless, the gulf which separated the officer from the lower ranks was almost unbridgeable, certainly in the early Victorian period. Officers in Wellington's army had been drawn almost exclusively from the classes which dominated civilian society, the aristocracy and the landed gentry. Civil enfranchisement depended on a certain level of wealth, and this was reflected in the composition of the officer class. Wellington, whilst he admitted that breeding did not always produce military skill, did believe that only the gentry had that innate sense of authority which made them fit to rule; in his eyes, the terms 'officer' and 'gentleman' were indivisible. Furthermore, no-one who did not possess a comfortable private income could ever hope to function properly as an officer. An officer's pay, whilst obviously far superior to that of the rank and file, was nonetheless quite insufficient to meet his expenses, and also remained largely static throughout the nineteenth century. An ensign – the lowest officers' rank, replaced by sub-lieutenant in 1871, and later by second lieutenant – was paid 5s 3d

(26.25p) a day, whilst a lieutenant-colonel received 17s (85p, with a further 3s, or 15p, if he commanded a battalion), rates which were fixed in 1806 and not substantially changed in Queen Victoria's time. Against this, the parents of an aspiring officer would have to find fees of £175 a year if he was to be enrolled as a cadet at the military college at Sandhurst. Until 1871, anyone seeking a commission into the infantry or cavalry was expected to purchase his rank at a fixed fee of £450 for an ensign, £700 for a lieutenant, £1,800 for a captain, £3,200 for a major, and £4,500 for a lieutenant-colonel. Ranks above lieutenant-colonel could not be bought, whilst the Artillery and Engineers did not follow the purchase system, and indeed, some officers were appointed without purchase, since the Commander-in-Chief could find posts at his discretion for those who had passed through one of the military colleges.

The expenses did not stop at the official purchase price, however. They were accompanied by a range of extra charges which reflected the

*Above: A famously languid portrait of Colonel Fred Burnaby of the Blues in the 1870s suggests something of the enormous social gulf which separated the officer class from the other ranks. (National Portrait Gallery)*

popularity of certain regiments, and facilitated transfers between them, as well as a high incidence of illegal or unofficial payments which were used to influence the system. Commissions in fashionable cavalry regiments, in particular, demanded fees well above regulation level, and were seldom short of applicants; these fees might amount to a further £750 for a lieutenant, and over £8,000 for a lieutenant-colonel. Promotion within the regiment was also dependent on purchase, up to the rank of lieutenant-colonel, or captain in the Foot Guards. Once he had received a commission, the aspiring officer would then have to buy his own uniform, perhaps £200 for an infantry officer in the last half of the century, but four or five times that for a cav-

alryman, who had to provide his own horse and equipment. In the most fashionable regiments it was impossible for officers to maintain their dignity without spending an enormous amount on thoroughbred horses and smart uniforms. On top of that there were mess bills, and a level of high living was similarly *de rigeur*. In the late Victorian army it has been estimated that an infantry officer could not subsist on less than £100 a year private income, whilst a cavalryman could not be comfortable on much under £700.

The system, of course, led to some conspicuous abuses. James Thomas Brudenell, the Earl of Cardigan, a haughty eccentric who achieved lasting fame leading the Light Cavalry Brigade to destruction at Balaclava in

the Crimea, is said to have paid £40,000 in 1836 for the command of his regiment, the 11th Hussars (then Light Dragoons), and spent a further £10,000 a year on the troopers' uniforms; and this despite the fact that he had lost command of a previous regiment, the 15th Hussars, because of his unreasonable behaviour. Such excesses were not typical, but the early Victorian army saw little wrong in the system of purchase. As far as the government was concerned, it was a useful source of revenue, and for individual officers it served as an investment which provided a pension when they 'sold out' of the army at the end of their service. Its most serious drawback was that it almost entirely separated promotion from performance; an officer needed no special merit or even efficiency to rise through the ranks, as Cardigan had proved. When purchase was finally abolished, however, promotion through merit was found to be equally unreliable and equally vulnerable to abuse or influence. Promotion instead became largely dependent on seniority, and as a post became vacant within a regiment, so the man below rose to fill it. In peace-time, therefore, there was something of a log-jam, as regiments went for years with no vacancies at the higher levels, and many officers advanced towards middle age whilst stuck in the junior ranks. As a result, the outbreak of active service was usually regarded with enthusiasm, not only because it broke the monotony of peace-time soldiering, and

offered the prospect of distinction, but because it was bound to thin out the ranks and improve the chances of promotion.

The attitude towards the army among the civilian class from which officers were drawn was almost exactly the opposite to that which prevailed among the other ranks. Whereas the ordinary soldiers were despised outcasts from their own class, officers were highly regarded within theirs. Amongst the gentry it was far from dishonourable to serve as an officer and, indeed, many families who aspired to that class, who had made money in industry and commerce and bought land, found that the presence of a son in the army was an aid to social acceptance. Thus if the gentry carried their attitudes and ideals into the army, there was an equal exchange in the opposite direction; officers continued to enjoy the sort of field sports that they had pursued as civilians – hunting, shooting, fishing – and with long periods of leave allowed to them, they moved freely between

army and civilian life. As the gentry were conservative, traditionalist and patriotic, so, too, was the officer class. Indeed, the army was a God-send to many a younger son of an established county family: under the system of primogeniture, family estates were habitually left to the eldest son. Daughters might be found suitable marriages, but the options available to younger sons were strictly limited; since trade was barred to them as vulgar and beneath their dignity, the cliché had it that they were left with a choice between the army and the Church.

Unlike their men, officers had plenty of time to mix with members of the opposite sex, since their duties in peace-time were hardly demanding, and up to half the year might be spent on leave. Marriage, however, was only marginally more acceptable. Officers were expected to refrain from marrying too young – the informal rule was that 'subalterns cannot marry, captains may marry, majors should marry, colonels must marry'. As a result, the

*Right: Women and the army: Paymaster Henry Duberly of the 8th Hussars and his adventurous wife, photographed in the Crimea. (Private collection)*

number of wives supported by officers was small, and it was not unknown for an officer who made a marriage which his colleagues thought inappropriate to be ostracised and forced to resign. Officers clearly did not have to suffer the indignities inflicted on their other rank counterparts, but even so, married life was scarcely comfortable when a regiment was overseas or on campaign. Although it was not impossible for officers to return from overseas postings on furlough, and therefore visit wives left at home, it was common for wives to accompany regiments posted to India, if only because of the length of time the regiment was likely to be overseas. Even then, the wives spent much of their time in the cool hill stations whilst their husbands soldiered in the hot plains, and long periods of separation were still common. Nor was it unknown for wives to accompany their husbands to operational theatres; numbers did so in the Crimean war, including the famous Fanny Duberley, wife of the paymaster of the 8th Hussars. A number of officers' wives accompanied their husbands to South Africa for the wars of the 1850s and 1870s but the practice began to die out thereafter.

On almost all levels, therefore, officers had nothing in common with the men they commanded. They had money, education and power, and were confident of the privileges afforded by their niche within the status quo; they had their own values, their belief in tradition and personal honour, and their own pastimes; even their language differed noticeably from that of their men. The rankers had no individual worth or influence within their regiments, and many happily accepted this lot, with its blissful absence of responsibility, as pre-ordained by the nature of society. Physically, officers and men scarcely mixed, particularly in peace-time, since officers had their own lodgings or quarters, and messed together. For the most part they encountered their men only on the parade-ground, and even then the bulk of routine duties fell to a limited

number of officers – the adjutant, for example, or the musketry instructor – whilst the practical daily command of the other ranks fell to the senior NCOs. Many officers served for years with their regiments having very little knowledge of the men beneath them, nor any real understanding of their problems. This was not, however, a universal trait, for probably the majority adopted the paternal attitudes which came increasingly to influence their class in the last half of the century, and they accepted the responsibility for the welfare of their men to a greater or lesser degree, without ever for a moment considering that they were social equals.

## Allegiance to the Regiment

It was under such circumstances that the outward symbols of regimental unity and *esprit de corps* achieved their significance. With little else in common, officers and men were tied together by a common allegiance to Queen and country, bound by a regimental tradition which framed their lives, and reflected the discomfort and danger they faced together on active service. Regimental history, with its emphasis on past heroism, became increasingly important, since it stressed the continuity of regimental life, and provided expectations which all ranks strove to fulfil. Regimental devices – facing colours on tunics, different badges, even peculiar practices which had a particular significance only within the regiment – all helped to stress the differences between the various units, and to infuse their members with a sense of pride and belonging. Foremost amongst these were the Colours, which were presented to each battalion by the Queen, either in person, or by an important individual on her behalf. Although each infantry battalion carried a Queen's Colour – the national flag – minor differences between these were jealously guarded, and each regiment also carried its own Colour, bearing its unique regimental devices and battle-honours. Although the Colours had a practical purpose, as a means of indicating the core of the regiment on the battlefield, their

*Above: An infantry battalion on parade in the Crimea; note the Colours in the centre. (Private collection)*

true significance was emotional. They represented not only the army's commitment to the nation and royal family, but also the trust vested in that regiment by the sovereign in return, and the accumulated honour of the regiment. The Colours were, in effect, a regiment's soul, and they bound both officers and men to them, subjugating their otherwise very real differences to a common unity of tradition.

## The Crimea and its Effects

Of course, the Victorian era was no more static in the military field than it was in civilian life. Bad practices, cruel discipline and harsh living conditions which were accepted by society at large in 1837 became less so as the century wore on, and perhaps the greatest single stimulus to reform in the Victorian era was the

unprecedented public outcry which greeted Britain's conduct of the Crimean War. The Crimean campaign was unique in Victorian military experience, in that it was the only European-style conflict undertaken by Britain in the century between Waterloo and the First World War. Unlike colonial campaigns up to that time – and to a large degree after it – it could not be waged with troops drawn from a nearby garrison, and it had been necessary to mobilise an expeditionary force specifically to meet its needs. On the whole it functioned well enough at its lower levels, triumphing at each of the main battles, and there had been no lack of gallantry or endurance, but the campaign demonstrated deep-seated weaknesses which had taken root since the end of the Napoleonic Wars. There had been an almost complete absence of any plan for the systematic raising of such a force, whilst the long years of retrenchment, pursued by successive governments, had left

too few men to fill the ranks. Once men in the first expedition – just 26,000 of them – became disabled through disease or injury, there was no ready means to replace them; new units were sent out as reinforcements, but many units finished the war with drastically reduced numbers. Furthermore, at the beginning of the war, transport and supply facilities were chaotic, whether run by the army or by civilian contractors unused to the army's needs. The senior commanders had no experience of working together with each other, let alone with their French, Turkish and Sardinian allies; indeed, the presence of one or two eccentric personalities who bore an intense dislike for each other – notably Lord Lucan, who commanded the Cavalry Division, and his brother-in-law Lord Cardigan, who led the Light Brigade under him – undoubtedly contributed to the problems of command co-ordination at the higher levels.

In all of these respects, the Crimean War was scarcely any differ-

ent from many of its predecessors. With no established structure of planning and support, the army was inevitably accustomed to muddling through. No doubt, by the time of the Crimea, its commanders were stale and out of practice, but a period of settling in, of establishing *ad hoc* systems in the field, was to remain a characteristic of British military experience in the nineteenth century – nor, indeed, was it unique among the imperial powers in that. What made the Crimea different, however, was that it was the first war to be covered extensively by the press. Journalists who were allowed almost unlimited access to the front sent home reports which became increasingly critical, not of the fighting men themselves, but of their apparently inept and inefficient leaders. Most notably, the despatches of William Howard Russell, published in *The Times*, amounted to an exposé of folly and inefficiency, and concentrated in particular on the suffering of the men in the ranks. The frequent recurrence of cholera in the over-crowded camps, the onset of the desperate winter of 1855, which the army faced under canvas and with an insufficient supply of warm clothing, the endless delays in moving food and other supplies the seven miles from the harbour at Balaclava to the siege lines, and lastly the plight of the sick and wounded, with too few doctors to treat them and hardly any proper facilities to house them, were all described in merciless detail. Both the British public – who had hitherto shown little interest in the condition of the army – and parliament, whose support for reform had always been

*The narrow harbour at Balaclava. The wooden barrack huts in the foreground were not built until after the harsh winter of 1854–5. (Private collection)*

tempered in the past by parsimony, were shocked out of their lethargy. A number of highly publicised attempts, both private and official, were made to alleviate the suffering, perhaps the most famous being Florence Nightingale's mission to build a base hospital at Scutari.

## The Post-Crimean Period and Cardwell's Reforms

The public outcry which followed the Crimean campaign proved short-lived. Once the war had petered out the story disappeared from the headlines, and the traditionalists closed ranks. Furthermore, the Crimea was followed, almost before it was over, by that other great crisis of the mid-Victorian period, the Mutiny in India. Much of the fighting there fell to local troops, augmented by reinforcements sent out piecemeal from Britain, so that any inefficiency and

errors were not as conspicuous as they had been in the Crimea. This war was, in any case, presented to the public in very different terms; it was portrayed as a righteous war of revenge, in which stalwart Christian soldiers accomplished prodigious feats of heroism and endurance to overcome treacherous and barbarous heathens. If anything, the Indian Mutiny restored something of the public's faith in the army, and for a decade afterwards the pace of army reform was scarcely greater than in the years before the Crimea.

The first major attempt to reform the army's administrative structure as a whole was undertaken by Edward Cardwell, the Secretary of State for War from 1868 to 1874, during Gladstone's first administration. Like his predecessors, Cardwell was primarily concerned to curb army expenditure but, unlike them,

*Right: This engraving from* **The Illustrated London News** *of 1882 suggests that the army had succeeded in creating a rather more amiable image of the recruiting sergeant. (Rai England Collection)*

he was prepared to tackle the root of the problem. His reforms were profound and far reaching, and generally carried out in the teeth of opposition from the traditionalist party, personified by the Duke of Cambridge. The Duke, the Queen's first cousin, had seen active service in the Crimea, and dominated the military establishment throughout the second half of the century, until his retirement in 1895, first as Field Marshal Commanding-in-Chief, and later as Commander-in-Chief. He was in effect the military head of the army and, though perhaps more liberal in his outlook than Wellington, nonetheless stepped into his role as the arch-conservative for the new age. The Duke was generally opposed to any sort of reform on the grounds that it eroded the army's spirit, and he was jealous of both his own prestige, and of the non-political, pro-royalist stance embodied in his post. Despite his immense personal power, however, he at best succeeded in moderating or curbing Cardwell's reforms, never in blocking them completely; and perhaps Cardwell's greatest achievement was in simplifying the senior administration of the army – which had hitherto been split between a number of military departments – and bringing it effectively under government control.

Cardwell's reforms were prompted in part by events in Europe, where a wave of political instability culminated in the surprisingly easy Prussian victory in the Franco-Prussian War of 1870. The Prussian success prompted a certain amount of soul-searching in Britain, especially when Cardwell admitted that under existing structures, he doubted if Britain could put together an expeditionary force of 20,000 men, should it be called upon to defend its alliances in Europe. Cardwell was inclined to make military service more attractive to a better class of recruit, whilst at the same time making provision for a standing reserve which could – as Prussia had done – be mobilised quickly and efficiently in time of national crisis. Both objectives could be achieved by the introduction of a new short-service form of enlistment, where a man was no longer required to join up, in effect, for life, but could – in its final manifestation – serve just six years with the Colours (with an option of re-enlistment), and a further six in the Reserve. Short service was not in itself a new idea; it had been mooted in the 1840s, but had foundered on that occasion in the face of the Duke of Wellington's implacable opposi-

tion. The military establishment believed that short service would rob the army of its tried and tested veterans and replace them with young men who would no sooner learn their trade than leave. Nevertheless, Cardwell's system was finally approved in 1870, the first of several important measures which gradually changed the outlook and composition of the army over the remainder of the century.

It was also Cardwell who attempted to curb the widely resented abuses in the recruiting system itself. Enlistment bounties were abolished, whilst recruiting agents were proscribed from setting up their business in pubs. Those seeking to persuade recruits to take the Queen's Shilling were expected to paint a more realistic picture of army life, and anyone who could prove that he had enlisted under false promises was entitled to be released from his duty. These reforms were only partly successful, in that recruiting agents either ignored them completely, or merely abandoned the interior of a pub for the street outside, but they did help to create a climate of enlistment which was less overtly based on drink and deceit.

Furthermore, Cardwell finally abolished the system by which officers purchased their commissions. Ironically, Cardwell did not object to the purchase system itself, but merely to the abuses, the excess and unofficial payments, which it fostered. However, when trying to curb these, he came to the conclusion that it would be more effective in the long run to abolish purchase entirely. In this, of course, he was opposed by the Duke of Cambridge and by a number of influential senior officers, and his measures were only passed by parliament after a prolonged political battle in both Houses. To sugar the pill, the government accepted that all officers, even those who had not been required to purchase their commissions, would be compensated to their full value, and the final bill was in the region of £8 million.

Cardwell's other important long-term reform was an attempt to tie the infantry battalions to particular regions within the United Kingdom. This was intended both to foster local loyalties, in the hope of easing the perennial shortfall in recruitment, whilst at the same time providing a new administrative framework to regularise the garrisoning of the overseas colonies. The Localisation Bill of 1872 established sixty-six territorial districts within Britain, each of which had a brigade depot. Each depot was supposed to have two infantry battalions, two Militia battalions, and a number of Volunteer units attached to it. One infantry battalion was always supposed to be at home whilst the other

was abroad, and they were to be regularly rotated; as a result, no more than 50% of the regular infantry would, in theory, be out of the country at any given time. The first twenty-five regiments of the line already had two battalions, although the links between them had hitherto been notional rather than practical; the idea was to link each of the remaining, previously unrelated, single-battalion regiments to form pairs. It was expected that the Militia and Volunteers would also benefit from regular training with their Line counterparts, and the capacity for home defence would therefore be immeasurably strengthened.

In this, too, Cardwell was only partially successful. His policy followed in the footsteps of a general trend, first implemented in the 1840s, to make the colonies more militarily self-reliant. By raising and training forces drawn from the local settler population, colonies were expected to shoulder more of the burden for their own defence, and free some of the long-standing British garrisons. In some colonies, such as New Zealand, where the move coincided with the reduction of Maori resistance to settler encroachment, this was moderately successful; in others, such as South Africa, the friction which accompanied the steady expansion of imperial rule meant that a strong military presence was inevitable. Furthermore, the outbreak of fresh bursts of violence upset the delicate balance inherent in the system; those battalions overseas which were under strength or suffered heavy casualties were brought up to scratch by drafts sent out at the expense of the home battalions, and, when a situation was particularly serious, the home battalions were ordered overseas as well. The result was predictable; in 1872, when the system was introduced, there were seventy battalions at home and seventy-one abroad, but by February 1879 – following the initial disasters in the Zulu War – the number had shrunk to fifty-nine battalions at home, and eighty-two overseas. Nor was the linking of battalions effectively carried out, since

many commanding officers were reluctant to see their long-standing traditions submerged in amalgamation. It was not until 1881 that Cardwell's idea was taken to its logical conclusion, and the old numbers and county affiliations which had characterised individual battalions were abandoned in favour of new local titles. To symbolise the change, much-loved uniform facings were discarded in favour of universal facings, though the army later won back the right to wear distinctive facings in its ceremonial dress.

### 'All Sir Garnet'

Although Cardwell's tenure in office was short – just six years – the spirit of his programme of reforms was continued and developed by his successors, whilst under his patronage a broadly sympathetic pro-reform school emerged in the army itself. In particular, Sir Garnet (later Viscount) Wolseley headed a small group of officers who were in favour of limited reform, and their influence spread with the dazzling success of Wolseley's own career; he eventually succeeded the Duke of Cambridge as Commander-in-Chief in 1895 although, ironically, parliament had by that time stripped the office of much of its authority. As a subaltern, Wolseley had fought in a typical selection of mid-century wars – the Second Burma War, the Crimea (where he was wounded and lost the sight of one eye), the Mutiny, and the Second China War. He had earned a reputation for personal courage and a knack for thorough planning. In 1869 he produced a manual, *The Soldier's Pocket Book*, which was highly regarded, and in 1870 he was given his first command, the Red River Expedition in Canada; faced with the prospect of suppressing recalcitrant Franco-Indians, Wolseley was required to transport his force hundreds of miles across difficult and rugged terrain, and he managed it with such despatch that the enemy melted away on his arrival without fighting. In 1873, when ordered to defend British possessions on the coast of West Africa against an invasion by the inland Asante (Ashanti), he personally selected a Staff from young like-minded officers, many of whom had served with him in Canada. He assembled an expeditionary force by plundering the best troops from those available on home service, kitted them out with a practical uniform, and carefully planned their transport and supply. The Asante campaign was Wolseley at his best; the expedition was well thought-out, swift, and successful, and it had a deep affect on his career. In his sub-

sequent campaigns, Wolseley relied where possible on the same group of officers – among them Redvers Buller, George Colley, John McNeill, Evelyn Wood, William Butler and Henry Brackenbury – and this so-called 'Ashanti Ring' became adept at working together under his leadership and were later immensely influential. When frustrated in dealing with the Duke of Cambridge or with politicians, Wolseley did not scruple to appeal to the press, whom he affected to despise, but whose

approval he courted. Thanks to this exposure, he soon became a well-known and much admired figure amongst the British public, and the press on occasion championed him as 'Our Only General'. 'All Sir Garnet' was a catch-phrase implying efficiency and order. He failed to secure a command in the Zulu War until the fighting was over, but his swift and successful campaign in Egypt in 1882, culminating in the battle of Tel-el-Kebir, crowned his active service career in a glory which was only slightly tainted by his failure in the Sudan in 1885.

Yet in many ways Wolseley's attitude to reform was limited. He was very much a product of his time and class, and he shared many of its prejudices. Personally a snob, he accepted implicitly the belief that only the upper classes had the necessary character to become officers, and at a time when many officers of limited means sought to serve with regiments based in India – where a higher standard of living could be enjoyed at a lower cost – he tended to look down on officers with a background of Indian service. Although the composition of his ring of favourites was never static, it earned the widespread resentment of those who were excluded from it and encouraged the formation of a rival 'India Ring', which centred upon Lord Roberts. The existence of these two mutually antagonistic schools was to prove damaging late in the century, when they were brought into direct conflict over the prosecution of the Anglo-Boer War. Indeed, although members of the Ashanti Ring enjoyed a high public profile, which contributed towards their rapid promotion, their greatest successes dated from the years when they were under Wolseley's personal command. Colley, given an independent command in the 1881 Transvaal War, lost every battle and was killed in action, while Buller, when commanding during the early stages of the Boer War, displayed lit-

*Left: That very model of a modern Major-General, Sir Garnet Wolseley in the 1870s. (Author's collection)*

tle of the sure touch he had exhibited in Zululand. Wolseley's approach to Staff matters was individualistic; he preferred to make appointments himself, oversee his subordinates' actions, and was, on the whole, opposed to the concept of a formal Chief of Staff. When he had the opportunity to create such a post as Commander-in-Chief, he refused to do so. Indeed, in many ways Wolseley's career typifies the Victorian army in the 1870s, 1880s and 1890s: when dealing with small actions, it displayed initiative, resourcefulness and flair, but only so long as those qualities were reflected in the personality of an individual commander. It lacked the capacity to look beyond the confines of essentially localised campaigning, and to adopt structures which were self-supporting.

For all Cardwell's reforms, the composition of the officer elite did not change after the abolition of purchase. Many of those who had bought their commissions before 1870 continued to serve and their attitudes, if anything, became more influential as they rose in rank. Family tradition had always been a powerful factor influencing sons of the gentry to join the army, and most had been inculcated with the necessary attitudes by the public school system. By the 1890s the officer class was increasingly self-perpetuating, and many senior officers had sons following in their footsteps.

### Gentlemen Rankers

The practical gulf which existed between officers and their men survived well into the twentieth century. It was theoretically possible for men to rise through the ranks and become officers, and it was quite common for senior NCOs to accept appointments as quartermasters. Quartermasters, however, although they messed with officers, were regarded in much the same manner as the gentry regarded tradesmen; their job was a very necessary one, but they formed a subordinate class of their own in the pecking order. A few 'gentlemen rankers' – gentlemen who had enlisted in the ranks, often

to escape a past indiscretion, and in the hope of finding promotion – did make a successful transition, but for a true ranker to become an officer required a moral courage which few were willing to hazard. Some did; Hector MacDonald, a Scottish crofter's son who rose through the ranks to become a general and achieve a knighthood, was one, and so was Sir William Robertson, who, in the title of his autobiography, went *From Private to Field Marshal*. Such men were, however, the exception, and it is no coincidence that both had relied on extensive Indian service. It was painfully difficult for such men to find the necessary income expected of them; Frank Bourne, who as a colour-sergeant had been one of the heroes of Rorke's Drift, recalled that in recognition of his services he was 'awarded a commission, but as I was the youngest of eight sons, and the family exchequer was empty, I had to refuse it at that time'. Bourne later followed the typical quartermaster's route into the officers' mess, and finally reached the rank of lieutenant-colonel in the aftermath of the First World War. Generally, however, men promoted from the ranks had a difficult and lonely time, seldom able to fit in with their colleagues, their origins betrayed by their outlook, habits and speech. There is even a suggestion that Hector MacDonald's fall – after he was involved in a sexual indiscretion – was encouraged by an establishment keen to see an outsider put in his place.

Nevertheless, the pace of army reform might fairly be said to have accelerated in the 1870s, 1880s and 1890s. The almost flippant disregard for the basic skills of their job, affected by fashionable officers in the years before the Crimea, had given way to a growing respect for professionalism. The Staff College had been established at Camberley in 1858, and attempted to instruct officers in some of the skills necessary to manage an army in the field; its graduates had not at first been popular, since it was widely regarded that attending Staff College was

merely an excuse to avoid regimental responsibilities, but the fact that Wolseley was a graduate, and that his favoured Ring had almost all been through Staff College, helped change attitudes. Tactical theory, too, underwent significant changes. The American Civil War and Franco-Prussian War were widely studied, although the fighting in Europe differed so much from the British colonial experience that the lessons drawn from it were superficial and confusing. Nevertheless, a further shift away from the dense Napoleonic formations employed in the Crimea, towards a greater emphasis on open-order and flexibility, characterised the manuals of the period. In addition, the army itself was immeasurably better armed. The 1860s had finally seen the widespread adoption of breech-loading rifles, culminating in the issue of the efficient single-shot Martini-Henry in 1871. The first magazine rifle – the Lee-Metford – was introduced in 1888, allowing individual infantrymen a much greater rate of fire. This process reached its logical conclusion with the issue of the improved Lee-Enfield in 1895, a rifle which, in modified form, remained the standard British infantry arm until the 1950s. Machine guns were experimented with in the 1870s and 1880s, cumbersome hand-cranked guns like the Gatling and Gardner, and although they proved unreliable, they offered a glimpse of what such weapons might achieve. This promise was fulfilled with the invention of the efficient and fully automatic Maxim gun in 1891.

### Easing the Burden, 1870–1900

There is no doubt that Cardwell's reforms had some effect on the life of the ordinary soldier. Private Donald MacDonald's second letter to his family suggests both the continuity of army routine, and the changes that were underway:

In the hut which I live in there are about 15 men – you are supposed to get up at six o'clock every morning, make our beds, clean our brasses, gun and bayonet, brush our boots and be on parade properly dressed at seven OC, when we get an hour's drill. We breakfast at eight, get ready again for commanding officer's parade at 10 OC, when we get another hour's drill. We dine at a quarter to One, then get ready again for parade at 2 OC, get an hour's drill as before. Then we go to school from 5 to 7 every night except Saturdays – the examination is to take place very shortly and I want if possible to get a Second Class Certificate which is the highest that is generally taken. In Arithmetic we have to know Vulgar Fractions all the Comp. Rules, Reduction etc, Banking a/cs, Mess a/cs, and so forth. Of course I knew all these before when at school, but it requires practise to bring them to your recollection. The schoolmaster gives me great praise for my work. I forgot to say that we had tea at a quarter past four. Our breakfast consists of a 1/4th of dry bread and a basin of coffee. Our dinner is generally very good, beef and potatoes daily, and soup perhaps twice or three times per week. We sometimes get a dough but very seldom. Our tea is the same as breakfast and a basin of tea.

Women remained, on the whole, unwelcome in a fiercely single-sex environment, but from the 1880s the first married quarters were introduced in home garrisons. Official provision was made for wives to receive a proportion of their husband's pay, and in 1881 the first annuity was granted for widows of men killed in action. With the establishment of a School of Cooking at Aldershot in 1870, the first steps were taking towards improving the monotonous diet. In an attempt to wean the men away from their dependence on drink, the army attempted to provide alternative ways of spending leisure time, notably in the form of games rooms,

where men could relax over the billiards or card tables. In this respect they were encouraged by the militant anti-drinking campaigns waged by the increasingly popular non-conformist religions in civilian life; the Wesleyans, in particular, did all they could to encourage more wholesome pursuits, and went so far as to establish 'Soldiers' Homes' in garrison towns, where the men could while away their free time in an alcohol-free environment. The logical conclusion of this tee-total evangelism was the creation of the Army Temperance Association in 1893.

Nevertheless, it took time for many of these improvements to take effect. William Robertson, who enlisted in the 16th (Queen's) Lancers in 1877 when not yet eighteen, left a record of his first impressions of barrack-room life, at a time when the ranks contained a mix of short-service recruits and 'old sweats':

Regiments were … still composed mainly of old soldiers, who, although very admirable comrades in some respects and with a commendable code of honour of their own, were in many cases – not in all – addicted to rough behaviour, heavy drinking, and hard swearing. They could not well be blamed for this. Year in and year out they went through the same routine, were treated like machines – of an inferior kind – and having little prospect of finding any decent employment on the expiation of their twenty-one years engagement, they lived only for the present, the single bright spot in their existence being the receipt of a few shillings – perhaps not more than one – on the weekly pay day. These rugged veterans exacted full deference from the recruit, who was assigned to the worst bed in the room, given the smallest amount of food and the least palatable, had to 'lend' them kit which they had lost or sold, 'fag' for them in a variety of ways, and, finally, was expected to share with

them at the regimental canteen such cash as he might have in the purchase of beer sold at 3d a quart …

True, recruitment in the late Victorian army grew steadily – the army rose from a strength of just under 184,000 men in 1876 to nearly 225,000 in 1898 – but this reflected a more vigorous enlistment drive rather than any significant increase in the appeal of service life. The Localisation Bill was only partly effective in creating an army with strong local ties; although the existence of a regional depot inevitably attracted a number of recruits from that area, it did not necessarily reflect the origins of the men themselves, especially if the depot was situated near an urban centre which attracted a large pool of itinerant labourers. Indeed, few brigade districts could support the battalions associated with them on their own, particularly if they were in rural areas, and many recruits were drawn from outside. Furthermore, many recruits expressed a desire to serve with a particular regiment, not necessarily their local one, and this was accommodated where possible, whilst all arms of the service continued to draw recruits from Ireland and Scotland. Probably the most that can be said is that from the mid-1870s a greater proportion of men in the ranks bore some connection with their brigade districts than had been the case before.

## Civilian Attitudes to Army Life

Paradoxically, although the British public still regarded army life with the greatest suspicion, it began to display an increasing romanticism towards the exploits of its soldiers overseas as the century wore on. This change had much to do with the improved facilities for communicating news, and with a more strident patriotism which became evident from the 1870s. It had been the newspapers which had first alerted the civilian population to the army's inadequacies in the Crimea, provoking an unprecedented wave of sympathy. Although photography was in its infancy, and it was in any case quite impossible to reproduce photographs in newspapers, journals illustrated with engravings became popular from the 1840s onwards. Increasingly, the British public were able to see images of contemporary warfare in their very homes, and within a few weeks of the events themselves taking place. Such images were often extraordinarily accurate; some Crimean ones were based on James Robertson or Roger Fenton photographs, and it was common for officers serving at the front to send home sketches to be published in engraved form. The pictures were, of course, sanitised, and sometimes unashamedly patriotic. By the 1870s, the more popular illustrated papers – *The Illustrated London News* and *The Graphic* – employed 'special artists', whose job was to travel the world in the footsteps of Victoria's armies, and chronicle them in a suitably dashing style. By the 1880s this had produced something of a personality cult, with the more famous 'specials' happily mixing their own exploits into their reports, and creating the impression that warfare was a high adventure; Tommy Atkins was the great hero, and the 'special' embodied the vicarious thrill of the civilian public looking over his shoulder at his feats of derring-do. All of this stimulated and encouraged a growing awareness of Britain's Imperial mission, which combined with the popularity of ideas of 'social Darwinism' – which were interpreted to stress the supremacy of British ideals and systems – to produce a brash patriotism characterised as 'jingoism'. The phrase jingoism was first coined in 1878, from a music-hall song which, composed in the wake of a threatened confrontation with Russia, aptly summed up an increasingly truculent pride in Britain's military might: 'We don't want to fight, but by jingo if we do, we've got the men, we've got the ships, we've got the money too!'. This renewed interest in the sharp end of Empire was reflected, too, in the art world, where a small number of artists who specialised in military scenes – notably Lady Elizabeth Butler and Richard

Caton Woodville – found a ready market for their visually stunning but rather stagy recreations of the great battles of the day. Nevertheless, the army stoutly performing its duty overseas was one thing; a garrison of redcoats, drinking, whoring and fighting in the city streets at home was quite another, and the public continued to despise army life in the form which it most frequently encountered. Rudyard Kipling, that great poet of the ambiguity of empire, perfectly summed up the public's double standard when he wrote,

> It's Tommy this, and Tommy that,
>     and chuck 'im out, the brute!
> But it's Saviour of 'is Country,
>     when the guns begin to shoot...

In the field, the qualities of the short-service recruits continued to be the subject of bitter debate. They were first used in large numbers in the Zulu War of 1879, where their showing was poor; the latter stages of the campaign were marked by a general unsteadiness amongst the troops and by a high incidence of false alarms at night. Whilst critics of the system argued that this showed the erosion of character produced by the system, the true fault lay not so much in short service *per se*, but in the fact that these men had been rushed out to Zululand hurriedly to make good the losses at Isandlwana. Many had scarcely learned the basic drill required of them, and they were greeted on arrival with exaggerated tales of the prowess and ferocity of their enemy. When the same men had had proper time to learn their trade, they proved every bit as reliable as the tough 'old sweats' of yore: the 3/60th Rifles, for example, were put into action at Gingindlovu in 1879 within a few weeks of their arrival in South Africa, but their nervous performance there was not repeated when many of the same men were pinned down all day under accurate Boer rifle fire at Ingogo in the 1881 Transvaal War. Similarly, 'B' Company, 2/24th, which held Rorke's Drift at the start of the Zulu War consisted of short-

service men, but had already undergone its baptism of fire in several months of hard campaigning in the Ninth Cape Frontier War.

### The Challenge of the Boer War

Perhaps the major success of the Cardwell reforms was to create a pool of reservists where none had existed before. It was put to the test when the Anglo-Boer War broke out in 1899 and, on the whole, more than proved its worth. Although when the war broke out the prevailing opinion was that the Boers would be no match for a trained modern army, the troops available on garrison duty in South Africa were still thought insufficient to meet the threat. Certainly, they were barely able to contain the initial Boer advances, and a significant contingent had to be despatched from India to reinforce them. Furthermore, it was decided to mobilise the 'First Army Corps' – those regiments based at home who could be readily brought up to strength with the first line of reservists – and send it to South Africa. A total of 47,000 men – thirty-three infantry battalions, seven cavalry regiments, and nineteen batteries, plus support corps – were efficiently raised and shipped out to the front. Its initial performance in action was poor, but this had little to do with the quality of the troops themselves. A combination of strategic and political circumstances – chiefly the British disasters at Stormberg Junction and Magersfontein – led to the Corps being sent into action before it was ready, and in the face of serious tactical difficulties. The defeat at Colenso, greeted with shock at home, was the result of hurried and poor planning, and of the excellence of the Boer position, neither of which indicate fundamental flaws in the reservist system. More damaging, however, was the fact that the army went into the Boer War with its senior organisational structures scarcely better prepared than in the Crimea, and Colenso clearly showed that battalion commanders were unused to working in brigades, and brigade commanders within a Corps, whilst Staff work still

*The Boer War demonstrated the willingness of the Colonies to support the Mother Country: Canadian troops storming a kopje, c 1901. (National Army Museum)*

relied heavily on the attitude of individual generals.

The Boer War, indeed, proved to be the ultimate test for the British army. For a war that was confidently expected to be over by Christmas 1899, it was to drag on until May 1902, and involve an unprecedented commitment of resources. Every British regiment, cavalry or infantry, except one (the 15th Hussars) – a total of 256,340 officers and men – fought in South Africa at some point, together with 109,048 Militia and Volunteer troops, a large number of non-regulation volunteer units, 30,633 volunteers from the colonies, and over 50,000 white South Africans settlers. Thousands of local civilians, black and white, worked as transport drivers, and, despite the fact that both sides attempted to propagate the myth that it was a 'white man's war', both used Africans as servants in the field and scouts, and neither scrupled on occasion to employ them in the firing line. Unlike most previous colonial campaigns, the war defied easy tactical solutions, and the army was forced to learn on its feet in a series of pitched battles and sieges, and then a protracted period of guerrilla war. Much of the war was waged

against practical difficulty as much as the enemy; the British struggled to maintain their troops in the field, tied to cumbersome supply trains, whilst the mobile Boer commandos, who lived off the land, ran rings around them. Although the British gradually honed down their forces, and made increasing use of mounted infantry and mobile machine- and quick-firing guns, they never quite rid themselves of the burden of supply, and even at the end of the war could seldom move beyond the fastest pace of their infantry. In the end, the struggle turned into a war of attrition, in which the immeasurably greater resources of the British ultimately won the day. Lines of blockhouses and barbed wire were built across the veld, to tie the Boers down, whilst their women and children were moved off the land into concentration camps, and their farms destroyed to deny the so-called 'bitter-enders' logistical support. These techniques have remained highly controversial, because in the squalid and badly run camps the Boer non-combatants were prey to hunger and disease, and the death rate among them was appalling. They were, however, ultimately successful in forcing

*Above: The 1st Army Corps lands in South Africa: the 2nd (Queen's Royal West Surrey) Regiment entraining at Durban docks, Boer War, 1899. (Bryan Maggs Collection)*

the exhausted and dispirited commandos to lay down their arms.

The Boer War had shown how far the British army had come in the 63 years that Queen Victoria had ruled the Empire. It had proved itself capable of meeting a serious challenge through sustained campaigning a long way from home, but it had nevertheless exposed many of the fallacies of the colonial era. At its higher levels it had been cumbersome and inefficient, and many of its generals clung to outmoded tactical theories. It had adapted to the circumstances in which it found itself, but slowly, and painfully; the Boers had taught a harsh lesson many times before it was finally learned. The close of the war encouraged a deep introspection and self-analysis, and provoked some far reaching reforms. The consequences of these would be tested in a very different type of warfare in Europe, with the outbreak of the First World War in 1914.

# 2
# BRITISH CAMPAIGNS, 1837–1902

## THE CRIMEA

The Crimean War (1854–6) was unique in British military experience in the Victorian period in being, in every respect, a European war. It had come about, not because of a need to secure or protect a colonial possession, but through a failure of international diplomacy on a grand scale. It was a direct clash between the greatest world powers of the age – with Britain, France, Sardinia and the Ottoman Empire ranged against Tsarist Russia – and it was fought entirely according to European conventions of war. There were no great disparities of outlook, organisation or tactics between the opposing armies, and indeed the fighting was conducted with weapons and methods which had altered little since the Napoleonic period. In many ways the Crimean War foreshadowed the First World War; both were great collisions of Empires, drawn into dispute following a clash in the Balkans, and in the field, the major battles comprised only a small part of the fighting, which was characterised instead by prolonged trench warfare. For Britain the Crimea was a watershed, the point at which the military practices and attitudes of an older order were seen to be outmoded, inefficient and costly, and which saw the first tentative steps taken towards a modern age.

The principal cause of the Crimean War was an abiding British suspicion

*The height of the battle of Inkerman: British and French troops fighting side by side to repulse the Russian attack. (Rai England Collection)*

of Tsarist Russia. During the struggle against Napoleon, Russia had seemed to Britain a heroic ally, but this image changed in the years that followed. British politicians and public alike began to fear that Russia, at once powerful, backward, exotic and alien, held designs on British imperial possessions overseas. Russia, it was widely believed, wanted to extend her influence westwards, into Europe, and southwards, into the independent Moslem khanates of Central Asia. Both areas nominally fell within Ottoman Turkey's sphere of influence, but Turkish power was on the wane, and successive British governments felt that this posed a real long-term threat to the security of their own overseas possessions. If Russia could secure a safe passage of the Bosphorous, the way was open for her fleet, based at Sebastopol in the Black Sea, to move freely into the Mediterranean, threatening the supremacy of the Royal Navy. Worse, by seizing large tracts of land in Central Asia, Russia could open the back door to Persia and Afghanistan, and beyond Afghanistan lay the most prized British possession of them all, India.

Ottoman Turkey had been in decline since the 1820s, and Russia had attempted, on a number of occasions, to pick up the pieces. By 1850 Tsar Nicholas I was prompted to describe Turkey as 'the sick man of Europe', and to hint that her European possessions should be carved up between the great powers. This solution was not acceptable to either Britain or France, and war came about ultimately because of an obscure quarrel over rights of access to the Christian holy places in Jerusalem. Although Jerusalem was part of Turkey's middle eastern empire, the Christian churches traditionally kept the sites, and in 1850 a wrangle between the Catholic and the Orthodox Churches over access to them led to a political showdown between France – who backed the Catholics – and Russia, who championed the Orthodox Church. This provoked Russia into moving troops into the Turkish Balkans to support the oppressed Orthodox communi-

ties there, and in July 1853 open war broke out between Russia and Turkey. The Russian advance faltered, however, in the face of a strong Turkish stand on the Danube, but in November the Russian navy caught a Turkish fleet in harbour and destroyed it with high explosive shells, which caused outrage in Europe. Britain and France promptly demanded Russia's withdrawal, and when it was not forthcoming, declared war in support of Turkey in March 1854.

It was not, however, immediately clear where this war was to take place. Royal Navy ships were sent into the Baltic, to bombard Russian ports, and during the course of the war there was to be sporadic Naval action against the Black Sea port of Odessa, and as far afield as the Russian Pacific coast. Nevertheless, the options for land operations were limited by the question of logistics and the need to support Turkey. Troops would clearly have to be sent abroad, but where to? Should they fight in the Balkans, or attempt to strike at Russia elsewhere and, if so, where? In the event, British troops were embarked before the Allied ultimatum expired, and were sent to the Dardenelles with no very clear objective in mind; their final destination would be dictated by unfolding events. This was the largest force sent out from Britain since the Napoleonic Wars, consisting of ten cavalry regiments, two horse artillery troops, eight field batteries, a siege train, 300 sappers and thirty infantry battalions. Before hostilities ended, a further four cavalry regiments, one troop of horse artillery, three field batteries, 115 siege guns, 460 sappers and twenty-two infantry battalions would be despatched as reinforcements, so that by 1856 nearly half the British army was committed to one campaign. The contribution of their French and Turkish allies was somewhat larger.

The British force was placed under the command of a number of senior officers, most of whom were veterans of Wellington's campaigns. The Commander-in-Chief was Fitzroy James Henry Somerset, Baron

Raglan. Raglan had been Wellington's Military Secretary in the Peninsula, and his personal courage was legendary; he had lost an arm at Waterloo, and when the surgeon carried off the amputated limb, Raglan coolly called him back and removed a ring, given to him by his wife. He had spent the years since in administrative posts, however, and had never commanded an army in action before the landing in the Crimea; furthermore, he was 64 years old at the start of the campaign. Indeed, few of his divisional commanders were much younger (their average age was 63), and most, like Raglan, had seen little active service since Wellington's day. Most were quite unused to commanding larger formations – brigades and divisions – whilst some, such as the Earl of Lucan and his brother-in-law, Lord Cardigan, had such a personal dislike for one another that it was almost impossible for them to work together. The youngest divisional commander was the Duke of Cambridge, just 35, the Queen's first cousin, who was appointed largely to represent the Royal family on the battlefield.

The expeditionary force had sailed from Britain at the end of February, amidst scenes of public jubilation; in the manner of all such expeditions, there was a firm belief that the troops would all be home by Christmas. The carnival atmosphere continued into the Mediterranean, but by the time it put ashore at the Dardenelles, the first signs of chaos and confusion were unmistakable. The troops were eventually landed at Varna on the Black Sea coast, but within a few weeks cholera had broken out, sweeping first through the French camp and then into the British, where over 600 men died in one week alone. A month later there was a devastating fire in Varna, which swept through the rickety buildings and destroyed many of the stores.

Even at this late stage, the exact Allied objectives had not been decided. Then, by a curious twist of fate, Russia abandoned her Balkan campaign and promptly withdrew

*Right: The Highland Brigade advancing with Colours flying and bayonets fixed at the Alma. (Rai England Collection)*

her forces. This offered the Allies a way out of their dilemma, but both Britain and France had invested so much prestige in the campaign that they felt unable to withdraw without first making an effective demonstration. Instead, they decided to strike at Sebastopol in the Crimea, the main base of the Russian Black Sea fleet, despite the fact that very little was known about either the Crimea, or Sebastopol itself. The Crimea is shaped like a diamond, lying on its side, and connected to the Russian mainland at the northern point. To the west and south it is surrounded by the Black Sea; to the east, by the Sea of Azov; and Sebastopol lies near the southern point. After some initial wrangling, the Allies opted to land at the ominously named Calamita Bay, on the west coast. They were singularly unprepared for a contested landing, but in the event the local Russian forces had already withdrawn towards Sebastopol, and the first troops were put ashore without opposition on 14 September. On the first night it rained heavily, soaking the troops, whose tents had not yet been put ashore – a foretaste of the discomforts to come.

The advance to Sebastopol began on the 19th. The line of advance took them south, with the coast on

their right, and was bisected at intervals by rivers running out to the sea. Lord Cardigan, leading the Light Cavalry ahead of the advance, ran into trouble almost at once, running into Russian Cossack cavalry beyond the River Bulgarnek. He immediately deployed the 11th Hussars and 13th Light Dragoons in a line, screened by skirmishers, and the first shots of the land war were fired. But before he could commit his men fully, Cardigan was ordered to withdraw by Raglan, who had spotted Russian infantry massing beyond the river, in a fold of ground invisible to Cardigan. British artillery hurried forward to cover Cardigan's retreat. The Russians also withdrew, and the reason for their apparent reluctance to give battle became clear the next day. Beyond the Bulgarnek, the next geographical obstacle was the river Alma. The river itself was only a stream but, whilst the northern side – from where the allies were advancing – sloped gently down towards the Alma, the ground rose sharply on the southern side, to a height of 500 feet or more, crested here and there with rocky cliffs. The road to Sebastopol wound up between the hills. As the Allied force approached the river early on the morning of the 20th, it immediately became clear

that the Russians had occupied the heights opposite in force. Nearly 40,000 men and over 120 guns were positioned along the upper slopes and crest, and to the (Allied) right of the road, the Russians had constructed two earthwork redoubts, effectively blocking the way.

The subsequent battle was essentially a Napoleonic contest, a vindication of the preferred British tactic, the assault in line, as advocated by Raglan's mentor, Wellington. The British took the left of the front, and the French the right. The French attacked in column, screened by skirmishers, but their attack became bogged down as they pressed up the heights towards the Russian position. By contrast, Raglan deployed two divisions in line next to one another, with one in support and two more in reserve. The attacking divisions crossed the Alma under fire, but began to lose formation as they pressed on up the heights, and much of the attack was carried out almost in skirmishing order. The Russian redoubts were captured, and a strong Russian counter-attack – in column – was met in line and broken up by volley-fire. British batteries were rushed up to an advanced position to enfilade the Russian line, and the Russians at last fell back. The battle lasted for about three hours, and both Allied armies were heavily engaged. Royal Navy ships, cruising off the coast, had added their fire in support, and shelled the crest of the hills. The advantages of the line formation over column had been vindicated, but the battle had showed the weakness of British divisional commanders in co-ordinating the attack, and Raglan himself had only exerted limited control. The battle was largely won by the initiative of the battalion commanders and by the courage and spirit of the men in the ranks – not for the last time in the Crimea. Nevertheless, the victory had proved costly, the British losing some 2000 men killed and wounded, the French 1300, and the Russians as many as 5000. The heights were strewn with dead and dying, and, tested for the first time in a severe action, the British medical facilities proved quite unable to cope with the flood of casualties.

For two days the Allies camped above the Alma whilst the wounded were collected and the dead buried, and in the meantime the Russians retired into Sebastopol. On the 23rd the advance began again. The Allies' natural line of advance would lead them to attack Sebastopol from the north, but the Russians had built an impressive line of fortresses to guard against any such threat, and instead the British and French opted to march around the port's flank, to encircle it, and to attack from the less well-protected south. Unknown to them, the Russian commander, Prince Meshikov, had decided not to remain in Sebastopol, but to retire inland along the valley of the Tchernaya river. This movement was carried out even as the Allies advanced, and the two armies almost blundered into one another. By the time the Allies had completed their manoeuvre, Sebastopol was guarded by a reduced force of just 16,000 men.

The Allied move effectively left them in unchallenged occupation of the Sebastopol peninsula, with the exception of the port itself. There were a number of viable landing places on the coastline, and Raglan chose the harbour at Balaclava –

seven miles from Sebastopol – for the British. Superficially it seemed ideal, a small harbour guarded by hills all round, but when the British occupied it on 26 September, after only a token resistance by the Russian garrison, they found it almost totally unsuitable as a supply depot. The harbour itself was tiny, an inlet just 1000 yards long and only 300 wide, with the town perched precariously on steep hills which rose sharply on all sides. The only easy route out of the bay was at the northern end, at the tip of the inlet, where a road ran though open country for a few miles before rising onto a ravine-scarred plateau that lay between Balaclava and Sebastopol. Although British engineers did their best to improve the port's rickety jetties, Balaclava would remain impossibly congested throughout the war. The French, who had been allocated two bays on the open coastland to the west, found them far more suitable for landing supplies.

The choice of landing beaches effectively dictated the Allied dispositions around Sebastopol, with the French taking the left of the line, and the British the right. The Russians had used the delays in the Allied advance to erect a chain of redoubts, linked by trenches, around the town's southern approaches, so that it was already too late to attempt a *coup de main*. The allies responded by erecting their own system of opposing trenches, and the fighting around Sebastopol degenerated into siege warfare. The Allies were still hampered by confusion and indecision; on the 17 October they directed an intensive artillery barrage against the defences, but failed to follow it up with an assault.

Instead, it was the Russians who struck first. Prince Menshikov, whose troops had been steadily reinforced by new battalions arriving via the Sea of Azov, spotted that the British line of communication was at its weakest around Balaclava itself. Some attempt had been made to fortify the hills above the bay, but the British line rested otherwise on a thin line north of the town. Here the undulating country was bisected by a

ridge running east to west, which the British had christened the Causeway Heights. No less than six redoubts had been hurriedly erected here, but they were not heavily fortified and were only lightly held by Turkish troops. The main British presence consisted of a single battalion of infantry, the 93rd Highlanders, placed on a rise below the Causeway Heights. The British Cavalry Division, commanded by Lord Lucan, was also camped near the western end of the Heights.

Early on the morning of 25 October, Menshikov struck at the Heights, advancing down the Tchernaya with a force of seventeen infantry battalions, thirty squadrons of cavalry, and sixty-four guns. The redoubts were rolled up from the Allied right, with the Turks making little effort to defend them. Raglan, hurrying to the scene, ordered troops down from Sebastopol, but in the meantime the Russians struck at the 93rd. Four squadrons of cavalry crested the Heights between the captured redoubts, and advanced towards the ridge. The 93rd's brigade commander, Sir Colin Campbell, deployed his men in a single line two deep; to those watching the developing battle, they seemed pitifully few, a 'thin red streak, tipped with steel'. As the Russian cavalry trotted towards them, however, Campbell gave the order to fire, and a volley rippled down the line. The cavalry shied off to their left, apparently hoping to outflank the Highlanders on the right. Campbell ordered his companies on the right to refuse the flank, and they loosed another volley which caught the Russians in the side as they moved across their front. This was enough to discourage the cavalry, who fell back on their supports beyond the Causeway Heights.

The Highlanders' stand had been remarkable, rebuffing a cavalry charge with just two volleys, and with very few casualties on either side. It was to be followed, however, by two more even more extraordinary events. Beyond the Causeway Heights, the main Russian cavalry force – some 2000 men – had been steadily advancing, and they now crossed the Heights to the west of the first attack. This route took them directly across the front of the stationary British Cavalry Division, to the west of the Heights. Sir James Scarlett, in command of the Heavy Brigade, immediately moved forward to intercept them. Surprisingly, the Russian cavalry had halted ahead of him, perhaps uncertain of their objective. With several squadrons lagging behind, their advance disrupted by obstacles, Scarlett led the first of the day's two great cavalry charges. Heavily outnumbered, his men rode up the gentle slope ahead and smack into the stationary Russian mass. There was a brief flurry of fighting, a congested melee amidst a press of men and horses, and the British survivors emerged on the far side. As they rallied, British artillery, which had been rushed up in support, opened fire, and the Russians retreated back across the Causeway Heights. The Heavy Brigade had lost seventy-eight men in the charge; the Russians 270.

The demoralised Russian cavalry were now vulnerable to a vigorous attack by the Light Brigade, who were well-placed to charge into their flank. Cardigan, however, felt that his orders allowed him no opportunity to move, and he allowed the moment to pass. The stage was set, instead, for the great tragedy by which this day would be remembered. To observers on the heights towards Sebastopol, it seemed that the Russians were now preparing to withdraw, taking with them the guns captured in the redoubts. The only troops in a position to stop them were the Light Cavalry Brigade, and Raglan therefore sent an order to Lucan ordering him to make a demonstration against the redoubts. Unfortunately, from his position on the northern edge of the Heights, Lucan could not make sense of the order, and Raglan was prompted to send a second, with fatal consequences: 'Lord Raglan wishes the cavalry to advance rapidly to the front, and try to prevent the enemy carrying away the guns. Troop of horse artillery may accompany. French cavalry is on your left.'

Presumably Raglan meant that the cavalry should cross to the southern side of the Heights and advance below the redoubts, thereby outflanking the Russian positions, but from the foot of the Heights the only Russians Lucan could see were directly in front of him down a valley at the northern end of the Causeway Heights. The Russians commanded this valley on both sides, and Lucan was incredulous; Raglan's message had been carried by his ADC, Captain Nolan, and when Lucan questioned the order, Nolan, gesturing towards the battery ahead, snapped: 'There, my lord, is your enemy; there are your guns.' Astonished, but reluctant to disobey a direct order, Lucan gave the order for the cavalry to advance. The Light Brigade, deployed in squadrons, were on the left and slightly in front, with the Heavies now to the right rear. Cardigan himself led his brigade. As they advanced, Captain Nolan broke ranks and rode across their front, shouting wildly; if he had realised the error, however, he had no opportunity to correct it, for at that moment a Russian shell exploded overhead and Nolan was killed by a splinter.

As the pace quickened, the cavalry came under fire from both sides of the valley and Lucan, realising that the attack was folly, called back the Heavy Brigade. The Light Brigade, however, rode on through a storm of shot and shell and reached the guns, cutting down the gunners. Behind the Russian battery, Cossack cavalry belatedly came forward to protect the gunners, and the Light Brigade's impetus carried it in amongst them. After a fierce tussle, which broke up what remained of their formations, the Light Brigade began to rally on its officers and, having completed its objectives, retired back down the valley. Considering that they had charged into the very 'jaws of death', their casualties were surprisingly light; out of a total 673 men who had begun the charge, 113 had been killed, and 247 wounded. Cardigan, who had led from the front throughout, was quite untouched. The most devastating blow, however, was that

475 horses had been killed, and forty-two injured, and this alone meant that the Light Brigade ceased to exist as an effective force.

The Charge of the Light Brigade dominates the memory of Balaclava. In fact, in most other respects, the battle had been a British victory; a strong Russian force had been checked, and, although Russian troops occupied the eastern end of the Causeway Heights for several weeks more, the line of communication between Balaclava and Sebastopol remained open. However, wrangling over the fate of the Light Brigade began almost before the last shots were fired, as Raglan greeted Lucan with the comment: 'You have lost the Light Brigade!' It was the first salvo in a battle which lasted for years, and was fought out in lawsuits and parliamentary debates. Cardigan himself did not stay long in the Crimea; with the onset of winter, he took the opportunity to resign his command and return to Britain.

On the 26th, the day after Balaclava, the Russians mounted a sortie from Sebastopol against the right of the British line. It was repulsed, but it foreshadowed a much greater Russian offensive in the same area. Sebastopol was not completely cut off by the Allies, since the British right fell some way short of the river Tchernaya, and one road remained open to the Russians. This allowed the town garrison the chance to coordinate its movements with Menshikov's forces inland, and on 5 November the Russians mounted a joint attack on this sector, just above the ruins of the village of Inkerman. Here the ground sloped up sharply from the river to the heights where the British right was posted. The ground here was extremely broken, a maze of tangled gullies which scoured the slope, obscured here and there by patches of bush. The attack involved some 40,000 troops and began early on the morning, when the heights were shrouded in thick fog. The Russians pushed up the corrugated slope and blundered into the first British picquets, but instead of withdrawing them, the local British commander, realising the danger to his flank, ordered up supports to reinforce them. Thus began the hardest fought battle of the war, a confusing series of piecemeal actions which lasted for most of the day and almost defy description. Both British and, later, French troops were rushed from elsewhere along the line to hold back the Russian advance, and they were fed into a narrow front where the fighting raged back and forth over the slopes and gullies. Much of the fighting took place in a gloom of fog and mist that limited visibility to a few yards and was often hand to hand, using bayonets, rifle-butts, stones and even boots. It was impossible to maintain any sort of ordered formation, and the fight was controlled at battalion level or below; the brunt of the fighting often fell to small groups, commanded by NCOs, who were required to mount fierce attacks or stubborn defences on their own ini-tiative. By late afternoon the Allied pressure was beginning to push the Russians down the hill, and at last they retreated. It had proved a very costly assault: nearly 11,000 Russians had been killed, wounded or cap-tured, including six generals and 256 officers. The British lost 597 killed, and 1860 wounded, including thirty-nine officers killed and ninety-one wounded. The French lost 130 killed and 750 wounded.

Inkerman had proved to be a sol-diers' battle, and the Allies had tri-umphed solely through the courage and tenacity of the men in the ranks. Yet the effect was to produce some-thing of a stalemate, paralysing active operations for much of the rest of the war. The repulse seriously damaged the Russian capability to make such assaults, and despite a constant flow of reinforcements, they never felt able to chance such an attack again. In this respect the Allies – particularly the British – were in a similar position; their losses could only be made good by inexpe-rienced drafts from home, who took time to reach the front. Indeed, the high proportion of fresh troops exposed in the later fighting around Sebastopol was reflected in perfor-mance in the field; such troops did not lack courage or enthusiasm, but they did not possess the tenacity and endurance of those who had faced the enemy before.

After Inkerman, the war degener-ated into the sort of trench warfare which later characterised the West-ern Front during the First World War. Both sides made occasional probes, forays or night attacks to test the other's defences, but major activ-ity was further hampered by the onset of bad weather. A terrible storm blew up on 14 November, dev-astating British shipping anchored off Balaclava and flattening many of

*Russian skirmishers attacking British positions outside Sebastopol, October 1854. (National Army Museum)*

*Right: The slender comforts of campaign life: Colonel Hallewell of the 28th Regiment and his servant in the Crimea. (Private collection)*

their camps. It was the first taste of a Crimean winter, for which the Allies – who had expected the war to be over long before – had made no provision. Among the British, the supply of winter clothing was negligible. In the absence of a proper commissariat, civilian contractors struggled to move supplies up to the front from Balaclava, and there were desperate shortages of food. Disease broke out in the cramped and insanitary conditions in the trenches to add to the miseries of exposure and frost-bite. Many of the new drafts sent out from Britain fell ill as soon as they were exposed to conditions at the front, and were promptly sent back again. There was no effective system for evacuating the sick or

injured, and the regimental medical staff were hopelessly overworked. The worst cases were sent back to a base hospital at Scutari, on the Bosphorous. Conditions here were equally grim. News of the suffering prompted Florence Nightingale to raise thirty-eight volunteer nurses and sail to Scutari in an attempt to improve the conditions there.

With the improvement of the weather in spring 1855, the Allies prepared for a new offensive, reinforced by Sardinia's decision to enter the war, and by the arrival of 15,000 of her troops. Nevertheless, the Allies were still hampered by indecision and rivalry between themselves. In April a prolonged bombardment lasted for the best part of eight days, but the only assault that was mounted was an ineffectual night attack by part of the British Light Division. Towards the end of May, there was a joint expedition against the Russians in the Tchernaya valley, in which the French bore the brunt of the fighting, but the results were inconclusive. At the beginning of June, another prolonged bombardment preceded an attack on some of the key defensive points around Sebastopol, but the results were dis-

appointing and the Russian line held. On 28 June Lord Raglan died.

Not until winter loomed again did the tide finally swing in the Allies' favour. At the beginning of September fresh assaults were made against the Russian redoubts, with the usual lack of success. This time, however, the Russian garrison decided to pull out and fall back across the Tchernaya, abandoning Sebastopol to the Allies. After having been fought over for so long the town proved a disappointing prize. Nor did its capture end the war, as the focus of conflict had now shifted away from the Crimean front. In Armenia, the Russians had attacked the fortified Turkish city of Kars, where British advisers helped to orchestrate the defence. Kars was besieged for five months before starvation finally forced the defenders to submit. Frustrated at a lack of success in the Crimea, Britain stepped up her naval attacks on Russia, bombarding the forts at Odessa, and patrolling the Pacific Coast. In Sebastopol, the British and French prepared for another Crimean winter, but this time they were much better equipped to face it. Heavy sheepskin coats were issued to the men, who

were moved out of their tents and into the abandoned barracks and buildings of Sebastopol. By spring 1856, the Allied armies were ready for a fresh offensive, but the British and French governments, sick of war, were prepared to negotiate. In February Austria offered to mediate between the warring parties, and on 30 March the Treaty of Paris was agreed. Under its terms, the Black Sea and Dardenelles were forbidden to Russian warships, and Austria, Britain and France guaranteed the integrity of the Ottoman Empire.

The original British objective – to safeguard her naval supremacy in the Mediterranean – had therefore been secured, and by July 1856 the last British troops had been evacuated from the Crimea. The whole campaign had cost the British army 1933 killed in action, 1921 dead from wounds, a staggering 15,724 dead from disease, and 2874 discharged

through disease or wounds. The Treaty of Paris lasted until 1871, when the Russians abandoned it, fortified Sebastopol once more, and began to reconstruct its Black Sea Fleet.

## INDIA

By the time Queen Victoria came to the throne in 1837, India was already, in an apt if clichéd phrase, the 'jewel in the crown of Empire'. Britain ruled, directly or through alliances with local potentates, an area of 1.6 million square miles, which stretched from the Indus river in the west to Burma in the east, and encompassed high mountain ranges, baking lowland plains, and humid jungles. British rule affected the lives of 400 million people, and the need to secure India internally, or defend it against external threats from rival

empires, dominated British foreign policy throughout the century. In particular, the vulnerable western border, which for centuries was the traditional route into India for would-be conquerors, proved a source of constant concern, and required continual policing. Furthermore, the 1850s saw an internal challenge to British rule which, had it succeeded, would have jeopardised British influence across southern Asia, and jeopardised the basis of the Empire itself.

### The Origins of British Power

Until 1857, Britain ruled India through the Honourable East India Company (EIC). The Company had originally been a purely commercial concern, granted a monopoly of British trade across half the world – the area between the Cape of Good Hope and Cape Horn, excepting those areas ruled by Christians, who

*Opposite page: The* entente cordiale*: British cavalry sergeants share a glass with a French infantry-man in the Crimea. (Private collection)*

*Right: The harsh and forbidding terrain of the North-West Frontier, the security of which plagued British India for more than a century. (Bryan Maggs Collection)*

were graciously permitted to trade with whom they liked – by Queen Elizabeth I in 1600. This monopoly allowed the Crown to benefit from the activities of its merchant adventurers whilst maintaining a safe political distance. The British, French, Portuguese and Dutch all vied for the lucrative spice trade, and, forming local alliances within India, brought their wider quarrels with them, provoking a series of struggles which ultimately saw the British victorious, and left the Company itself the dominant power in the sub-continent. By 1837 the last Mughal emperor was little more than a Company pensioner, and many apparently independent Indian princes ruled only with Company approval. The Company, meanwhile, had lost much of its original trading focus. Its authority was made subject to the British government, and it was effectively transformed into an agent of the Empire. It ruled India through three self-contained Presidencies – Bombay on the west coast, Madras on the east, and Bengal in the north-east – and all three Presidencies maintained a large military establishment. The backbone of the Company military system was the Indian regular soldier or sepoy (from the Persian *sipahi*), who was trained to fight according to European drill systems, in largely British uniforms and with British weapons, and under the command of both white and Indian officers. Although the Crown maintained the fiction of the Company's independent status, units from the British army (usually known as King's or Queen's regiments, to distinguish them from EIC troops) were required to serve in India, albeit at Company expense. In due course, Indian troops would be employed in support of the Crown in countries outside the sub-continent. One significant feature of military life which characterised the history of British rule in India, however, was that Indian officers were considered inferior to British officers of the same rank.

## Strategic Concerns, 1837

By the time of Queen Victoria's coronation, the greatest threat to British rule seemed to be largely external. British influence ended at the line of the Indus and Satlej rivers in the west, beyond which lay the independent Sikh kingdom of Lahore to the north, and the amirates of Sind to the south. These, in turn, gave way to the rising hill country that ended in the Afghanistan massif. Beyond Afghanistan, 2000 miles north-west of the Satlej, was the River Oxus, the border with Central Asia, and the first outposts of the Russian empire. Despite this broad buffer zone, however, Britain was acutely sensitive to the possibility of Russian influence in India, and whatever her true intentions, Russia was not averse to playing the India card when it suited her broader strategic concerns. Rumours that the Russians were poised to strike into Afghanistan were rife from the 1820s; in 1828 Russia established a pro-Russian Shah on the Persian throne, and in 1837 Persia, with Russian support, attacked the western Afghan city of Herat, a move which seemed to Company officials in distant Calcutta to be heavy with menace.

The Company responded by attempting to establish a pro-British regime in Afghanistan. A palace coup in 1810 had resulted in the incumbent Amir, Shah Shuja, fleeing to exile in Lahore. The British now proposed to return Shuja to his throne in return for his future support; although some Afghan resistance was anticipated, it was widely believed that the Afghans would be no match for a British army. There were two routes into Afghanistan: through the Khyber Pass in the north, and through the Bolan in the south. The Company controlled nei-

ther of these. The route to one lay through the kingdom of Lahore, whilst the other was in the territory of the amirs of Sind. The kingdom of Lahore, ruled by able and astute Sikh Ranjit Singh, was broadly sympathetic to the Company's cause, having its own quarrels with the Afghans, but refused to publicly commit itself by allowing EIC troops free passage. The Company decided, instead, to enter Afghanistan through the Bolan, taking the opportunity instead to impress the amirs of Sind along the way, and in February 1839 an army consisting of Queen's and EIC troops in almost equal numbers, and supported by an enormous train of non-combatants, crossed the Indus. There was little fighting in Sind itself, although Afghan hillmen contested the passage of the Bolan. The British occupied Kabul and restored Shah Shuja to his throne, but the Afghan adventure soon turned sour. Shuja's regime proved deeply unpopular, and in 1841 the Afghans rose up, and when the British garrison at Kabul tried to retreat to India it was cut to pieces. Although British

troops were hurried into Afghanistan and suppressed the Afghans, the mission had been a political disaster, and by 1843 the Company had abandoned all involvement in Afghanistan.

## The Conquest of Sind, 1843

The failure of intervention in Afghanistan left the western border as open as ever. Furthermore, the fighting had largely alienated both the amirates of Sind and the kingdom of Lahore. In a belated attempt to shore up its influence, the Company entrusted the eccentric but dynamic General Sir Charles Napier with the task of annexing Sind. Napier's approach to the affair was decidedly pragmatic; 'We have no right to seize Sind', he wrote, 'yet we shall do so, and a very advantageous, humane and useful piece of rascality it will be.' Another commentator observed that, 'Coming after Afghanistan, it put me in mind of a bully who had been kicked in the street and went home to beat his wife in revenge.'

Napier provoked a war by presenting the amirs with a treaty he knew

they could not accept. A British resident at Haiderabad, in southern Sind, was attacked, and Napier promptly crossed into Sind in February 1843 at the head of 2600 troops, including a single Queen's regiment, the 22nd Foot. The Amirs attempted to block his advance with nearly 20,000 men, mostly Baluchi tribesmen. The Baluchis deployed in a strong position in a river bed at Miani, but, undaunted by the odds against him, Napier immediately attacked, on 17 February 1843. The superior discipline and firepower of the Queen's and EIC troops prevailed, and the Baluchis reluctantly gave way. Napier had lost twenty officers and 250 men, against an estimated Baluchi loss of 7000. Reinforced, Napier pressed on towards Haiderabad, only to find his way blocked again outside the village of Dubba. Once again, the Baluchi position was well chosen, with one flank resting on a river, and the other on a wood, and the line screened by entrenchments. Napier once more attacked with vigour, and the infantry drove the Baluchis out of their position, so that they were exposed to Napier's cavalry. When the amirs inquired what terms Napier offered, he replied bluntly: 'Life and nothing more. And I want your decision before twelve o'clock, as I shall by that time have buried my dead, and given my soldiers their breakfast.' The amirs had little option but to submit.

The Sind campaign had been short, sharp, but successful. Nevertheless, as in Afghanistan four years before, the defeat of the main enemy concentrations did not entirely pacify the countryside, and Napier was faced with continuing low-intensity warfare in the border regions. He countered the threat with locally raised irregular troops, who were vigorous in patrolling and counter-raiding, a pattern of events which soon came to typify British experience along the Indian frontiers.

*Opposite page: The 22nd Regiment attacking Baluchis at the battle of Miani, 17 February 1843. (National Army Museum)*

### The '48 Hours War': Gwalior 1843
In 1843, the Company also embarked on a swift campaign against the Maratha state of Gwalior, the so-called '48 Hours War'. The Maratha princes had long been opposed to Company rule, and in 1843 an apparent build-up of Maratha forces at Gwalior, east of Delhi, seemed to threaten Company influence in northern India at a time when it was preoccupied with affairs in the west. The Company mounted a pre-emptive campaign, and in December General Sir Hugh Gough, a Napoleonic veteran, was sent to annex Gwalior at the head of an army of 12,000 men. It was not expected that the Marathas would oppose the expedition, but at the village of Maharajpore on 29 December Gough ran into a force of 14,000 Maratha infantry, 3000 cavalry, and as many as 100 guns. Gough was not a particularly imaginative commander, and placed great faith in frontal assaults made with the bayonet. At Maharajpore he attacked across ground seamed with gullies and in the face of a withering Maratha fire; the village itself was successfully stormed, and the Marathas driven back through a succession of defensive positions. Gough's tactics condemned his men to enormous casualties – over 800 men killed – but ultimately his troops were able to endure the grim slogging match for longer than the Marathas, who finally withdrew at a cost of 3000 men and fifty-six guns. Coincidentally, another British column advancing on Gwalior was attacked at Punniar on the same day. The Marathas had occupied a ridge overlooking the road, but were driven from it in a series of well co-ordinated flank attacks, a distinct contrast to Maharajpore. Within a few days the converging British columns occupied Gwalior, and the Marathas were forced to accept terms.

### The Sikh Wars, 1845–9
The occupation of Sind meant that the Punjab – the region west of the Satlej river – was the only area along the Afghan foothills not controlled by the Company. This was the terri-

tory of the Sikhs, originally a reformist religious sect, who had acquired a militant edge, and who had been forged into a kingdom in the early nineteenth century by Ranjit Singh. The kingdom of Lahore boasted a large army – the Khalsa – trained and uniformed along European lines by French veterans of the Napoleonic Wars. Ranjit Singh had been an ally of the Company, but after his death in 1839 the army became the dominant force in Sikh politics. The mood swung against the Company, fuelled by suspicion of its intentions in the aftermath of the Afghan debacle, and by 1845 tension had reached such a pitch that a Sikh army crossed the Satlej and struck at Company territory, besieging the town of Ferozepore.

Sir Hugh Gough, the victor of Maharajpore, was despatched to halt the Sikh advance. Moving without proper scouting arrangements, Gough was surprised by a Sikh army of 22,000 men and twenty-two guns which had moved to intercept him. The Sikh gunners took up a position masked by low jungle beyond the village of Mudki. Despite the fact that his troops were exhausted by the day's march, Gough launched a frontal assault on the Sikh position on the evening of 18 December 1845. Gough's infantry suffered heavily from the Sikh artillery, but on either flank his cavalry easily routed its dashing but disorganised Sikh counterpart. Rather than risk being cut off, the Sikhs withdrew under cover of darkness to their camp at Ferozeshah. The Khalsa lost fifteen of its guns and hundreds of men killed, but Gough sustained 872 killed and wounded, a high price to pay for his tactical unsubtlety.

Just three days later, apparently learning little from his mistakes, Gough attacked the camp at Ferozeshah. Here the Sikhs had some 35,000 infantry and seventy-three guns heavily entrenched behind a breastwork chest-high and a mile long. Delayed by the need to await reinforcements, Gough once again launched a frontal attack in the late afternoon. Despite horrific casualties from the Sikh cannonade, the British

*Above: The 9th Regiment overruns Sikh guns and attacks their camp at Ferozeshah, 1845. (Private collection)*

infantry pressed on to reach the enemy entrenchments, and the battle raged at close quarters until darkness fell. By this time Gough realised that his attacks had lost momentum; his men lay out on the field all night exposed to Sikh musketry, but in the morning returned to the attack. They successfully stormed the Sikh artillery, until the sudden arrival of Sikh reinforcements threatened to cheat them of success. The new arrivals remained uncommitted, however, and indecision and intrigue amongst the Sikh officers finally cost them the battle. Gough had won the day, but at the cost of over 2400 men.

In the immediate aftermath of Ferozeshah both armies regrouped. A siege train was despatched from Delhi to reinforce Gough, but the Sikhs moved out to intercept it. Gough despatched Sir Harry Smith to head them off, and Smith attacked the Sikh camp at Aliwal on 28 Janu-

ary 1846. Showing rather more tactical flair than his commander, Smith softened up the position with a heavy bombardment, suppressing much of the Sikh artillery, then launched a cavalry attack on the Sikh left and centre. The Sikh regulars formed squares to receive them, but the cavalry drove through them in an action which effectively demonstrated the inadequacies of Sikh bayonet training. The Sikhs abandoned the field in disorder, and Smith captured all their guns.

The successive British victories broke all of the Sikh positions east of the Satlej except one, at Sobraon, where 30,000 men were entrenched with their back to the river. Gough approached Sobraon in his usual style on 10 February, and the fighting was a repetition of the earlier engagements. Initial assaults were driven back with heavy casualties, but eventually forced a breach in the Sikh line. A ferocious melee drove the Sikhs back to the river, and as the Khalsa attempted to withdraw over a single bridge of boats, the bridge collapsed under the weight, and hun-

dreds of men were swept away. Sikh casualties were estimated at between 8000 and 12,000, and all their guns were captured; Gough's men, however, had again paid a high price, with over 2300 killed. Nevertheless, on 8 March the kingdom of Lahore submitted to the Company. The Sikh army was dissolved, and the kingdom itself declared a Protectorate, with EIC officials distributed around the Punjab to administer it.

Yet the country was by no means pacified, and many in the old army felt that they had not been defeated in the field, but betrayed by their own high command. The result was a popular uprising which in April 1848 claimed the lives of two Company officials at Multan. The EIC garrisons around the country despatched troops to besiege Multan, but even as they did so members of the Khalsa flocked to join the rebellion. Gough was once more given command of an army to suppress the Punjab, but at the river Chenab at Ramnaggar on 22 November he found his way blocked by boggy ground and Sikh artillery. He was

*Left: British cavalry charging the Sikhs at Sobraon. (Rai England Collection)*

The political repercussions of Chillianwallah were such that Napier was sent to replace Gough, but in fact Gough brought the war to a close before he arrived. Multan fell to the besiegers, and a siege-train was sent to reinforce Gough. Encouraged, he advanced on the Sikh concentration at Gujerat. On 10 February 1846 he opened fire with a heavy barrage which suppressed most of the Sikh artillery; his infantry then drove off the Sikh foot, whilst British cavalry dispersed their Sikh opposite numbers on the flanks. The Sikh rebellion collapsed in the light of this uncharacteristically adroit victory, and on 12 March the Khalsa formally surrendered. This time the kingdom of Lahore was annexed outright, the army broken up, and a new internal security force raised along EIC lines.

## The Indian Mutiny, 1857–9

The Company's campaigns in the west, particularly the Sikh Wars, were the hardest they had yet fought on Indian soil. Although British regulars of the Queen's regiments had been heavily involved, the majority of the troops employed were nonetheless Indians in the Company's armies. India could not, therefore, have been won or held without the complicity of its own subjects. The extent of Company dependence on its subjects became all too apparent in 1857, when the army of the Presidency of Bengal turned against its master, precipitating a desperate struggle in which the future of British rule itself was at stake.

It was a fundamental part of Hindu belief that Indian society was divided into four pre-ordained, immutable classes. These classes were appointed particular roles in the great scheme of things, and intimate contact between the classes was to be avoided at all costs, since it might lead to a spiritual contamination that had lasting repercussions in the afterlife. Each class was further sub-divided into innumerable castes, which were

forced to withdraw and cross the river elsewhere, outflanking the Sikh position. On 13 January 1849 he blundered into a large enemy force well placed above the village of Chillianwallah. The Sikhs had placed their guns on a low rise overlooking marshy ground and surrounded by jungle. Gough had not intended to

*Below: 'At them with the bayonet': the final destruction of the Khalsa at Sobraon. (Rai England Collection)*

attack, but an opening barrage from the Khalsa guns provoked him. 'The impudent rascals fired on me', he said, 'They put my Irish blood up and I attacked them.' The British force had to advance across broken ground in the teeth of a terrible barrage, and when it reached the Sikh line, fighting raged at close quarters until nightfall. The Sikhs eventually fell back, but only to a more secure position in the rear, and this ineffectual victory had cost Gough 2400 killed and wounded.

based not only on class, but upon racial or tribal origin, and profession. In the armies of the Madras and Bombay Presidencies, caste had not been allowed to interfere with military discipline, and differences were effectively subordinated to the common brotherhood of the soldier, at least while the men were in Company service. The Bengal Presidency, however, had recruited heavily from the princely states of north-eastern India, which were traditionally conservative in their beliefs. On the eve of the uprising, the Bengal establishment was a large one – ten regiments of regular cavalry, eighteen of irregular cavalry, seventy-four infantry regiments, and twenty-two artillery batteries. Approximately two-thirds of these men belonged to the higher castes, whilst the rest were either lower-caste Hindus, Moslems or Christians, all of whom were considered 'untouchable' by their high-caste colleagues.

The effective management of such an army required no small amount of understanding of the soldiers' beliefs, and tact in dealing with them, but the first half of the nineteenth century was a time of great change. Growing ideas of racial superiority caused many younger British officers to despise all things Indian, whilst the Company's attempt to introduce western ideas of progress aroused suspicions that it was intent on undermining Indian religious beliefs. In 1856 a new Enlistment Act required sepoys to accept the possibility of overseas service – which was never popular, since the confinement on board ship carried a great risk of contamination of caste – whilst at the same time denying them extra payments, which were often spent on purification rituals. That same year the Company annexed the kingdom of Awadh (Oudh), where many of the Bengal sepoys had been recruited, an

unpopular move which deprived many sepoys of privileges they had previously enjoyed at the king's court. Amongst the conservative upper classes, it seemed that the Company was bent on attacking their traditions and beliefs on all sides.

It was against this background that the infamous issue of the greased cartridges achieved such significance. In 1856, the Company attempted to replace the outdated smooth-bore 1842 model percussion musket with the Enfield rifle, which had proved far more effective in the Crimea. To load the Enfield it was necessary to bite one end off the cartridge, then pour part of the powder down the

*Below: The outbreak of the Great Mutiny caught the East India Company by surprise. Here Mutineers from the 9th Bengal Infantry attack their officers. (Author's collection)*

barrel. The cartridge was then rammed home, and to make this easier it had been lubricated with grease. This grease the sepoys regarded with deep mistrust, since a rumour soon spread that it was a mixture of cow and pig fat. The cow was a sacred animal to the Hindu, and the pig an unclean one to the Moslem, and to allow such fat into the mouth was an abomination to both. In fact, there may have been some truth to the story, since many contractors, opting for the cheapest alternative, waxed the cartridges with tallow, which did indeed contain animal fats.

Mutiny was by no means unusual in the Company's army. Refusing pay, and in extreme cases refusing orders, was a traditional method of demonstrating discontent within the Indian military system. There had been many mutinies in the past. Most were resolved before they led to violence, although a few had been ruthlessly suppressed. None, however, were as severe as the Great Mutiny of 1857, either in scope or consequences. When news of sepoy discontent reached Company ears, many European officers tried to calm their soldiers' fears by offering to replace the suspect cartridges with those greased with harmless vegetable fats, but the sepoys' reluctance to accept this was indicative of the depth of their discontent. Other officers reacted harshly, bullying or disarming those men who refused the new rifle. The results were shocking; on 29 March 1857, Mangal Panday, a sepoy of the 34th Native Infantry stationed at Barrackpore, went berserk, attacking his officers and calling on his fellows to join him. He was overwhelmed – ironically by Indian members of his regiment – and later tried and executed, but the Company failed to recognise the extent of the discontent. Then, at Mirath (Meerut), an important garrison on the Grand Trunk Road which connected Calcutta in the east to the Punjab in the west, the 3rd Light Cavalry and 11th and 20th Native Infantry at first refused the new cartridge, and then, on Sunday 9 May, fired on their officers at Church Parade. Mirath exploded into incendiarism and violence as the soldiers, urged on by the bazaar mob, attacked white officers and civilians alike. When the news of the uprising spread, garrisons across Bengal followed Mirath's example.

The Great Mutiny was to prove the severest test of British rule in India, and, indeed, one of the greatest crises of Queen Victoria's reign. Nevertheless, it was not a co-ordinated challenge to British rule across the sub-continent; had it been, it is unlikely that the British could have maintained their hold on the whole country. The mutiny itself was almost entirely confined to the Bengal army, since although a few regiments in the Madras and Bombay Presidencies showed signs of wavering loyalty, there was no outbreak comparable to that in Bengal. More surprisingly, perhaps, the Punjab remained loyal to its new masters, providing an immensely important resource for the British, who drew heavily on Sikh troops to augment the slender number of EIC European troops and British regulars. Even in Bengal, many Indians remained loyal to the Company, for not all EIC regiments mutinied, and many among the civilian population either sheltered British fugitives during the initial uprisings, or joined British troops as irregulars or servants. Thus, without Indian assistance, the British could never have restored their authority.

Furthermore, the rebels were weakened by internal divisions, by differing motives, and by no very clear objective. On the very evening that the mutiny erupted at Mirath, the mutineers set out on the road to Delhi, to the court of Bahadur Shah, the last of the Mughal emperors. Delhi had already joined the rising, and with the arrival of the Mirath garrison, the mutineers proclaimed Bahadur Shah their leader. The emperor accepted the role reluctantly, but in doing so, he shifted the emphasis of the revolt away from a purely military protest towards a conservative national rebellion. Delhi became a focus for the rising, a symbol of a golden age of pre-colonial independence, but neither the emperor nor his 'mutineer court' had any definite idea how this ideal could be transformed into reality.

The outbreak of the Mutiny took the British by surprise, and they reacted slowly to the challenge. The nearest concentration of British troops was at Ambala in the Himalayan foothills, 160 miles from Mirath, and it took several days to prepare them for the march. Even then they were able to advance only at night, because of the stifling daytime heat. Cholera broke out, decimating the ranks and striking down one senior officer after another. At Badli-ki-Serai on 8 June the British column encountered and defeated a rebel force outside Delhi, but it soon became apparent that they could not hope to recapture the city immediately. Delhi lay with its back to the River Jumna, and was protected by high walls and ditches. Furthermore, rebels from all over Bengal were making their way there, and the British were heavily outnumbered. The best they could do was take possession of a ridge overlooking the city, and try to invest it whilst waiting for reinforcements.

Meanwhile there had been sporadic outbursts of violence across northern India, and the situation was particularly severe in Awadh, where Company rule was new and fragile. The first mutinies broke out in the capital, Lucknow, at the end of May, and the British commissioner, Henry Lawrence, took steps to fortify the complex of buildings which comprised the residency. In early July Lawrence decided to make a sortie against rebels concentrating outside the city. His troops – a mixture of British regulars and volunteers – blundered into the enemy and were defeated; they fell back on the Residency, which the rebels promptly besieged. Although the position was relatively secure, the garrison was constantly exposed to sniper and shell-fire, and Lawrence himself was killed by a shell fragment.

One of the most brutal incidents of the whole rising occurred at Kanpur (Cawnpore), on the borders of

*Left: The devastation inflicted on the city of Lucknow, besieged by both the rebels and later the British. (National Army Museum)*

*Left: Troops in typical Mutiny campaign dress – shell-jackets and covered forage caps – pose in front of Colonel Wheeler's cantonment, pockmarked by shell-fire, at Kanpur. (National Army Museum)*

Awadh. The British commander here, General Wheeler, had withdrawn his command to two old brick-built barrack buildings outside the city, which he had hastily fortified, this position coming under attack in early June. At Kanpur, the rebellion was to produce one of its most significant leaders, the adopted son of a dead Mahratta prince, known as the Nana Sahib, who had been largely dispossessed by the Company, and who thereby personified many of the movement's grievances. The Nana Sahib sent terms to Wheeler under a flag of truce, guaranteeing the British safe conduct out of his territory. Wheeler agreed, and at dawn on 27 June his force, and their civilian dependants, marched out of the barracks and down to the nearby River Ganges, where the Nana Sahib had provided boats for them. As the British climbed into the boats, however, the first shots rang out – whether by planned treachery or simply through the tension of the moment has never been resolved – and the boats were raked with fire. Most of the British were slaughtered in the shallows, or butchered as they staggered ashore. One boat managed to escape, but many of the women and children were killed on the spot, and the rest – over 200 of them – were taken prisoner.

For both sides, the fate of Delhi, Lucknow and Kanpur came to symbolise the progress of the rebellion. The rebels needed a decisive victory to spread their cause, but they were weakened by uncertain planning among their high command and by poor tactical co-ordination. Each week that went by worked in favour of the British, for whom the beleaguered cities became a focus for the restoration of their authority and prestige. If Delhi could be taken and the beleaguered garrisons relieved, the British could afford to ignore the patchy rebellion in the countryside so long as they kept the main trunk roads open. A steady trickle of reinforcements flowed into Bengal, first from across British India itself, and ultimately from the wider Empire abroad.

In early June, troops from the Madras army – mostly from the Company's Madras European Fusiliers – were hurried up to Benares and Allahabad. They were commanded by Colonel James Neill, a stern disciplinarian who considered it his Christian duty to inflict a terrible punishment on the rebels. The initial stages of the rising had been characterised by sudden outbursts of ferocious violence, often carried out by the bazaar mobs in the first anarchic hours of mutiny, and exaggerated tales of the horrors inflicted on white civilians were widely believed amongst Neill's men. With the occupation of Allahabad, the first serious atrocities committed by British troops took place, as Neill's men ravaged the city and surrounding countryside, burning homes, and hanging all Indians they suspected of involvement in the rising. Later, when the story of the fate of the British prisoners at Kanpur became known, the slaughter reached levels of inventiveness which seem positively macabre to twentieth-century sensibilities; victims were hanged from makeshift gallows or from trees by the dozen, their bodies left in grotesque patterns, whilst others were blown from the mouths of guns – a traditional Mughal punishment for mutiny – or forced to perform disgusting and degrading acts of repentance before they were killed.

At the end of June General Henry Havelock arrived at Allahabad to take over command from Neill, and a fortnight later he struck out for Kanpur. Havelock forced a way through on 17 July, only to find that the British prisoners had been murdered the day before. Ironically, they had been slashed and hacked to death and their bodies thrown down a well in the apparent hope that the British would be discouraged and abandon the attempt to save them. In fact, in an age when middle-class Victorians were accustomed to venerating their womenfolk, and when the theory of racial superiority carried with it a deep-seated sexual fear of other races, the sight of the blood-soaked *bibighar*, the 'lady's house' where the massacre had occurred, and the terrible spectre of the well, merely provoked the British to a greater frenzy of revenge. Neill went so far as to order that any captured rebels must be made to lick clean a patch of the bloody floor before they were executed.

Between Kanpur and Lucknow lay a sizeable rebel concentration. Havelock's first attempt to march on the besieged capital could not find a way through, and he was compelled to fall back on Kanpur and await reinforcements. They arrived in the middle of September, under the command of General Sir James Outram. Together, Havelock and Outram made a thrust towards Lucknow, and reached the Residency on 25 September. Having got in, however, they found they couldn't get out, and the relieving force proved little more than a reinforcement for the garrison. The siege continued for a further two months, until the arrival of a new British Commander-in-Chief – Sir Colin Campbell, the hero of Balaclava – prompted a fresh attempt at relief. Campbell finally relieved the city on 17 November.

In the meantime, Delhi had fallen. For three months the British had clung to their exposed position on the ridge, despite frequent rebel attempts to dislodge them. At last, with the arrival of reinforcements – chiefly troops from the Punjab – they felt confident enough to mount an attack. Early on 14 September, engineers exploded a charge against the bricked-up Kashmir Gate, and thereby opened a breach in the city walls. Storming parties streamed through, and fierce fighting raged through the streets. The British made no distinction between mutineers, rebels and non-combatant civilians, and during the height of the attack all were slaughtered indiscriminately. Many rebels managed to escape across the River Jumna, but Bahadur Shah was captured, together with most of his sons; three were shot dead to prevent their rescue, and a further twenty-three subsequently hanged.

Such retribution did not end the rebellion, however; indeed, it may have stiffened the resolve of those committed to it, and it certainly alienated much Indian civilian support. Even as Colin Campbell struggled to relieve Lucknow, a new rebel coalition emerged to threaten his rear. Two small states south of the River Jumna, Jhansi and Gwalior, were alive with a disaffection which epitomised the resentment of the old Indian elite towards British rule. In early June, the EIC troops in both states mutinied. In Jhansi, where the rebellion focused upon the figure of the widowed Rani, who had been dispossessed by the Company, fifty-five Europeans were murdered. The rebels were brought into the wider world of the uprising by a former commander in the employ of the Nana Sahib's father, Tantya Tope, who visited Jhansi and Gwalior to raise men for the recapture of Kanpur. He reached Kanpur shortly after Lucknow had been taken, forcing Campbell to abandon the latter and face about. Tantya Tope captured Kanpur on 27 November, but Campbell drove him out after stiff fighting on 6/7 December.

The fighting then raged through Awadh and Central India for more than six months. Campbell returned to Lucknow, which the rebels had occupied after his withdrawal, and stormed it on 21 March 1858. Meanwhile, fresh troops from Bombay, under the command of General Sir Hugh Rose, had advanced on Jhansi. Tantya Tope moved to oppose Rose, but was defeated on the last day of March, and Rose stormed Jhansi three days later. After stiff fighting the British sacked the city and slaughtered many of its defenders, but the Rani slipped away to joined Tantya. Their combined forces moved north towards Gwalior, with Rose in hot pursuit. The Rani was killed in a skirmish with British cavalry on 17 June, and three days later Rose stormed Gwalior. By now the rebel forces were in disarray, driven onto the defensive by constant British

pressure. Tantya Tope continued to try to rally disaffected rulers to his cause, but with little hope of success, and in April 1859 he was betrayed to the British. He was later hanged for rebellion – a charge which in fact had little basis, since he had never been bound by loyalty to the Company – and with his death the Mutiny came largely to an end.

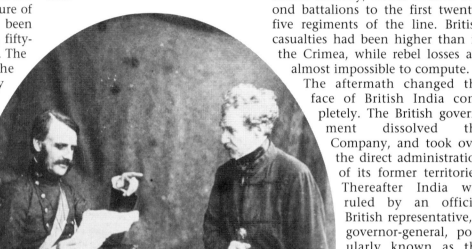

***Two British heroes of the Mutiny: Major-General Mansfield (left) and General Sir Colin Campbell. (National Army Museum)***

It had proved far and away the greatest test of British arms on Indian soil. By its end more British troops had been involved in the fighting than had fought in the Crimea, together with thousands of Indians who had remained loyal to the Company. To ensure that there were sufficient troops to counter the

*Right: British cavalry watching storming parties force the Kashmir Gate into Delhi; water-colour by Orlando Norie. (National Army Museum)*

threat without making other areas of the Empire vulnerable, the Duke of Cambridge had authorised the raising of twenty-five new battalions of British infantry, which became second battalions to the first twenty-five regiments of the line. British casualties had been higher than in the Crimea, while rebel losses are almost impossible to compute.

The aftermath changed the face of British India completely. The British government dissolved the Company, and took over the direct administration of its former territories. Thereafter India was ruled by an official British representative, a governor-general, popularly known as the Viceroy. The implications for the Queen's and the Company's army were immense. In effect, the Company's soldiers were taken over by the Crown, and they transferred their allegiance from the Company to the Queen herself. This move met with some resistance among men who felt that their original oath of allegiance was not transferable, and after some disturbances the Crown had to allow the option for men to be discharged if they did not wish to accept the new arrangements. There were, in any case, other more drastic changes. It was decided not to maintain the Company's old European troops, and these regiments – three from each Presidency, nine in all – were recon-

*Right: British troops fighting their way through the streets of Delhi. Possession of the city achieved great symbolic importance for both sides, and it was only captured after a bitter struggle. (Private collection)*

*Left: The Indian Mutiny came to assume all of the characteristics of a race war, and both sides fought with desperate valour. (Author's collection)*

*Opposite page: The Afghans were a tough and formidable enemy, perfectly at home in their mountain environment. Typically, they are shown here sniping at an enemy from the heights. (Author's collection)*

stituted as single-battalion British regiments. To ensure that the proportion of white troops on the subcontinent remained favourable, British regiments were posted there with greater frequency, but for a maximum of twelve years at a time. As a result, most soldiers in the British army served part of their time in India, even when the short-service system was introduced in the 1870s. Furthermore, three new British regiments were raised from amongst the European troops of the Bengal Light Cavalry and from amongst the pool of spare EIC white troops – the 19th, 20th and 21st Light Dragoons. The Indian regiments themselves were reorganised, and the number of men under arms reduced. After careful study, it became official policy to mix men within the ranks regardless of caste and origins, in an attempt to prevent the dominance of high-caste men from a particular locality which had been such a feature of the Mutiny. In effect, however, this move was only partly successful, because senior officers remained prejudiced against lower-caste soldiers and in favour of those they considered better fighting material.

To ensure that Indian troops would be unable, in future wars, to turn on the British so effectively, practical steps were taken to keep their military effectiveness subordinate to British regulars. The Company's European artillery was transferred to the Royal Artillery, while the Indian artillery was entirely disbanded. The superior qualities of the Enfield rifle had not gone unnoticed, and for the remainder of the nineteenth century Indian troops were armed with inferior firearms to their British counterparts. Thus Indian troops only received the Enfield when the British adopted the breech-loading Snider, and the Snider when the British received the Martini-Henry, and so on. Furthermore, the post-Mutiny Indian army abandoned the Company's policy of dressing its soldiers as closely as possible in a British style, and new uniforms were introduced which more closely reflected local styles.

In fact, the Mutiny proved to be the last major campaign fought by the British on Indian soil. The British had proved themselves masters in the field, and by the time it was over India was entirely under British control, either directly or through compliant local rulers, and its capacity for armed resistance negligible.

## AFGHANISTAN AND THE NORTH-WEST FRONTIER

The security of the north-western frontier concerned the British for as long as they ruled India. This wild and inhospitable country, rising in a series of hot plains and jagged mountains to the Hindu Kush massif in Afghanistan – the 'killer of Hindus' – was the overland gateway to the west. Beyond Afghanistan lay Iran (Persia) in the south, and Central Asia to the north, with Russia beyond. Therein lay the cause of British concern, for though they did

not wish to control the overland route themselves – Britain's access to India was from the sea – they wished to deny it to others. For nearly 200 years – at least until the collapse of the Soviet Union – the fear of successive Indian administrations was that Russia would one day march into the sub-continent via Afghanistan. Nor was this fear entirely unfounded; although it was perhaps unlikely that, in Palmerston's memorable phrase, 'the Cossack and the Sepoy' would ever be brought into direct confrontation in the shadow of the Hindu Kush, the Tsar undoubtedly

sought to influence events in the border states in pursuit of broader international strategy.

Afghanistan became the chessboard in this great contest of intrigue between the British Lion and the Russian Bear, known as the 'Great Game'. A harsh land of dizzying peaks and narrow fertile valleys, of stifling summer heat and frost-bitten winters, Afghanistan's people possessed a toughness of spirit that matched their environment. They were divided into two main groups, the Afghans proper to the south and west, and the Pathans to the north and east. Both were tribal, with each tribe further subdivided into clans; although each tribe had a recognised leader, the Afghan character was marked by a fierce independence of spirit which bred a loathing of authority, and made any form of government a precarious and dangerous business. Feuds between tribes, clans and individuals were common, and any insult to an acutely honed sense of honour could only be expunged in blood. Despite this, however, the Afghans were quite prepared to set aside their internal squabbles in the face of a common outside threat, or to defend the call of Islam, to which most were enthusiastic adherents.

Inevitably, among such a people, politics in the higher levels of government were a ruthless and cutthroat business, and it was to exploit apparent divisions in the Afghan court that the British first became involved in Afghanistan. In 1810 the reigning Amir, Shah Shuja ul Mulk, was ousted in a palace coup and fled to the court of Ranjit Singh in Lahore. This left power in the hands of the rival Barakzai clan under the leadership of Dost Muhammed, who by the 1830s found himself faced by a crisis on his western borders, provoked by increased Russian activity in the region following the installation in 1828 of a pro-Russian Shah on the Persian throne. The situation became increasingly tense as, throughout the next decade, the Shah pressed a claim to the western Afghan city of Herat, and laid siege to it with the help of Russian advisers.

To the British, it seemed that Dost Muhammad was incapable of halting the Russian advance, and in 1838 the EIC despatched an envoy, Alexander Burnes, to gain greater influence in the court at Kabul. The Russians responded by sending an envoy of their own, and the British, in an attempt to forestall them, adopted a more radical and long-term solution to the security of the frontier: to invade Afghanistan and restore the former Amir, Shah Shuja, to the throne.

Little was known about the Afghans, and it was widely believed that they would welcome back an ousted legitimate leader, and that even if they did not, they would be incapable of opposing an army equipped and trained along European lines. Since Shah Shuja had few adherents of his own, and since the Company could not persuade one of its local allies to do the job, Shah Shuja would have to be propped up by British bayonets. Thus Britain became committed to a military campaign that would prove one of the most disastrous it embarked upon during the nineteenth century.

After the kingdom of Lahore had politely declined permission for the British to use the Khyber Pass, the expedition was assembled instead at the mouth of the Indus, to reach Afghanistan via the arid wastes of Sind. The assembled force, the 'Army of the Indus', was typical of British armies in India at the time. It consisted of 39,000 men, a mixture of Queen's troops and EIC regiments, supported by an enormous transport train. Since Sind boasted few roads, all baggage was carried on pack animals, and over 30,000 camels were bought or hired to carry equipment and supplies. Even this total would prove inadequate and as the campaign wore on hundreds of animals succumbed to heat, thirst, and over-work. Furthermore, the army was accompanied by thousands of Indian civilians, including soldiers' wives, who provided all the services the army required – servants, water-carriers, grooms, camel-drivers, barbers, and traders.

The army was assembled by February 1839. It was 1200 miles to the Afghan capital, Kabul, but the march began well enough; the Amirs of Sind had reluctantly allowed it safe passage to the Bolan, and the pass was taken with little resistance on 10 March. The direction of the British advance apparently took Dost Muhammed by surprise, most of his troops having been concentrated astride the Khyber route, and the first Afghan cities encountered – Quetta and Kandahar – were taken with surprising ease. However, the next city along their route, Ghazni, protected by a strong fortress, was more vigorously defended. The British were hampered by the absence of their siege train, which had not yet come up, but an Afghan deserter brought them the news that one of the city's great gateways – the Kabul Gate – had merely been barricaded, not bricked up as was usually the practise in wartime. Early on the morning of 23 July a party of sappers took advantage of a raging gale to mask their approach, made a dash for the gate and exploded a charge against it. The Afghans, caught by surprise, tried to rally, but their morale collapsed as the British streamed into the city. Over 600 Afghans were killed and 1600 captured, for the loss of eighteen dead and 173 wounded on the British side.

The capture of Ghazni had been spectacularly successful, and the Afghan will to resist crumbled in its aftermath. On 7 August Shah Shuja entered Kabul at the head of an Anglo-Indian army. There were few conspicuous signs of welcome from his old subjects, but the new Amir soon settled into his administration, whilst his British allies set up camp outside the city. By the end of 1839, the Afghan expedition seemed to have achieved its objective with complete success. Yet all was not as it seemed. Both Dost Muhammed and his able and charismatic son, Muhammed Akbar Khan, were still at large, and clearly commanded considerable respect amongst the population at large. Although the British contingent settled down to the pleasures of garrison life, bringing up their women to join them and enjoying races and band-concerts in the extensive cantonment they had built outside Kabul, the country was not pacified. Trouble spluttered on in Kalat, and the chiefs in some outlying areas ignored Shah Shuja and the British with equal impunity. Furthermore, there was growing resentment in Kabul itself, where the loose ways of the foreign infidels outraged Moslem propriety. In particular, there were widespread rumours of womanising among both British officers and other ranks, and the diplomat Alexander Burnes was said to be particularly active in this regard. Though the British garrison remained blissfully unaware of it, the country was ripe for rebellion.

In 1841 the British decided to reduce the cost of the administration. Firstly, they cancelled the subsidies they had negotiated with the tribes who commanded the passes between Kabul and Jellalabad, and secondly they ordered Sir Robert Sale's brigade to return to India. The coincidence of events was unfortunate; Sale marched out along the Jellalabad road in September, and was promptly attacked by the outraged tribes. He got as far as the town of Gandamak, and dug in. Within a few weeks, sporadic risings broke out across the country, culminating in an incident in Kabul itself. On 2 November a mob gathered outside Burnes' house, and denounced him as a seducer. They broke in, set the house on fire, and Burnes and his associates were murdered.

Neither Shah Shuja nor the British commander, the elderly Major-General Elphinstone, made any attempt to punish the murderers. Sale was ordered to return to Kabul, but rather than risk the hostile passes again, he marched in the opposite direction, and occupied Jellalabad. Another force sat inactive at Kandahar. Emboldened, the Afghans in Kabul occupied a ridge overlooking the British cantonment, and began to fire down into the lines. Towards the end of November the British made a sortie to drive them off, but it was badly co-ordinated, and returned to the cantonment in such haste that the wounded were left on the field. A determined move to occupy the

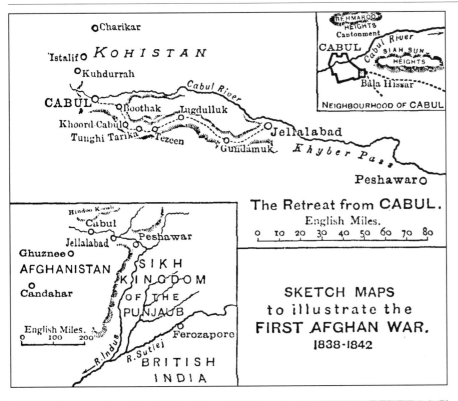

*Left: A contemporary map of the First Afghan War and the 'Retreat from Kabul'*

city's Bala Hissar fortress might have secured the garrison, but Elphinstone dithered until it was too late. By the middle of December, it was clear that the British position was untenable, and the senior political officer, Sir William MacNaughton, opened negotiations with Muhammed Akbar. MacNaughton tried to play the chiefs off one against another, but with disastrous consequences. At a meeting with Akbar on 3 December he was confronted with evidence of his duplicity, and murdered on the spot. His body was dismembered and the remains displayed in the Kabul bazaar. Elphinstone was now in a frenzy of indecision, whilst his officers wrangled bitterly amongst themselves. Akbar offered to allow the garrison to leave Kabul unmolested, and there seemed little choice but to accept his terms.

The march began on 6 January 1842. Elphinstone still had about 4500 troops at his disposal – among them one Queen's Regiment, the 44th Foot – but was hampered by about 12,000 camp followers, including a number of officers' wives. Many of the sick and injured had to be left behind. No sooner had the troops left the cantonment than the Afghans, probably in defiance of Akbar's wishes, moved in, looting what had been left behind and murdering stragglers. The camp followers panicked, and abandoned most of the baggage within a mile or two of the cantonment. The first day's march covered only five miles, and already the column showed every sign of falling apart.

Indeed, it took just a week for the Afghans to destroy the Kabul garrison entirely. The Afghan winter was fast closing in, and the Indians, in partic-

*Left: The destruction of the Kabul garrison. As discipline collapsed during the retreat from Kabul, the Afghans attacked and murdered soldiers and civilians alike. (Author's collection)*

*Above: On the domed hill in the background the last of the 44th Regiment were overwhelmed at Gandamak in 1842. This picture dates from the Second Afghan War (1879), and the original caption reads: 'Quantities of bleached human bones were found upon it when this spot was visited by our forces'. (Bryan Maggs Collection)*

ular, were acutely vulnerable to cold; hundreds died that first night. With each day's march their condition became worse. There was little or no command from the top, and the column soon degenerated into a shambling mob, whilst the Afghans hung on the flanks and rear, rushing down to make sudden attacks with impunity. Now and then an officer would try to rally his men for a counter-attack, but the respite was only temporary. On the second day as many as 500 regulars and 2500 camp followers were slaughtered in the narrow Khurd Kabul Pass, and the next morning Muhammed Akbar offered to take the British wives and children into his protection. The offer was accepted, and when the senior surviving officers went out to negotiate, they, too, were taken prisoner.

For most of those who remained, the end came in a terrible defile known as the Jagdalak Pass. A few of the 44th managed to keep together, and on the 13 January took up a position on a domed hill above the town of Gandamak. Here the Afghans offered to call a truce, but

as the tribesmen crowded round, scuffles broke out and fighting flared up. The 44th were overwhelmed; a few officers were taken prisoner, including a Captain Souter, who had wrapped the regimental colour around his waist. All of those who had survived thus far were either killed or taken prisoner; the only European to escape was a surgeon, William Brydon, who reached Jellalabad riding on an exhausted pony later that day. When the rising had broken out, Muhammed Akbar had promised that he would leave only one man alive to carry the news out of Kabul – and so he had. The destruction of the Kabul garrison left two British concentrations isolated within Afghanistan – 'Fighting Bob' Sale's force at Jellalabad, and General Nott's Kandahar garrison – as well as a number of smaller outposts. All now came under attack. Muhammed Akbar immediately moved on Jellalabad, but the city's defences proved too strong for the Afghans to take by storm – though they were badly damaged on one

occasion by an earthquake – and instead they besieged it. The siege continued until April, by which time the garrison, running low on supplies, was becoming desperate. On the 7th the British made a spirited sortie which took the Afghans by surprise; fighting in the open, the British and Indian troops used their firepower to good effect, drove the Afghans out of their camp, and captured several guns. At Kandahar, too, Nott tied down the Afghans by mounting sorties where he could.

By this time help was at hand. A British force had concentrated at Peshawar, commanded by the newly-arrived Major-General Pollock, and with the onset of the spring weather it marched into Afghanistan to relieve the beleaguered garrisons. Pollock's force was a strong one – over three regiments of cavalry, and seven battalions of infantry, the usual mix of Queen's and EIC troops. His objectives were limited to the evacuation of the garrisons, since in the aftermath of the Kabul disaster Britain had decided to abandon the occupation of Afghanistan. Pollock's advance lay through the Khyber Pass, which he attacked by surprise on 5 April. Deploying some of his Indian troops to distract the Pathans guarding the pass, Pollock sent flanking

*Below: General Pollock's army advancing past the skeletons of those killed in the Khurd-Kabul Pass during the retreat from Kabul, 1842. (National Army Museum)*

columns up the heights on either side, thus turning the Afghans own tactics against them. The Pathans, overlooked and shot down in the open, fell back, and Pollock thereby established a new principal in frontier warfare – that of 'taking the high ground'.

Pollock arrived at Jellalabad nine days after Sale's successful sortie. Although now under political pressure to withdraw, Pollock prevaricated, determined to rescue the survivors of the Kabul garrison. Several months slipped past until Lord Ellenborough, the Governor-General in India, reluctantly agreed that British prestige could only be salvaged by the release of the prisoners and by a punitive expedition to reoccupy Kabul. In July 1842 both Pollock at Jellalabad and Nott at

Kandahar were given permission to advance on Kabul; having freed the prisoners, they were to retire immediately. Both generals struck out, encountering Afghan opposition along the way. At the end of August Nott fought a tough battle outside the fortress of Ghazni – first stormed by the British three years before – and again took the city. Pollock, meanwhile, accomplished his advance in the face of almost constant Afghan opposition. He was advancing along the line of the Kabul garrison's retreat, where the skeletons of its dead still lay in heaps, working his men up into a fury of retribution. Pollock repeated over and again his tactic of seizing the heights, and gradually forced his way through the defiles. Muhammed Akbar made a stand at Tezin on 12 September, but Pollock's cavalry drove off a fierce but undisciplined charge of Afghan horsemen, whilst his infantry met the rush of *Ghazi* religious warriors with the bayonet. By the end of the battle the Afghans had suffered 1000 dead, to Pollock's thirty-two dead and 130 wounded. Four days later Pollock entered Kabul; Nott, disappointed, marched in on the 17th.

For a few anxious days the fate of the prisoners hung in the balance. They had been well treated so far, but it was feared they would be killed as the British advanced. In fact, a sortie led by Sale on the 20th found them a few miles north of Kabul; they included his own wife, the indomitable Lady Florentia Sale, and eleven other European women, twenty-two British officers, two clerks, twenty-five British soldiers, and twenty-two children. Pollock allowed himself the satisfaction of blowing up the Kabul bazaar, and burning several villages as retribution, before withdrawing. On 12 October 1842, the British once more marched out of Kabul, this time as victors. Nevertheless, the Afghan spirit was by no means crushed, and several soldiers were killed by Afghan snipers as the column made its way back to the border.

Despite the punishment exacted by Pollock and Nott, the First Afghan

War had been an undoubted failure. Instead of installing a pro-British regime in Kabul, it had achieved precisely the opposite, creating a climate of hostility and suspicion which denied the British any influence. In the immediate aftermath of the war, the British abandoned their forward policy and sought instead to secure the frontier along the borders of Afghanistan. By the mid-1840s, following the annexations of Sind and the kingdom of Lahore, this had been achieved. With almost all of the country east of the Afghan foothills under their control, the British became involved in policing the region, a duty which characterised their experience on the North-West Frontier for almost a century thereafter. Many of the border tribesmen had paid only lip-service to the central authority in the past, and to them the advent of British rule made little difference. They continued to raid the more settled lowlands much as they had before. British authority depended on a handful of young and adventurous administrators, backed up by locally raised irregular forces, which were themselves often composed of Sikhs or Pathans. Although low-intensity warfare remained endemic on the Frontier, it is some measure of British success that the border regions remained unaffected by the Great Mutiny, and, indeed, even supplied contingents to support British troops at Delhi.

## The North-West Frontier

Nevertheless, the Mutiny disturbances inevitably had an unsettling effect. In the 1850s a Moslem fundamentalist group, calling themselves by a curiously modern name – the *Mujhaddin*, the Warriors of God – established itself in the mountainous country north of Attock. Their numbers were swollen by bands of disaffected Moslem sepoys from the nearest Bengal Army garrisons, and in the early 1860s the *Mujhaddin* began to raid those tribes which had not converted to their cause, and to build up a power-base. The British decided to nip the movement in the bud, and in 1863 an expedition of 5000 men – a typical mix of British and Indian troops, commanded by Sir Neville Chamberlain – was sent against them. Chamberlain's plan was to cut through the Ambela Pass, to execute a turning movement, and circle round behind the *Mujhaddin* settlements, but the plan's success depended on the neutrality of the Bunerwal tribesmen who controlled the pass, and unfortunately this was not secured beforehand. Indeed, the sudden appearance of a British army unannounced on their doorstep provoked the Bunerwals into supporting the *Mujhaddin*, and Chamberlain found his way effectively blocked. The keys to the pass were a number of rocky spurs, jutting out from the tree-covered hills on either side, which dominated the route below. The British seized these spurs and established picquets upon them, but the outcrops were often so small that

*Below: Fighting around the 'Eagle's Nest' pickets, Ambela campaign, 1868. (Rai England Collection)*

they could be occupied by only a handful of men. These were protected by hastily built stone sangars, but they remained far from secure as the trees and boulders obscured all but their immediate field of fire. No sooner had the British established these picquets than the Bunerwals, exhorted by the *Mujhaddin*, attacked them. Fighting ranged around the crags for several weeks, many of them changing hands several times, as the British first gave way before a wild rush of tribesmen, only to regroup elsewhere and carry the picquet at the point of the bayonet. This type of warfare allowed both sides to rush reinforcements to the scene, and in this the British had a decided advantage, due to the superiority of their firepower. It was not until the beginning of December, however, that the Bunerwals could be persuaded to agree to terms, and to betray their alliance with the *Mujhaddin*. Eventually the Warriors of God were largely dispersed by local tribesmen with British support. A campaign planned to last for a few weeks had taken

three months, however, and cost the Anglo-Indian forces 238 dead and 670 wounded, compared to a loss of 3000 among the enemy. In many ways the Ambela campaign, with its curious mixture of ferocity and chivalry and its fierce fighting among narrow mountain passes, set the pattern for future military activity on the Frontier.

In the immediate aftermath of her defeat in the Crimea, the Russian threat to India seemed remote. By the early 1870s, however, the Great Game was afoot once more, as Russia began a new advance into Central Asia. British paranoia about the Tsar's intentions was fuelled by a new crisis between Russia and Turkey, which broke into open warfare in 1877. The old fear of Afghanistan's territorial integrity surfaced once again. In fact, Dost Mohammed's regime in Kabul had remained determinedly neutral since 1843, and that policy did not change when Dost Mohammed was succeeded by his son Sher Ali in 1863. Nevertheless, in 1877 both Russia

and Britain were prompted to send diplomatic representatives to the Afghan court. Despite the fact that a new Anglo-Russian agreement effectively took much of the heat out of the situation, the Government of India was still incensed when the British representative was turned back at the Khyber Pass in 1878. The British promptly presented Sher Ali with an ultimatum which expired on 20 November 1878.

### The Second Afghan War

The Second Afghan War ran a curiously parallel course to the first. The British invaded in three columns – Sir Donald Stewart led 12,800 men from Quetta in the south towards Kandahar, Sir Sam Browne struck at Kabul via the Khyber Pass in the north, and in the centre Frederick Roberts VC advanced up the Kurram valley. Stewart's advance was largely unopposed,

*Below: Lord Roberts (left of centre, with white beard) and his staff during the Second Afghan War. (Bryan Maggs Collection)*

*Left: The battle which made Roberts' reputation: the storming of the Peiwar Kotal, Second Afghan War. (National Army Museum)*

*Opposite page, top: A guard of honour awaiting the arrival of the Amir Yakub Khan at Gandamak, May 1879. (Bryan Maggs Collection)*

route lay up a ridge covered with pine forest and jumbled boulders, and the night was bitterly cold. By dawn Roberts' men were close enough to rush the nearest Afghan positions. Afghan resistance was stubborn, however, and Roberts' plan to roll up their line was thwarted by the terrain; nevertheless, his pressure on the Afghan flank drew attention away from the centre, and an assault by the troops he had left in camp broke through. The Afghan line collapsed, and Roberts was left in possession of the Peiwar Kotal and the road through the Kurram.

The British advance continued in the face of local opposition, but Sher Ali did not wait for it, fleeing Kabul to seek refuge with the Russians, and leaving the throne to his son, Yakub Khan. Yakub promptly agreed to come to terms, and rode into the British camp at Gandamak. On 26 May 1879 he signed a treaty which forced him to cede the Kurram and Khyber valleys – the gateways to Afghanistan – and to accept British control of Afghan foreign policy and a British representative at Kabul. This post was taken by Major Sir Louis Cavagnari, who arrived at the Residency in the Bala Hissar in July, accompanied by an escort of just seventy-five men of the Corps of Guides, under Lieutenant Hamilton VC. Stewart's and Browne's columns were withdrawn, but Roberts' force remained in occupation of the Kurram.

*Opposite page, bottom: Major Sir Louis Cavagnari on his appointment as British Resident at Kabul at the end of the first phase of the Second Afghan War. His murder provoked a renewal of hostilities. (Bryan Maggs Collection)*

and Browne overcame an Afghan stand at Ali Masjid by a skilful turning movement. It was Roberts, however, who stole the laurels in this first phase of the fighting. Aged just 46, Roberts had won his VC in the Mutiny, and held the local rank of major-general, despite the fact that he was only a major in his regiment. He was to face some of the stiffest opposition to the advance, and the skill with which he overcame it established his reputation as a field com-

mander. Roberts' column advanced up the Kurram valley, only to find its way blocked at the Peiwar Kotal (a *kotal* being a ridge connecting two outcrops of higher ground) by a strong force of Afghan regulars well placed along the heights. Rather than risk a direct assault, Roberts opted to make a bold outflanking move at night. Late on the evening of 1 December he took over 3000 men to turn the Afghan left. The approach was fraught with difficulties; the

Although the British occupation was minimal in 1879, compared to the expedition forty years earlier, the apparent calm which greeted the British victory was just as deceptive. Cavagnari had hardly been installed in the Residency for two months when trouble began. A detachment of Afghan regular troops from the western city of Herat – who had not been involved in the fighting – took over the garrison in Kabul. They reacted to Cavagnari's presence with

*Below: The defence of the Residency at Kabul by Cavagnari's escort of the Corps of Guides. (Author's collection)*

an ill-concealed disgust, and on 3 September an angry mob collected outside the Residency. Shots were fired, and the Herati troops broke out their arms. Hamilton and Cavagnari tried to organise a defence, but the Residency buildings were overlooked all round, and the Afghans, reinforced by the Kabul mob, poured in a heavy fire. Cavagnari himself was killed early on, shot through the head whilst firing from the roof-top. The Afghans brought guns close up to the walls to try to force a breach, and several times Hamilton led out sorties to drive off their crews. When eventually Hamilton and the other Euro-

peans had been killed an Afghan offer to the surviving Indian troops to let them surrender was contemptuously rejected. At the end the last six men alive charged out together, and were all killed. The fighting had lasted for nearly twelve hours.

The news of the massacre of the Residency caused uproar when it reached British India. The only force still on Afghan soil was Roberts' old Kurram column, now renamed the Kabul Field Force. Roberts immediately went onto the offensive, and the Amir, Yakub Khan, seeing which way the wind was blowing, promptly surrendered to him. Despite being hampered by a lack of baggage animals, Roberts pressed on towards Kabul. When, on 5 October, he encountered a strong Afghan force drawn up along a line of hills blocking his advance at Charasia, he had only 4000 men with him. Undaunted, he attacked the next morning, using the tactics which had triumphed at Peiwar Kotal. He made an attack on the Afghan left, and when the Afghan commander moved troops from his centre to support the left, Roberts punched through the centre. When the Afghans retired, Roberts unleashed his cavalry – the 9th Queen's Royal Lancers and 5th Punjab Cavalry – who chased them from the field in a dashing charge.

On the 8th Roberts occupied Kabul. Determined to restore British prestige, he executed a number of Afghans accused of involvement in the attack on the Residency and then, when the Bala Hissar was wracked by a series of explosions – which may or may not have been accidental – he ordered the rest razed. Nevertheless, Roberts was not fool enough to think that the Afghans were cowed, and he prepared a large walled cantonment at Sherpur, just outside the city, to protect his troops as winter drew on. He had only some 7000 men to defend a perimeter four and a half miles long, but the position was strengthened here and there with abatis and wire entanglements.

By December it was clear that tribal leaders in the hills around

*Above: A spirited charge by the 9th Lancers during Roberts' actions round Kabul. (Author's collection)*

Kabul were massing their forces for an attack on his position. Roberts moved first, however, sending out small columns to break up these concentrations. On 11 December 300 cavalrymen under Brigadier-General Massey blundered into 10,000 Afghans, and were forced to

bid a hasty retreat, losing four field guns which had accompanied them. An attack on the cantonment was clearly imminent, and Roberts tried to delay it by harassing the Afghan forces gathering on the hills whilst at the same time preparing for the defence. The attack came before dawn on the morning of 23 December; a huge force, 100,000 strong according to some accounts, streamed down on the cantonment.

Roberts, however, had been fore-warned of the attack, and star shells were used to illuminate the host so that a storm of rifle and artillery fire could be poured into them. Armed largely with swords and shields, the Afghans were cut down by the score, but here and there pressed right up to the walls. The first attack lasted until 10 am, and was driven off; the Afghans regrouped and tried a fresh assault, but were even more exposed to the British fire in daylight. By noon they had retreated to the hills, harried by Roberts' cavalry, and leaving about a thousand dead on the plains.

Roberts' losses were a trifling eighteen killed and sixty-eight wounded. Roberts reoccupied Kabul the next day, but the British seemed no nearer a political solution. Yakub Khan was so disillusioned with the state of affairs that he abdicated, and whilst the British pondered their options General Stewart was ordered to march from Kandahar to take over from Roberts in Kabul. Leaving a garrison in the city under the command of General Primrose, Stewart set out for Kabul. By now, however, trouble was brewing again, and Stewart found his way blocked by a strong tribal force at Ahmad Khel on 19 April. Stewart was hampered by a long baggage train, and was unable to deploy all his troops. The Afghans attacked with great ferocity, and part of Stewart's line collapsed. The remainder rallied on the 3rd Gurkhas and 2nd Sikhs, however, and the attack was driven off. Stewart reached Kabul in safety, and the British installed a new Amir, a nephew of Sher Ali by the name of Abdur Rahman. Then, just as it seemed that the British position was at last secure, the greatest blow of the war befell them.

The western city of Herat had so far escaped the fighting, and in July a brother of Yakub Khan, Ayub Khan, used it as a base for a surprise attack on Kandahar. The pro-British governor of Kandahar appealed to his allies for support, and General Primrose despatched a brigade under General Burrows to head off Ayub. Burrows' force stumbled across the Afghans near the village of Maiwand

on 27 July. Burrows was heavily out-numbered and his line crumpled under the onslaught. Burrows lost over 1000 men: the Queen's 66th Regiment was almost wiped out, the artillery lost two of its guns, and the survivors fled the field in confusion. Ayub Khan immediately followed up his success and laid siege to Kanda-har, where Primrose and some 5000 men under his command retired inside the city walls.

Roberts was now ordered to march to Primrose's relief. He was given 10,000 men – the pick of the Kabul garrison, including three British bat-talions (the 60th Rifles, and the 72nd and 92nd Highlanders), and the best transport animals – and set out on 8 August 1880. The subse-quent march caught the public imagination in Britain, and crowned the reputation Roberts had first earned at Peiwar Kotal. Marching across rugged country in extremes of

heat by day and cold by night, Roberts' command covered 280 miles in twenty days. On 31 August he marched into Kandahar and relieved the garrison, and the next day sallied out to attack the Afghan cordon. The Afghans had taken up a strong position anchored on a sad-dle known as the Baba Wali Kotal, and incorporating several villages. Once again Roberts offered a feint – an attack on the *kotal* – then deliv-ered his main thrust elsewhere. The Afghans put up a spirited resistance, and attempted to fall back on a new defensive line, but a charge by the 92nd Highlanders, supported by the 2nd Gurkhas and 23rd Pioneers, turned their flank. Ayub Khan's army abandoned the field, leaving its camp and artillery to the enemy.

Roberts' victory at Kandahar brought the military operations of the Second Afghan War to a close. Politi-cally, however, British objectives

*Above: British troops pose in front of the impressive Bala Hissar, the great fortress which dominated Kabul. (Bryan Maggs Collection)*

*Opposite page, top: The stand of the 'last eleven' of the 66th Regiment at Maiwand. (Author's collection)*

*Opposite page, bottom: Roberts' positions in the Sherpur canton-ments outside Kabul: Indian infantry manning a barricade of wagons and branches, with sup-ports in the rear. (Bryan Maggs Collection)*

remained confused; Gladstone's Liberal Government had come to power at home, and was opposed to a forward policy, the practicality of which had, in any case, been called into doubt. In the end it was decided to abandon Afghanistan to Abdur Rahman and, in another telling parallel with the experience of 1839-42, the last British troops marched out of Afghanistan in May 1881, having performed the job required of them, but achieved few lasting results.

Abdur Rahman's regime survived until his death in 1901. He proved a tough and resilient ruler, prepared on occasion to accept British influence, and to deny Russia's territorial designs. As a result, there was no further British intervention in Afghanistan during the Victorian period, and it was not until 1919 that British troops again marched and fought on Afghan soil.

## The Siege of Chitral

The Great Game, however, continued throughout the 1880s and 1890s. The line of the Frontier, from Baluchistan in the south to Chitral in the north, continued to preoccupy British officials, whose agents on the spot were charged with maintaining British influence and authority, usually with no more than a small garrison of Indian troops to support them. This was the great age of the Imperial Frontier, of intrigues amongst the tribes, of minor incidents, and punitive expeditions. In the 1880s, for example, unrest in the Black Mountain region, north of Attock and not far from the Ambela Pass, culminated in an attack on a party of Indian troops. An expeditionary force of five British and ten Indian infantry battalions, supported by artillery, was sent to punish them. After stiff fighting, the British destroyed the villages, the tribal leaders submitted, and the British withdrew, although the region was not finally pacified until 1891. That same year, the British began work on a road through the northern region of Hunza-Nagir, which resulted in a brief campaign which effectively overcame the objections of the local ruler.

These incidents were typical of the British experience on the Frontier. In 1895, however, one particular incident caught the imagination of the British public at home, and seemed to encapsulate something of the mood of the times and the character of the Empire. A remote little fort, in the northernmost corner of British India, was besieged by local tribesmen, and two British columns were obliged to fight their way through to it. Although the British garrison consisted almost entirely of troops from the Indian army, the siege became a symbol of British pluck and dogged endurance in the way that Rorke's Drift had during the Zulu War, and Mafikeng would in the Anglo-Boer War. The fort was at Chitral, a small mountain state on the eastern edge of the Hindu Kush. In 1892 its ruler had died, and the British intervened

*Below: Troubles on the Frontier: the Northumberland Fusiliers' officers' mess, Black Mountain expedition, 1888. (Bryan Maggs Collection)*

in the subsequent succession dispute. When their candidate was promptly murdered, however, they despatched a force of 500 Sikh and Kashmiri troops, under the overall command of a Surgeon-Major Robertson, to investigate. Robertson's attempts to install a new pro-British ruler provoked an uprising. Robertson, aware of the vulnerability of his force, had wisely installed himself in Chitral fort, a small square structure on the banks of the Chitral river. At the beginning of March 1895 Robertson sent out a reconnaissance to investigate the Chitrali movements, but this was ambushed and badly mauled. Robertson's command then found itself cut off and under siege. A party bringing up ammunition and supplies from a garrison nearby was also attacked, and two British officers captured. The garrison was in real danger from dwindling food supplies and a gradual increase in disease, exacerbated by Chitrali sniping, by occasional attacks on the water supply, and by attempts to undermine the walls of the fort.

When news of the outbreak reached the outside world, two columns were hastily despatched to the relief of Chitral. A small force of Kashmiri troops – 400 men and two guns – under the command of Colonel Kelly set out from the garrison at Gilgit, 220 miles to the east of Chitral, whilst a much larger force – three infantry brigades plus cavalry – was assembled under Major-General Low at Peshawar in the south. Both columns faced a difficult advance; Kelly's route lay over high mountain passes, which at that time were deep in snow, whilst Low would have to move through the Malakand and Swat valleys, where local tribesmen turned out to oppose him. Both columns pushed forward in early April, Kelly's in the face of almost insurmountable physical obstacles, Low's in the face of stiff resistance. Low's men had to fight their way down the length of the Malakand and Swat valleys, but in the event it was Kelly's little force which reached Chitral first, raising the siege on 20 April. Robertson's garrison had held out for forty-seven days.

*Above: British troops on campaign on the North West Frontier; note the baggage mules and civilian drivers. (Bryan Maggs Collection)*

### The Pathan Revolt

In 1897, a new outbreak spread a wider wave of unrest across the Frontier. The causes remain obscure, but seem to have been related to a growing resentment at the increase in British control, and an upsurge in religious fundamentalism. The first outbreak occurred in the Tochi valley, where a British agent and his escort were fired upon, and trouble soon spread to the Malakand pass. Here the British garrisons at Malakand and Chakdara were attacked and besieged, and an expeditionary force – the Malakand Field Force under Major-General Sir Bindon Blood – was hastily despatched to their rescue. Even while Blood's operations were under way, the rising spread to the Mohmand tribes, north of the Khyber Pass, and, most seriously, to the Afridis of the Khyber itself. The Khyber had been secured by garrisons of a

*Left: Seaforth Highlanders crossing the river Tochi on a foraging expedition during the Pathan Revolt of 1897. (Bryan Maggs Collection)*

locally-raised irregular unit, the Khyber Rifles, who garrisoned the three forts which commanded the road, including Ali Masjid. However, on 23 August, when the Afridis approached the forts, the Khyber Rifles abandoned them almost without a fight. The fall of the Pass was a serious blow to British prestige, and steps were immediately taken to punish the Afridis. One of the largest punitive expeditions ever fielded on the Frontier was mustered at Kohat, a total of 11,892 British and 22,614 Indian troops and 20,000 non-combatants, assembled from garrisons all over India. The force was commanded by Lieutenant-General Sir William Lockhart, and christened the Tirah Field Force, since its objective was to ravage the Afridis' summer retreat, the Tirah valley, an area which had hitherto seen hardly any British activity.

The Tirah Field Force set out from Kohat on 11 October. In order to enter the valley it had first to secure a steep ridge-top commanded by the village of Dargai. On 18 October Dargai was successfully assaulted by the leading British division but, with its supports delayed by bad terrain, it was thought unwise to leave the troops in an exposed position, and they were withdrawn. The Afridis immediately reoccupied the village, and on the 20th the attack had to be attempted again. This time the resistance was fiercer, and the leading companies, who had to advance up a steep slope exposed to a withering fire, became pinned down. In one of the most dramatic incidents in the military history of the Frontier, the 1st Battalion Gordon Highlanders stormed the heights as their pipers played *Cock o' the North*. One of them, Piper Findlater, fell shot

*Left: Gordon Highlanders storming the Dargai Heights, 20 October 1897. (Rai England Collection)*

*Above: King's Own Scottish Borderers in action with Maxim support, Pathan Revolt, 1897. (Rai England Collection)*

*Right: Destroying Afridi villages in the Tirah valley, 1879. (Rai England Collection)*

through both ankles but continued to play in a very exposed position, and earned himself the VC.

From Dargai, the column pressed forward into the Tirah, with the Afridis contesting every likely pass and ridge-top along the way. Once in the valley, the British burned villages, and sent out parties to harass the tribesmen in the surrounding hills. Often these columns were attacked by the Afridis in turn, who seldom missed a chance to raid a straggling baggage column, or rush an unwary rearguard. Not until 7 December did the force begin to withdraw, retreating via the Khyber, so as to restore the fallen forts. In the meantime, Bindon Blood had been suppressing resistance in Malakand and amongst the Mahmonds by similar means.

By the end of 1897, the great Pathan revolt was over. Although nothing more than a punitive expedition, it had proved a small war in itself, with the Tirah column alone sustaining over a thousand casualties, and the Pathans many more. It was not the last of the fighting, by any means, for the British would be troubled by their Afghan and Frontier policies until the Raj finally came to an end in 1947. Yet the Pathan Revolt was perhaps the last of the old-style Frontier disturbances, for the Great Queen's reign was drawing to a close, and times were changing. In 1901 both Victoria and Abdur Rahman died, and that same year that very superior Viceroy, Lord Curzon, created a new administrative district, the North-West Frontier Province. The Frontier was passing into the modern age, and when in due course British soldiers went to war once more in Afghanistan – in 1919 – theirs was a twentieth-century war, for they went armed with aeroplanes and armoured cars.

## Southern Africa

By the time Queen Victoria came to the throne in 1837, British Imperial entanglements at the southern tip of Africa had already produced a bitter legacy of conflict. Furthermore, the region would remain problematic throughout her reign, requiring a military commitment second only to that of India and the North-West Frontier. Indeed, at the very end of the century southern Africa was wracked by the most serious war yet experienced by the Empire, one that would take three years of hard fighting to resolve, test many accepted military truths, and require the services of almost every regiment in the British army, and many from the colonies.

The reasons for this persistent conflict lay in the diametrically opposed interests of the three main population groups in the region – the indigenous Africans, the Boers, and the British themselves. European involvement dated back to the seventeenth century, when the Dutch first established a provisioning station at the Cape of Good Hope, the southern tip of Africa, to service their ships on the long sea-haul to the Indies. The Dutch had easily displaced the Cape's aboriginal population, the semi-nomadic Khoi and San peoples, but had little interest in exploring the hinterland. Nevertheless, the settlers who subsisted on the edges of the tiny colony, by raising cattle and growing vegetables for the East India Company fleet, developed into a hardy and independent breed, roaming beyond its borders in search of good grazing land. By the late eighteenth century these settlers, known as Boers – mainly Dutch, with a sprinkling of French and German religious refugees – had drifted westward, until somewhere along the banks of the Great Fish River they met African groups moving steadily in the opposite direction.

These were the southern branch of a people known as the Nguni, and they were called the amaXhosa. Like the Boers, they were essentially pastoralists, and although the first contacts along the new frontier were friendly enough, it soon became apparent that Boers and Xhosa were in direct competition for an increasingly limited resource – land. As early as 1779 there occurred the first of a cycle of cattle-raids and reprisals dignified with the name of the Cape Frontier Wars. Over the next century there were to be eight more such wars (1793, 1799–1802, 1811–12, 1818–19, 1834–5, 1846–7, 1850–53, and 1877–8), and these were further complicated by great upheavals in the interior, which marked the emergence of the Zulu and BaSotho kingdoms in the 1820s and produced thousands of refugees to add further pressure to frontier districts. Thus, by the time the British arrived, there were few areas in central and eastern South Africa which had not already been liberally watered with blood. In time, the British redcoat would be called upon to shed his share.

The British first arrived at the Cape in 1795, inheriting it as a side-effect of the fluctuating political alliances in Revolutionary Europe. This first sojourn was a brief one – just long enough to become involved in the third of the Frontier Wars – before returning the colony to the Dutch. In 1806, however, the wheel of fortune took another turn: Britain found itself at war with Holland, and retook the Cape by force, largely to prevent the French seizing it and threatening the sea-route to India. With the Cape came all of the problems of the frontier, and British attempts to resolve them produced a new twist in the complex web of antagonisms. The British tried to fix the boundary between the colony and the Xhosa, and attempts to enforce it led to three further wars, each more ferocious than the last. Nor were the frontier Boers happy with the arbitrary British approach, which failed to pay sufficient attention to the complaints of fellow whites. Indeed, so disgruntled did the frontier Boers become, especially after 1833 when Britain abolished slavery (upon which many Boer farmers depended), that they rejected British authority entirely, packed their possessions into their ox-wagons, and trekked off into the interior in search of more congenial climes.

### Fighting the Voortrekkers

The Great Trek movement of the 1830s dragged British authority reluctantly in its wake, and shaped the pattern of conflict for the remainder of the century. The Boer movement thrust up through central southern Africa and brushed aside those African groups which blocked its path. The British refused to acknowledge that the Boers were anything other than fugitive British subjects, and watched the progress of the Trek with alarm. When the Boers entered Natal, on the eastern coast, and attempted to open contacts with rival European powers through Port Natal, the region's only viable harbour, the British resurrected a dormant claim to the area, awarded by the Zulu kingdom to British adventurers a decade before, as an excuse to block the Boer movement. Two companies of British troops under the command of a Captain Smith of the 27th Regiment were mustered on the Cape Frontier, and marched up overland to Port Natal. Smith

*Right: Boer rifle-men wait to ambush Captain Smith's column, marching along the shore beyond; Port Natal, 1842. (Killie Campbell Library)*

*Right: Boer rifle-men wait to ambush Captain Smith's column, marching along the shore beyond; Port Natal, 1842. (Killie Campbell Library)*

claimed the Port in the name of the Queen; the Boers refused to disperse, and on 23 May Smith tried a daring night attack on their camp. His force marched out along the beach at low tide, but the Boers discovered his approach and fired at him from the protection of a mangrove forest. Smith's force was thrown back in confusion, and retired on a makeshift earthwork fort, which the Boers promptly besieged. Smith was

in a difficult position, his fort cramped and insanitary and his men low on supplies, but he was saved by one of the British traders at the port, who slipped through the Boer lines and rode 600 miles to the Cape frontier to raise the alarm. Troops were immediately despatched by sea, and landed at Port Natal under the cover of a Naval bombardment on 26 June. The siege was lifted, and Britain took immediate steps to annex the Natal

hinterland – to the disgust of many Boers, who promptly trekked back into the interior.

The action at Port Natal was just the first of a series of interconnected clashes which affected most of the principal players in the south African drama in the 1840s. Inland, the Boers had established two independent republics north of the Orange (Senqu) River, which marked the Cape's northern boundary – the

*Right: Captain Smith's fort at Port Natal, showing the effects of the Boer siege, 1842. (Killie Campbell Library)*

Orange Free State, and beyond that the Transvaal. Sandwiched in a small triangle of land, between the eastern slopes of the Drakensberg (Kahlamba) mountains and the Orange, were a number of African groups who appealed to Britain to protect them from Boer land hunger. Britain agreed, and was promptly called upon to make a foray across the Orange. A sharp action took place at Zwartkopjes in April 1845, and the Boers were defeated. This had the effect of increasing British influence across the Orange, but before anything came of this a fresh war broke out on the Cape Frontier.

### The Troubled Frontier
In 1820 the British, in a somewhat cynical attempt to create a buffer zone between the Boers and the Xhosa, had encouraged immigration from Britain, and unceremoniously dumped on the frontier those who took up the offer. Many of these 1820 settlers were ill-equipped to survive in the veld, and the land given to them had, in many cases, formerly belonged to the Xhosa. A

bitter war resulted in 1834-5; peace had been patched up after extensive fighting, but the fundamental cause of conflict – the struggle for land – was not addressed. By 1846 tension had grown to such an extent that a Xhosa arrested for allegedly stealing an axe was freed by his friends, and a column subsequently sent to punish the Xhosa was ambushed as it made its way up a difficult mountain pass. This was the start of the Seventh Frontier War, the so-called War of the Axe, and it followed a pattern established in the sixth. When the Xhosa entered the colony, attacking settlements, troops rushed to the frontier and forced them back to their mountain strongholds after stiff fighting. Pitched battles in the open were rare, because the Xhosa, who knew they could not match British fire-power, avoided them; on one occasion, at the Gwangqa River on 7 June, the 7th Dragoons stumbled on a Xhosa army crossing their front in broad daylight, and in the ensuing charge caused bloody havoc. It was a different matter in their mountain

strongholds, however, where the Xhosa could move across rugged, bush-covered terrain at a pace which frustrated the British, who were hampered by unwieldy baggage trains. Here it was the British who were outclassed, and they resorted instead to a war of attrition, the Xhosa being subdued in the end by the wholesale destruction of their villages and crops.

### Boers, BaSotho and the War of Mlanjeni
With the end of the War of the Axe a new British Governor arrived at the Cape, a man whose flamboyant and eccentric personality would leave its mark on South Africa over the next few years – Sir Harry Smith, the egocentric Peninsular veteran and hero of the battle of Aliwal in the Sikh Wars. Smith was a man of extraordinary energy, who treated South Africans, black and white, with equal measures of sentimental paternalism or theatrical contempt. After imposing a new settlement on the war-weary Xhosa chiefs, Smith crossed the Orange to investi-

*Left: In the early Cape Frontier Wars, the British found themselves ill equipped to meet the Xhosa on their own terms in the bush. (Author's collection)*

*Right: Xhosa warriors ambushing British troops in the Boomah Pass at the start of the Seventh Cape Frontier War. (Author's collection)*

gate the situation there. Deciding that it needed tidying, he blandly announced that he intended to annex the area north of the Orange, and in February 1848 it became the Orange River Sovereignty. The results were immediate and predictable; the Boers were outraged, and gathered their forces to drive the British out. Smith promptly attacked, and in a neat outflanking movement dispersed them at the battle of Boomplaats on 29 August 1848. A British resident then began to disentangle the various overlapping land claims of the Boers, the BaSotho, and other local African groups.

On the Cape frontier, however, Smith's settlement, which had humiliated many of the leading Xhosa chiefs, soon collapsed. Smith sent troops into Xhosa territory in a show of force, and on 24 December 1850 a column was ambushed in the Boomah Pass. The next day the Xhosa once more invaded the colony. Smith had insufficient troops to mount an effective response, and had to wait until the initial Xhosa impetus faltered. He then went onto the offensive, driving them back into the hills. This,

the Eighth Frontier War – known to the Xhosa as the War of Mlanjeni, after a mystic who encouraged them to resist – would prove the toughest of them all, for the Xhosa had learned much from their previous defeats, and were led by resolute and daring commanders. In particular, the chief Maqoma, who orchestrated a series of raids from a stronghold known as the Waterkloof, ran rings around the British sent to capture him. The fighting dragged on throughout 1851 and became increasingly more brutal as British and colonial troops, frustrated by conventional methods of warfare, resorted to a war of extermination.

Meanwhile further trouble was brewing north of the Orange. The BaSotho kingdom had emerged in the 1820s under King Moshoeshoe, who had maintained friendly relations with the British; however, when trouble flared between the BaSotho and their African neighbours, the British took the side of the latter. The small British force sent into the troubled area was consequently attacked by the BaSotho at Konoyana (Viervoet) on 30 June 1851. Its African allies were lured

away by a decoy of cattle, and BaSotho horsemen made a fierce charge on the British camp. The presence of artillery saved the day, but the British force nonetheless beat a hasty retreat. Before they had time to consider their next move, Sir Harry Smith was recalled, and Sir George Cathcart took his place as Governor.

On the frontier, the fighting dragged on until March 1853, though the Xhosa had lost all hope of winning long before. Their armies broken up, their homes burnt or bombarded, their families killed without compunction, the last bands waged a desperate cat-and-mouse warfare, harried through the bush by increasingly ruthless British troops, until at last they were exhausted into submission. By that time Cathcart had made a further demonstration against the BaSotho too, but the results were more ambiguous. In December 1852 he had crossed the Orange to confront Moshoeshoe, advancing in three small columns against his famous mountain stronghold, Thaba Bosiu. On the 20th the BaSotho intercepted him. One British column, consisting chiefly of the 12th Lancers, was pinned against

*Above: 74th Highlanders in modified campaign uniform fighting in the Waterkloof, Eighth Cape Frontier War. (Author's collection)*

a cliff-face on Berea Mountain, and suffered over twenty-five dead. Elsewhere, Cathcart kept his troops well in hand when faced with another mounted charge, but by the end of the day his columns had all been halted, and he had suffered nearly forty killed. Before he could launch a fresh attack, Moshoeshoe, with the shrewd diplomacy which typified his reign, hastily submitted. In April 1854 the British, happy to be rid of the Sovereignty, formally abandoned all claims that Sir Harry Smith had made to the region. Most of it returned to Boer rule as the Orange Free State, though BaSotholand remained an independent sovereign territory.

### The Tightening Grip
The next two decades were a period of consolidation for the British and Boers, and despair for the Africans.

On the Cape frontier, the collective grief at the recent defeat and the alienation of land that followed manifested itself in an apocalyptic religious delusion; the Xhosa slaughtered thousands of their cattle as a sacrifice to the spirits of their dead heroes, in the hope that this would cause them to intervene and restore their former glory. But the spirits did not appear, and the people starved. The slaughter of its cattle, following so soon after the destructive Eighth War, largely broke the power of the Xhosa. The British secured their hold on the Cape, and began to develop Natal, while in the Free State and the Transvaal the Boers attempted to tighten their control of their African neighbours, including the BaSotho.

The period of comparative quiet which followed came as something of a relief to the British, for whom the cost of maintaining its possessions in South Africa had long outweighed its strategic significance. Yet the calm was no more than a lull, for the fundamental issues which had led to the earlier conflicts had in no

sense been resolved. With the discovery in 1868 of diamonds at Kimberley, just north of the Cape, these tensions were once more highlighted. Britain acted swiftly to annex the diamond fields in the face of rival Boer claims, but the discovery accelerated a process of economic disruption which had in any case been gathering pace. Diamonds at last offered a return on Britain's investment in the region, but in order to manage the resultant economic growth, it was necessary to construct a trade and transport network which cut across the boundaries of the mutually suspicious Boer, British and African possessions. In the 1870s, the solution devised by the Colonial Office in London was confederation – a loose association of locally administered states under British control. Of course, given the history of South Africa it was unlikely that confederation could be brought about peacefully, and a skilled and experienced statesman with an Indian background, Sir Henry Bartle Frere, was despatched to South Africa to bully Boers and Africans alike into joining the scheme.

Even before Frere arrived, the British had annexed the northern of the two Boer republics, the Transvaal. This was a vast country, thinly populated by the most independent-minded of the Trekkers – so independent-minded, indeed, that they rejected almost all attempts to govern them, and the region was largely bankrupt. The British took a hasty and highly selective canvas of opinion, then simply marched into the capital, Pretoria, in 1877, and raised the Union Flag. In the event, the annexation of the Transvaal was to prove the single most politically destructive act carried out by the British in South Africa. It resulted in an immediate wave of conflict, and created the climate of hostility which led to the outbreak of the Great Boer War twenty years later.

For one thing, the Transvaal was already embroiled in two territorial disputes with its African neighbours, which the British now inherited. In the far north-east, clashes with the Pedi confederacy of King Sekhukhune had led to desultory fighting in which the Transvaal had repeatedly come off worse. The British, opting to continue the Boers' hard line policy towards the Pedi, sent an expedition against them in October 1878 under the command of Colonel Hugh Rowlands VC. He had just 130 infantry and 338 mounted men, and was faced with a gruelling march through a hot, dry landscape, to reach Sekhukhune's capital, Tsate, which nestled in a hollow at the foot of the Leolu mountains. Rowland's column was harassed by the Pedi, but its real enemy was the environment – shortage of water, and the onset of horse-sickness. In the end, Rowlands was forced to admit that his force was too small to accomplish its task, and he withdrew.

## The Zulu War

A far more serious clash was brewing, meanwhile, on the Transvaal's south-eastern border. Here, on the Natal side of the Drakensberg mountains, the border overlapped land claimed by the Zulu king. This was a remote area, thinly settled by either side, but the rivalry had led to a good deal of tension between the Transvaal and the incumbent Zulu king, Cetshwayo kaMpande. Hitherto Britain, through Zululand's southern neighbour, Natal, had broadly supported the Zulu position, but after the annexation of the Transvaal it baldly assumed the Transvaal's claim. This in itself soured Anglo-Zulu relations, which were further marred by Frere's policies. Frere, keen to push the Confederation policy through, was anxious to prove to disgruntled Transvaal citizens the advantages of British rule, and it seemed to him that he could best do this by checking the Zulu threat. There was, in any case, a wave of discontent spreading through South Africa's hard-pressed black population; on the Cape frontier another rising had broken out in 1877 – the ninth, a half-hearted and sad affair which merely confirmed how broken Xhosa power was – whilst tension was building with a semi-independent chieftain on the BaSotho borders, Moorosi, who was in dispute with the Cape Colony. The Pedi were also clearly uncowed. Frere saw a common hand in all this, and was convinced that Cetshwayo, as the leader of the most powerful black kingdom left in the country, was behind a conspiracy to resist white expansionism. The home government was reluctant to embark on fresh campaigning in South Africa, but Frere gambled that he could provoke a quick war with the Zulus, and win it with the troops already at his disposal, before the Colonial Office could object.

In this Frere proved to be sadly mistaken. In December 1878 he presented the Zulu king with an ultimatum which had been carefully calculated to ensure its refusal. It expired on 11 January 1879, and the Anglo-Zulu War began. The senior British commander, Lieutenant-General Lord Chelmsford, was fresh from the Cape frontier campaign, where he had waged a frustrating war trying to pin down the elusive Xhosa bands. He was determined not to allow the same thing to happen in Zululand, and decided to invade in three separate columns, converging on the Zulu king's principal residence, oNdini. Chelmsford, who commanded the Centre Column of this pincer movement in person, crossed the border without opposition, but on 22 January all three columns encountered their first major Zulu resistance. The Right Flank Column, under Colonel Pearson, operating in Zululand's humid coastal belt, was just dragging its cumbersome baggage wagons across the Nyezane river when a Zulu force appeared on a range of hills across the track ahead. Pearson deployed his troops in a long firing line as a Zulu attack developed rapidly from the heights, sweeping down as if to outflank him. Although Pearson's line was over-extended, the Zulus proved unable to withstand a withering fire from artillery, rockets, Gatlings and rifles, and were driven off. Nevertheless, the battle was a sobering experience for Pearson's command, who were surprised by the tactical skill and sheer courage with which the Zulus pressed home their attack. Far away in the north, the Left Flank Column under Colonel Wood also saw action on the 22nd; but it was on the Centre Column that the hardest blow fell.

On 20 January Lord Chelmsford had established a base on the forward slope of a mountain called Isandlwana. By that time, his intelligence sources suggested that King Cetshwayo had despatched the main Zulu army against the Centre Column. On the night of the 21st, a reconnaissance party encountered Zulus about twelve miles from the camp, and Chelmsford, keen not to let them slip away, marched out with about half his force before dawn. Isandlwana was guarded by about 1700 men altogether, including two guns and 700 infantry from the 24th Regiment. While Chelmsford was away, however, scouts from the camp stumbled on a Zulu army, 20,000 strong, which had slipped round Chelmsford's flank, and lay concealed in undulating country about five miles from the

Isandlwana. The Zulu army immediately rose up and advanced rapidly on the camp. The garrison attempted to make a stand in front of the camp, but was outflanked, and the line collapsed; the Zulus overran the camp and killed over 1300 men. Chelmsford knew nothing of the battle until it was too late; by the time he had marched his column back to Isandlwana, the triumphant Zulus had ransacked the camp, and dispersed.

In the aftermath of the victory at Isandlwana, the Zulu reserve, about 4000 strong, cut across country to attack a small British garrison left to guard the border crossing at Rorke's Drift. The post consisted of two thatched buildings, held by less than 150 men – mostly from B Company, 2/24th – but it included a stockpile of supplies which had been due to go forward to the column. When the first terrified survivors brought news of Isandlwana, the senior officers, Lieutenant John Chard of the Royal Engineers and Gonville Bromhead of the 24th – opted to stand and fight. The post was barricaded with heavy sacks of mealie and boxes of army biscuit, and men posted to defend the buildings. The Zulus attacked at about 4.30 pm, and continued to assault the post throughout the night. One of the buildings was stormed and set on fire, but the garrison held out, and the Zulus withdrew before dawn. Over 500 Zulus had been killed for a loss of seventeen of the garrison; eleven of the defenders were subsequently awarded the Victoria Cross.

The destruction of the camp at Isandlwana effectively scotched Lord Chelmsford's initial invasion plan. On the coast, Pearson, following his victory at Nyezane, had occupied a deserted mission station at Eshowe. Left unsupported by the disaster at

Isandlwana, he dug in. For three months he was effectively under siege, shut up within the confines of the fort, low on food, his men prey to disease and constantly harassed by the Zulus. Similarly, Colonel Wood's Left Flank Column, which

*J.R.M. Chard, the hero of Rorke's Drift, photographed later in life as a Lieutenant Colonel. (Royal Engineers Museum)*

had established itself at Khambula hill in the aftermath of Isandlwana, could do little beyond harrying Zulus living in the vicinity.

In the meantime the British government rallied behind Chelmsford in an attempt to restore British pres-

tige. Reinforcements, denied to him before the war, were now sent out with alacrity. By the end of March Chelmsford felt able to go onto the offensive once more. His first task was to extricate Pearson's beleaguered garrison at Eshowe, and to distract the Zulus from his real intention he asked Wood to make a diversionary attack in the north of the country. Wood had long been troubled by Zulus operating from a mountain stronghold known as Hlobane, from which a highly successful attack had been launched against a convoy of the 80th Regiment at Ntombe River on 12 March. Wood decided to attack Hlobane on 28 March, assaulting the mountain with horsemen at either end, hoping to catch the Zulus in a pincer movement. In the event the plan misfired, and the British, once on top of the mountain, found themselves trapped by the unexpected appearance of the main Zulu army, 20,000 strong, which was en route to attack Khambula. The retreat from Hlobane was a rout, the worst debacle of the war after Isandlwana. It did at least warn Wood of the presence of the Zulu force, however, and when it attacked his camp the following day, he was fully prepared. For several hours the Zulus made determined assaults on his position, a chain of wagon-laagers and earthwork redoubts on the top of Khambula ridge, until they were eventually driven off by a particularly ruthless mounted pursuit.

Within a few days Chelmsford, too, would win a decisive victory on the coast. At Gingindlovu, midway between the border and Eshowe, his column was attacked by a large Zulu force on the morning of 2 April. Chelmsford's column was deployed in square, protected by a rampart of

*Above: A British battalion on the march: the 91st Highlanders, Zululand, 1879. (National Army Museum)*

*Below: Whilst the general tactical trend in the 1870s was towards open-order formations, the battles of the Zulu War, like oNdini pictured here, were won by concentrated British firepower. (Rai England Collection)*

earth, with a wagon-laager inside; once again, despite extraordinary courage, the Zulus were unable to penetrate the British fire-zone. The next day Chelmsford relieved Eshowe, and began to withdraw once more to the Thukela. The heavy defeats at Khambula and Gingindlovu, at either end of the country and within a few days of each other, badly damaged Zulu morale, and gave Chelmsford the time to prepare a new invasion of Zululand. This began at the end of May. As it wound slowly towards oNdini, however, Chelmsford was informed that he was to be replaced by General Sir Garnet Wolseley, who was being sent out from England. Chelmsford was determined to bring the war to a successful conclusion and banish the spectre of Isandl- wana before Wolseley arrived, and he reached oNdini at the beginning of July. Here, on the 4th, he marched his force in a hollow square close to the Zulu royal homesteads, and the Zulu charges dashed them-

selves to pieces against the storm of British firepower. He then resigned his command, leaving Wolseley with little more to do than pacify the country and capture King Cetshwayo.

### The Sekhukhune Campaign

Cheated of his glory in the Zulu War, Wolseley was at least allowed the chance to finally suppress the Pedi. In September 1879 he recommenced the operations Rowlands had aban- doned the year before, but this time with a much stronger force, consist- ing of British regulars – fresh from Zululand – supported by Swazi war- riors. The Pedi skirmished before Wolseley's advance, and fell back on the capital Tsate. Tsate was situated in a hollow, with the Leolu hills behind and a plain in front, broken by a solitary kopje which com- manded the approach. This kopje was strewn with boulders and pitted with caves, and the Pedi had further fortified it with stone sangars. Wolse- ley attacked on 28 November. The

'fighting kop' was bombarded at dawn, and rushed by British regulars, who overran the first line of barri- cades but were pinned down further up the slope. The Swazis were sent to attack the town by another route, however, and circled round through the hills, descending on Tsate from the rear. This had a demoralising effect on the Pedi, who fled the town. Those ensconced on the kopje held out throughout the day, how- ever, though many took advantage of a thunderstorm the following night to make a break for freedom. The remainder were either starved out, shot, or blown up over the next few days, and Sekhukhune himself was captured on 2 December. The power of the Pedi, which had once rivalled that of the Zulu, was effec- tively destroyed.

*Below: The final British assault on King Sekhukhune's capital, 1879; the 'fighting kopje' is in the centre of the picture. (Author's collection)*

## The Transvaal Revolt

Wolseley left South Africa shortly afterwards, handing over command to his protégé, General Sir George Pomeroy Colley, but even before he left it was clear that trouble was brewing in the Transvaal. By late 1880 the British had just one cavalry regiment and three infantry battalions, with support services, to garrison the entire Transvaal. The main concentration was at the capital, Pretoria, but small garrisons were stationed in small towns across the country, an unpopular duty for the redcoats, who found the remote and dusty towns dreary, the inhabitants surly, and the routine numbingly boring. By the end of 1880 Boer opposition had become so severe that troops were regularly used to support the civil administration. In December the republican party played its hand: 7000 Boers gathered under arms and proclaimed that the Transvaal was once more an independent republic. Shots were fired outside Pretoria, and a column of British troops – Lieutenant-Colonel Anstruther with two companies of the 94th Regiment – was moved from the northern town of Lydenburg to the capital. On 20 December, in open country near Bronkhorstspruit, Anstruther was met by a Boer deputation who called on him to abandon his march. Anstruther replied that he must follow his orders, and Boer riflemen on nearby slopes promptly opened fire. The 94th had begun the fight in extended column, guarding their baggage wagons, and the Boer firing was so accurate that they were unable to deploy fully to meet it. By the time Anstruther agreed to surrender, after perhaps just fifteen minutes of fighting, 150 of his men had been killed or wounded. Anstruther himself had been hit five times, and died a few days later.

The action at Bronkhorstspruit triggered a wholesale Boer rising. The principal British garrisons – at Pretoria, Pochefstroom, Rustenburg, Marabastad, Lydenburg, Standerton and Wakkerstroom – were all besieged. Some 2000 Boers crossed the border with Natal, and took up a position across the pass at Laing's Nek, blocking the main road into the Transvaal from that direction. Colley, who was in Natal when the rising began, concentrated 1200 men at the northern Natal town of Newcastle ready to march to the aid of the beleaguered garrisons.

Colley was undoubtedly one of the most intellectually gifted of Wolseley's famous Ashanti Ring, but his charismatic personality obscured the fact that he had an almost total lack of experience of battlefield command. The implications of this first became apparent on 28 February 1881, when he attempted to force a way through the Laing's Nek pass.

*Right: General Sir George Colley, photographed wearing the practical campaign uniform of the 1873–4 Asante War. (Royal Archives)*

He began by softening up the Boer position with artillery fire, but the Boers were well-protected behind breastworks. The attack was mounted by five companies of the 58th Regiment and four companies of the 3/60th, supported by Mounted Infantry on the flank. The infantry advanced up the steep slope in column, under a heavy and accurate Boer fire. The Mounted Infantry attack was driven back in confusion; the 58th pushed forward to within 150 yards of the crest and then attempted to deploy in extended line. By that time, however, they were exhausted by the effort of the climb, and the effect of the Boer fire at such close range was devastating. An attempt to mount a bayonet charge withered under a hail of bullets, and the 58th were driven back. Colley's force lost about 190 men killed and wounded, including a high proportion of officers. Boer casualties were less then 40 men.

The British reverse at Laing's Nek was followed shortly after by another almost as serious. Colley's camp was at Mount Prospect, a spot half way between Laing's Nek and Newcastle.

The Boers, encouraged by their success, sent small parties deep into Natal, which threatened Colley's line of communication with Newcastle. On 8 February Colley took five companies of the 3/60th, four guns and a small detachment of Mounted Infantry to clear the road in his rear. This lay through undulating country, and on a grassy plateau known as Schuinshoogte, above the Ingogo river, Colley was fired upon by about 300 Boers who had gathered to challenge him. Colley immediately deployed his men in a semi-circle in open order and returned the fire. The Boers then skirmished forward and attacked. The gunners were particularly exposed, and soon began to suffer heavily. The infantry crouched behind boulders to return the fire, but the Boers were excellent shots and steadily picked them off. Colley's force was pinned down for the best part of the day, and only just managed to extricate themselves after dark. British casualties were almost 150 killed or wounded; the Boers suffered less than twenty casualties.

Bronkhorstspruit, Laing's Nek and Ingogo had given the British a harsh lesson in the fighting capabilities of an enemy they had hitherto despised as undisciplined frontier farmers. Yet all three disasters were destined to pail into insignificance beside the final crowning catastrophe.

In the aftermath of Schuinshoogte, Colley received a trickle of reinforcements, chiefly the 92nd Highlanders, fresh from Roberts' victories in Afghanistan. The Boer position at Laing's Nek was overlooked to the British left by a high hill known as Majuba. At short notice on the night of 27 February, Colley assembled a force of less than 400 men – chiefly from the 92nd and 58th – and led them in person up a steep and difficult climb to the summit of Majuba. Although the position was a commanding one, it would have needed careful preparation as a base for an offensive against the Boer positions, and these Colley did not make. At dawn the next morning about 350 Boers assaulted the mountain, overran the summit, and shot Colley dead.

Majuba cost the British over 200 dead and wounded, whilst the Boers lost only a handful of men.

*Left: The battlefield of Schuinshoogte (Ingogo), showing the remains of artillery horses killed in the battle. (Bryan Maggs Collection)*

*Right: The final ignominy of the Transvaal War: British troops fleeing down Majuba under Boer fire. (Author's collection)*

*Left: The bulk of Majuba mountain, photographed from the British side, with O'Neill's cottage in the foreground. (Bryan Maggs Collection)*

*Below left: The final British collapse at Majuba. (Author's collection)*

*Right: Auctioning the effects of those killed on Majuba at Mount Prospect camp, to raise money for their families. (Author's collection)*

In the aftermath of the defeat, British political opinion swung in favour of peace, and on 14 March Colley's successor signed an armistice with the Boer leaders at O'Neill's Cottage at the foot of Majuba. The news was greeted with disgust amongst the besieged garrisons, who had held out since the beginning of the year in difficult circumstances, often in the face of frequent Boer attacks. Wood's agreement was ratified by the Pretoria Convention signed in August, which formerly returned the Transvaal to Boer hands, whilst allowing Britain an ill-defined right to interfere in Transvaal affairs. Although the settlement brought hostilities to a close, few regarded it with any satisfaction – it was one of the few wars undertaken by the British Army in the Victorian period which was undeniably a defeat – and its ambiguities paved the way for the much greater conflict of 1899-1902.

**Imperial Power-Play**

The Pretoria convention spelt the final end of the Confederation policy, which had been mortally wounded by the Zulus at Isandlwana. On the whole, the Liberal govern-

84

ment in London in the 1880s was set against fresh Imperial adventuring, yet the fundamental problems which beset South Africa remained unresolved. In Zululand, the failure of the British to adopt a firm post-war policy led to civil war, which finally erupted into a minor rebellion in 1888, and redcoats had to march into the field once more to put it down. BaSotholand, abandoned by Britain after the collapse of the Orange River Sovereignty, had suffered two debilitating wars against the Free State, and the ageing Moshoeshoe had appealed to Britain to intervene once more. BaSotholand had been annexed in 1868, but by 1880 the colonial administration was proving so irksome that the BaSotho also rebelled. The subsequent war was waged almost entirely by colonial troops, and the two sides fought each other to a standstill. In the interior, the economic disturbance caused by the discovery of diamonds at Kimberley led to the British to seize both Griqualand West in 1878, brushing aside local Tswana resistance, and – with-

out firing a shot – Bechuanaland in 1885.

These moves effectively isolated the Boer republics and kept them outside the developing mining economy. In 1885, however, gold was discovered on the Witwatersrand in the Transvaal, and the latent hostility between the British and the Boers was once more thrown into relief. Thousands of foreign miners, known to the Boers as *uitlanders*, flocked to the gold-fields, but the Transvaal, led by the hard-line and deeply conservative republican leader Paul Kruger, refused to grant them political representation. Influential figures like Cecil Rhodes, the diamond magnate, attempted to undermine Kruger's support; in 1890 Rhodes' British South Africa Company occupied the area of modern Zimbabwe. This had the effect of blocking any possible Transvaal movement to the north, although Zimbabwe (then known as Rhodesia) proved lacking in the mineral reserves Rhodes had hoped for, and involved his company in protracted campaigns against the local Ndebele and Shona groups. Frus-

trated, Rhodes and his associates tried direct action; in 1895 his lieutenant, Dr Jameson, led a raid into the Transvaal to provoke the *uitlanders* into rebellion. In the event the *uitlanders* did not rise, and Jameson's followers surrendered after a fight at Doornkop, outside Johannesburg, on 2 January 1896.

The Jameson Raid was a turning point in the decline of Anglo-Boer relations. The Boers, believing a wider clash imminent, began preparations for it, whilst a new British administration at the Cape adopted a more aggressive policy. In June 1899 an attempt at a negotiated settlement collapsed, and the *uitlanders* began to flee the Transvaal. The Orange Free State, although not directly involved in the quarrel, declared its support for the Transvaal. British troops on garrison duty were moved up to guard vulnerable border towns, whilst troops were mobilised in the United Kingdom in expectation of a clash. Kruger, opting to seize the initiative, issued an ultimatum demanding that the troops on the borders be removed. It expired on 11 October 1899, and the Anglo-Boer War – known to the Afrikaners as the *Tweede Vryheidsoorlog*, the second war of freedom – began.

## The 'Great Boer War'

The opening stages of the Anglo-Boer War were waged by British officers who had learnt their skills in earlier, more straightforward conflicts, whose outlook was conditioned by those experiences. They tended to despise the Boers as untrained frontier farmers, and their fundamental conservatism was ill-suited to the profound changes in tactical thinking and weapon technology which were taking place. Consequently the war began with a series of startling British defeats.

The Boer republics had perhaps 40,000 men at their disposal, mostly armed citizens, stiffened with small numbers of regulars armed and trained along European lines. With Majuba very much in mind, the Boers opted for an offensive strategy, hoping to strike quickly into the British colonies and inflict sufficient heavy defeats to bring the British to the negotiating table before the resources of the wider empire could be mobilised. In the west, they struck at the diamond town of Kimberley – where Cecil Rhodes himself had the misfortune to be trapped within the Boer cordon – and, further north, at the dusty frontier town of Mafikeng, which commanded the road to Zimbabwe. In the south, a further strike was made into the Cape Colony, in an attempt to encourage Cape Boers to rise to the republics' support. By far the greatest thrust, however, was made into Natal. Here the main Transvaal forces, under Commandant-General Piet Joubert – a hero of the 1881 war – and supported by commandos from the Free State, poured across the Laing's Nek pass, past the grim bulk of Majuba, and started on the road to Durban. The British commander in South Africa, General Penn-Symons, assembled 4500 British troops at the northern Natal town of Dundee to block their advance. On 20 October the Boers occupied Talana hill outside the town, and Penn-Symons drew his men up and rushed the hill in style. The Boers were driven off, but the British suffered severely from a heavy and accurate Boer fire as they scrambled up the rocky slopes; Penn-Symons himself was mortally wounded. The next day, with the Boers still in the vicinity, Penn-Symons' successor decided Dundee was indefensible, and made preparations to retire. In short, Talana was a good introduction to the costliness, confusion and futility which would characterise many of the battles of the Boer War.

## The Siege of Ladysmith

The Dundee garrison retired on Ladysmith, in central Natal. For a number of years Ladysmith – the 'Aldershot of South Africa', named after Sir Harry Smith's wife – had housed the main British garrison in Natal. Strategically, it was not well-placed, lying north of the significant barrier of the Thukela river; when the first British reinforcements arrived in Natal – 10,000 troops sent from India under the command of General Sir George White – their first inclination had been to abandon Ladysmith in favour of a better line nearer the port at Durban. White felt that Penn-Symons' stand at Dundee had compromised such a plan, however, and he moved north to Ladysmith. He arrived just before the action at Talana. As the Dundee garrison fell back, White made a foray to prevent the Boers from cutting it off, and caught the Free State commandos at Elandslaagte station on 21 October. In almost textbook style White's troops drove the Boers from one kopje to another, and finished them off with a grim lancer charge. Yet White did not follow up his victory, preferring instead to concentrate his forces. Piet Joubert's Transvaal commandos promptly took advantage of this delay, and advanced rapidly to seize a circle of hills surrounding Ladysmith. White tried to break out of the trap, and on the night of 29/30 October he mounted a bold attack on Boer positions at Pepworth Hill and Nicholson's Nek. Unfortunately the plan badly miscarried, the darkness added to the confusion, and daylight found the attacking British badly exposed to the fire from Boers securely concealed on the hills. The British attack collapsed, and White's men fell back on Ladysmith. White now found his 13,000 troops, together with their 2500 servants and 5400 civilians, surrounded in a little town of tin-roofed bungalows, at the mercy of heavy Boer artillery which shelled them with impunity from the surrounding heights.

Whilst the events of the initial Boer invasion were being played out, the British army at home had mobilised its First Army Corps of 47,000 men and sent it out to South Africa under the command of General Sir Redvers Buller. Buller was a big, bulldog of a man with a famously gruff manner; he had won the VC during the debacle at Hlobane in the Zulu War, and was widely regarded by a jingoistic British public as a hero who could do no wrong. When Buller left England, he shared the popular belief that the quickest way to win the war was to strike up through the interior from the Cape, following the line of the railway, first to the Free State capital of Bloemfontein, then to Pretoria. He arrived in South Africa just in time to hear of White's investment at Ladysmith, however, and opted instead to split his force; leaving the smaller part under Lord Methuen to try to relieve Kimberley, he despatched the remainder to Natal.

## The British Counter-Attack

After the frantic events of October, November 1899 saw something of a lull. The Boer assaults lost their impetus, and frittered away their resources in long and ultimately pointless sieges. With White bottled up in Ladysmith, Natal was acutely vulnerable to an attack on Durban, which, if it fell, would have denied the British the great advantage of their world-wide maritime transport network. To the disgust of younger, more adventurous leaders, however, the cautious and conservative Joubert refused to seize the opportunity, and the younger commandants became pinned down under a hail of rifle and pom-pom fire. The fighting had reached a stalemate by nightfall, but the Boers abandoned their positions under cover of darkness. They took up a new position a few miles away, along a low ridge known as Magersfontein. Methuen spent a fortnight regrouping, then prepared to attack.

### 'Black Week'

The second week of December saw a resumption of fighting on all the main fronts with unprecedented ferocity, and circumstances contrived to deliver three defeats to the British in quick succession, a string of disasters so shocking that they were known collectively as Black Week. The first occurred in the eastern sector of the northern Cape, where Free State Boers had been threatening the strategically important Stormberg Junction. On 10/11 December General Gatacre took 3000 troops out in a daring night march to clear the Boers away, but the darkness, imperfect maps, and imprecise orders combined to confuse Gatacre's command completely. Dawn the following morning found the British forces widely scattered and at the mercy of the Boers, who killed and wounded nearly 150 and took 600 prisoner. The very next day Methuen himself suffered a serious reverse at Magersfontein. Realising that the Magersfontein ridge was a strong position, he had been reluctant to mount a frontal assault in the dark, so had planned a careful night attack. In the event the plan miscarried, and dawn caught the leading brigades still in close formation, fatally exposed to Boer fire. The attack collapsed in confusion. Methuen lost 950 killed and wounded compared to less than 300 Boer casualties – and this time the Boers stayed in their trenches. The defeat was all the more humiliating because it had fallen most heavily on the Highland and Guards Brigades, which enjoyed such a high reputation within the army.

The news of Stormberg and Magersfontein reached Buller in Natal at a critical time. The Boers

*Above: General Sir Redvers Buller was a national hero when he was appointed to command the 1st Army Corps in South Africa, but the difficulties of his campaign to relieve Ladysmith ruined his reputation. (Author's collection)*

had to be content with a minor raid into Natal. The respite gave the British time to organise their forces, and by the end of November, as Buller's troops began to disembark at Durban, Methuen was ready to go on the offensive in the west. He had 10,000 men at his disposal, and pushed up through the arid wastes of the northern Cape, following the railway line. On 23 and 24 November he won two minor actions at Belmont and Graspan, whilst the Boers fell back on the line of the Modder River, which blocked the road to Kimberley. The Modder was a good natural defensive position, meandering through largely open and featureless country. The Boers, under General Piet Cronje, secured themselves in slit trenches along the banks, so that any British advance would have to be made across miles of flat open country. On 28 November Methuen attacked the Modder, with predictable results; his assaults

*Opposite page, top: Naval Brigade guns under fire from the Boer positions overlooking the Thukela river at Colenso, December 1899. (Author's collection)*

*Opposite page, bottom: Hart's Brigade pinned down under heavy Boer fire: 'Thukela loop', battle of Colenso. (Author's collection)*

had taken up a strong defensive position along a line of hills on the north bank of the Thukela river, which blocked any British advance on Ladysmith. The British advance would inevitably take them across open, undulating country where they would be exposed to the full weight of Boer fire. Buller was reluctant to take such a risk, but whilst he pondered his options the news of Stormberg and Magersfontein forced his hand. With the need to restore British prestige paramount, he opted for a frontal assault on the village of Colenso, which commanded the main route to Ladysmith. Buller had about 18,000 troops available – the Boer commander, Louis Botha, had less than 7000 – but Buller's men had only recently arrived in South Africa, and the brigade commanders were not used to working together. This soon became all too apparent when Buller made his attack early on the morning of 15 December. He planned to assault the Thukela line with two infantry brigades, with two more in support. In the event, his artillery drew ahead of their supports, and took up an exposed position closer to the Boer line than had been planned, and immediately came under heavy fire. The leading

brigade on the left became confused by the topography of the river, advanced in close order into a loop in the Thukela, and was brought to a halt by a withering frontal and enfilading fire. Buller, seeing the danger to the artillery, devoted his attention to extricating them, and failed to make the best use of his reserves. Disheartened, reluctant to sacrifice his men's lives unnecessarily, he called off the assault after an hour, compelling his gunners to abandon ten out of twelve guns to the Boers.

Colenso cost Buller 900 men killed or wounded – the majority wounded – and was the crowning humiliation of Black Week. In fact, it had hardly affected the strategic situation in Natal at all, but such was the outcry among politicians and the Press at home that Buller was sent a fresh division of reinforcements, and a new overall commander, Lord Roberts, was despatched to South Africa. The choice of Roberts was an unfortunate one for Buller, who was a member of Wolseley's Ring; Roberts was not only the darling of the rival India Ring, but his son, Lieutenant Freddy Roberts, had served on Buller's staff and been killed at Colenso. Meanwhile the Boers largely failed to follow up their victories, though they did step up the pressure on Ladysmith, launching an attack on British positions outside the town on 6 January 1900, which was narrowly repulsed. Buller, well aware that he could not dawdle before the Thukela heights indefinitely, waited for the arrival of his reinforcements and then made a second attempt to break through.

## Spioenkop

Buller resorted to his original plan. Fifteen miles upstream from Colenso there was an alternative crossing point on the Thukela, and he resolved to try to outflank the Boer line at this point. His troops began an assault on the Boer positions on 19 January, but soon became pinned down on the rocky hillsides under heavy fire from above. On the spur of the moment one of Buller's divisional commanders, General Warren, suggested that the key to the Boer position was a whale-backed ridge in the centre of their line, known as 'Look-out Hill' – Spioenkop. The battle of Spioenkop would prove the greatest disaster of the Natal campaign. On the night of 23/24 January British troops scaled the slopes and drove off a Boer picquet on the summit. When dawn rose the next morning, however, the British line proved to be badly sited, and exposed to both Boer artillery fire and determined infantry assault. During a day of bungling and confusion, the troops clung to the summit whilst Warren and Buller failed to mount effective supporting attacks. By nightfall the British casualties were so heavy that the commander on Spioenkop decided to withdraw. The attack cost the British 300 dead, 1000 wounded, and 200 captured, and by the time it was over, they were back precisely where they had

*Below: The summit of Spioenkop. The British ascended on the left, the Boers on the right; the British held the crest, centre, whilst the Boers held the outlying spurs. (S.B. Bourquin)*

*Above: Bodies tossed haphazardly from their inadequate trench on the summit of Spioenkop. (Transvaal Archives Depot)*

*Right: 'Dulce et decorum est, pro patria mori'; a grim photograph of partially buried British dead on the summit of Spioenkop. The photographer has cut two slightly different negatives showing the same scene together to give the impression of a row of corpses. (Transvaal Archives Depot)*

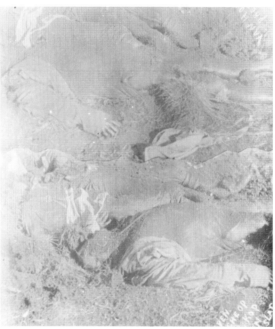

started. A few days later an attack on the Boer position a few miles to the east, at Vaalkraanz, was also abandoned in the face of resolute Boer resistance.

**The Western Front**

Whilst Buller struggled to overcome his very real difficulties before Ladysmith, Lord Roberts brought a fresh energy to the war on the western front, and gave the British their first major victory of the campaign. By early February Roberts had amassed nearly 37,000 men; the Boers were still in position at the Magersfontein ridge, but rather than confront them head-on Roberts planned to outflank them. Striking out to his right, he hoped to surprise the Boers by abandoning the line of the railway. He was right; he began his move on 12 February, and, despite some opposition, his cavalry circled wide of the main Boer line, and entered Kimberley on the 15th, relieving it after 124 days of siege, which had cost the lives of thirty-five soldiers and five civilians. Roberts' main force followed in the cavalry's wake. Their line was very extended, and vulnerable to Boer counter-attack – on the same day that Kimberley was relieved Christiaan de Wet caught a supply train crossing the Riet river and captured or destroyed 1600 draught oxen – but the threat it posed to Cronje at Magersfontein was obvious. Cronje decided to

*Left: British artillery in action during the defence of Kimberley. (Bryan Maggs Collection)*

*Right: Lord Roberts receives the surrender of General Cronje after the battle of Paardeberg. (Author's collection)*

abandon his position, and retire east towards Bloemfontein. He was encumbered by a long wagon train and by several hundred non-combatants, and his route took him right across Roberts' line of advance. Brought to bay by British cavalry, he laagered his wagons at Paardeberg on the Modder River, and deployed his men along the banks. The British were desperate to break up his force – the largest Boer concentration on the western front – and on 17/18 February, whilst Roberts was absent sick, his chief-of-staff, Lord Kitchener, launched a direct assault. The attack was badly co-ordinated, however, and broke up after suffering heavy casualties, but it did at least surround Cronje and prevent further retreat. Cronje finally realised the hopelessness of his position, and surrendered his command of over 4000 men on 27 February – the anniversary of Majuba.

## The Relief of Ladysmith

By this time the tide had turned in Natal too. Buller had returned to the old Colenso road. On the extreme right of the old battlefield were a series of ridges and broken kopjes which were separated from the main Boer position by the Thukela river. In the first battle, Buller had made no more than a diversionary attack against them, but on 14 February he began a series of intensive assaults. By now his troops had learned to work well together, and the hills were taken after a series of open-order attacks closely supported by artillery fire. By 18 February the British had cleared the ground up to the river, and were preparing to cross at a point where it flowed through a narrow gorge. On the other side of the Thukela the ground rose up in a series of hills, each well-entrenched by the Boers – Wynne's Hill, Hart's Hill, Pieter's Hill and Railway Hill. Buller began his attack on the 22nd, his troops advancing up out of the Thukela valley in the wake of an effective creeping barrage.

The Boer resistance was stubborn, and several attacks were pinned down, but this time Buller was res-olute, and outflanked the main Boer positions. On the same day that Cronje surrendered at Paardeberg, the Boer line cracked, and they suddenly abandoned their positions. Buller was content to let them go, and on the 28th the first British cavalry reached the beleaguered garrison. The siege of Ladysmith had lasted 118 days, and cost the lives of over 200 men killed in action; a further 600 soldiers and civilians had died of disease; Buller's losses were twice that number. The entire Natal campaign had probably cost the lives of 400 or 500 Boers.

The British successes of February 1900 undoubtedly marked a turning point in the war. The Boer invasions of British territory had been steadily repulsed, and the British were poised to go onto the offensive, and to take the war into the Boer republics themselves. In the west, Roberts pressed on towards Bloemfontein, the Free State capital; the Boers attempted to stand at Poplar Grove, but the heart had temporarily gone out of them. On the 13th Roberts'

*Above: A group of men from the Manchester Regiment defending Caesar's Camp on the Platrand during the fighting around Ladysmith. By the time of the Boer War the nature of warfare had changed radically from the early Victorian era. (Author's collection)*

troops entered Bloemfontein. To the British it seemed that the war was all but over; that there remained only the capture of the Transvaal capital, Pretoria, to ensure a complete Boer collapse. For seven weeks Roberts lingered in Bloemfontein, reorganising his transport system and accumulating supplies. The enforced wait had an unfortunate consequence for his troops, who were afflicted by an outbreak of typhoid which at times almost reached Crimean levels of suffering. The Boers took advantage of the lull to regroup, and at the end of March de Wet mounted a lightning attack which caught a British wagon convoy off guard at Sannah's Post in the Free State. The British lost 170 killed and wounded and de Wet took 400 prisoners; it was the first hint that, far from being over, the war was about to enter a new phase.

In the meantime, the British won their last successes of the conventional war. On 16 May, Mafikeng was relieved. The little garrison had held out for 217 days, though it had only been severely tested in the last few days before the relief, when the Boers mounted a last desperate attempt against it. The siege had caught the imagination of the British public, and Mafikeng achieved an emotional importance out of all proportion to its strategic significance; its relief was greeted with immense celebration in Britain, and the garrison commander, Lieutenant-Colonel Baden-Powell, became a public hero. By this time Roberts had begun his march on Pretoria. After desultory fighting he took Johannesburg on the 30th, and on 2 June Kruger and the Transvaal government abandoned Pretoria. Three days later Roberts entered the city in triumph. Buller, meanwhile, had been advancing cautiously but steadily up through Natal, suppressing Boer resistance in the Drakensberg passes. On 12 June he crossed into the Transvaal, and the next day Roberts' troops fought the last battles with Boers retreating east of Johannesburg, towards the Mozambique border. On all fronts it seemed that the British were triumphant.

## The Guerrilla War

This impression was, however, profoundly misleading. If many of the older, slower, most conservative Boer leaders – men like Cronje or Joubert – had died or surrendered, a new, more flexible and resolute generation had risen to take their place. Freed from the need to defend the capitals, men like de Wet, Botha, Viljoen, Herzog and Smuts were able to use what resources remained to them to their best advantage, and

92

*Right: Relieved at last: Buller's troops marching into Ladysmith, February 1900. (Bryan Maggs Collection)*

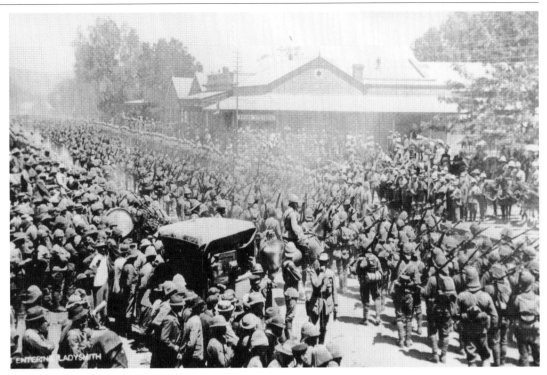

the Boers became a fast moving guerrilla army. Their numbers never totalled more than 25,000 men, and they had nearly 150,000 square miles to roam in. The British held the main towns and the railways – the main arteries by which their garrisons were supplied – but it was almost impossible for them to control the countryside; the Boers knew the veld infinitely better than they, and could move at the fastest speed of their horses and carts, while the British were tied to the slowest pace of their infantry.

At first, the guerrilla war had some discernible pattern. Roberts, determined to bring the Free State commandos to bay, attempted in June and July 1900 to trap them in the Brandwater Basin, against the BaSotholand border. Although 4000 Boers were captured, 1500 escaped, among them de Wet, who displayed an astonishing ability to avoid capture. This episode, known as the 'First de Wet Hunt', suggested that the British were incapable of co-ordinating their movements well enough over a large area to bring a cunning enemy to bay. De Wet slipped into the Transvaal, running rings around his pursuers. In the north-eastern Transvaal Botha went onto the

defensive, attempting to keep the British back from the Mozambique border, where Kruger still maintained a government in exile. On 27 August, however, combined troops from Roberts' and Buller's command broke through the cordon at Bergendaal and pushed up to the border at Koomati Poort. Kruger fled before their advance, and left the country on 11 September, to die shortly after in Holland. Even before he had gone, Roberts had proclaimed the Transvaal a British colony once more. The Natal Army was formally broken up, and Buller returned to England. Roberts, too, was keen to quit the war, but it was not until the end of November that he felt able to hand over supreme command to Kitchener.

**Kitchener's War**

The war now degenerated into its last bitter phase. Kitchener himself has been blamed for this, and his coldly methodical approach certainly exaggerated the shift to a war of attrition. Yet, in truth, the war was merely following a logical course set in motion by the outbreak of the guerrilla war. As early as June 1900 Roberts had authorised the burning of farms belonging to Boers known

to be still in the field. Unable to catch and destroy them, Roberts was striking at their supply base; Kitchener simply went one stage further by adopting a proper scorched-earth policy. Boer non-combatants – women and children – could not be left unprotected on the veld, and were rounded up and housed in makeshift refugee camps – known as concentration camps. The camps, however, were crowded and insanitary, food was poor, and the administration inefficient. Disease soon broke out, and before the war ended over 26,000 Boer women and children would die in the camps, leaving a scar on the soul of the Afrikaner nation which has still not fully healed. This exaggerated the bitterness between the 'hands-uppers' – those Boers who had surrendered to the British, or even joined their forces – and the 'bitter-enders', who were determined to resist to the last, and the last year of the war took on overtones of a civil war.

Initially the scorched earth policy was counter-productive, and probably served to prolong the fighting, since it stiffened the resolve of the 'bitter-enders' and relieved them of the need to protect their farms and families. In November and December de Wet slipped out of the Free State, and struck into the Cape Colony. The British were no more able to catch him in this, the 'Second de Wet Hunt', than they had been in the first, but Boer hopes that Afrikaners living in the Cape would rise to join them proved largely unfounded, despite the fact that some commandos penetrated as far as the coast in the Western Cape. The British fixation with de Wet led to a dangerous complacency elsewhere in the country, and on 13 December a British camp was captured at Noitgedacht, only forty miles west of Pretoria, and over 600 troops taken prisoner. In January and February 1901 de Wet once again went onto the offensive in the 'Third de Wet hunt', cutting British lines of communication, attacking convoys and destroying railways. By now, however, the British were developing a strategy of

containment. Blockhouses were built across the country – over 8000 in all – protecting the railways and, later, the main roads. Columns of British horsemen, often Colonial Mounted Infantry, still slow by Boer standards but much faster than the old infantry columns – mounted co-ordinated 'drives', sweeping through the country, pushing the Boers towards the barrier of the blockhouse chains. By this time the larger Boer forces had been broken up, and most commandos were only about 200 strong; men had become irreplaceable, and each one killed or captured was one less for the British to fight. With their ammunition running out, the Boers took to raiding the British for supplies, attacking convoys or simply searching through a camp area for loose rounds after the British had moved on. Viljoen and Botha regularly harassed the Delegoa Bay rail-

way in the eastern Transvaal, but when Botha attempted a strike into Zululand in September 1901 he was easily checked. By the beginning of 1902 the Boers had clearly lost the war of attrition, and in May they met British representatives at Vereeniging, outside Pretoria, and finally agreed to surrender.

The Boer War had been immensely destructive. Some 8000 British troops had died in action, and a further 13,000 from disease. Over 4000 Boers had been killed, in addition to the civilian losses in the camps. The economy of South Africa was devastated, and the war cost Britain over £220 million. The legacy of bitterness it provoked affected the history of South Africa until recent times; a

*Below: War of attrition: British troops foraging at a Boer home, August 1900. (Private collection)*

hardening of Boer attitudes in the post-war years contributed to the philosophy of racial segregation and oppression which characterised the country until the 1990s. It is perhaps fitting that the war had outlasted Queen Victoria, who died in January 1901, for it was both the last of the old wars of Empire and the first of a new, more brutal, and recognisably twentieth-century style of warfare. It had both exposed the failings of the army – its conservatism and inflexibility – and paved the way for reform. In that respect it was a timely preparation for the darker events to come, and the lessons learned in the Boer War would stand the British army in good stead during the holocaust of the Western Front, just twelve years later.

## NORTHERN AFRICA

In 1868, Britain embarked on the first of a series of wars in some of the most inhospitable country in the world – the deserts of North Africa. Unlike later campaigns, however, which were prompted by important strategic considerations, the Abyssinian expedition was little more than a punitive foray, the result of a clash of national pride following a very minor diplomatic incident.

### The Abyssinian Campaign

From the middle of the nineteenth century, Abyssinia – modern Ethiopia – was ruled by Emperor Tewodros II, who was known to the British, under an anglicised version of his name, as 'Mad King Theodore'. The British had a habit of crediting their opponents with mental instability, presumably because of the presumed insanity of challenging the Empire in the first place; Tewodros, however, does seem to have had a decidedly mercurial and unpredictable temperament. Abyssinia possessed a largely feudal system of government, in which regional tribal groups were ruled by hereditary leaders known as *rasses*. In a series of skilful campaigns in the 1850s Tewodros had conquered and subdued the more powerful *rasses* and brought them under his control. A Coptic Christian, Tewodros seems to have been driven by a desire to modernise his backward country in the face of determined internal opposition, and he looked to Europe for support. In particular, he encouraged a number of European missionaries to establish themselves at his court at Magdala, and he invited a British representative to join them. One was duly sent, but unfortunately killed by Abyssinian rebels, upon whom Tewodros inflicted suitably dire retribution. Another envoy was sent, and with his help Tewodros composed a letter of friendship to the British government. Despite the fact that Britain was keen to establish trading links in the Red Sea area, this letter apparently languished in a Colonial Office file, and no reply was sent. Tewodros, feeling that he had been slighted, promptly imprisoned the British envoy, who was soon joined, first by a group of German missionaries, and then by another British representative, sent to negotiate the release of the first.

The plight of the hostages suddenly brought Abyssinia to the forefront of British attention, and the government demanded their release. Tewodros, who seemed determined to provoke a confrontation with a superior power whom he much admired, refused. An expeditionary force was therefore assembled in India, consisting of both Queen's and Indian regiments, and placed under the command of General Sir Robert Napier, a hero of the Mutiny. Indian troops were selected not only because they were physi-

*Right: General Sir Robert Napier and his staff, Abyssinia, 1868. On his left is his Deputy Adjutant General, Sir Frederic Thesiger, later Lord Chelmsford. (Bryan Maggs Collection)*

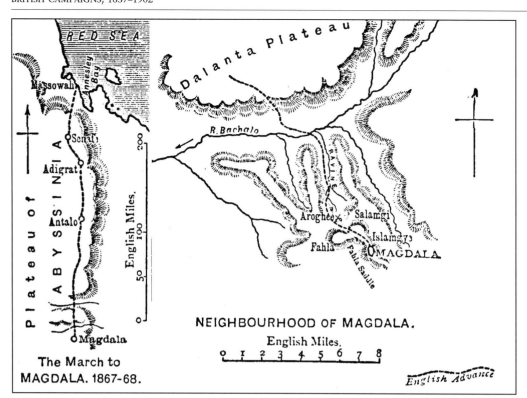

The March to MAGDALA. 1867-68.

NEIGHBOURHOOD OF MAGDALA.

English Miles.

*Left: In the Abyssinian campaign of 1868, the harsh and inhospitable terrain was as much of an enemy as King Tewodros' forces.*

*Right: The battle of Aroge. (Rai England Collection)*

*Below: A British infantry battalion in the field: the 4th Regiment, Abyssinia, 1868. (Bryan Maggs Collection)*

cally closer to the theatre of operations, but also because they were more acclimatised to the extremes of weather likely to be encountered. Nevertheless, Napier faced an extraordinary logistical challenge. Magdala was over 400 miles from the Red Sea coast. The coastal plains were baking hot, and in the dry season, when Napier landed, there was no water. His columns would have to make roads as they went along, bridging huge chasms, until they reached the less humid inland heights, where the weather alternated between burning sunshine and chilling downpours. The Abyssinian army was something of an unknown quantity, although its traditional weapons – swords and spears – were thought to have been augmented with large numbers of obsolete firearms and even a few artillery pieces. Napier's force –

13,000 troops, 19,000 non-combatants and 55,000 transport animals, including Indian elephants – began its march from the port of Zula in January 1868.

During his campaigns of conquest, Tewodros had been able to put armies as large as 15,000 men into the field, but the British arrival coincided with a number of internal rebellions which prevented him contesting Napier's approach, and left him with just 7000 men to guard Magdala. Magdala itself was situated on a spectacular plateau, which dropped a thousand feet to the valley below. By 10 April Napier had reached his goal, and his men deployed on the Aroge plain on the slopes of the Magdala massif. With a thunderstorm as a dramatic backdrop, Tewodros' army descended to the attack.

Napier's men opened fire with rockets and cannon. The Abyssinian charge wavered slightly, but then came on in a wild rush. Here and there it struck home, and there were brief flurries of hand-to-hand fighting, but for the most part it was scythed down by Napier's carefully controlled volley-fire. The Abyssinian artillery proved ineffective and soon fell silent. Several times Abyssinian leaders gallantly rallied their men and led them back to the charge, but each time they were repulsed. At last they drifted from the field, leaving behind 700 dead and 1200 wounded; Napier's troops had suffered just twenty wounded, of whom two later died.

Tewodros had not joined the fighting, and remained secure on the summit of Magdala, watching the spectacular defeat of his army. Rather to the surprise of the British, Tewodros now released his prisoners unharmed, but he refused to surrender. On 13 April Napier decided to storm the summit. The approach was via a single narrow track, commanded by a fortified gateway. A storming party rushed up the track in the face of light but determined Abyssinian resistance, and burst through the gate; as they did so the Abyssinian commander at the gate put a pistol into his mouth and pulled the trigger. When the fighting was over and the body examined, it was found to be Tewodros himself.

Napier had achieved his objective: the prisoners were released and Tewodros punished. All that remained was to destroy Magdala. Engineers spiked the Abyssinian guns, and blew up the larger buildings on the summit; the rest were destroyed by fire. On 16 April Napier began the long march back to the sea.

Unlike most British colonial wars, there was no attempt to impose a settlement or establish a new regime on Abyssinia – it was simply left to pick up the pieces after the British

*Left: British troops guarding the Kafir-Bur gate, Magdala, 1868. (Bryan Maggs Collection)*

departed. In time a new emperor would emerge, and the centralising process would begin anew; ironically, within twenty years Abyssinia would be strong enough not only to withstand the intervention of one of Britain's imperial rivals – Italy – but to resist the rise of the emerging Mahdist state in the Sudan, which was itself the main cause of British military activity in the region until the end of the century.

## The Egyptian Entanglement

Britain became involved in the Sudan because of her perennial concern for the security of the maritime routes to India. Until the 1860s, this effectively meant the long haul around southern Africa, since the shorter route, via the Mediterranean, was largely impractical because it meant crossing Egypt overland: until, that is, the Suez canal was built. The canal was the inspiration of a Frenchman, Ferdinand de Lesseps, and when it was opened in November 1869, it cut several weeks off the sea voyage to India. Yet the building of the canal provoked a political crisis within Egypt. Nominally a part of the Turkish empire, Egypt was actually under the control of a dynasty of Khedives, who had gained a considerable degree of independence from Turkey. The extravagant and extrovert Said Pasha had authorised the building of the canal, and welcomed the European involvement that had come with it. However, by 1875 he was unable to service the debt he had taken on to pay for it. The British Prime Minister, Disraeli, seriously concerned at the strategic implications, secretly bought up the Khedive's shares, at once securing British interests and forestalling the French. Nevertheless, Said's successor Isma'il was left so much in debt to foreign banks that Britain and France were almost able to dictate his policies at will. This

*Left: Troops standing guard in Magdala. (Bryan Maggs Collection)*

aroused considerable popular discontent within Egypt, where the ruling Turco-Circassian elite was already unpopular among native Egyptians. This resentment soon crystallised around the army. The Egyptian officers elected as their leader a Colonel Ahmad 'Urabi, an eloquent speaker who damned not only Isma'il and his successor, Tawfiq, but the foreign powers who appeared to be propping them up. Thus a purely internal squabble was transmuted to a nationalist uprising, which threatened important British interests, and soon drew Britain and 'Urabi into confrontation. Tawfiq's administration was forced to recognise 'Urabi's position, and anti-European rioting broke out in the streets of Alexandria. Alarmed, Britain began to assemble a fleet in Alexandria harbour, provoking 'Urabi to place the harbour's chain of forts on full alert. After a flurry of diplomatic activity, in which France declined to become involved, the British fleet opened fire on 11 July 1882.

The bombardment of Alexandria lasted most of the day, and most of the Egyptian forts were reduced to rubble. 'Urabi moved his troops south of the town, abandoning Alexandria to the mob, which roamed the streets, murdering Christians, burning and looting. The British put ashore parties of sailors and marines, who clearred the streets with warning bursts from Gatling guns, and within a few days occupied the city completely.

In Britain and India, meanwhile, a force had been assembled with the aim of suppressing 'Urabi and returning Egypt to the compliant Tawfiq. Command of the expedition was given to Sir Garnet Wolseley, and he planned it with typical precision, laying a complex trail of false information to deceive 'Urabi as to his intentions. In the first week of August nearly a hundred transports packed with troops, horses and provisions left England alone. By feinting with several sorties from Alexandria, Wolseley convinced 'Urabi – and some of his own officers – that he planned to march directly up the Nile to attack Cairo. In fact,

he did nothing of the sort, and on 18 August occupied Port Said at the northern end of the Suez canal, while troops sailing from India landed at Suez, at the southern end. By the end of August both contingents had rendezvoused at Ismailia, midway along the canal. From Ismailia another waterway, known as the Sweet Water Canal, cut westwards to join the Nile delta at Zag-a-Zig, some fifty miles north of Cairo. Wolseley's plan was to push rapidly forward along the line of the Sweet Water Canal and confront 'Urabi before he had time to secure his defences. The move undoubtedly caught the Egyptians off-guard, and 'Urabi was still manoeuvring into position when the British struck.

A division under Major-General Graham advanced as far as Kassassin Lock, where they encountered the enemy trying to take up a position in front of them. Graham sent back a message asking for cavalry support, but attacked on 6 September without waiting for it to arrive. The Egyptians fell back, and when the cavalry arrived that night they walked straight into the retiring Egyptian left flank. In the spectacular 'moonlight charge' which followed, the heavy cavalry fell on the disorganised Egyptian battalions and virtually annihilated them.

'Urabi's main position was at Tel-el-Kebir, at the western end of the Sweet Water Canal. By the time Wolseley reached it a week later, the Egyptian force numbered as many as 25,000 regular infantry, 30,000 irregular cavalry, and seventy guns. These were securely entrenched behind a solid earthwork – a rampart screened by a ditch – which straddled both sides of the canal. Wolseley, reluctant to mount a frontal assault in daylight, planned to attack at dawn. This meant manoeuvring into position in the dark, a notoriously difficult feat over broken ground in enemy country. Nevertheless, Wolseley prepared his advance well, and the attack took place before first light on 12 September. The Indian Division took the left flank – south of the canal – with the British infantry on the

*Above: 'After the Battle': Sir Garnet Wolseley's arrival at the Bridge of Tel-el-Kebir. (Private collection)*

*Left: Sergeant-Major Green and NCOs and privates of the Gordon Highlanders photographed in Egypt in 1882. (Royal Archives)*

*Below: Alphonse de Neuville's stirring study of the Highland Brigade's dawn attack on the Egyptian trenches at Tel-el-Kebir. (Anne S.K. Brown Collection)*

right, north of it, and the cavalry on the extreme right. The Highland Brigade had advanced successfully to within a few hundred yards of the trenches when dawn broke, and the first grey light revealed their red coats. The Egyptians immediately opened a heavy fire, and the Highland Brigade broke into a charge, storming the parapet. As crowds of disorganised Egyptian troops fell back along the canal, both British and Indian cavalry gave chase.

Tel-el-Kebir broke the back of Egyptian resistance. Wolseley despatched the Indian cavalry to secure Zag-a-Zig, whilst the British cavalry cut across the desert to Cairo. The expected Egyptian stand there failed to materialise, and a few days later 'Urabi surrendered his sword. Wolseley returned to Britain a conquering hero, and in truth the expedition was an undoubted success; it had been mounted with the same determination and despatch as the Asante campaign, and it secured Wolseley's reputation as a thorough and courageous commander.

In Egypt the Khedive was restored with the overt support of the British, and the Egyptian army was reorganised, this time with British officers. In effect, control had passed into British hands. Whilst this may have ensured the safe management of the Suez canal, it brought with it a problem which would involve the British army in prolonged bloodshed, and would tarnish many glittering reputations, not least that of Wolseley himself.

## The Sudan

The source of conflict was Egypt's southern colony, the Sudan, and its causes had little enough to do with Britain. 'When God made the Sudan', an Arab saying has it, 'He laughed', and it is easy to see the divinity's grim humour in this vast and inhospitable tract of desert and semi-desert. Any form of communication and administrative control was almost entirely dependent on the life-line of the Nile, but the Egypt of the Khedives lacked the resources to govern the Sudan efficiently. Even before Tel-el-Kebir the Sudanese tribes, discontented with Egyptian interference, taxation and corruption, were ripe for revolt.

The rising, when it came, crystallised around the person of a Danaqla Arab from the Dongola province of northern Sudan, a mystic by the name of Mohammed Ahmad ibn al-Sayyid Abdullah. Mohammed Ahmad's early life was characterised by a scholarly devotion to Islam, and in 1881 he proclaimed himself *al-Mahdi*, 'the proclaimed one', an apostle of the Prophet whose coming was foretold in the beliefs of some Islamic sects. The Mahdi's initial supporters were from the poorest sectors of the riverine Arab community, for whom the promise of paradise had an immediate appeal, but his cause spread rapidly, offering as it did both fundamentalist religious certainty

'Osman Digna'), raised the semi-nomadic Beja tribesmen of the Red Sea littoral to the Mahdi's cause, and laid siege to an Egyptian outpost at Suakin.

In London, the British government was aware of the impending crisis, but Gladstone's Liberal administration was profoundly opposed to Imperial expansion, and refused to intervene directly in Sudanese affairs. Instead, it appointed a special representative, who was sent to the Sudanese capital, Khartoum – still in Egyptian hands – to organise the evacuation of Egyptian nationals. The man it chose for this singularly unappealing job was a soldier who had earned his reputation whilst on loan to the Chinese government, whose 'Ever-Victorious Army' he had commanded during the Taiping Rebellion in the 1860s, and who had served in an administrative capacity in the Sudan once before – Colonel Charles 'Chinese' Gordon, RE. At first glance Gordon appeared the ideal man for the job: charismatic, determined, resourceful, one who would stick by his duty to the death. Gordon was a complex character, however, driven – perhaps even tormented – by a deep faith, and above all was his own man. Once safely installed in Khartoum, he refused to abandon it to the Mahdi, and bombarded the Government in London with telegrams advocating alternative strategies. In March 1885 the Mahdi moved his forces to the Nile, and, setting up a camp at Omdurman, on the opposite bank to Khartoum, laid siege to the capital.

In the meantime, Egyptian fortunes had also sharply declined on the Red Sea coast. Another Egyptian expedition under the command of a British Officer – Valentine Baker Pasha, had been sent to relieve the Suakin outposts. Baker's column had marched out to confront Uthman Diqna at El Teb, but his army fell apart in the face of a furious attack on 2 February 1885, and over 2000 men were slaughtered in the desert.

and a nationalist rejection of the ungodly ways of the 'Turkish' oppressors. The Mahdi, guided by a divine vision, strove to drive the Egyptians out of the Sudan, and to that end he proclaimed a *jihad*, or holy war. His initial successes were so spectacular that his followers could easily see the hand of God in them. When the Egyptians sent troops to arrest him, they were easily overcome by his followers – whom he called *ansar* (helpers) – and by January 1883 he was so strong that he was able to storm El Obeid, the capital of the western province of Kordofan. This victory gave the Mahdists not only an enormous moral victory, but, with the capture of El Obeid's arsenal, a

huge stockpile of military hardware. Britain regarded the Mahdist revolt as a purely Egyptian affair, and was reluctant to sanction the use of British troops; instead, an army of 8000 Egyptians under the command of a British officer, General William Hicks – Hicks Pasha – was despatched into the Sudan. The Mahdi lured it out into the wastes of Kordofan. When Hick's force began to disintegrate from exhaustion and lack of water, the Mahdi attacked and destroyed it at Shaykan in the first week of November 1883. Hicks himself was among the dead, and his demise provoked fresh outbreaks across the country. In the east Uthman Diqna (known to the British as

*Right: Charles Gordon (right) photographed as a young Engineer officer with a colleague, Captain Hay. (Royal Engineers Museum)*

To stave off the imminent Egyptian collapse all along the coast, the British despatched their first troops to the Sudan, nearly 3000 infantry supported by cavalry, artillery and a Naval Brigade, under the command of Major-General Sir Gerald Graham. Graham occupied Suakin, and marched out to attack El Teb towards the end of February. His men were formed into a large square formation, protected on one flank by cavalry, which remained outside the square. As they reached the village of El Teb, passing the remains of Baker's men who lay unburied nearby, Uthman Diqna's followers opened fire with field guns captured from Baker. Graham halted his command and his artillery and machine guns

*Below: Graham's Anglo-Indian force watches as an observation balloon is inflated during the march on Tamai, 1884. (Author's collection)*

103

returned the fire. Diqna's Beja then sprang up from the cover of rocks and scrub and mounted a fierce charge which carried right up to the square, despite heavy casualties, and was only just driven back. Graham's square then advanced and took the village of El Teb, in the face of fierce resistance. The British cavalry charged the Mahdists as they retreated, only to find that rather than flee the enemy threw themselves on the ground and tried to hamstring or trip the horses as they passed. Eventually the Beja abandoned the field reluctantly, and Graham, believing he had dealt them a severe blow, marched back to Suakin.

In fact, despite being undoubtedly a British victory, the second battle of El Teb did little to alter the strategic situation around Suakin: the Anglo-Egyptian force held the port, but Uthman Diqna controlled most of the countryside beyond. In the middle of March, Graham sallied forth again, this time to confront a Mahdist force gathering near the village of Tamai. On 13 March Graham's force advanced to the attack in two divisional squares. A large khor – a dry ravine – lay between Graham and the village, and as the square on the right approached it the Beja suddenly appeared in large numbers and charged. One side of the square opened a furious fire, obscuring the enemy approach with smoke, whilst the front continued to advance at a quicker pace than the sides. Gaps therefore appeared in the sides, and the Beja, spotting the opportunity, rushed into them. The naval contingent's Gatlings were overrun, and the square was driven back in confusion. The situation was only saved by the determined support of the other square, whose supporting fire caused the Beja to draw off. The broken square rallied, reformed, and advanced to capture Tamai. Once again, Uthman's attacks had been highly skilful and very tenacious, and only the superior firepower of Graham's force had won the day. Nevertheless, the victory achieved nothing, for at the end of March Graham was ordered to withdraw most of his force from Suakin and return to Egypt, leaving Uthman Diqna still in possession of the hills beyond.

### Gordon and Khartoum

Whilst Graham and Uthman Diqna were waging their local war, almost without interference from the outside world, the Mahdi's pressure on Gordon had grown, and provoked a moral crisis in Britain. Khartoum, built at the confluence of the White and Blue Niles, was by no means indefensible, and Gordon, the Royal Engineer, had repaired the old walls and ditches surrounding the city and added modern refinements – such as mines and wire entanglements – of his own. He infused the garrison and civilian population with something of his indomitable spirit, but inevitably a shortage of supplies, and occasional fighting with the Mahdists, eroded morale. In Britain, the public was outraged at Gladstone's apparent willingness to leave a national hero to his fate. In August 1884 Parliament forced a reluctant Government to approve funds to mount a relief expedition.

The job was given to Wolseley, who, in the light of his victory at Tel-el-Kebir, seemed ideally suited to it, but it was no easy task. To begin with, Wolseley would have to assemble his

*Left: The battle of Tamai, 1884. (National Army Museum)*

*Right: Sir Garnet Wolseley and his staff on board the SS Queen, Sudan, 1885. (Bryan Maggs Collection)*

*Below: Colonel Fred Burnaby of the Blues is unhorsed as the Mahdists burst into the square at Abu Klea; he was killed a few moments later. (Author's collection)*

troops – over 7000 British regulars alone – on the Sudanese border. He would then have to cross several hundred miles of extremely difficult terrain, presumably in the face of fierce Mahdist opposition, before the Mahdists overran Gordon. After careful consideration, Wolseley decided to transport his entire column up the Nile. A flotilla of small boats, including steamers from the travel company Thomas Cook, was hired to transport the troops, under the guidance of 300 Canadian boatmen known as *voyageurs*, whose skill Wolseley remembered from his Red River days. The advance began in October, but, for all Wolseley's careful preparations, progress was slow, and by January the column had only reached Korti. This was 200 miles across the desert from Khartoum, but further by the meandering course of the river. Messages smuggled out of Khartoum suggested that the garrison's plight was desperate, and Wolseley decided to form a flying column to push overland by the quickest route. At the beginning of January 1885, 1800 men under the command of Brigadier-General Stewart struck out across the desert from Korti towards Metemmeh.

Stewart followed a line of wells, and on the 17th he approached the

well at Abu Klea. His men were drawn up in a square formation, but the baggage camels, in the centre, were difficult to control, and the formation bulged out at the rear. Suddenly a large Mahdist army rose out of the broken ground, and rushed straight at the left front corner of the square. Stewart's men opened up with volley and machine-gun fire, and the Mahdists changed direction, swerving round to attack the left rear. This corner had been particularly disrupted during the advance, and the Mahdists charged up, overwhelmed a naval brigade party guarding the angle, and poured into the square. Fortunately the confusion of baggage animals in front checked their impetus, allowing the troops on the front face to turn their rear rank about, and fire on the enemy behind. The men on the broken face stood their ground in small clumps, and the Mahdists were gradually driven out and fell back. The crisis had lasted only a few minutes, but the British had come within an ace of being overwhelmed. The bat-

tle cost Stewart seventy-four men killed and many more wounded.

Stewart's column pressed on the next morning. The Mahdists were still gathering before Metemmeh, and the column was harassed by long-range sniper fire, Stewart himself being mortally wounded. Command passed to Sir Charles Wilson, who opted to leave part of the force in a protected zareba, overlooking the next set of wells, at Abu Kru. On the 19th Wilson took a detachment forward in square formation, and the Mahdists rushed down to attack him on three sides. On this occasion, however, the well-directed fire from the square, supported by shell-fire from the zareba, prevented the enemy from getting closer than fifty yards. On the 21st Wilson advanced to the Nile close to Metemmeh, where he found four armoured steamers, sent by Gordon, waiting to greet him. Wilson paused for a day or two to allow his men to recover, and to prepare for the last stage of the advance, then embarked as many of his men as he could on the steamers,

*Above: The desperate hand-to-hand fighting as the Mahdists are driven out of the damaged square at Abu Klea. (Author's collection)*

and set off for Khartoum. The journey took three days, much of it under fire from Mahdists in positions lining the shore. When Khartoum came in sight on the 27th, however, there was no sign of Gordon or his command. The Mahdi, determined not to have his prize snatched from him at the last moment, had mounted a heavy assault on the 25th, and, after 317 days of siege, Khartoum had been overrun just two days before Wilson arrived. Gordon himself had been killed, apparently fighting desperately at his palace, and, against the orders of the Mahdi, his head had been cut off and taken to Omdurman.

The news of the fall of Khartoum and the death of Gordon profoundly shocked Victorian Britain, and Gordon himself soon achieved the status of a Christian martyr. Wolseley was quite prepared to carry on the fight;

*Above: The making of an Imperial martyr: in this famous version of the scene, Gordon fatalistically awaits his death as Khartoum falls to the Mahdi. In fact, Mahdist sources suggest that he died fighting in defence of his palace. (Anne S.K. Brown Collection)*

*Above right: An atmospheric representation of the last moments of Khartoum. (Author's collection)*

indeed, the river column, still toiling down the Nile, was attacked at Kirbekan on 10 February. The column had met the Mahdists in line, rather than the ubiquitous square, but still repulsed them. Gladstone's Government, however, decided to cut its losses, to abandon the Sudan to the Mahdi, and Wolseley was ordered back to Egypt. Thus the Gordon Relief Expedition ended on a decidedly sour note of failure; it had been Wolseley's greatest challenge to date,

and neither he nor his Ring emerged from it with their reputations unscathed.

## The Eastern Sudan

The British decided to retain one toehold in the Sudan, at Suakin, where they planned to build a railway across to the Nile to improve their lines of communication. General Graham was sent back to Suakin with about 13,000 men, to find that the Egyptian garrisons still held no more than the coastal enclaves, while Uthman Diqna controlled the interior. Graham marched out to attack a Mahdist concentration at Hashin Wells, and dispersed them on the 20 March 1885. Within just two days of this promising start, however, his command came within an ace of suffering one of the first reverses of the war. To protect the line of the proposed railway, Graham ordered the establishment of a number of protected supply depots in the

desert, and on the 22nd a force under the command of Major-General Sir John McNeill, consisting mainly of the Berkshire Regiment and three battalions of Indian infantry, began to construct a thorn zareba at Tofrek. It was a desperately hot day, and a glare rising off the desert made it difficult to see. The zareba was only partly finished when reports came in that the enemy were approaching, and suddenly the Beja appeared in large numbers only a few hundred yards away, charging furiously. A large herd of baggage camels lay between the zareba and the enemy, and the Beja immediately rushed into it, driving the terrified animals back on the troops. The Berkshires were unable to form up properly before a horde of maddened camels, mixed up with the enemy, streamed amongst them. Many noncombatants fled in panic, and were cut down. Only the steadiness of the Indian regiments on the far side of the zareba, and of a detachment of Royal Marines who formed a square, prevented it from being swept away completely. After a few moments of chaos and pandemonium, the Mahdists were driven out, and the British were able to reform, and drive the enemy away with concentrated volley-fire. In just twenty minutes the British lost 100 dead and 140 wounded, whilst 900 camels were killed or had to be destroyed.

At the beginning of April Graham occupied Uthman Diqna's headquarters at Tamai without fighting, but the victory was a hollow one since the British Government then decided to abandon the Sudan entirely. In June Graham's force was withdrawn from Suakin.

In the aftermath of the British withdrawal, it was left to garrisons of the Anglo-Egyptian army to hold the Sudanese frontier. Curiously enough, the Mahdi did not long survive his greatest victory, and he died in June 1885, probably from typhus. His successor was one of his senior disciples, the Khalifa Abdullahi, who attempted to consolidate the *Mahdiyya*, the Mahdist state, and to establish a central framework of administration, based on Islamic law, that cut across tribal loyalties. The *Mahdiyya* remained essentially expansionist in outlook, following the Mahdi's original inspiration, but any early hopes of invading Egypt were blocked when the *ansar* were defeated by an Anglo-Egyptian force at Ginniss on 30 December 1885 – a battle chiefly remembered in the British army as being the last occasion when scarlet was worn into action in a major battle. Instead, the Khalifa turned his attention to his eastern neighbour, Abyssinia. The Abyssinians, being Christians, were enemies of the faith, but despite severe fighting in 1887, the Mahdists were unable to defeat them. A concerted attempt to invade Egypt was defeated by the Egyptian army in a series of fights in 1889, culminating in the battle of Toski on 3 August.

**The Reconquest**
In Britain, public pressure to avenge Gordon remained intense, but it was not until the mid-1890s that a combination of factors made this possible. Gladstone's Liberal Government had given way to a Conservative administration with a more expansionist outlook, whilst rival European empires – notably France and Italy – were threatening to expand in central Africa at the expense of British interests. In 1896, therefore, the Egyptian army, which had been thoroughly reorganised under British officers, was ordered to reconquer the northern Sudanese province of Dongola. Under the command of the Sirdar – the commander-in-chief – General Sir Herbert Kitchener, 18,000 men were assembled on the Sudanese border. To circumvent the transport problems which had so plagued Wolseley, Kitchener ordered the construction of the Sudan Military Railway along stretches of the Nile, a remarkable feat of engineering, masterminded by a Royal Engineer and built with conscripted Egyptian labour. By early June 1896 Kitchener had crossed into the Sudan, and on the 7th he defeated a Mahdist force sent to oppose him at Firket. From here he advanced slowly and cautiously to the town of Dongola itself, which was taken after brief skirmishing.

The reconquest of Dongola had been surprisingly easy, a triumph of methodical planning and logistics.

*Left: The construction of the Sudan Military Railway, the key to Kitchener's reconquest. (Rai England Collection)*

*Above: The 1/Cameron Highlanders firing over the zareba into the Mahdist camp on the Atbara, covering the entrance of the storming parties. (Author's collection)*

Nevertheless, it was clear that if the a final confrontation with the Khalifa was to be provoked, Kitchener would need more than his Egyptian troops. At the end of 1897 he asked for British troops as reinforcements, and was sent enough for a brigade. As they arrived at the front, the Khalifa, well aware of the impending crisis, despatched an army of 12,000 Mahdists under an able commander, Mahmud wad Ahmad, who established an entrenched camp on the Atbara river, near its confluence with the Nile, blocking Kitchener's advance. Kitchener, his preparations complete, advanced on Atbara with a force of 14,000 men, twenty-four guns and twelve machine-guns. The troops were in position before dawn on 8 April 1898, and for once the Mahdists were content to fight a defensive battle. The British artillery opened fire at dawn, and after several hours of close-range bombardment the infantry formed into line and attacked. Mahmud's camp was protected by a thorn zareba, but this was easily pulled aside, and, covered by volley fire, the assaulting companies rushed into the maze of huts, rifle-pits and ramparts which constituted the camp. The Mahdists defended them fiercely as the advancing line swept over them, but finally gave way, and were exposed to a merciless fire as they fled. The Anglo-Egyptian force lost over eighty officers and men killed and nearly 500 wounded, but the Mahdist losses were over 3000. Mahmud himself was bayoneted through the leg and captured.

After Atbara Kitchener received another brigade of British reinforcements, and by August he was ready to continue his advance. By the end of the month Omdurman was in sight. The Khalifa did not contest his advance, but gathered a large army at Omdurman itself. On the night of 1 September, Kitchener bivouacked on the banks of the Nile, a few miles from the city. His force was formed up in an extended line, protected by a shallow shelter-trench and thorn zareba, and was curved so that both flanks rested on the river. The next morning British gunboats shelled Omdurman, and the Mahdist army – as many as 40,000 strong – came into view from behind hills to the left. They advanced rapidly in close formation, the British opening up with a storm of shot and shell as they

*Above: The charge of the 21st Lancers at Omdurman. (Author's collection)*

*Below: 'Three Cheers for the Queen': Grenadier Guards and Cameron Highlanders celebrating the victory at Omdurman. (Bryan Maggs Collection)*

came within range. The Mahdists pressed forward with extraordinary courage but, exposed on open ground without cover, they were cut down in their hundreds. Once they began to retire, Kitchener ordered his troops to pursue and drive them from the field. The victory was comprehensive, and surprisingly easy; for the loss of little more than 100 men killed, Kitchener had inflicted over 20,000 casualties on the Mahdists, nearly 10,000 of whom were killed. Kitchener immediately occupied Omdurman, and two days later representatives of every unit present with his force attended a religious service in the ruins of Gordon's palace across the river in Khartoum.

Omdurman effectively broke up the *Mahdiyya*. The Khalifa himself fled into the wastes of Kordofan with what remained of his following. The campaign was largely over, but Kitchener marched south to Fashoda, where a French force under a Major Marchand had raised the Tricolour. Here, in one of the remotest parts of Africa, the representatives of the two great European

*Above: Kitchener's staff examining the ruins of Gordon's palace in Khartoum after the fall of Omdurman. (National Army Museum)*

*Below: The price of glory: the burial of a British officer after Omdurman. His damaged sun helmet is on top of the grave. (Bryan Maggs Collection)*

empires faced one another down, until diplomats in Paris and London agreed that Marchand should withdraw. The Sudan became Egyptian again, and the British supplied its administrators. Mahdism still lingered in the outlying provinces, and it was not until 22 November 1899 that the Khalifa was killed. Uthman Diqna was not captured until January 1900; he lived until 1926.

British involvement in the Sudan led indirectly to another series of small campaigns, which began at the very end of the Victorian period. Along with the Sudan, Britain had taken over the Egyptian province of Somaliland, in the Horn of Africa. In 1898, Sayyid Muhammad Abdullah Hassan – inevitably known to the British as 'the Mad Mullah' – attempted to unite the semi-nomadic Somali tribes by preaching *jihad*. The British waged no less than five separate campaigns against him between 1900 and 1920, mostly with Indian troops. On occasion they received support from both the Italians, who had interests in the region, and the Abyssinians. Few of these campaigns were entirely successful, and some were downright disasters; at the battle of Gumburu in April 1903, for instance, the Somalis overran a British square and killed 196 officers and men. Sayyid finally died from influenza in 1920 and his rising collapsed.

## New Zealand

In pre-colonial times the Maori of New Zealand were a robust tribal society who laid claim to ownership of all of the North Island, and much of the South. They were essentially a stone-age people using a variety of skilfully worked wood and stone tools and weapons. Indeed, their limited technology had not prevented the evolution of a highly sophisticated code of warfare, and conflict was endemic in their culture. Tribes fought with one another over land claims, or to enhance a chief's *mana* – his prestige, reputation and spiritual power. Any shedding of blood called for *utu*, a fierce payment in kind,

which could be satisfied at the expense of any one of the transgressor's tribe. Some tribes were locked in cycles of revenge which went on for generations, a fact which the *pakeha* – the white man – was quick to recognise and exploit. To protect themselves against the threat of such violence, the Maori had become adept at the construction of fortified earthworks, known as *pas*. In pre-colonial society, *pas* were a complex combination of trenches, ramparts and screens of wood and flax, overlooked by watch-towers. From about 1820, however, the first firearms were introduced among the Maori, who

rapidly appreciated their value; as a result tribal conflict increased, and the style and shape of *pas* was gradually altered to take account of the new weapons. By the 1860s, when the British used artillery extensively against them, most pas had become complex earthwork redoubts, with little in the way of palisades.

European contact with New Zealand increased after Britain established a

*Below: The Maori had a robust fighting tradition and took naturally to European firearms: a warrior photographed in traditional dog-skin cloak. (Tim Ryan)*

penal colony in Australia in 1788, and the first permanent settlements sprung up among the islands a decade or so later. These were mostly anarchic shanty-towns, composed of run-away convicts and adventurers, which catered for the needs of passing whalers. The Maori tolerated them, and traded extensively, but in return were introduced to the dubious delights of European diseases, prostitution and liquor. Given the lawless nature of these settlements, clashes were inevitable, and prompted the British to intervene in 1840. In an attempt to put these settlements on a formal footing, the British offered to extend their protection to the Maori if they accepted British suzerainty. The idea was a controversial one – many chiefs saw no reason why they should give anything away to the *pakeha*, let alone their birthright – but in February 1840 several hundred Maori chiefs accepted British protection by signing the Treaty of Waitangi. It is not entirely clear whether they realised the full implications of this, but shortly afterwards Britain formally annexed New Zealand as a colony. Within a few months the first settlers arrived from Britain to establish a colony.

The influx of settlers exacerbated a growing tension between the Maoris and the *pakeha*, and led to the first shots in a struggle that would last nearly seventy years: a defiance that equalled that of the Xhosa on the Cape frontier, or the Pathans in the Afghan foothills. The ensuing campaigns were known by the British simply as the Maori Wars, but to the Maori they were known as the *Te Riri Pakeha* – the white man's anger – or, most recently and significantly, as the Colonial Land Wars. The first outbreak occurred in the north of the South Island, where two chiefs who had crossed over from the North Island harassed a party of surveyors marking out land for settlement. A shot was fired, the wife of a chief was killed, and the Maori immediately fell on the surveyors and slaughtered them. They then retired to their villages on the North Island, and prepared to be attacked. In the meantime another outbreak

had occurred in the north, around the settlement of Kororareka in the Bay of Islands. This was the home of the powerful Ngapuhi tribe, whose chief, Hone Heke, had been one of the first to sign the Treaty of Waitangi. However, when the new British governor had established his capital at Auckland, not Kororareka, the settlement declined, and with it Heke's trade. This seemed poor recompense for his loyalty to the Crown, and Hone Heke expressed his frustration by cutting down a flagstaff, which he himself had erected on a hill overlooking the town. Over the next eight months, the British put the pole back up three times, and each time Heke cut it down. On the final occasion, in March 1845, Heke led his warriors in a raid against the settlement itself, killing ten soldiers and seamen, driving off the settlers, and setting fire to their homes. The action immediately provoked a split among local Maoris, some of whom sided with the British, others with Heke.

This called for a serious response. There were few enough British troops in the colony, but these were reinforced by men who were on penal duty in Australia, chiefly from the 58th, 96th and 99th regiments. These were marched up to the Bay of Islands, and after some preliminary fighting Heke built a *pa* named Ohaeawai. In July 1845 the British tried to soften up Heke's *pa* with an artillery barrage – confined largely to rockets fired by a Naval contingent – then tried to take the place by storm, only to be driven back with heavy losses. The British called off the attack on Ohaeawai, which Heke promptly abandoned; this was in accordance with Maori practice, since most *pas* were intended to be no more than temporary strongholds, to be held until they had inflicted the maximum casualties on the enemy, and then abandoned. Heke built a new *pa*, Ruapekepeka, 'the bat's nest', which the British attacked in January 1846, storming it on Sunday the 11th only to find that it was largely empty: Heke, being a Christian convert, never suspected that the British would attack on a Sunday, and had

taken most of his warriors off into the bush for a church service.

The capture of Ruapekepeka effectively brought the northern war to a close. Heke was increasingly isolated among the Maoris, and even his own followers were tiring of war, and he successfully sued for peace. In the meantime, however, trouble had flared up in the south of the North Island. Te Ruaparaha and Te Rangiheata, the chiefs responsible for the earlier massacre of the survey party, had been drawn into increasing conflict with settlers in the Hutt river valley. In May 1846 their followers attacked an outpost of the 58th Regiment, killing several pickets. Troops were immediately moved into the area, and in a particularly bold operation Te Ruaparaha was seized from his village one night and arrested. Te Rangiheata then built a *pa*, Horokiwi. The British bombarded it for three days, but were unable to find a way through the entrenchments. In the end Te Rangiheata slipped away with his followers and abandoned Horokiwi; he went to the most remote part of the country he could find, and lived the rest of his life away from the detested influence of the *pakeha*.

The action at Horokiwi proved the last major outbreak of the First Maori War. However, the wars soon lived up to the old Maori name for their preferred type of conflict, 'the fire in the fern'; no sooner is it beaten down in one place than it spreads across country unnoticed and flares up in another. Indeed, the Maori wars were essentially a series of local conflicts as each tribal group in turn came under pressure from white settlement, and either chose to compromise or to resist. Throughout the 1840s and 1850s immigration increased, and the settlers discovered that to be viable their farms required large amounts of land to support stock. To them, it seemed that much Maori land was under-utilised, but to the Maori all land was held in common ownership, and even those areas which they did not cultivate remained the haunt of their ancestors. Whilst some Maoris agreed to allow the whites to settle on their land, few understood the concept of parting with it in perpetuity, and these fundamentally different attitudes led to frequent misunderstandings and tension. In the 1850s, tribes living in the Waikato – an area of central North Island, largely untouched by white settlement – banded together to elect a king, to act as a spokesman in their dealings with the whites; the 'king movement' was a peaceful expression of resistance to European economic penetration, but it was regarded with suspicion by the settlers, and in the early 1860s events slid rapidly into open warfare.

The first outbreak occurred in the Taranaki district, near the Waikato. Here settlers had been anxious to buy a particular slice of Maori territory for some time, but ownership of the land was disputed between two rival chiefs, and the more senior, Wiremu Kingi, was adamantly opposed to it. The Governor thought it judicious to support the other claim, and the settlers began to survey their land, but the 'Waitara purchase' became notorious among the Maoris since it suggested that the authorities were prepared to use any means, no matter how dubious, to prise them from their lands. Wiremu Kingi promptly built a *pa*, and troops were moved into Taranaki. On 17 March the British achieved a minor success against a small Maori force, but within days one of their sweeps through the bush had been ambushed and badly mauled. Even away from their *pas*, in the dank and claustrophobic fern forests the Maoris were, man for man, more than a match for the British. On 27 June a major assault was made on Wiremu's *pa* at Puketakauere, but the attack was poorly co-ordinated and the storming parties were halted by the warren of trenches and driven back. This embarrassing series of reverses led to a change in the British high command, and Major-General Thomas Pratt arrived in New Zealand to take over the colony's defences. Pratt went onto the offensive in October with over 1000 men, chiefly of the 12th and 65th Regiments, and proved to be a thoughtful commander, careful of his soldiers' lives. Rather than make costly frontal assaults on the *pas*, he preferred to drive saps close to them; although settlers derided this approach as slow and costly, the Maoris found it disconcerting, and Pratt took several *pas* with very little fighting. Kingi and his followers concentrated on a new *pa* at Te Arei, which Pratt attacked at the beginning of February 1861. Despite Maori counter-moves, Pratt drove his sap to within 200 yards of the *pa*'s outer defences. In desperation the Maoris tried raiding the British works at night, but were driven off after several fierce melees, and on 19 March the defenders of Te Arei surrendered. Kingi retired to the Waikato, and the First Taranaki War was over.

In the aftermath of the Taranaki campaign, the Governor, Sir George Grey, promised an enquiry into the Waitara purchase, but the 'Kingite' Maoris still complained bitterly of the injustice of the deal. Under pressure

from settlers Grey began to build a military road through the bush towards the Waikato. The Kingite chiefs took this as proof of his hostile intentions, and in May 1863 violence flared up again, both in Taranaki and the Waikato. Grey appealed for reinforcements, and troops crossed into the Waikato. General Sir Duncan Cameron – who had commanded a brigade at Balaclava – advanced, in the face of constant skirmishing, on the main Kingite concentration at Rangiriri. The Rangiriri *pa* was a massive affair, a complex of redoubts linked by deep, wide trenches, but without traditional palisades. Cameron's force numbered about 1300 men from the 12th, 14th, 40th, and 65th regiments, supported by artillery and a naval detachment. Cameron planned to take the *pa* in a pincer movement by direct assault on 20 November, but the flanking parties took too long to get into position and Cameron ordered the main thrust forward unsupported. The storming parties were trapped in a maze of trenches and shot down by well-positioned Maoris above them. Nonetheless, when parties of British troops moved round behind the *pa* the following day, and Cameron started work on a sap, the defenders abandoned Rangiriri.

The capture of Rangiriri allowed Cameron to advance up the Waikato valley. After a series of minor actions, the Kingites fell back on a *pa* at Orakau. Cameron's forces surrounded it on 30 March, but after an initial repulse decided to besiege it. The Maoris were short of water supplies, and a number of women and children were inside the *pa*; under a flag of truce the British offered them terms, but a Maori responded with a shout which became famous as a symbol of defiance; 'Friend, we shall fight against you for ever and ever!' In fact, the Maori position was hopeless, and after enduring British fire for several days, they suddenly broke out of the *pa* and fled into the bush. The capture of Orakau effectively ended the Waikato campaign, but Maoris retreating from Cameron's advance spread the rising across other parts of the country. In February 1864 it erupted along the coastline of the Bay of Plenty, to the east of the Waikato. Here resistance concentrated on a *pa* built near a gap in a fence which marked off Maori and missionary land – the Gate Pa. The Gate Pa was by no means the largest or most complex Maori fortification in the wars of the 1860s, but the action there achieved notoriety for the fierceness of the fighting. The British attacked the position on 29 April. The outer trenches were carried by storm, and the defenders abandoned their position. As they fled, however, they ran into another British force positioned in their rear, so promptly turned and charged back into the *pa*, colliding with the original storming party. A fierce close-quarter fight broke out and the storming party was repulsed, the British losing over 120 killed and wounded. Nevertheless, such was the weight of numbers that the British and their Maori allies were able to bring to bear that the Bay of Plenty tribes submitted in June.

The wars had, in any case, entered a new phase. In the aftermath of the fighting in Taranaki a new Maori movement had emerged, a mixture of Christian ideology and Maori traditional belief known as *Pai Marire*, 'good and peaceful'. This began as an attempt to bring Maori and *pakeha* together, but soon became bitterly disillusioned by the wholesale confiscation of Maori land which followed each campaign. Known as 'Hauhaus'

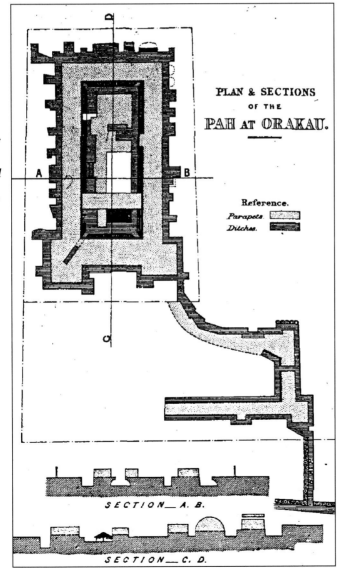

*Right: A plan of the* pa *at Orakau, the last Maori bastion in the Waikato campaign.*

*Left: Maori prisoners taken in the campaigns of the 1860s, under guard at Rutland Stockade, Wanganui, by men of the 18th (Royal Irish) Regiment. (Tim Ryan)*

PLAN & SECTIONS
OF THE
PAH AT ORAKAU.

Reference.
Parapets
Ditches.

SECTION__A. B.

SECTION__C. D.

from a shout ('Hau! Hau!') which formed part of their rituals, members of the cult became a focus for violent resistance to colonial rule. In early April 1864 a party of troops burning rebel crops was attacked, and the head of Captain T.W.J. Lloyd of the 57th was cut off, smoke-dried in traditional Maori fashion, and passed around the tribes as proof of the movement's *mana*. Although a Hauhau attack on a British redoubt was repulsed at Sentry Hill on 30 April 1864, the movement spread quickly, especially after the murder of a white missionary by Hauhau followers. The Hauhau campaign followed the broad pattern of previous fighting, although on a smaller scale. Although individual Maori tribes continued to build *pas*, there was a greater emphasis on raiding, and fighting in the bush. Each tribe that had accepted the call of the Hauhau movement had to be reduced in turn, and war-bands roamed across large areas of uninhabited bush. In this regard, volunteer units raised from among the settler population, such as the famous Forest Rangers, proved themselves more adept at bush fighting than the regulars. They were supported by large numbers of Maoris who rejected the Hauhau movement, or had long-standing feuds with the Hauhau tribes.

The Hauhau wars dragged on for the best part of eight years. The main groups had been largely defeated by 1866, and British troops began to withdraw from New Zealand, passing the prosecution of the war over to colonial volunteers. In 1868 the rising received a new boost when a chief named Te Kooti, who had been wrongly arrested as a Hauhau and imprisoned on Chatham Island, escaped with his followers. Troops were sent to capture him, but Te Kooti brushed them aside, and on 10 April 1868 he killed 70 whites and Maoris in a counter-attack on the settlement at Hawke's Bay, and then fled to the mountains. Te Kooti was to prove the most daring and resolute of the last Maori guerrilla leaders, and

continued the fight for a further four years. In the end his followers were whittled down by clashes with colonial patrols, and he finally abandoned the fight after a skirmish in February 1872. He was allowed to settle unmolested in territory still owned by the Kingites.

*The unfortunate Captain Lloyd of the 57th Regiment, whose head was cut off in one of the first skirmishes with the Hauhau, and passed amongst the tribes as encouragement to fight. (Keith Reeves Collection)*

Maori losses in the wars between 1845 and 1872 have been estimated as 2000 killed, with a similar number wounded. British and colonial forces lost 560 killed and over 1000 wounded, whilst Maoris fighting for the British lost perhaps 250 killed. In

the end, most land was opened up for white settlement, but the wars engendered an enduring legacy of bitterness which has continued into the twentieth century.

## WEST AFRICA: ASANTE

Despite a climate so inhospitable to Europeans that it had been christened 'The White Man's Grave', the ready availability of gold and slaves drew the European powers to West Africa long before the nineteenth century. Even so, the heat and high incidence of malaria and yellow fever made colonial settlement impractical, and European settlements remained little more than enclaves, often literally shut up in castles on the shore. Their tiny numbers belied their economic influence, however, for their willingness to pay for their favourite commodities with desirable goods such as firearms set up patterns of trade which extended far into the hinterland. The Dutch and British, in particular, competed vigorously for the lucrative Gold Coast trade which was generated among an inland power, the Asante ('Ashanti'), but conducted through the intermediary of the coastal Fante tribes. The complex manoeuvring between the four parties, as each sought to profit at the expense of the rest, resulted in a series of wars which gradually became a contest for supremacy between the Asante and the British.

The Asante state was basically a confederation of forest groups. Their king – the *Asantehene* – ruled a 400 square-mile area from a palace at Kumase, and exerted control over the confederation by means of a golden stool, a symbol of immense mystical power which represented the spiritual unity of the Asante people. The River Pra, sixty miles from Kumase, marked Asante's southern border, and the boundary with the Fante. By the 18th century the Asante were already heavily involved in trade with Europeans, but were resentful of the Fante's role as middle-men. In 1806 the Asante attacked the Fante, and provided the British with the first proof of their own military impotency. The British were keen to maintain the status quo, but maintained no troops in the area, and were quite helpless to prevent the Asante sweeping through Fante territory, and slaughtering Fante refugees quite literally under the walls of a British coastal fort.

In 1824 a British governor at the Cape Coast, Sir Charles Macarthy, attempted to organise a Fante army to put the Asante in their place, but it was so severely defeated that Macarthy literally lost his head, which was carried as a trophy to Kumase. This debacle persuaded Britain to maintain its distance from local politics until 1873, when a dispute over the ownership of several coastal trading posts provoked an Asante invasion, and led to a direct confrontation with British troops. Initially, the British government tried to fight the war by proxy, sending Sir Garnet Wolseley to organise

Fante resistance, but Wolseley soon realised that this idea was impractical, and applied for British troops. Wolseley tackled the subsequent campaign with thoroughness and gusto, and it made his reputation. He devised a practical uniform for his men, abandoning scarlet in favour of a neutral grey, expended huge amounts of his prodigious energy in organising transport, ensured competent medical facilities for the inevitable task of evacuating the sick and wounded, and wrote copious detailed instructions on the tactical complexities of forest fighting.

In fact, the main Asante army had already retired across the Pra by the time Wolseley's troops arrived. Asante armies traditionally had problems sustaining themselves in the field for long periods in Fante territory, where the different climate of the more open terrain made them prone to disease. In January 1874 Wolseley concentrated his forces – the 23rd and 42nd Regiments, a battalion of the Rifle Brigade, the 1st and 2nd West India Regiments, a

battery of mountain guns, a force of black auxiliaries and a detachment of Engineers – on the Pra, and began last minute negotiations with the *Asantehene*, Kofi Karikari. By now it was Britain that was making demands, and when King Kofi proved unwilling to comply Wolseley crossed the border. His plan was to strike up the principal trade route to Kumase with his main force, whilst a supporting column, consisting largely of African auxiliaries, entered Asante from a route to the east. Wolseley commanded the main column in person, and had not progressed far when on 31 January his scouts ran into an Asante army deployed near the village of Amoafo.

Wolseley had stressed the importance of men remaining calm when fighting in the gloomy forest environment. The Asante were armed with trade guns, but although these

*Below: A stalwart Wolseley directs the fighting amidst the forest gloom, Asante, 1873. (Anne S.K. Brown Collection)*

produced a terrifying volume of noise and smoke, they were not particularly effective. Wolseley's troops fanned out on either side of the track, keeping close together, and trying to form a hollow box. They came under a heavy fire from an enemy who was almost completely concealed. Wolseley had deliberately picked a high proportion of officers to accompany the column, but the psychological effect of fighting an invisible enemy at close range in the smoky forest gloom was nevertheless trying. The Asante were able to manoeuvre quickly, bringing their firepower to bear on apparent weak spots, and attacks on the flanks alternated with disconcerting rapidity. At one point Wolseley's headquarters was hard pressed, and several times Asante gunmen had infiltrated between British lines, or slipped round to retake ground that had already been cleared. In the end Wolseley pushed his column forward in short rushes, supported by salvoes of cannon-fire, and the Asante melted away into the forest.

From Amoafo Wolseley pressed on towards Kumase. Nearing the village of Odasu a few days later he ran into a stockade across the road. There was a familiar crash of Asante musketry, and there followed a repetition of Amoafo. Wolseley's men stormed the village, then spent several hours defending it against Asante counterattacks. At last Wolseley managed to punch a way through, barely overrunning a number of well-placed Asante ambushes. So swift was this advance, however, that it carried right on into Kumase itself, apparently taking the Asante by surprise. When Wolseley entered the capital it was full of curious crowds, among them many warriors who had clearly just come from the fight. Wolseley seized the royal palace, and began to round up as much Asante gold as he could find. Kofi Karikari himself had fled, however, and overnight most of the population deserted Kumase. With heavy rains threatening, Wolseley organised a rapid return to the coast.

His expedition was hailed as a great success in Britain, and it had certainly achieved its principal objective

of defeating the Asante in battle. Yet the Asante army had not been broken up, and neither had Kofi Karikari been deposed; in fact, it was clear that Wolseley's force could not have sustained itself so far from the coast for much longer. It was a curious type of victory, and it left the Asante to their own devices. A period of political turmoil followed, which did not end until the accession of *Asantehene* Prempe I in 1888. Prempe, indeed,

*Above: Wolseley's men, in their practical campaign uniforms, emerge into a clearing on the road to Kumase, 1874. (Author's collection)*

asked the British to support his claim, and thereby encouraged a new wave of colonial interference in Asante affairs. Britain responded by trying to bully the Asante into joining a newly formed Gold Coast Protectorate, but

Prempe refused. The British response was to mount another expedition to Kumase in 1895-6. Although the British regarded this as a military invasion, the Asante did not resist, and troops occupied Kumase without a fight. Prempe submitted, and was promptly arrested and sent into exile. The British built a fort at Kumase to house their representative.

The Asante kingdom simmered with resentment at this move, and in June 1900 were provoked into revolt by a heinous insult from a new British governor, Sir Frederick Hodgson. Hodgson marched up from the coast, and at his first meeting with the assembled Asante chiefs demanded to know why, as the senior power in Asante, he had not been offered the Golden Stool to sit upon. No Asante had dared to sit upon the Golden Stool, and to suggest such a thing was blasphemy. Within a few days the Asante had risen in arms, and Hodgson and his escort of 750 African troops, with a handful of white officers, found themselves besieged in the fort at Kumase.

With Imperial commitments in South Africa and China, there were few regular troops to spare for his rescue, and the task therefore fell to colonial troops from across West Africa. For two months the siege continued, moments of occasional eccentricity – the British responded to Asante war-songs by playing 'Rule Britannia' on a gramophone – masking the garrison's desperate plight. Food and medical supplies ran low, and the Asante harassed the post with continual sniper-fire. On 23 June Hodgson decided to fight his way out; leaving a small force behind to guard the sick and wounded, he broke out with the survivors and fought his way down the forest road. Three days later, he met a relief column coming in the opposite direction. It was not until 14 July that the relief column fought its way through to Kumase, relieving the fort in the nick of time. It took three months of incessant skirmishing for the British to put down the revolt. In 1902 Asante was formally annexed by Britain, and today it forms part of

modern Ghana. The Asante had hidden the Golden Stool away from Hodgson, and its whereabouts remained a secret until workmen building a road unearthed it in 1920.

## CHINA

To the minds of acquisitive Westerners, China at the start of the nineteenth century seemed another India – a plum of the East, ripe for the plucking. Within its enormous boundaries were 400 million potential customers for the goods produced with increasing efficiency by the processes of the Industrial Revolution, whose unsaved pagan souls were a spur to missionary endeavour. Furthermore, the administration of the ruling Manchu Quing (Ch'ing) dynasty seemed hopelessly introverted, archaic, bureaucratic, inefficient and corrupt, and China's military forces were weak and anachronistic. Yet the Quing rulers of the Celestial Empire singularly failed to see the benefit of contact with Europeans who, from the majesty of the Imperial Palace at Beijing (Peking), seemed no more than so many uncouth barbarians. The resultant frustration of the European powers was to be cruelly vented on China, making the nineteenth century a time of turmoil and conflict.

The first British traders had established a 'factory' (compound) at the port of Canton in 1757 but, like their Portuguese and French counterparts, had largely been forbidden to move outside its confines. The British soon found China to be a lucrative market for opium, which was grown on the plains of north central India, and for a while proved to be the British East India Company's most profitable export. The Chinese readily took to the drug, which soon brought the British and Quing authorities into conflict. The Imperial court disapproved of the opium trade, whilst the British were deeply frustrated at the restrictions imposed on their commerce. Chinese attempts to stamp out the opium trade in Canton in 1839 led to the first of several wars against the European powers. The principal

cause was the issue of free trade, but was complicated by radically different perceptions of the world and the human condition. By twentieth-century standards it is therefore particularly ironic that the first of these wars was, in effect, fought by the British to force the Chinese to buy opium, to the detriment of tens of thousands of ordinary Chinese citizens. The Opium War, or First China War, lasted from 1839 to 1842 and set a pattern for later conflicts; it was marked not by continuous violence, but by occasional outbursts of varying ferocity, interspersed with long negotiations. The most serious fighting occurred between 1840 and July 1841, when British troops under the overall command of Sir Hugh Gough occupied the heights above Canton, and stormed a number of towns around Nankin. The Chinese fought with great courage and ferocity, but were no match for the superior discipline and firepower of Gough's troops. The Chinese army consisted largely of a hereditary levy of Manchu 'Bannermen', whose administration was cumbersome, and who fought mainly with swords, spears and bows. Before Gough could capture Nankin, the Imperial authorities sued for peace, and the Chinese were forced to allow the British access to four more ports. They continued to refuse to receive foreign representatives at the Imperial Court, however, and refused to deal with them as the agents of independent governments of equal status.

In 1854 the Opium War treaty came up for revision, and the Chinese attitude showed no signs of relenting. In October 1856 a Chinese ship, the *Arrow*, sailing under the Union Jack and with a British captain, was boarded by Chinese officials, and her crew arrested as pirates. The British representative in Canton demanded an apology, and fighting broke out. The French, no less frustrated than their British counterparts, were quick to join in pursuit of their own grievances. In December 1857 Canton was captured by an Anglo-French expedition, and in May 1858 the Allies attacked the strategically important forts at Dagu (Taku) at the mouth of the river

Peiho, only 100 miles from Beijing. The forts – large earthen redoubts, surrounded by trenches full of sharpened bamboo stakes – were bombarded by a flotilla of French and British gunboats and abandoned when landing parties threatened to storm them from the rear. The demonstration was sufficient to force the Emperor to reluctantly agree to accept foreign representatives at his Court.

When, however, British and French troops arrived to escort their representatives to Beijing in June 1859, they tried – against the terms of the treaty – to sail up the Peiho, and the Dagu Forts opened fire. This time Allied attempts to take the forts were spectacularly unsuccessful: six British gunboats were disabled, and the attempt of a small landing party to wade knee-deep through clinging mud at low tide exposed it to the full exotic array of Chinese firepower – artillery, antiquated fire-arms, arrows, rockets, fire-balls and stink-pots – which inflicted 448 casualties.

*Below: The assault on Canton. (National Army Museum)*

The war resumed. After the inevitable round of delays, evasions, negotiations and ultimatums, the British and French, reinforced from Europe and India, assaulted the Dagu Forts anew in August 1860. Some 11,000 British and Indian troops under the command of General Sir Hope Grant, and about 6000 French under General de Montauban, landed about eight miles up the coast from the mouth of the Peiho. The Allies marched inland, avoiding the coastal swamps, and struck the Peiho upstream of the Dagu Forts, defeating an Imperial army in the field on 12 August. From there they advanced down the course of the river, effectively attacking the Dagu Forts in the rear. The Forts consisted of two large works on either side of the river mouth, with a third smaller one further inland. The Allies therefore encountered the smaller fort first, and on 21 August Grant began bombarding it with over forty guns and light mortars, whilst British ships off the coast shelled the outer forts. The approaches to the inland fort were so narrow that only 2500 British (chiefly of the 44th and 67th Regiments) and 400 French troops

could mount the assault. Although the storming parties came prepared with a pontoon bridge and ladders, they were still greatly hampered by the mud and swamp. When they reached the outer defences they were met by a terrific fire at close range, and were trapped in a confused tangle at the bottom of the trenches. The Chinese pushed away their scaling ladders, and tossed grenades and spears among them. Some officers tried making a ladder by driving their swords into the rampart walls, and gradually the Allies managed to force one or two openings in the Chinese line. The British and French vied with each other to be the first to raise their flags inside the fort, and the honour fell to Lieutenant Chaplain, who planted the 67th's colours above a high central bastion. The Chinese resistance was stubborn, but at last they broke, many being killed as they fled by impaling themselves on their own barriers of stakes. British losses were twenty-one killed and 184 wounded, whilst the Chinese are thought to have lost 400 dead. The remaining forts surrendered without further fighting,

*Right: A stirring, if rather romanticised, drawing of the storming of the Dagu Forts, 1860. In fact most of the troops wore sunhelmets rather than covered shakos. (Author's collection)*

and the Allies pushed on in the face of vacillating Chinese opposition to the outskirts of the capital itself, defeating the Chinese army in two large-scale engagements en route. The Emperor fled, and the Quing dynasty seemed on the point of collapse. At the last minute, as Allied siege-guns prepared to open fire on the walls of Beijing, the Chinese declared themselves willing to accept Anglo-French demands, and the invaders withdrew, having secured their rights to be represented in the Court and to expand their trading activities.

The treaty which followed the end of the Second China War led to almost four decades of peace between the Celestial Empire and the West, but offered little respite for the beleaguered Quing dynasty. With their authority supreme over such a vast area, across so many geographical zones, and over so many disparate ethnic groups, the Quing had to deal constantly with the threats of natural disaster and rebellion. In the last half of the nineteenth century, a series of floods killed thousands of ordinary Chinese, disrupted the

*Below: Fierce fighting between British and Manchu troops. (Rai England Collection)*

provincial administration, and unsettled the survivors. In 1851, a major rebellion broke out which threatened the survival of the dynasty itself. The Taiping Rebellion was both a religious and political movement, and it spread rapidly across central China. During the 1860s the foreign powers offered limited support to the Imperial government: men such as 'Chinese' Gordon were allowed to take commissions on the Emperor's behalf, foreign instructors trained and led units of Chinese troops, and British and French regular troops and naval brigades took the field against the rebels. However, most of the fighting fell to Imperial Chinese troops, and was extraordinarily destructive; by the time it was over, it had cost the lives of some 20 million people.

The Quing reacted to the Taiping challenge by introducing a number of minor military and political reforms, but these proved too little too late to secure China's political and territorial integrity. The 1880s was the great decade of European Imperial rivalry, and the world powers seemed ready to carve up China just as they were carving up Africa. Newly modernised Japan seized Manchuria, France took Tonkin, Annam and Cochin China (Vietnam) from Chinese control, and the Russians captured Port Arthur. In all of these campaigns the immensely proud Manchu army had proved quite incapable of resisting even considerably inferior western forces. Foreign missionaries, forced on the Imperial government, began vigorous programmes of evangelism amongst the native Chinese, and their influence was widely resented. All of this intense activity stirred the fundamentally conservative nature of the Chinese peasantry, and found expression in an anti-foreign movement known as the *Yi-he quan*, the 'Fists United in Harmony', which emerged in the northern Shandong province in the spring of 1898. Secret society movements were by no means unusual in Imperial China, and the *Yi-he quan* followed an established tradition in which political

opposition to the Quing was merged with religious dissent and martial arts to produce a revolutionary movement. They were unusual, however, in that rather than challenging Confucian orthodoxy or the Imperial government, they supported both at the expense of foreign influence, their creed being summed up in their slogan *'Fu-Quing mie-yang'* – 'Support the Quing, destroy the foreign'. The *Yi-he quan* practised a form of spiritual possession whose rituals, involving basic *gong-fu* (kung fu) techniques, were easy to learn, and which among foreigners earned them the nickname Boxers. Soon the Boxers began attacking Christian converts and destroying examples of Western technology, such as telegraph wires and railways. Although the Imperial authorities publicly disavowed the Boxers, many in the Court supported their aims, among them the powerful Dowager Empress, Tz'u-hsi. Tz'u-hsi had always been violently opposed to foreign interventionism in Chinese affairs; her subtle influence helped the movement to grow, and from June 1900 the Imperial Court openly supported the Boxers. The Boxers had no access to sophisticated weapons, and their creed in any case rejected all things European, but the Imperial government had raised a number of regular regiments, organised and armed along Western lines, and these joined the attacks on foreigners. Whites in outlying districts were attacked, and the Boxers began to converge on Beijing, to demonstrate their support for the Quing and to attack the foreign legations.

The foreign representatives in Beijing had been confined to a small area, overlooked by the walls of the Imperial city. When the rising began Westerners and Christian converts fled to the protection afforded by the small detachment of troops each legation maintained. Eventually some 400 military personnel – British, Americans, French, Italians, Russians and Japanese – were crowded into the narrow confines of the legation district, together with more than 500 European civilians and 350 Christian Chinese. The Legations were sur-

rounded by both Imperial troops and Boxers, who began bombarding them on 20 June, and mounted occasional fierce, but largely ineffective, attacks on the perimeter. When news of the attacks reached British ships anchored off the mouth of the Peiho, Vice Admiral Sir Edward Seymour organised a relief column from a flotilla of Allied ships lying there. He assembled a force of over 2000 men consisting of troops from all the foreign powers represented – the first time the major world powers had set aside their imperial rivalries and united to impose their will on an independent sovereign state. They marched to Tianjin (Tientsin), and from there advanced by train towards Beijing. The Boxers, however, had destroyed the track and bridges along the way, forcing Seymour to abandon the railroad. Indeed, the Boxers gathered in such numbers that Seymour was forced to abandon his march completely, and retire on Tianjin. The retreat was harried by Chinese troops and Boxers all the way, until another international force sent out from Tianjin rescued him. Seymour's first attempt to relieve Beijing had cost him sixty-nine dead and 207 wounded.

Indeed, by the time Seymour got back to Tianjin the town had become a focus for Chinese resistance. Thousands of Boxers and Imperial troops had surrounded the town to prevent the Allied troops which had landed at Dagu and assembled there – some 12,000 of them, mostly Russians and Japanese, but including the Royal Welsh Fusiliers sent up from Hong Kong – from breaking out. Chinese artillery bombarded the town, whilst the Boxers mounted daring attacks on the Allied perimeter. The siege was finally lifted on 14 July after several days' heavy fighting, culminating in the storming of the Chinese quarter, which had become a Boxer stronghold.

With the relief of Tianjin, the Allies were able to consolidate their position, and reinforcements were shipped in. An international force of 20,000 men – the British detachment consisted of the Royal Welsh Fusiliers, the Royal Marine Light

Infantry, Royal Engineers and an Indian contingent – was assembled under the command of a German Field-Marshal, Count von Waldersee. On 4 August this mixed force began its advance up the Peiho river. The Chinese tried to block it at the village of Peitang on the 5th, but were driven off by a textbook attack by the Japanese contingent. It was a difficult advance, carried out in the face of constant skirmishing, and made worse by extremes of heat. When fighting occurred it was usually ruthless; captured Boxers and Imperial troops were summarily beheaded – a common enough retribution in the aftermath of an unsuccessful rebellion in Imperial China. By 13 August the relief force had reached the city walls of Beijing. The garrison in the Legations was still holding out, although by now exhausted and short of supplies. On the 14th the relief force stormed the city and relived the Legations. The siege had lasted for fifty-five days.

The relief of the Legations was a turning point in the Boxer Uprising. The Allies went onto the offensive, shelling more defences at the mouth of the Peiho, and capturing several cities still in Boxer or Imperial hands. In January 1901 the Quing sued for peace, and finally admitted defeat in its long struggle to keep the influence of the 'foreign devils' at bay.

## BURMA

The kingdom of Burma, based at Ava on the central reaches of the river Irrawaddy, lay in a strategic position which caused the British some concern. It framed their Indian possessions to the east, and was also a potential gateway to the imagined riches of China. It was regarded 'by the Supreme Government as part of the glacis encircling India's lines of defence'. In the early nineteenth century, the kingdom was militarily robust, and followed an expansionist philosophy which seemed to threaten India itself. Its soldiers had marched into the Indian border towns of Chittagong and Assam, whilst the British found diplomatic

negotiations with Ava to be unpredictable and frustrating. In 1824 a dispute over an East India Company trading post had led to a full-scale war, in which British troops had fought in red coatees and wearing their full dress shakos. The fighting took place in steamy jungle thickets, where heat-stroke felled men just as surely as the Burmese. Although the British army was undoubtedly technologically superior – the First Burma War was characterised by an extensive use of Congreve rockets – the Burmese fought behind well-built stockades of bamboo and teak, and the conflict was bloody. It won the British some territorial concessions, but once the troops had withdrawn Ava behaved as if its position was unchanged.

The British found this attitude exasperating, and in 1852 the tension overflowed into violence when a British official attempted to resolve a dispute by ordering Royal Navy ships to open fire on Burmese stockades on the Irrawaddy. The result was the Second Burma War, which seems to have caught both sides largely by surprise. The British sent an expeditionary force which consisted of four Queen's battalions – the 18th, 35th, 51st and 80th – and an EIC contingent. Because of the difficulties of operating in jungle terrain, the British troops were

*Below: British troops storming the Shwe Dagon pagoda, the climax of the Second Burma War, 1852. (National Army Museum)*

*Above: A skirmish with dacoits. The Third Burma War petered out into a long campaign to suppress dacoit bands consisting of a mixture of bandits and Burmese loyal to Thibaw. (Author's collection)*

*Opposite page, top: British infantry and Burmese pagodas, Third Burma War, 1888. (Bryan Maggs Collection)*

*Opposite page, bottom: 'Action in the Wuntho Jungles': although this picture is obviously posed, it does suggest something of the difficulties of pursuing dacoit bands through the Burmese bush. (Bryan Maggs Collection)*

embarked on a flotilla of steamers, and operated almost entirely from navigable rivers, chiefly the Irrawaddy. On 5 April Burmese stockades at Martaban, at the mouth of the Irrawaddy delta, were stormed, opening up the river for an advance on Rangoon, where the Burmese had fortified the complex of pagodas which lay at the heart of the city with stockades. On 11 April Dalla, on the opposite side of the river to Rangoon, was shelled, and a landing party stormed the pagodas there. The following day troops were put ashore in two storming columns on the Rangoon side, and advanced rapidly through the jungle towards the city. Although the Burmese stood bravely

by their stockades, they were driven out by EIC artillery, and by evening the British had captured the outer defences around the pagoda complex. Early the next morning an assault was mounted on the heart of the complex, the Shwe Dagon pagoda itself, under the cover of a furious artillery barrage. The Burmese had erected three tiers of stockades around the temple, but the storming party breasted their fire, broke through the Burmese line, then charged up the steps and carried the pagoda with a cheer. The action cost the lives of five British officers – two from sunstroke – and seventeen men, whilst 132 were wounded. The number of Burmese casualties is unrecorded.

The capture of Rangoon was of immense symbolic importance, but in fact British control extended over only a small part of Burma. Over the following weeks expeditions were mounted to reduce the town of Bassein, also on the Irrawaddy delta, and, ironically, to put down an anti-Burmese revolt in the province of Pegu. These actions were typical punitive expeditions, in which small parties of troops were shipped to their objectives, destroyed Burmese stockades, often after a stiff bout of fighting, and then returned to Rangoon. The British also constructed a military road to improve communications between Calcutta and the Irrawaddy. On the whole, however, the Kingdom of Ava refused to accept the reality of defeat, so the British simply annexed Lower Burma – the area of the Irrawaddy delta around Rangoon – and maintained an army of occupation there. This was not an entirely satisfactory situation from the British point of view, and Anglo-Burmese relations began to deteriorate following the accession of Thibaw as King of Ava in 1878. Thibaw's reign was characterised by a capricious level of political violence and, worse, by an apparent even-handedness when dealing with foreign trade delegations. In 1885 Thibaw signed a commercial treaty with the French which raised the dreadful spectre of French influence so near the Indian border.

125

The British responded by trying to annex Thibaw's kingdom at gunpoint. The resultant campaign was described by one commentator as 'not a war at all – merely a street row'. The British thrust was towards Thibaw's court at Mandalay – the campaign inspired Kipling's poem, *The Road To Mandalay* – and, once again, was conducted by means of the arterial Irrawaddy. The Kingdom of Ava had made some attempt to update its army in the aftermath of the 1852 campaign, but it remained no match for the British force of 12,000 men commanded by General Prendergast, consisting of three Queen's battalions and several Indian regiments, which set out from Rangoon on 10 November 1885. The Burmese attempted to make a stand behind stockades at Minhla, but the British pressed forward in the face of a heavy fire and Burmese resistance collapsed. Prendergast entered Mandalay unopposed on 28 November. Thibaw surrendered with members of his family, and was sent into exile, and Upper Burma annexed.

The victory proved illusory, however, since British control only extended as far from the Irrawaddy as their guns could reach. Even the Kingdom of Ava had found it difficult to exert tight control in outlying areas, where dacoitry – banditry – was endemic, both for economic reasons and as a form of political protest. After the fall of Mandalay, thousands of soldiers from the former Burmese army retreated to the jungles, and were joined by patriots, romantics mourning a golden age of Burmese independence, and those simply after a quick profit. For five years the British were forced to wage a campaign of pacification against the dacoits, who moved through the jungles almost with impunity. On two occasions dacoit bands threatened Mandalay, and in January 1891 the town of Kwalin in Upper Burma was besieged, necessitating the despatch of a relief column including three Queen's battalions and an Indian contingent. In 1889 Wolseley himself commanded an expedition to Ponkan, and another expedition was mounted to Wuntho.

By 1890, however, the steady pressure on the dacoit bands had reduced their numbers and killed many of their leaders, and resistance to British rule finally petered out.

## CANADA

Late in 1837, the very year that Queen Victoria came to the throne, Canada, the last British possession on the continent of North America, was riven by revolt. The uprising, a patchy affair, was the result of a number of social factors resulting from the growth of the colony early in the century; of political and religious tensions between the English and French-speaking settlers; and of the spread of radical and republican ideologies. It was particularly severe in the settlements along the St Lawrence River, around Montreal. Detachments of the 24th, 32nd, 66th and Royal Scots regiments were put into the field, supported by local militia. There were several skirmishes around the villages of St Denis and St Charles, on the southern bank of the St Lawrence, in November 1837. These first attempts did not break the back of the rebellion, however, because the troops were hampered by the onset of the severe Canadian winter. In December, the rebellion spread north of the St Lawrence, and Sir John Colbourne marched on a rebel concentration at the village of St Eustache. He attacked on the 13th, and the rebels were driven out of the village after bitter street-fighting. St Eustache proved to be the toughest fight of the campaign, after which many rebels took to the woods. Sporadic outbursts of guerrilla warfare continued for another year.

In the 1860s, Canada was the setting for a minor campaign which resulted from the activities of an Irish republican group, the Fenian Brotherhood. The Fenians had a great deal of support amongst the immigrant Irish community in America, and mustered a small private army, consisting largely of Irish veterans of the American Civil War, with the intention of raiding into Canada. Their objective was to embarrass the British government, and force the United States to put pressure on Britain to withdraw from Ireland. In the event the raids were small affairs; in April and May 1866 the Fenians crossed the border but were dispersed by Canadian militia. In May 1870 they made a more serious attempt, but were again dispersed after a brief fight at Trout River. The Fenian campaign had proved daring but ineffectual, and after Trout River the republican movement abandoned the idea of further raids into Canadian territory. In 1870 the Hudson Bay Company, which still administered tracts of south-west Canada, signed over a district known as the Red River Colony to the Canadian government. This remote area was home to the Metis, a group of mixed French and native Canadian descent, who lived largely through hunting and trapping. The Metis were neither consulted nor informed of the transfer of their lands, and when the news broke it provoked them to armed rebellion. About 500 Metis gathered under arms and seized a Company post at Fort Garry, electing a former classics student, Louis Riel, as their leader. The Canadian government appealed to Britain for support, and an expeditionary force of 1200 men – of which the 60th Rifles provided the infantry backbone – was transported to Lake Superior under the command of Colonel Garnet Wolseley, who was then Deputy Quartermaster-General in Canada. The subsequent campaign was largely bloodless, and is chiefly remembered for the ingenuity with which Wolseley kept his men provisioned, and transported them across 600 miles of wilderness country, using waterways for roads. Wolseley's force reached Fort Garry in the third week of August 1870, after a journey of three months, but the Metis were so taken by surprise that the rebellion collapsed and Riel fled to America. In 1885 a more serious Meti Rebellion broke out, and Riel returned from America to lead a breakaway government; the rebellion was put down by Canadian troops without the use of British regulars.

# 3

# UNIFORMS AND WEAPONS

'The Queen's Army took an idiotic pride in dressing in India as nearly as possible in the same clothing they wore at home ... Could any costume short of steel armour be more absurd in such a latitude?'

Viscount Wolseley, speaking of the Second Burma War, 1851–3

The period immediately before Queen Victoria's accession was characterised by the most extravagant approach to uniform in the history of the British army. For perhaps twenty years after the defeat of Napoleon, there had been no large-scale wars; it was an era of national celebration, a time when the army's ceremonial role was pre-eminent, and the army's tailors were allowed to indulge the prevailing victorious spirit. By the 1830s, however, the financial consequences of this approach, coupled with an increase in warfare along the fringes of the colonies, encouraged a gradual shift towards a practical fighting costume which characterised the development of British uniform during Victoria's reign. Until the widespread adoption of rifled firearms, with the resulting increase in accuracy and capacity for destruction, few military thinkers considered it strange that the British soldier should march into battle wearing a bright red jacket, with white straps crossing conveniently in the centre of his chest, and on his head a cumbersome head-

*The kitchens of the 8th Hussars in the Crimea. Most of the men are wearing stable jackets and forage caps; the man centre left wears his full-dress braided jacket and busby. Note one of the soldiers' wives in the background. (Private collection)*

dress with a conspicuous badge plum in the centre. Not until the 1880s was there any serious concession made to convenience in the field, and by that time the dangers and discomfort of scarlet had been made brutally apparent by Boer and Afghan marksmen and by the harshness of life in the deserts of the Sudan. Indeed, it was not until the 1890s, as Victoria's reign drew to a close, that ceremonial and service dress became completely divorced, and the soldier wore one uniform at home, and another, drab and practical, in the field.

Until about 1860, however, the soldier fought in ceremonial dress, modified to various degrees according to the conditions of terrain and climate, the flexibility of his commanding officer, and the vagaries of supply. Any survey of uniforms in the early Victorian period must therefore begin with those specified by officers' Dress Regulations and by Horse Guards directives. Despite its name, however, the soldier's uniform was seldom that, and any number of factors affected what a particular unit wore at any given time. It was quite common for several regiments to serve in the same campaign in very different uniforms, whilst apparently all adhering to the same dress regulations. Each soldier had two orders of dress, full dress – basically a smart uniform for all important occasions – and undress, a more relaxed order of dress for working. Which one he wore on any given occasion depended largely on the whim of his commanding officer, whether he preferred his men to 'make a show' and look smart on active service, or whether he permitted them the greater degree of comfort undress allowed. Indeed, some more adventurous battalion commanders even approved the issue of practical fighting uniforms, adapted to the needs of the operational theatre, though the majority did not. In theory, uniforms were required to last for a year – two in India – and new ones were issued annually on 1 April. Any changes in uniform design authorised at home would therefore be reflected in the next

official issue; but whereas troops stationed at home would receive them almost immediately, it could be up to two years before the same uniforms were issued to troops stationed in India. It was therefore quite common for obsolete items to be worn long after they had been officially replaced, particularly in the more remote garrisons. Furthermore, since they purchased their own uniforms, officers were allowed far greater latitude than their men, and when they replaced them they usually did so according to the latest pattern, so that new styles might be found in use amongst officers months before they were issued to their men. Regimental attitudes and local conditions also played a part; in South Africa during the Eighth Cape Frontier War, for example, it was common for troops to fight in a costume which was largely indistinguishable from civilian dress, but in the Crimea, just two years later, full dress was the norm, at least in the early part of the war.

## Uniforms c.1837

In 1837, the standard dress uniform jacket, worn with variations by almost all arms of service, was the coatee. For infantry officers and sergeants, this was scarlet, double-breasted, with long tails at the back, and cuffs and collar of the regimental facing colour. The extravagant gold lace around the buttons on the front of the coatee, a characteristic of the styles of the 1820s, had been removed, but there were still bars of lace either side of the buttons which decorated a slash, or flap, on the outside of the cuff, and more around the buttons on the skirt-flap at the back, and either side of the collar opening. Until the 1860s, when they were formally abolished, each infantry regiment, apart from Rifles, maintained the fiction that one company consisted of grenadiers, and another was a light company. In fact, grenadiers had not carried grenades since the eighteenth century, and the increasing emphasis on open-order tactics meant that even by the early Victorian period most battalions were trained in the skirmishing techniques

which had been the preserve of the light company. Nevertheless, the distinction continued to be reflected in the pattern of uniform. Officers of battalion companies wore gold epaulettes on their shoulders, whilst those of the grenadier and light companies wore extravagant wings.

Line other ranks wore a simplified version of the officers' coatee. This was single-breasted, but made of a coarser, brick red cloth, that was noticeably dull by comparison. The facing colours were on the collar and cuffs, and all braid was white worsted. Unlike the officers' coatee, the ORs' had braid loops across the front, on either side of the buttons, but it followed the officers' in that the cuff slash (which was the same colour as the coatee) was also braided. Battalion companies wore shoulder straps of the facing colour, edged in braid, whilst grenadier and light companies wore wings.

Headgear for both consisted of a large 'bell-topped' shako, decorated with a woollen ball on the top, and a brass regimental badge on the front. Trousers were dark blue/grey 'Oxford mixture' for winter issue, with a red welt down the outside seam, and white linen for summer wear, although trousers of a lighter blue were often authorised for wear in India.

Highland regiments followed broadly the same pattern, but with slightly shorter tails at the back of the coatee, and, of course, feather bonnets instead of the shako, and regimental tartan – either a kilt or trews – instead of trousers. The Guards regiments wore bearskins instead of shakos, as did Fusilier regiments, but of a slightly different pattern. The Rifle regiments – the 60th (King's Royal Rifle Corps) and the Rifle Brigade – wore uniforms of very dark green. Their shakos were of the same pattern, with a black tuft and bronze bugle-horn badge. Officers of both regiments wore a Hussar-style jacket, with black braiding, a pelisse, and a crimson sash. The men of the 60th wore a single-breasted jacket, with red facings on the collar and cuffs, three rows of buttons down the front, and short tails; the men of the Rifle

Brigade wore a double-breasted coatee, with black facings, longer tails, and two rows of buttons at the front.

In undress, the infantry wore a short 'shell' jacket, cut off at the waist, with no tails behind. This was quite plain: although it had the facing colour on the collar and cuffs, it had no braiding. The officers' version had either gold epaulettes or gold cords on the shoulders, though many officers preferred to wear a long, dark-blue frock-coat, which hung down almost to the knees, and bore no lace. The appropriate head-

*Below: An officer's bell-topped shako, Light Company, 19th Regiment, 1836–44. (Army Museum's Ogilby Trust)*

gear for undress was the forage cap. In 1829 a broad-crowned woollen cap was authorised, in dark blue for Line regiments, and green for Light Infantry. This had a coloured band around the crown – red for Royal regiments, of the facing colour for Line regiments, and diced red-and-white for Highlanders. These caps were officially replaced in 1834 with a plain dark blue or green 'pork-pie' forage cap, but the earlier type continued to be worn long after. Officers' caps had black leather peaks, and these were also authorised for ORs to wear in hot climates. Officers' caps had a band of black oak-leaf lacing around the crown, and usually had the regimental badge embroidered in gold on the front; it was

common for ORs to wear regimental badges or numerals on the front of the 'pork-pie' cap.

Amongst the cavalry, the early nineteenth-century fascination for classical influences was still evident amongst the Dragoon Guards, who started Queen Victoria's reign wearing a brass Roman-style helmet with a black fur crest which could be replaced with a lion's head device. They wore a plain single-breasted scarlet coatee, with epaulettes for officers and shoulder scales for ORs. Trousers were dark blue, with gold stripes for officers and yellow for ORs. The Light Dragoons escaped the heavy helmet, and wore instead the bell-topped shako and a double-breasted scarlet coatee with short tails, epaulettes or shoulder scales. Trousers were dark blue with double gold or scarlet stripes. The Hussar regiments wore dark blue jackets, with five rows of buttons on the front, heavily braided in gold for officers or yellow for ORs. In addition they wore scarlet pelisses, also heavily braided and edged with fur, barrelled waist-sashes, and trousers with a single broad stripe of gold or yellow. Headgear was a busby of dark-brown fur with a scarlet or crimson bag. Lancer regiments began the reign with characteristic 'lancer caps', and scarlet jackets similar to those of the Light Dragoons, but in 1840 all but the 16th Lancers reverted to blue jackets. Trousers were blue with a double stripe, gold for officers, and red, yellow or white, according to regimental differences, for the ORs. In undress, most cavalry regiments wore forage caps and a short stable-jacket, which were broadly similar to the infantry's 'shells', although the Hussars retained their lacing across the front.

The Foot regiments of the Royal Artillery followed infantry styles, but in dark blue. In 1837 they wore a bell-topped shako, a double-breasted coatee with red facings, and dark blue/grey trousers with a broad red stripe in winter, and white trousers in summer. Undress consisted of a blue stable-jacket with red facings, and either a broad-topped forage cap with a red band, or a plain blue forage cap. Horse artillery followed the Hussar style, with braided jackets and black fur busbys with a scarlet band. In undress they wore braided stable-jackets with forage caps.

### Campaign Dress, 1837–54

The early campaigns of Queen Victoria's reign were fought in bitter extremes of temperature. In Canada, for example, where British troops were employed suppressing French-speaking insurgents, there were initially few concessions to the weather. Troops went into the field wearing their coatees and dark Oxford-mixture trousers, and shakos with black 'oilskin' covers. Indeed, it was unusual for the shako to be worn in action without some sort of cover, since the soldier was responsible for replacing it if it got lost or damaged, and it was expensive; the 'oilskin' cover was waterproof, and therefore protected the shako from both the elements and the worst of the knocks and scuffs that it could expect on campaign. At first, in the harsh Canadian winter, the troops had little protection beyond their greatcoats; these were of thin grey cloth, with a cape over the shoulders. Officers' greatcoats were of better quality, with longer capes. Not until after the Crimean War were troops issued with the single most obvious aid to comfort in the field – a waterproof sheet or blanket, which would have saved them, in a way the greatcoat never could, from all the discomfort, aches, pains and disease inflicted on them by being unprotected from the rain. However, by their second winter in the field (1838) they had adopted some practical items of local dress, notably heavy fur mittens, fur-lined boots, and caps with fur earflaps.

By contrast, in India and Afghanistan the initial problem was the heat. During the early stages of the First Afghan War (1839), the 16th Lancers apparently went into the field wearing full home-service dress, and suffered an appalling incidence of heat-stroke as a result. The infantry were hardly any better off; in the fighting at Ghazni and else-

where they are depicted as wearing their coatees and shakos with a white linen cover (the equivalent of the 'oilskin' for hot climes). Trousers were of a plain medium-blue dungaree, a type commonly authorised for Indian service. Officers wore forage caps without covers, and either shell-jackets or blue frock-coats. By the time the 17th Regiment were withdrawn from Afghanistan in November 1839, during the operations against the Khan of Khelat, the shakos and coatees had been abandoned in favour of the old-style broad-crowned forage caps and shell-jackets. During the disastrous retreat from Kabul in the winter of 1841-2, the 44th Regiment were wearing greatcoats, and some of the officers had acquired the local Afghan sheepskin coat, the *poshteen*; although in a famous late-Victorian painting the regiment is depicted making its 'last stand' at Gandamak in uncovered shakos, in reality these were probably in 'oilskin' covers, given the winter conditions. At Jellalabad, during the siege, the 13th Light Infantry are depicted making a sortie dressed in shirt-sleeves or shell-jackets, green forage caps with a yellow band, and blue dungaree trousers. This was a surprisingly relaxed regime, and it was very unusual for the early Victorian soldier to be permitted to fight in his shirt-sleeves; however, it no doubt reflected the fact that the 13th were operating under the guns of Jellalabad, and had no need to carry their equipment with them on what was essentially a raiding foray. Similarly, during General Pollock's march to relieve Jellalabad some troops were also apparently allowed to fight in shirt-sleeves, particularly when taking the high ground, an innovative tactic which required speed and determination, and the minimum of encumbrances. By the later stages of the fighting, the frock-coat had apparently become unpopular amongst officers, as it singled them out from their men, and made them targets for Afghan snipers. As for cavalry, the 3rd Light Dragoons fought in Afghanistan wearing their home-service coatees, but with white quilted covers over their shakos.

In Sind and Gwalior in 1843, the soldiers seem to have fought in coatees and blue dungarees with covered forage caps. At Miani, the 22nd Regiment, the only Queen's regiment involved, fought in just that, with the shako replaced by a peaked forage cap with a white cover and curtain at the back of the neck. The officers wore uncovered forage caps, and either frock-coats or shells. In the Gwalior campaign the British infantry fought in similar head-dress and trousers, but wearing the shell-jacket in preference to the coatee. Similar orders of dress prevailed in China in 1839-42, where the men wore the local blue trousers, but were still required to fight in coatees and covered shakos, or, at best, shells and forage caps. In New Zealand, during the First Maori War, the 58th Regiment went into action wearing shell-jackets and forage caps (both types) without peaks or covers.

Of course, much of the fighting in India and the East was carried out by the East India Company's armies, whose troops – both European and Indian – prior to the Mutiny largely followed the model of the Queen's uniforms. However, a study of EIC forces falls outside the scope of this book.

In the 1840s there were a number of changes to uniform patterns, and some of these reached India before the outbreak of the Sikh Wars. The most striking was a change in headgear; the bell-topped shako was abandoned in favour of a new pattern, which was almost cylindrical, tapering slightly towards the top, and with a peak fore and aft. It was topped by a ball tuft, and a regimental badge was worn on the front. Known as the 'Albert' shako, after the Prince Consort who supposedly influenced its design, it was the last pattern of shako destined to be worn extensively in action. There were other changes to head-dress, too: in 1845 the Light Dragoon shako was made more cylindrical, whilst in 1847 heavy cavalry – Dragoons and Dragoon Guards – were issued with a new pattern of brass helmet, with a black horsehair plume replacing the old woollen crest. At the same time,

*Left: The most practical campaign kit of the 1840s and 1850s, the shell jacket and forage cap. This is the uniform of Ensign Bray of the 39th Regiment, killed in the Gwalior campaign of 1843. The marks where the shot struck him can still be seen on the chest and arm. (Devon and Dorset Military Museum)*

at Aliwal they were also wearing their dress Lancer caps with white linen or black oilskin covers. During the First Sikh War, the most common order of infantry dress was shell-jackets with blue dungaree trousers, and Albert shakos with white covers. At Sobraon the 31st and 50th Regiments wore wide-crowned forage caps with white covers in place of the shako. During the Second Sikh War, the differences in appearance according to the attitudes of commanding officers were even more acute. The 10th Regiment fought in the trenches outside Multan in covered shakos, coatees and blue trousers, whilst the 32nd, on the same front, wore white shell-jackets – which were authorised for wear in the hot season in India – and white covered foraged caps. At Chill-ianwallah, the 24th fought in coatees, covered shakos and lavender trousers, whilst the more relaxed 29th wore undress shell-jackets and forage caps, with local blue trousers. In all cases, by this time, it was becoming common for officers to adopt items of local clothing, even amongst the more self-consciously 'smart' regiments. Turbans were often improvised by winding cloth around the forage cap or even the shako, and quilted coats were often worn over shell-jackets.

South Africa provided some contrast to India and, indeed, the first faltering steps towards the evolution of a practical fighting costume occurred on a small-scale in South Africa at least a decade before the more widespread, and better-known, developments in the Indian Mutiny. As early as the Sixth Cape Frontier War (1835) the 72nd Highlanders had abandoned their trews of 'Prince Charles Edward Stuart' tartan in

the skirts at the back of their tunics were shortened, and a new undress introduced. This was similar to the infantry pattern, and consisted of a forage cap and stable jacket, the equivalent of the infantry's shells. In 1846 the infantry's white summer trousers were abolished, except in hot climes, and replaced by lavender ones. In 1841 Foot Artillery lost their white trousers, and in 1847 their winter ones were made dark blue.

The Sikh Wars (1845-6 and 1848-9) were waged in a typical mixture of dress and undress. The 3rd Light

Dragoons, who fought in both campaigns, went into the first with all ranks wearing forage caps with white covers, but at Rumnaggar and elsewhere in the second wore the new shako with a white linen cover. In both campaigns officers wore stable jackets whilst ORs wore the cavalry equivalent of the coatee, a pattern which was broadly followed by the other cavalry regiments, the 14th Light Dragoons and 16th and 9th Lancers. The 16th were the only Lancer regiment to wear scarlet jackets, and during their famous charge favour of locally made leather trousers, and the regulation cross-belts were replaced with a waist-belt with a large pouch at the front. Coatees were retained, but forage caps (at that time broad-crowned, with diced bands) were embellished with leather peaks. In 1842, the 27th Regiment, which occupied and defended Port Natal against the Boers, took both their coatees and shakos with them, as individuals are shown wearing them, but clearly preferred forage caps and shell-jackets. At Zwartkopjes in 1845 the 7th Dragoons wore their old-style helmets, with brass lion device in place of the plume, and undress stable jackets. By the time the Seventh Cape Frontier War proper had erupted, however, the regiment had abandoned the helmets in favour of the blue broad-crowned forage cap with a yellow band, and the men were dressed thus during the charge at Gwangqa river in June 1846. The Artillery likewise fought in forage caps and shell-jackets, as did most of the infantry, although the 91st Foot apparently wore their coatees with all the lace stripped off. Improvised peaks were added to the forage caps, often back and front. Most officers preferred shell-jackets, and they were in any case ordered not to wear frock-coats, presumably because they made them unduly conspicuous.

Similar practice soon became common during the Eighth Cape Frontier War (1850-3), the most serious, longest and most brutal of the cycle. Most of the war was waged in an inhospitable environment of rocky hillsides, ravines and dense bush, where full dress was so constricting as to be almost entirely impractical. As was so often the case in South Africa, the British were desperately short of cavalry, and relied heavily on the locally-raised Cape Mounted Rifles; the one regular regiment present, the 12th Lancers, charged the BaSotho at Berea mountain in December 1852 looking remarkably smart in white-covered forage caps and stable jackets. By that time most infantry battalions were looking decidedly war-worn, a far cry from the smart appearance specified for home ser-

vice. They fought in shell-jackets or coatees, apparently with the lace and wings removed. Most regiments started the war in forage caps, but these gradually gave way to local civilian 'wide-awake' (wide-brimmed) hats or even woollen night-caps. Equipment was kept to a minimum, and often replaced with locally made belts or pouches. Trousers were officially white summer wear or light blue, but were often replaced with corduroy or tanned leather alternatives. Officers became increasingly civilian in their appearance, adopting comfortable 'frontier jackets' of various patterns and local *veldschoen* shoes. As the dull red jackets of the men weathered to a deep maroon colour under the constant round of intense sunshine or teeming rain, the army lost all trace of spit and polish and gradually assumed an appearance which blended with its environment. Although the military establishment remained ambivalent to such changes, some commanders went out of their way to encourage it. Colonel Fordyce of the 74th Highlanders issued his men with loose smock-frocks, which were usually worn on long sea-voyages to protect dress uniforms, and these were dyed to a dull brown colour using local vegetable dyes. These soon weathered to a light grey/brown, not dissimilar to khaki. The 74th wore trews, not kilts, and officers and men alike fought in forage caps. The men wore a locally-made substitute for their equipment, and the officers armed themselves with shotguns for effective close-quarter fighting. Although this innovative fighting costume did not catch on among other regiments, it did foreshadow the widespread use of similar dress during the Indian Mutiny.

### Equipment, 1837–71

During the Napoleonic wars the British soldier had generally been expected to carry around all his necessary possessions on his person. His officers might have the luxury of baggage wagons or mules, and could therefore afford to take a remarkable number of home comforts with them into the field, but nothing was

provided for the other ranks until at least the Crimean War. Indeed, the accoutrements with which the ordinary soldier was issued were essentially Napoleonic in design, and did not change fundamentally until the introduction of the first Valise pattern equipment in 1871, which was the first attempt to design an integrated set of equipment which was both functional and comfortable.

The infantry knapsack equipment, first introduced in 1808, remained in service with only minor variations until 1871. It consisted of a large canvas box, painted black, worn between the shoulders. In an attempt to make it keep a proper soldierly shape, it was reinforced at the corners with leather, and had board reinforcements inside. It was carried by two vertical straps around the shoulders, which were further held in place by a horizontal strap across the chest. It was, generally, hated by the soldiers, because it was heavy and uncomfortable; the internal reinforcing boards had a habit of sticking into the back at odd angles, and jarring against the spine on a long march, whilst the retaining straps either cut into the shoulders, or pressed tightly across the chest, making breathing difficult. In full marching order – in other words, when carrying all necessary equipment on campaign – a rolled grey greatcoat was carried in straps above the knapsack, with a kidney-shaped mess-tin wrapped in an oilskin cover and attached below the greatcoat. Ammunition and bayonet were carried in broad leather straps across each shoulder, which crossed on the chest, so that the scabbard and black leather cartouche box (containing 60 rounds) hung on each hip. A brass plate, bearing a regimental device, served to hold the cartouche belt together and was positioned so as to cover the point where the straps crossed one another on the chest. All equipment straps were white for Line infantry and Highlanders, and black for Rifles.

Items such as blankets, water-bottles and haversacks were considered 'camp equipage' and issued by the Board of Ordnance as the soldier went into the field. Until the 1860s, the water-bottle was a small wooden cask, called the 'Italian pattern'; it was suspended from a leather strap over the shoulder. It was not particularly effective (it leaked) or hygienic (any germs from bad water tended to soak into the wood), and was in any case seldom issued in India, where civilian water-carriers – *bhistis* – usually accompanied armies in the field and supplied water from pig-skins. Where water bottles were carried in India, they were often bought locally, glass soda-water bottles, often wrapped in wicker or buckram, being particularly popular. The haversack, when issued, was primarily intended to carry food.

It was not unusual for a soldier to carry whichever order of dress he was not wearing – undress or full-dress – in his knapsack, and certainly troops were often ordered into the field carrying spare boots, shirts or trousers. In light marching order – when these items were not carried – the greatcoat was packed in the knapsack and the blanket strapped above it. As a result, the soldier's equipment often weighed about 60 lbs, no insignificant weight when sweating across the Indian plains or scrambling through South African thorn-bush. There was an inevitable desire to do without the knapsack if at all possible, and here the soldier was once again at the mercy of his commanding officer. In India, from the 1830s, EIC sepoys wore a waist-belt with the bayonet attached by a frog, and some commanders of Queen's regiments allowed their men to follow this practise in Afghanistan and during the Sikh Wars. In South Africa, during the Sixth, Seventh and Eighth Cape Frontier Wars, the cross-straps were sometimes abandoned in favour of locally-made waist-belts with a large pouch on the front and a bayonet frog at the back. It was also quite common for troops fighting the Xhosa to leave their knapsacks either in store or with the regimental baggage, and to carry their possessions rolled up in the blanket or greatcoat, carried in the knapsack straps. By the end of the Eighth Cape Frontier War a number of regiments

had adopted the even more simple expedient of carrying such items in a rolled up in a blanket worn *en bande-role* – across the shoulder and tied at the hip. In 1850 a waist-belt was authorised to replace the bayonet cross-belt, but this took so long to issue that most regiments had not received it at the start of the Crimean War.

Infantry officers were required to carry little more than a sword, either in a broad shoulder belt for infantry and Royal Artillery officers, or from slings attached to a waist-belt for the rest. As the century wore on, the more conscientious officers took to providing their own pistols or revolvers, and spy- or field-glasses. For the most part their personal luxuries continued to be carried in the baggage train, but those who expected to be away from camp for any length of time wore a haversack in which to carry their food.

Cavalry equipment was, of course, more simple, since it was impossible for a rider to wear a knapsack on horseback, and their accoutrements consisted largely of a pouch-belt, worn across the shoulders, with a black cartouche belt in the small of the back and a swivel ring, to carry a carbine when mounted. A sword-belt – wider for heavy cavalry than light – had slings for a sword-scabbard, and a sabretache, a flat black leather wallet whose principal purpose was to protect the horse from being injured by the scabbard when the cavalryman was mounted. On prolonged campaigning the cavalry were issued with water-bottles and haversacks similar to the infantry patterns. These were supposed to be worn one over each shoulder, but in practise this made it difficult to use the sword-arm, so both were often worn over the right shoulder. Foot Artillery accoutrements generally followed infantry patterns, and Horse Artillery followed cavalry styles.

## The Crimea
In many ways the Crimean War was anachronistic, even by the standards of the 1850s. Whereas so much of the army's practical experience since 1837 had involved small-scale cam-

paigning, where more flexible skirmishing tactics had slowly and painfully begun to develop, the Crimea was an old-fashioned European slogging match, fought by brigades and divisions in close-order formations which, outside the Punjab, had seldom been employed in the colonies. So, too, the gradual shift towards fighting in undress was halted in the Crimea, where the need to face down a major Imperial rival encouraged the belief that British soldiers should take to the field looking their most splendid. Before the army left Bulgaria for the Crimea, Queen Victoria had approved wide-sweeping changes in uniform across all branches in the army, but such were the delays in issue and manufacture that these uniforms only reached the Crimea towards the end of the campaign, and the army therefore faced its first major challenge in forty years fully resplendent in uniforms that had already been superseded.

Because the army had trusted to luck to find transport and supply services when it landed – and there was precious little available – the troops were landed in marching order, and spent the first week of the campaign, including the battle of the Alma, wearing what they stood up in. For the infantry this meant coatees, shakos and, since summer trousers were ordered to be left onboard ship, just one pair of Oxford-mixture trousers. Knapsacks, too, were left on board, and the men were ordered to take a spare shirt, extra pair of boots, socks and a forage cap wrapped up in their greatcoats, and carried in their knapsack straps. Officers, used to the luxury of having their possessions carried in the baggage train, were also ordered to land with only what they could carry. Most wrapped these up in their greatcoats, and wore them *en banderole*, but a few begged knapsack straps from their men and carried them on their backs. The men's accoutrements, of course, now consisted of just a cartouche shoulder-belt and waist belt with bayonet, and the haversack and water-bottle. The Highlanders wore their full feather bonnets, but there were slight concessions to practicality

133

*Above: A group of men of the 68th Regiment in the Crimea. They are wearing coatees, forage caps and 'Oxford mixture' trousers, and carrying Enfield rifles. Note that the sergeant's coatee, centre, is double-breasted but has no braid on the front. (Private collection)*

amongst the mounted men; the cavalry and artillery were ordered to remove the plumes from their head-dress, and the Light Dragoons, Royal Artillery and Lancers covered their shakos with oilskins. The Scots Greys – part of the Heavy Cavalry Brigade – wore their full bearskins, but generally the cavalry were allowed to take off their expensive epaulettes and shoulder scales, and the Hussars – apart from Lord Cardigan himself – left their pelisses behind. The 13th Light Dragoons and 17th Lancers, incidentally, were the only two cavalry regiments to have been issued with experimental grey trousers. The 11th Hussars were famous for an extra touch of sartorial elegance, their crimson breeches, with gold stripes for officers and yellow for

ORs, which had earned them the dis-respectful nickname of 'The Cherry-Bums'. Unlike the Light Brigade, the Heavy Brigade adopted the practice of issuing 'booted overalls' – trousers with leather reinforcements on the inside leg and around the ankles – before they arrived in the Crimea. Most General Officers wore long blue undress frock-coats, initially with conspicuous cocked hats, but later with the infinitely more practical forage caps, although one or two clung stubbornly to more ostentatious costume.

The army was dressed thus when, within six days of landing, it fought the first pitched battle of the war at the river Alma. It perhaps says something for the popularity of the shako amongst the troops that as they went into action, those most heavily engaged tossed their shakos aside, and took out their forage caps. After the battle, most had to go back and retrieve them, for Lord Raglan was a stickler for correct orders of dress, but nevertheless many men contrived to lose them as quickly as possible. Once the army had established

a base at Balaclava it was no longer necessary for the men to carry everything around with them, and most of the subsequent fighting was done without knapsack equipment, although they still possessed only what they had landed in. The 93rd at Balaclava repulsed the Russian cavalry wearing coatees and feather bonnets, rather than shells and forage caps. Both the Heavy and Light Cavalry Brigades went into their famous charges in the uniforms already described. Sketches of the trenches around Sebastopol show that most infantry went on duty in coatees with forage caps, though the Guards regiments had a more attractive flat braided side-cap. By the time of Inkerman – 5 November 1855 – the weather had begun to deteriorate, and the since the battle began early on a cold and misty morning most of the men involved wore greatcoats. Although some went into action in shakos, the majority probably fought in forage caps, causing some confusion since the Russians were also fighting in greatcoats and forage caps.

When the expeditionary force had embarked for the Crimea, no-one, either present or at home, expected it to be still in the field in the winter. In October 1855 a supply of warm clothing had been sent out to the front, but it was lost when several ships were sunk during a devastating storm off the mouth of Balaclava harbour on 14 November. By December 1855 the weather was bitterly cold, the icy Crimean winds carrying first rain and then snow into the trenches. The men's uniforms were in any case beginning to show obvious signs of wear and tear. Coatees were faded and torn, shakos were battered and falling apart, and boots were worn through. Many troops adopted a common expedient of patching their clothes with coarse sacking cut from sandbags used in the defences, and sketches of men on picquet duty show them huddled in greatcoats, with blankets wrapped around them like shawls against the cold. The process of repair was not helped by the fact that most men had left their 'housewives' kit – needle and thread – in their knapsacks, although replacements were sometimes looted from dead Russians, together with their long knee-boots and greatcoats, which were cut up for patches. Replacement warm-weather clothing finally arrived at Balaclava in January 1855, but was further delayed because of the almost complete breakdown of the transport system between the harbour and the lines around Sebastopol. When it was at last issued, it proved to be highly practical, even if the images taken by the photographer Fenton caused something of a stir when they were exhibited or published as engravings at home. The British public was taken aback to see its army living in long boots, wearing sheepskin coats, usually with the fur inside, hooded coats, fur caps and heavy fur mittens.

When the weather began to improve in the spring of 1856 the winter clothing was withdrawn, and some attempt was made to return to a proper military appearance. Officers began to appear increasingly in shell-jackets, and forage caps were almost universal, but the men were

*Captain R.G. Cunningham, 42nd Highlanders, in the Crimea, wearing double-breasted coatee and forage cap. Captain Cunningham died at Malta from illness contracted in the trenches. (Black Watch Museum)*

still restricted to their coatees. The new uniforms authorised before the start of the campaign were issued in April 1855, but apart from a few officers, who had the latest patterns sent out to them, very few reached the

Crimea much before the end of the year. By that time, the fighting was largely over.

### Uniform Changes, 1855–6

The new uniforms marked the first significant break with tradition since the Napoleonic Wars, and were a decided improvement in terms of comfort. Instead of the old tight coatee, all branches of service (except for Royal Horse Artillery) were issued with a tunic. This was double-breasted for infantry and Lancers, and single-breasted for all other branches, and instead of the coatee's tails it had full skirts all round, which offered some protection below the waist in wet weather. The colour of the tunic remained the same, with regimental facing colours on the collar, cuffs and shoulder-straps, and the slashed panel on the cuffs. There was white lace around the buttons on the cuff slash, and the tunic was piped white around the edges, collar, cuffs and shoulder-straps, but the lacing across the front, which had been such a feature of the coatee, was abandoned. Officers abandoned their expensive gold epaulettes and wings, and rank badges were worn instead either side of the collar opening. Highland regiments received a doublet, with shaped skirt panels rather than full skirts. Shell or stable jackets remained for undress – white drill was specified for summer wear in India – although in Highland regiments sergeants and ORs wore white shells instead of red. Infantry regiments were also issued with a new shako, influenced by Continental designs, which was lower than the Albert pattern, and angled towards the front. Forage caps were modified slightly, but the old patterns continued to be worn for a number of years. There were minor changes, too, to the accoutrements; infantry company officers lost their shoulder-

*Captain Brown, 4th Light Dragoons, and his servant, wearing the warm sheepskin coats and fur hats which did not reach the Crimea until after the worst of the winter of 1854–5. (Private collection)*

belts in favour of waist-belts, bringing them into line with all other branches, and in 1856 the haversack ceased to be 'camp equipage' and became standard issue. The 60-round cartouche box was replaced about this time with a smaller box containing 40 rounds, and a black leather expense round, for 20 rounds, was added to the right front of the waist-belt. Pouches for percussion caps, which had hitherto been worn mostly in a pocket on the right of the

coatee, were added to the cross-belt.

Revolutionary though the new uniforms were, they were modified almost immediately, and from April 1857 all new infantry tunics were made single breasted. With only minor changes in cut and cuff designs, the 1857 tunic was worn as home-service dress throughout the remainder of the nineteenth-century.

## The Indian Mutiny

The Indian Mutiny differed radically from the Crimea in that the troops almost never went into action in full dress, and, indeed, even shell jackets were often replaced with a variety of drab and practical substitutes. These changes went beyond even those introduced in the Eighth Cape Fron-

tier War, and for the first time the majority of British troops went into the field in a costume which was primarily designed for comfort and convenience. The determining factor was the heat; traditionally, the British soldier in India had avoided fighting in the summer months, or working during the heat of the day, but the Mutiny forced him to accomplish prodigious feats regardless of time or season. Under these circumstances some concession to comfort was vital.

For the most part, British and EIC troops fought in similar uniforms during the mutiny. Since the fighting began in the summer, those Queen's regiments already based in India were wearing white summer undress. The practice of discolouring these had begun amongst Punjab irregular units in the 1840s, although neither British nor EIC troops had followed it in the Sikh Wars. The colour achieved was called khaki, after the Hindustani word *khak*, meaning dust. Although some units fought in the first skirmishes of the Mutiny in white, the practice of dyeing their shells and trousers khaki began early on. Dyes were improvised according to the means available, from tea and coffee to vegetable dyes, inks and even curry-powder. No two units were ever therefore likely to appear in the same hue, which varied from nut-brown, through grey to dust colour, and even a washed-out purple. Furthermore, few of these dyes were fast, and the clothing soon faded or washed out to all manner of muted greys and browns. The local blue dungaree trousers were often worn in preference to dyed whites.

When the uprising began, two battalions en route to China, the 90th and 93rd, were diverted to India. These had been issued with plain brown single-breasted 'boat-coats', which had been thought practical for the expected service in Chinese paddy-fields, and they were taken into the field in India instead. Indeed, many regiments sent out from England preferred to wear the smock-frock issued on board ship – as

*Left: The mid-Victorian soldier: Corporal James Sinn, 95th Regiment, photographed on his return from the Crimea, wearing the short-lived double-breasted tunic and knapsack equipment with waist-belt, and aiming his Enfield rifle. (Royal Archives)*

the 74th Highlanders had done in South Africa – and these were also dyed khaki. Some infantry regiments preferred to dispense with jackets altogether, and fought in shirt-sleeve order, and these too were dulled down by staining. Although one or two battalions may have retained shakos with white linen covers, with a curtain over the back of the neck, the most popular head-gear was the covered forage cap. In many units it was common for both officers and men to wind a length of cloth around the crown to produce a turban. Sometimes the combinations of dress were positively bizarre; some Highland regiments (the 79th and 93rd) continued to wear their feather bonnets, kilts, sporrans, hose and spats, but with dyed smocks. Mounted units tended to be more conservative; the 2nd Dragoon Guards (Queen's Bays) wore their scarlet tunics and

*Right: Troops in the typical campaign dress of the Indian Mutiny: white summer dress shells and trousers, stained khaki, and forage caps with turbans wrapped around. Note the officers wearing 'airpipe' helmets, right. (Keith Reeves Collection)*

137

brass helmets in the fighting outside Lucknow, in temperatures which must have made both insufferable. The 9th Lancers wore their white undress uniforms in the summer of 1857, but did not dye them; with the onset of the cooler weather they switched to blue undress, then back to white in 1858. Most cavalry regiments seem to have preferred a combination of home-service 'booted overalls' and khaki jackets or even shirt-sleeves. Covered shakos soon gave way to covered forage caps, with or without improvised turbans. The Royal Horse Artillery continued to wear their heavily-frogged blue stable jackets and blue trousers, but with turbans instead of busbys.

The proliferation of such unusual fighting kit was, as usual, more popular in some theatres and amongst some battalions than others. The widespread use of khaki had begun at Delhi, where the harsh conditions of life on the ridge among the hotch-potch of troops thrown together by circumstance encouraged a relaxed attitude towards uniform. Here many officers adopted outlandish civilian embellishments, such as quilted jackets, sun-helmets and 'wide-awake' hats. Units sent out from England tended to present a more uniformed appearance, at least early in the war. When the summer of 1857 passed, however, there was a general movement back towards scarlet and blue tunics or shells, not for the sake of conformity, but simply because these were warmer.

Sun helmets, now regarded as emblematic of the Empire period, were first worn extensively during the Mutiny. They had been popular amongst white civilians for some time, and a few officers had purchased them during the Sikh Wars. They were often worn with a coil of cloth wound round them as a pugga-ree, to keep them cooler. It was not until the middle of 1858, however, that they were privately purchased by some units and issued wholesale to the men. The shape and style of these helmets varied, but the most popular had a fluted air-vent or 'air-pipe' running up the spine at the

*Above: The 9th Lancers capturing a Mutineer baggage train outside Delhi, 1857. They are wearing white summer dress and covered forage caps; unlike most regiments the 9th did not dye their whites khaki. (Keith Reeves Collection)*

back, and were generally made of canvas stretched over a light wicker frame.

By the end of the Mutiny, the troops in the field presented a very motley appearance, but the experiment proved only temporary, for as soon as the fighting was over the troops returned to scarlet, and khaki was not seen again in action for another twenty years.

### Changes and Campaigns, 1859–71
The 1860s saw a number of improvements in the uniform field. Although the 1855 pattern shako – updated in 1861 and again in 1869 – continued to be worn with full dress until the introduction of the home-service helmet, it was not worn into the field. Instead, troops continued to

*Above: The practical campaign uniform adopted during the Second Maori War in New Zealand: men of the 68th Regiment in blue frocks, Oxford mixture trousers, and forage caps, with possessions carried in blankets worn* en bande-role. *(Tim Ryan)*

wear the forage cap. In 1855 a new forage cap was introduced for officers; for infantry this was dark blue with a black embroidered band and a flat peak, and was usually worn with a regimental numeral or badge on the front. In 1868 the familiar glengarry cap was officially adopted for all ranks, though many officers continued to wear their forage caps into the 1880s. In 1858 airpipe helmets replaced the forage cap as undress wear in India. From the late 1850s the familiar shell-jacket was replaced with a more comfortable five-button frock with full skirts. This was red or blue, as appropriate to the unit, and initially plain, without facing colours or piping, but with a pocket-flap on the left breast. Variations at

the end of the 1860s added the facing colours and a simple system of piping. In India, during hot weather, a white drill version of the frock was issued. From 1859 black leather leggings were authorised for wear at the commanding officer's discretion.

ORs' accoutrements remained largely unchanged from the Mutiny patterns. Officers were still only required to provide a waist-belt and sword, but most by this time armed themselves with revolvers, and telescopes or field-glasses, a compass, pocket-book and watch were all recommended. Field-glasses – binoculars – had been invented in the 1820s, but most officers preferred telescopes into the 1860s. Waterproof covers were also increasingly carried. In 1867 a dark blue patrol jacket was authorised for officers' undress wear. This was loosely cut, and fastened down the front with hooks and eyes, and decorated with rows of braiding across the front, which was secured at the opening with olivets. The pattern of braiding varied according to the branch of service.

These changes were evident to varying degrees in the campaigns of the 1860s. In 1857-58, during the first phase of the Second China War, the 59th Regiment fought in the brown 'boat coats' which had also been worn in the Mutiny, with covered forage caps. By the time fighting broke out again in 1860, however, forage caps had largely been replaced by airpipe sun helmets, and most of the troops seem to have worn red serge frocks and Oxford-mixture trousers. Knapsacks were usually carried on the baggage train where possible, and certainly seldom worn into action. The King's Dragoon Guards seem to have started the campaign in brass helmets, but soon abandoned these in favour of sun helmets.

In New Zealand, during the protracted fighting of the Second Maori War, the standard fighting uniform was a local variation on the scarlet frock, being a blue version of the same, which was more suitable to the fighting in dense fern-bush which characterised much of this

*Left: Soldiers of the 4th Regiment at Magdala, Abyssinia, wearing grey khaki uniforms and 'airpipe' helmets. (Bryan Maggs Collection)*

campaign. Some officers wore a loose blue smock, rather like the ship's smock-frocks common in the Mutiny, and the universal headgear was the forage cap. Knapsacks were rarely worn, and instead a soldier's possessions were carried in his greatcoat or a blanket, rolled up and worn *en banderole*.

On the Indian frontiers, British troops mostly fought in smocks and airpipe helmets or forage caps. In the Ambela campaign the scarlet frock was the norm, worn over trews or kilts, sporrans, hose and spats for Highlanders. Troops on the march seem to have worn airpipe helmets, but in the field reverted to forage caps.

In Canada, during the Fenian troubles of the 1860s, the troops similarly wore red frocks, forage caps, and greatcoats carried *en banderole*. In the winter months, the greatcoat was worn with the addition of winter clothing – fur caps, long boots and mittens. On Wolseley's Red River Expedition the 60th wore frocks and forage caps (of regimental green), but, since they spent most of their time on boats, worked in shirt-sleeves and locally-acquired moccasins.

In the Abyssinian campaign of 1868, the troops expected to have to work in extremes of temperature, from the heat of the coastal plain to the cold nights of the inland mountains, and those who started from India took both white drill uniforms and red smocks. The white drill was dyed with improvised dyes to make khaki – an expedient which became almost universal in India in the 1870s – although on this occasion the results produced a greyish colour rather than brown. In cooler weather the red frocks (blue for Royal Artillery) seem to have been worn with white trousers, whilst both khaki and scarlet frocks were worn in action at Aroge and Magdala. Headdress was the airpipe helmet, with a puggaree wound round it, and greatcoats were carried *en banderole*.

### The 1871 Valise Equipment
In 1871 the army finally approved a new set of accoutrements which was destined to do away at last with the old Napoleonic knapsack. Throughout the 1860s pressure had grown to develop some system which would include a knapsack of sorts, incorporate ammunition pouches, and distribute the weight evenly over the body, so as to make it more comfortable to wear. The principal component of the 1871 issue, as the name suggests, was the valise, a streamlined version of the knapsack, made of varnished canvas reinforced with leather, but without the painful board stiffeners. The valise was supported in the centre of the back, just above the waist-belt, by a system of braces which were interconnected by straps to the waist belt. This helped take some of the pressure off the braces, and reduced the constriction of the arms and chest which had been such a feature of the knapsack. A D-shaped mess-tin was carried in an oilskin cover above the valise, and on top of that the greatcoat, folded flat, strapped to the shoulders. Ammunition was carried in two pouches of twenty rounds apiece, worn either side of the waist-belt, and in a black leather 'expense' pouch or ball-bag, which was attached to the waist-belt, and either carried on the right hip or, when the valise itself was not worn, at the back. The bayonet was carried in a frog from the waist-belt at the left rear. The haversack, slightly modified, was to be

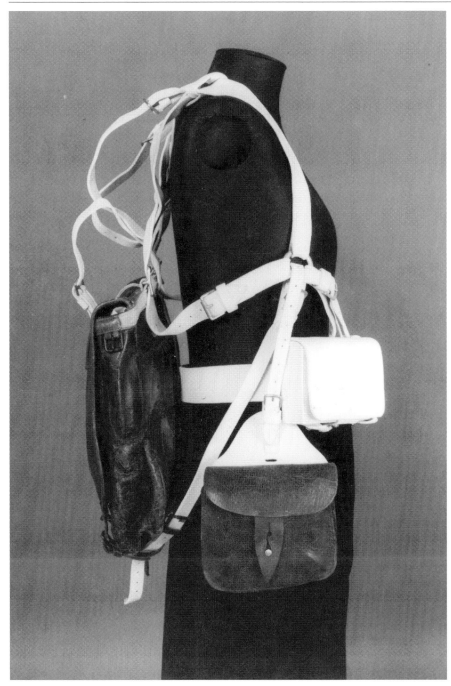

top of the skirts at the rear, and the weight of the valise on these caused chafing. The ball-bag, in particular, did not close properly, and it was common for soldiers scrambling about in action to lose loose rounds. As a result there were minor modifications in 1882, which replaced the two waist pouches and ball-bag with two larger pouches each containing 40 rounds, raised the height of the valise, and spread some of the weight by attaching straps to the back of the waist-belt. In 1888 a comprehensive review led to significant changes.

Although the Valise equipment was approved in 1871, it was several years before it was universally issued to troops overseas. It was standard issue amongst troops fighting in Zululand in 1879, but many of their counterparts in the Second Afghan War, which was raging at the same time, were still using the old knapsack cross-belts. Indeed, the Oliver pattern water bottle was scarcely if ever used in India where, since the Mutiny, it had been commonplace for battalions to equip themselves with locally produced glass soda-water bottles, which were usually cased in leather and carried on a shoulder strap. Officially officers were still only required to wear sword-belts, but since many now carried revolvers – and pouch belts with cartridges – these became obsolete. Some officers merely added their revolver holsters to the front of the belt, and fitted the pouch wherever there was room, but this was not an ideal arrangement, and in the 1870s it was common to carry the revolver in a holster attached to a belt slung over the shoulder. In the 1860s, however, General Sam Browne, an

worn over the right shoulder, whilst a new pattern water-bottle, a small wooden barrel known as the 'Oliver' type, was worn over the left shoulder.

The original ammunition pouches were of black leather, but these were replaced with buff leather ones in 1877. Indeed, all straps were of buff leather for Line infantry, whitened with 'blanco' for parades, but black for Rifles.

The Valise equipment was a vast improvement on the knapsack, but

not without its problems. Since the length and width of the straps was variable, there was a degree of individual selection implicit which had never been the case with the knapsack; if the complex web of straps did not quite suit the physique of an individual soldier, the balance was upset, and the straps could still constrict. The valise itself was cumbersome, and hung too low in the back; when first issued it was worn with a tunic which had two buttons at the

Indian veteran who had lost his left arm in action, invented a new belt which integrated both principles, and included a waist-belt with a simple buckle, a shoulder strap to support the weight, a revolver holster and sword-slings. Browne's intention had been to develop a system which he could use easily despite his disability, but the result worked so well that it became highly fashionable amongst officers fighting in Afghanistan, and later spread throughout the army as a whole.

### Campaign Dress, 1871–81

Shortly after the introduction of the Valise-pattern equipment, the army went to war wearing the first uniform specifically designed to meet the needs of a particular campaign. Sir Garnet Wolseley, with the meticulous planning for which his early career was famous, designed a uniform specifically to meet the needs of West African forest fighting in the Asante (Ashanti) campaign of 1873-4. This consisted of a loose plain frock, made of a grey/brown material known as 'Elcho tweed'. It was worn with trousers of the same material, and a new pattern of sun helmet,

*Left: The wooden 'Oliver' pattern water-bottle of the 1870s and 1880s. (Author's collection)*

*Left: Officers of the 72nd Highlanders in the Second Afghan War. A few are wearing scarlet doublets for the camera, but most are wearing khaki frocks with trews. The most popular fighting kit was that worn by the officer on the right; note the rolled blanket and 'Sam Browne' belt. (Bryan Maggs Collection)*

*Right: A rather faded but fascinating photograph of the 51st Regiment at Ali Masjid early in the Second Afghan War. They are wearing Afghan poshteen coats over old-pattern scarlet frocks with a single loop of braid on the cuff. (Bryan Maggs Collection)*

*Below: Officers and NCOs of the Royal Horse Artillery, Second Afghan War, wearing khaki frocks, forage caps and home service trousers. (Bryan Maggs Collection)*

based on a style which had replaced the airpipe pattern in India in 1870, and would be adopted as the universal head-dress for overseas service in 1877. This was made of light cork, and instead of the crested air-vent had a small, simple cap on top, with perforations around the edge of the cap to allow ventilation. In India such sun-helmets were white, but Wolseley specified that they should be light brown, and they were to be worn with a puggaree wound round them. Instead of the regulation black leggings, the troops were provided with rather longer canvas leggings. Each man was issued with two of the frocks, and a pair of tweed trousers and lighter duck trousers, in broadly the same colour. Equipment was the Valise pattern, but worn without the braces, as the valise was carried with the baggage, transported on this occasion by local African porters. The officers were recommended to provide themselves with Norfolk jackets, loose trousers, brown gaiters and shooting boots, and to carry the long saw-backed Elcho sword-bayonet,

issued to the men, instead of swords. The 42nd Highlanders grumbled that the new uniform meant the loss of their distinctive tartan and hose, but they were placated by being allowed to wear a red hackle on their helmets, as a regimental device.

Wolseley was not entirely satisfied with his experiment, but it had certainly proved more practical in the field that the scarlet frocks worn elsewhere. Nevertheless, when the Second Afghan War broke out in 1878, the troops despatched to the front were issued no such fighting kit, and had to make the best of whatever was available. This consisted of scarlet frocks for infantry (plain red had been abandoned for ORs in 1872) – of a pattern a few years out of date elsewhere, with facing colour on patches either side of the collar opening, and a single loop of braid on the cuffs – or white drill summer uniforms. White drill was always dyed khaki first, and it became common practice for battalions to send their whites to be dyed in their local bazaars before departing for the

*Above: Squadron of 9th Lancers photographed after Roberts' battle around Kabul, wearing quilted khaki jackets, home service trousers and forage caps. (Bryan Maggs Collection)*

front. Whilst Highland regiments retained their kilts and trews, many English battalions adopted the Indian practice of wrapping *puttees* – cloth bandages – around the legs as protection and support.

In cold weather it was common for men to wear a mixture of khaki and coloured items: the Royal Artillery, for example, were photographed dressed entirely in khaki, and wearing khaki frocks over the warmer blue trousers with red stripes. The 9th Lancers seem to have taken both their blue dress uniforms – now with a plastron front in regimental facing colour – and their khaki drills, as well as a quilted khaki jacket, whilst the 10th Hussars were photographed in khaki frocks with home-service trousers. Headgear was the white sun-helmet, worn with a

*Above: Officers of the 6th Dragoons in khaki frocks and home service trousers, with camel transport behind; Afghanistan, 1879. (Bryan Maggs Collection)*

*Right: Other ranks' scarlet frock, c 1880, with regimental facings on collar and cuff patches, and one 'long service and good conduct' stripe. Both this tunic and the frock equivalent – five buttons, and no piping down the front – were worn extensively in South Africa, 1877–81. (National Army Museum)*

khaki cover. Some regiments had been issued with the Valise equipment, but many had not; thus the 66th fought at Maiwand in khaki drill with Valise equipment with the old black pouches, whilst the 92nd Highlanders were also in khaki, but with knapsack cartouche belt and greatcoat *en banderole*.

Curiously, given the extent to which the Eighth Cape Frontier War had pioneered the use of practical campaign kit, the burst of fighting in South Africa between 1877 and 1881 was waged without the benefit of Indian khaki, and fought almost entirely in scarlet and blue home-service uniforms. For the most part the infantry fought in the five-button frock, which by this time had white trefoil piping on the cuffs and around

*Left: Unidentified colonel, Zulu-land 1879, in undress frock with white piping and gold braid, and glengarry. (Killie Campbell Library)*

the shoulder straps and bottom of the collar. Regimental facing colours were worn on tabs either side of the collar opening, and in some battalions on the cuff patches. Most battalions seem to have had the tunic with them too – which had seven buttons and was piped down the front – as both orders of dress appear in photographs. Officers wore either blue patrol jackets or their version of the scarlet undress frock, which had a collar of the regimental facing colour, was piped down the front, and had gold lace on the scarlet cuffs. Trousers were dark blue with a red welt. Artillery wore either a plain blue frock, similar to the old India pattern, with blue overalls with a wide red stripe, or a blue frock with red collar and yellow piping instead of the infantry's white. Headgear was the white foreign service helmet, and equipment was the Valise pattern, usually with white pouches, though the valise itself was mostly carried in transport wagons. A brass regimental shako-plate was authorised for wear on the front of the helmet, but the troops soon learned to remove this and to dull down both the helmet and pouch-straps from dye made from tea, coffee or even cow-dung, to make them less conspicuous as targets. The 3/60th Rifles wore rifle green frocks with red piping, including a single loop on the cuff, and had black accoutrements; the dyes used to make 'rifle green' were so dark at this time that the cloth appeared almost black. Undress head-dress consisted of the 1855 pattern forage cap for officers and the glengarry for ORs. The 91st Highlanders – the only Highland regiment to take part in these campaigns – wore doublets and trews. The Royal Engineers wore scarlet undress tunics with blue facings and gold or yellow braid, and blue trousers with a red stripe.

For most of the time in South Africa, the British remained short of cavalry. The only regular regiments to take part – the 1st King's Dragoon Guards and 17th Lancers – arrived during the

*Above: The white foreign-service pattern helmet of the 1870s and 1880s, with the shako-plate badge of the 57th Regiment. In South Africa the badge was usually removed and the helmet stained light brown. (Keith Reeves Collection)*

*Above right: Officers' tunic and pouch-belt, 17th Lancers, 1870s. This particular uniform belonged to Captain E.V. Wyatt-Edgell, killed in action at the battle of oNdini. The 17th wore their dress tunics in action, but with the plastron front buttoned over to show the blue reverse side. (Family collection)*

*Right: Infantry officers' forage cap, 1870s. (Author's collection)*

*Left: Infantryman's kit, c 1880, recreated by The Die-Hard Company. Note the biscuit on the plate, foreground!*

whom they fought. The 58th had the current Valise equipment, but wore scarlet; the 92nd wore the more practical khaki but carried equipment that had been rendered obsolete a decade earlier.

### The Transition to Khaki, 1881–99

The organisational changes which took place in 1881 had a small but significant effect on uniform. Although a new seven-button frock was authorised for home service, the standard overseas issue undress remained the five-button frock – scarlet for infantry, Engineers and heavy cavalry (except the 6th Dragoons) and blue for all others except Rifles. With the amalgamation of battalions, however, traditional facing colours were done away with, and were replaced by national ones – white for English and Welsh regiments, yellow for Scottish, and green for Irish. These colours were worn on round cuffs, instead of the trefoil patch design, and all the way round on the collar. Officers' frocks were of plain tunic colour, apart from among Highland regiments, whose officers wore similar frocks to their men, with rounded skirts at the front and gauntlet cuffs.

Apart from a small contingent sent from India – who fought in khaki drill – it was in this dress that Wolseley's expeditionary force took part in the 1882 Egyptian campaign. The Guards, fighting overseas for the first time since the Crimea, changed their white undress frocks for the scarlet of the Line battalions, and wore sun-helmets instead of bearskins. As in South Africa, sun helmets were universal, worn in some regiments with a coloured puggaree; most helmets were stained off-white with the usual dyes. Trousers were dark blue with a red stripe for infantry and cavalry as appropriate. Highland regiments wore kilts or, in the case of the Highland Light Infantry, trews. The Royal Marine Light Infantry wore blue frocks and trousers. Royal Artillery frocks were dark blue with yellow

closing stages of the Zulu War. Both wore home-service uniforms – scarlet tunics with blue facing and gold or yellow braid for the KDGs, and dark blue tunics with white plastron fronts and piping for the lancers. Trousers were dark blue with a gold or yellow stripe for the KDGs and blue with a double white stripe for the Lancers. In both cases, however, home-service head-dress was abandoned in favour of sun-helmets, and the 17th soon learned to button their plastrons over to show the blue reverse side rather than the brilliant white.

The 2/21st, 3/60th, 58th and 94th all fought in the 1881 Transvaal War in the same uniforms – often quite literally – that they had worn in Zululand. They were reinforced by the 92nd Highlanders, who were sent out from Afghanistan and arrived in time to play a significant part in the battle of Majuba. The 92nd were still wearing the uniform they had worn in India: khaki drill frock, helmets with khaki covers, kilts, sporrans, hose and spats. They were still equipped with the old knapsack cartouche belts, with soda-water canteens, and wearing their greatcoats *en banderole*; thus dressed they presented an interesting contrast to the 58th alongside

*Above: NCOs of the 2nd Life Guards in campaign dress, Egypt, 1882. (Royal Archives)*

*Below: 'Fighting isn't quite the sort of work that can be done in that rig', was John Bull's comment on the defeat at Majuba; but in fact the reasons for the British failure in 1881 went beyond mere uniforms. (Author's collection)*

braiding, and the 60th wore virtually the same uniform as they had in South Africa. Leggings were worn by the infantry and Royal Artillery, cavalry wore either boots or blue puttees. ORs' equipment was the 1871 Valise pattern, with buff pouches, the recent variation not having been issued before the campaign started. By this time most officers had acquired General Sam Browne's utilitarian belt. Although the men were issued with goggles and veils, to protect them against sand and flies, they do not seem to have been much worn.

Although the Egyptian war had proved entirely successful, it was becoming apparent that scarlet, blue and green were perhaps no longer the most appropriate colours in which to be waging a modern war. Certainly, in the desert conditions of Egypt the bright uniforms had become very grubby very quickly, but there was also a growing awareness of the increasing importance of concealment in an age of rapidly improving weapon capabilities. In fact large numbers of khaki uniforms – plain

frocks and trousers – were sent to Egypt, but arrived after the fighting was over. They were, however, issued to those troops who remained to garrison the country, and were therefore the uniforms in which British troops first encountered the Mahdists. On this occasion the khaki was of a decidedly grey hue, rather different to the dust-colour which had become standard in India. In the early fighting around Suakin, therefore, troops sent from Egypt wore this grey uniform, whilst the Indian contingent wore the more familiar khaki drill. Of the cavalry regiments, the 10th Hussars wore khaki frocks, home-service trousers and blue puttees, whilst the 19th Hussars wore grey frocks and brown Bedford corduroy breeches.

For the fighting in the Bayuda desert during the Gordon Relief Expedition of 1885, most troops wore grey, including the members of the various units brigaded into the Mounted Infantry Camel Regiment. The Camel Corps wore cord breeches and blue puttees, and carried their ammunition in bandoliers, rather

than the infantry's Valise pouches. Helmets were the usual foreign service pattern dyed brown. The Guards contingent took their red frocks with them, and loaned them to the Royal Sussex companies who made the unsuccessful dash to Khartoum by steamer, on the grounds that, according to Gordon, the Mahdists were likely to be overawed by the sight of British soldiers fighting in scarlet. For the same reason, during the last battle of the campaign at Kirbekan, the 1/South Staffs and 1/Black Watch also fought in scarlet frocks.

Although the army was clearly, by this stage, committed to fighting in khaki in practice, if not in principal, scarlet would not go away. In the second Suakin campaign, 1885, troops fought in both Indian khaki drill – some of which had been sent out especially to re-equip the Guards – and Egyptian grey. Indeed, the

*Right: The universal infantry campaign uniform of the 1890s: modified Valise equipment (Slade Wallace), khaki uniform and puttees. Usually a khaki cover would be worn over the helmet; this can be seen on the step behind. (Private collection)*

1/Berkshires seem to have been issued with both types, and to have worn both at Tofrek. Although this campaign was fought entirely in one type of khaki or another, scarlet was worn in action at Ginniss in December 1885. Again, the troops were ordered to put on their serge quite deliberately to impress the enemy; three out of four battalions did so, the other fighting in khaki. Ginniss, indeed, proved to be the last major battle fought in scarlet, although the last shots fired in anger by British troops in scarlet were those expended by the Royal Scots during the skirmishing which characterised the 1888 Zulu Rebellion. Even so, scarlet was not yet finished; scarlet home-service dress was worn by several battalions during the march to Kumas in Asante in 1896 – a campaign which, in the event, resulted in no fighting.

The fighting on the Indian borders during the 1880s and 1890s – the Third Burma War and various North-West Frontier expeditions – was characterised by a greater uniformity of dress than prevailed elsewhere, largely because khaki drill had long been standard issue in India, and in 1885 it was officially confirmed as service dress there. As a result there were few differences between regiments in the field over this period. Some infantry battalions adopted quilted neck-covers, to give extra protection in the sun, whilst others did not; among Scottish regiments the frocks were cut away to a rounded front, in the manner of their scarlet equivalent. Cavalry regiments preferred blue puttees, infantry khaki in various shades. In cold weather the men wore their greatcoats, whilst Afghan poshteen coats remained popular amongst the officers.

In 1888 a new variation on the Valise-pattern equipment was authorised, the Slade-Wallace, named after

*Right and left: Two VC winners from the 21st Lancers' charge at Omdurman: Captain P.A. Kenna (left) and Trooper Burn (right). Captain Kenna has armed himself with another ranks' lance; note the quilted neck-cover worn around the trooper's helmet. (Private collection)*

the two officers who invented it. This did away with the old large valise, and replaced it with a lighter version, worn higher on the back. The mess-tin and greatcoat were strapped to the waist-belt. The design of ammunition pouches underwent several changes over the next decade, reflecting the change from the .450 Martini-Henry to .303 ammunition. The first issue held 40 .450 rounds in the left pouch and 30 in the right; with the switch to .303 ammunition in 1889 the pouches were modified to hold 50 and 40 rounds respectively, but in 1890 a new pattern was issued, which opened from the back, and held 50 rounds in each pouch. Like every other piece of uniform or accoutrement, it took some time for the Slade-Wallace equipment to reach troops in all stations, but it seems to have been in general use by the time of the Chitral and Tirah expeditions.

In 1897 khaki was adopted as service wear on all overseas postings, not just India, so that in the Sudan in 1898 all British troops fought in largely the same uniform. Khaki was universal for all arms, infantry wearing helmets with khaki covers and large quilted neck-curtains, khaki trousers and puttees. Battalions were distinguished by large flashes sewn to the outside of the cover. Equipment was the Slade-Wallace set for ORs, and Sam Browne's for officers. Officers wore a new type of sun helmet, the Wolseley pattern, which was lower in height and had a wider brim. The 21st Lancers were also dressed entirely in khaki during their famous charge, and wore leather ammunition bandoliers rather than infantry pouches. By this time the Oliver pattern water-

frocks to their helmets as identification; these were mostly red for infantry and cavalry, with the regimental name embroidered in white, green for Rifles, red and blue for Artillery, dark crimson for medical services, and yellow for Engineers. Highland regiments used a piece of regimental tartan instead. Initially, these flashes were large and conspicuous, but once it became clear that the Boers used them for target practise, they were modified to less obvious proportions. For the same reason officers abandoned their impractical swords early in the war, and took to carrying carbines or rifles, which made them more difficult to pick out from their men.

Units of colonial cavalry, and later the Yeomanry regiments sent out from Britain, wore wide-brimmed 'slouch' hats, similar to the Boers', and these were so obviously practical that they were taken up by many infantry battalions. Indeed, by the end of the war regiments being sent out as reinforcements were issued them as a matter of course. Equipment generally remained the Slade-Wallace type, although the valise was usually carried on regimental transports, and the haversack was often slung between the shoulders instead. Given the prodigious amounts of marching accomplished by most infantrymen, it was quite common for rounds to become lost, particularly when the men snatched a few hours sleep at an overnight bivouac. Indeed, the Boers came to rely on this, and searched through British camp areas in the hope of finding a few rounds to replenish their supply. Partly as a result of this, a new webbing bandolier was issued to some regiments in the closing stages of the war in place of the pouches.

By the end of the Boer War many infantry battalions finished up looking a good deal like their enemy – in battered and weathered slouch hats, dull and dusty uniforms, and with bandolier equipment. They had indeed come a long way from their counterparts at the beginning of Queen Victoria's reign, resplendent in red coatees, shakos and glittering badges.

bottle had been replaced with a flat round type, covered in felt.

## The Boer War, 1899–1902

The Boer War marked the culmination of the gradual shift towards practical and inconspicuous fighting kit which had taken place over the previous two decades. Although some Boers, who remembered the Majuba campaign, had hoped to see the British wearing scarlet, the war was in fact fought entirely in khaki. At the beginning the troops looked much as they had in the Sudan, but without the quilted neck-covers. Here and there a few touches of the home-service dress were retained, such as the blue puttees worn at first by the Artillery, but these were soon abandoned for khaki. Similarly, Lowland Scots regiments began the war in trews, but gave them up for khaki trousers. Officers, who still provided their own uniform, usually bought helmets in a plain khaki colour, whilst ORs wore white helmets, usually with a puggaree and a khaki cover. Most regiments sewed patches taken from the shoulder straps of the home-service scarlet

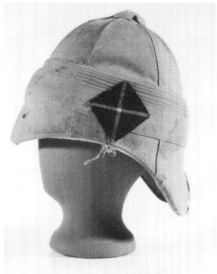

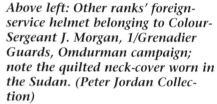

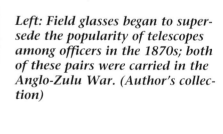

*Above left: Other ranks' foreign-service helmet belonging to Colour-Sergeant J. Morgan, 1/Grenadier Guards, Omdurman campaign; note the quilted neck-cover worn in the Sudan. (Peter Jordan Collection)*

*Above: Infantry officers' foreign-service helmet, 1899, belonging to Captain C.R.C. Ellis of the Cameronians, who was wounded at Spioenkop; it shows signs of shrapnel damage and bloodstains. (Peter Jordan Collection)*

*Left: A squad of Grenadier Guards under inspection, Omdurman campaign, 1898. (Bryan Maggs Collection)*

*Left: Field glasses began to supersede the popularity of telescopes among officers in the 1870s; both of these pairs were carried in the Anglo-Zulu War. (Author's collection)*

*Right: Officers of the Lancashire Fusiliers, photographed during the Spioenkop campaign, January 1900. Although most still wear Sam Browne belts, some have already begun to carry rifles rather than swords. (S.B. Bourquin)*

## WEAPONS

### Infantry Small Arms

1837 was a time of change in weapon technology. Hitherto the British army had gone to war armed with weapons that were only slightly updated versions of the smooth-bore Brown Bess flintlock which had won the Napoleonic Wars. The British military flintlock musket of the 1830s was 4 ft 7 ins (1.4 m) long, weighed nearly ten pounds (4.53 kg), and fired a simple lead ball. Tests showed that, given ideal conditions, a steady and experienced marksmen could fire it three times in a minute, and score a significant number of hits on a target 100 yards (91.5 m) away. At ranges beyond that, however, the unpredictable flight of the ball made it impossible to predict any degree of accuracy. Indeed, the weapon had no rear sight, because it was never intended to be aimed; all fighting was expected to take place in close order formations at close range. The soldier was taught to load and fire on command; he marched into place, pointed his weapon at a dense mass of the enemy and fired without any expectation of seeing where his shot went. Such a technique may have been successful in the grand battles of the Napoleonic era, but it rapidly became out of date in colonial conflicts where the fighting seldom took place in the open, and the enemy was often moving rapidly in open order, and making good use of cover.

The advantages of percussion over the flintlock system had been recognised for some time, and the first percussion firearms were issued just in time to serve in Canada, the first campaign of the new Queen's reign. The old flintlock system had been simple enough, if prone to errors. A squeeze on the trigger released the hammer, which held the flint, so that it struck a metal plate, creating a spark which fell into a pan primed with powder; the pan flared, thereby igniting the charge in the barrel and firing the ball. There was always a chance that the flint might not strike a spark, and that the pan would not ignite; or that it would 'hang fire' for a split second before pan and charge went off, and perhaps thereby singe the fingers or the face of the firer. In wet weather the troops had to go to extraordinary lengths to keep their powder dry, or the whole system failed completely. By contrast, the percussion system was much more reliable. Instead of the flint and pan, a small brass detonator was pressed onto a nipple which gave access to the charge. The hammer was cocked, released by the trigger, and struck the cap, thereby igniting the charge. The proportion of misfires was much lower for percussion guns, the danger of an unexpected 'flash in the pan' was done away with, and the whole system still worked in wet weather.

As early as 1831 the Board of Ordnance, which approved firearms for issue to the British army, decided in principal to change from the flintlock to the percussion system. It took time to find a suitable design of weapon, however, and no less than four patterns were sent to Canada in 1838, including some which had been converted from flintlocks. The majority of troops were still armed with flintlocks, however, and indeed it was well into the 1840s before they had all been recalled and replaced. In 1839 a standard pattern percussion musket was officially authorised and issued, and this was modified slightly and replaced by the 1842 pattern. Both were 4 ft 7 ins (1.4 m) long for ORs, and 6 ins (0.15 m) shorter for sergeants, whilst cavalry regiments were issued with a carbine version 3 ft 6 ins (1.07 m) long; Royal Artillery and Sappers and Miners' carbines were 3 ft 10 ins (1.17 m) long. The musket was issued with a seven-inch socket bayonet. Unlike the flintlock Brown Bess, the percussion musket came with crude fore and back sights, which did at least make aimed fire a possibility. In tests, when firing at a screen six feet high and twenty feet wide (1.83 x 6.1 m) – presumably representing a column of the enemy – roughly 75% of shots hit the target, although this declined sharply at longer ranges, and at 400 yards (366 m) only 4% of shots were hits. Even the 1839 pattern came too late for service in the First Afghan War, where the old flintlocks predominated – and, incidentally, were easily outranged by the long-barrelled Afghan jezails – but the percussion musket became the predominant weapon by the 1840s.

Rifling, too, had been recognised as advantageous since Napoleonic times. Rifling was simply a system of grooves cut on the inside of the barrel, twisting evenly down its length and thereby imparting a spinning motion to the projectile in flight, which increased both range and accuracy. Some Napoleonic systems had relied on brute strength for loading, and the marksman simply hammered the bullet into the barrel by means of a ramrod and mallet, so that the soft lead of the ball was forced into the rifling grooves. This system was, inevitably, both imperfect and time-consuming. In 1837 a new rifle adopted for use by Rifle regiments – the 3 ft 10 in (1.17 m) Brunswick – overcame the technical difficulties by incorporating a barrel with just two grooves, opposite one another, and a ball with a raised belt around it which was designed to fit the grooves. The Brunswick also included a more sophisticated and adjustable back sight and, although it saw little active service, results suggest that it was noticeably more accurate than the standard musket, since a good marksman could put the majority of his shots into a two-foot square target at 200 yards' (183 m) range. Because the bullets only fitted into the barrel when correctly aligned with the grooves, however, loading was a fiddly and slow process, and to overcome the risk of the enemy rushing in to attack before it could be achieved, the Napoleonic expedient of issuing a few ordinary musket cartridges, for rapid unaimed fire, was followed.

Although some Guards' sergeants were issued with rifles in the 1840s, it was not until 1851 that the smooth-bore musket was officially replaced. After numerous trials, a design invented by a Belgian, Captain Claude Etienne Minié, was approved. Minié's rifle solved the problem of fitting bullet to rifling by developing a

.577 calibre bullet that was not round but cylindrical-conoidal – basically a stunted version of the shape familiar today – which offered a flat base to the charge, thereby maximising the surface area exposed to it, but which was hollow at the base and expanded under pressure from the explosion to fit the grooves. The rifle was some 4 ft 6 ins (1.37 m) long, weighed 9 lbs (4.3 kg), and was the first to include a perfected sliding ladder backsight, which could be raised or lowered according to range – a system which remained standard throughout much of the nineteenth century. The Minié was sighted up to 1000 yards (915 m), although it took a very good shot to make much practice at that range, even under ideal conditions. Nonetheless, it was a significant improvement on both the Brunswick and the 1842 musket. Small numbers of Miniés were sent out to South Africa, where the musket had proved singularly inappropriate for the bush fighting which characterised the war against the Xhosa, and their improved performance was noted with some satisfaction.

By the time the Crimean War broke out, the Minié had still not been fully distributed, despite being authorised three years before. In some cases rifles were issued only at Varna, and the troops had to make what practice they could with them before they landed in the Crimea. The 1842 musket remained in evidence throughout the war, but all the evidence suggests that the Minié did give the British infantryman an advantage over the Russians, who were still armed with smooth-bores. Russian tactics favoured Napoleon's method of attacking in dense columns; these required a high volume of fire to disrupt them before they struck home, and the Minié allowed the British to open fire at longer ranges, and sustain an accurate fire for longer, thereby causing maximum damage to the head of the attacking column. It is even said that at close range the Minié bullet had enough power to pass clean through several men before being spent, and the dense Russian columns were, therefore, particularly vulnerable to its fire.

In the event, although the Minié was undoubtedly a significant weapon – it was the single most common type used in the American Civil War, for example – it soon became obsolete in the British army, for in 1853 the Board of Ordnance approved the issue of an improved rifle, to be manufactured at the factory at Enfield. The Enfield rifle, basically an improved version of the Minié; was 4 ft 6 ins (1.37 m) long and differed externally from the Minié in that it was the first British rifle to have the barrel fixed to the stock by means of three (in the standard version) iron bands. A shorter version was produced for sergeants, and a carbine version for cavalry and artillery. It had ladder back-sights, sighted up to 1200 yards (1098 m), and like all its predecessors it was a muzzle loader. The .577 bullet came sealed in a paper cartridge which also contained the powder. The soldier had to bite off the end of the cartridge, pour the powder down the barrel, and ram the bullet down after it. Partly to keep the cartridge waterproof, and partly to lubricate the bullet, the cartridge was thinly spread with grease. The nature of the grease was not specified when the cartridges were ordered from contractors, many of whom used the cheapest type available – tallow, which contained animal fats. It was the new Enfield cartridge, and the rumours that the grease had been specially chosen to defile the religions of both Muslims and Hindus, that provoked the outbreak of the Indian Mutiny.

The first Enfield rifles were issued in time to reach the Crimea shortly before the fall of Sebastopol. Although by that stage the fighting was largely static, the new rifle was nonetheless favourably received. Most British troops were armed with it during the Indian Mutiny and, ironically, their success on a number of occasions was due to the fact that the Enfield, which the sepoys had refused to accept, outranged the older patterns carried by the rebels.

In Europe during the 1850s firearm design underwent something of a revolution with the invention of the Prussian 'needle-gun', which

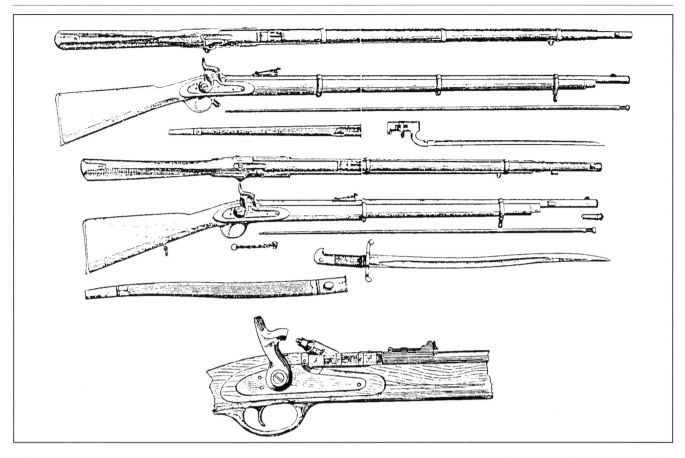

*Above: The Enfield rifle, the most effective infantry weapon of the 1850s.*

*Right: The Snider system enabled Enfield rifles to be converted to a breech-loader.*

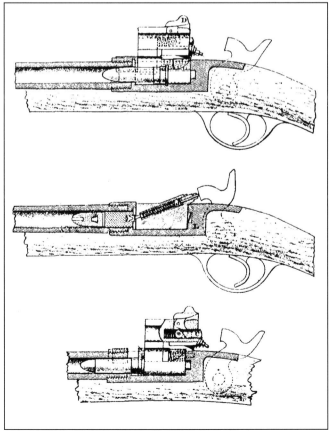

foreshadowed modern weapons in that it was a crude breech-loader which fired a metal cartridge by means of a firing pin, in this case an elongated 'needle' which struck a detonator in the centre of the base of the cartridge. The British army was heavily committed to the percussion system, but by the end of the decade was actively seeking a means of converting its muzzle-loaders to breech-loaders. A number of designs were tested, including those by Terry and Westley Richards, but the system eventually adopted was the Snider. This converted the standard Enfield rifle into a breech-loader by cutting out a section of the barrel to make a breech, and closing it with a hinged breech-block. Although still a percussion weapon, the Snider fired a metal cartridge of the same .577 calibre as the Enfield. From 1866 large numbers of Enfields were taken in for conversion, and the new weapons were therefore the same length as those already in service, but were noticeably lighter. The Snider was sighted up to a range of a thousand yards.

The chief improvement in the Snider system was that it did away with the cumbersome drill of pouring powder and ball down the barrel and ramming it home; the rifle was now loaded simply by opening the breech block and inserting a cartridge. As a result the rate of fire improved dramatically, and this was very evident in the two campaigns in which the Snider was used, in Abyssinia in 1868 and Asante in 1873–4. At the battle of Aroge some 300 men of the 4th Regiment met a charge of 7000 Abyssinians with a volley fired at 250 yards' (229 m) range. The men were then ordered to switch to independent firing, which enabled them to loose off as many as ten shots in a minute, and certainly seven or eight, even under the more stressful conditions of the battlefield. The 4th's line, therefore, was probably producing thirty or forty shots a second – a staggering rate by comparison with the Enfield, and certainly astonishing to the Abyssinians, whose own firearms were obsolete matchlocks or flintlocks. In the rain-forests of Asante, much of the fighting took place at thirty or forty yards' range, but because of the dense undergrowth the enemy could seldom be seen. The enemy's presence was usually therefore revealed by the smoke from their firing, and the British response was to suppress this by firing low, fast volleys in the direction of the smoke. This tactic required the ability to produce a terrific volume of fire at crucial moments, and the Snider was far more capable of this than the Enfield had been.

Nonetheless, the Snider was only a stop-gap, and it was replaced from 1874 with arguably the most famous of late-Victorian firearms, the Martini-Henry. The Martini-Henry represented a complete break with the percussion system, being a single-shot centre-fire falling block weapon; the mechanism was opened by depressing a lever behind the trigger-guard, which caused the block to fall, opening the top of the chamber. The bullet was inserted, the lever pulled back up, the breech closed, and the rifle was ready to fire. It was a simple, robust and effective system which was even quicker to use than the Snider, allowing for up to a dozen shots a minute to be fired. The infantry version was 4 ft (1.22 m) long and weighed 10 lbs (4.76 kg), and a carbine version was produced for cavalry and artillery. The Snider, although displaced amongst regular troops, remained in service with the Volunteers and Militia, and in the Indian army, for at least another decade.

The Martini-Henry was the universal weapon in the Second Afghan, Ninth Cape Frontier, Zulu, Sekhukhune and Transvaal campaigns, and the Sudan expeditions of the 1880s. It was sighted up to 1200 yards (1098 m), but was particularly effective at ranges of less than 400 yards (366 m), when the rear sight-ladder was laid flat, allowing the marksman to aim without craning his neck away from the butt. It fired a lighter bullet than the Snider (.450) and there was some concern that it lacked the 'stopping power' which many soldiers considered was necessary to drop a charging enemy in his tracks. Certainly the old Snider had been capable of producing some horrific and incapacitating injuries, whilst the narrower bullet of the Martini-Henry, and its slightly higher velocity, could clip through flesh producing small, neat injuries which might be overlooked in the heat of battle. Nevertheless, the effect of the bullet striking bone was quite literally

*Above: The Mark II Martini-Henry rifle, the standard infantry firearm of the 1870s and 1880s. (Author's collection)*

shattering, since it had a tendency to flatten on impact with a bone and thereby splinter it lengthways, causing dreadful injuries to limbs, and horrific head wounds; both the Snider and Martini-Henry produced the classic damage mentioned by Kipling, 'a round blue hole in his forehead, and the back blown out of his head'.

The Martini-Henry had other defects, too. After about ten rounds or so the mechanism began to foul and the recoil became more pronounced, so that after very prolonged firing it caused heavy bruising to the shoulder – so much so that, after Rorke's Drift, some soldiers admitted that after perhaps 200 rounds they could only hold their weapon at arm's length, resting on the barricade, and fire away wildly. Furthermore, the weapon became very hot, and it was difficult to support the stock without burning the fingers on the barrel. The first type of cartridge, the Boxer pattern, was of thin rolled brass, and once the weapon was heated the cartridge had a tendency to break apart, causing jamming; either the extractor grip would tear off the base, leaving the rest in the breech, or pieces from the side would stick to the chamber. These defects had been noted in Afghanistan and Zululand, but became particularly apparent in the Sudan, where the terrific rate of fire needed to stop the Mahdist shock-charges, the extreme heat of the desert, and the sand, which got everywhere, combined to produce a disturbingly high incidence of jamming. As a result a new

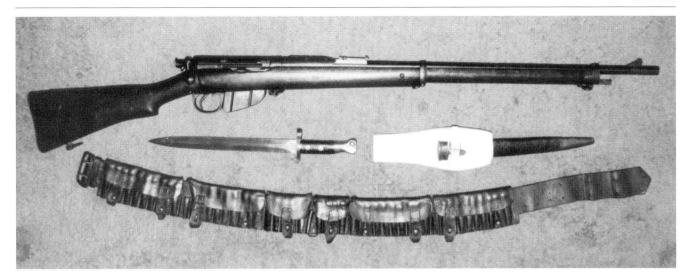

*Above: The first magazine rifle: the bolt-action .303 Lee-Metford, shown here with bayonet and Boer War period bandolier. (Ian Castle Collection)*

*Right: 'Like snowdrifts': despite its poor quality, this photograph gives a revealing glimpse into the devastation wrought by magazine rifles at Omdurman, 1898. (Bryan Maggs Collection)*

cartridge of stronger drawn brass replaced the rolled type from 1885.

In 1888 the British army abandoned the single-shot principal and introduced the first magazine rifle. This was the bolt-action Lee-Metford Mark I, which was 4 ft 1 ins (1.26 m) long, weighed 9 lbs (4.3 kg) and had a rear sight graduated from 300 to 1900 yards (275 to 1739 m). The rounds were fed into the breech from a magazine positioned underneath, in front of the trigger-guard. The Mark I magazine held eight rounds, loaded individually, though a cut-off could be used to convert it to fire single shots. The rate of fire was twelve rounds per minute with the cut-off, or twenty-five per minute from the magazine. In 1892 a slightly revised Mark II was issued, which had an improved ten-round magazine. At about the same time the army approved the issue of cartridges with cordite in place of the old black powder, which burned with less smoke, thus making it almost impossible to detect the position of a concealed

marksman. In 1895 the Lee-Metford was replaced with the Lee-Enfield, which had almost all the same specifications, but with an improved rifling system in the barrel. In 1892 the Martini-Henry carbines carried by cavalry were converted into Martini-Metfords with the addition of the Metford barrel, but in 1896 the Lee-Enfield carbine, just under 4 ft long (1.22 m), was issued to cavalry. Artillery batteries were armed with Martini-Metfords and, from 1896, Martini-Enfields.

The Lee-Metford and Lee-Enfield remained the army's principal small-arms through to the end of the Victorian era and beyond. The 1898 reconquest of the Sudan was largely accomplished with the use of the Lee-Metford, and the majority of troops

began the Boer War with the same rifles, though these were steadily replaced with Lee-Enfields. Both fired the same .303 bullet, and there was some concern that the smaller, slimmer slug lacked the stopping power of the old Martini-Henry. Certainly there were numerous reports of individuals – particularly those in a state of religious ecstasy – being shot many times before they were brought down, and for a while troops were issued with hollow-nosed bullets made at the arsenal at Dum Dum in India. These flattened out on impact causing more damaging wounds, but they were soon withdrawn, and later banned by the Geneva Convention. Indeed, against mass targets any lack of stopping power was more than compensated for by the Lee-Metford's extraordinary rate of fire. This was demonstrated spectacularly in the Sudan, where a veritable hailstorm of fire left Mahdist corpses piled up like snowdrifts. At Atbara the war correspondent G.W. Stevens reported that 'the Warwicks ... were volleying off the blacks as your beard comes off under a keen razor'. At Omdurman a private of the Seaforth Highlanders recalled that 'when they came to 1300 yards we fixed bayonets and rose, firing section volleys, each volley aiming just below a flag. We fired 97 volleys right off'. After the battle many on the British side were deeply moved by the sight of the ground occupied by the Mahdists, strewn as it was with thousands of corpses, but, sadly, the implications of warfare where both sides were armed with such weapons had not been fully appreciated when the Anglo-Boer War broke out a year later.

## The Bayonet

The British soldier began the Victorian era with a socket bayonet which had scarcely changed since the eighteenth century, and which did not alter fundamentally until the adoption of the Lee-Metford rifle in 1888. It had a 17-inch (0.43 m) triangular-section blade with a curved neck which attached to a socket that slotted over the muzzle of the rifle, with a simple zigzag slot to take the foresight. This principal continued into the percussion era, though the 22nd Regiment had found at Miani that they had to tie their bayonets in place

*Below: The Enfield and Martini-Henry socket bayonets of the 1870s.*

with cord to prevent the Baluchis snatching them off, and this was recognised in the 1842 musket by the addition of a spring catch to keep the socket in place. Rifle Regiments, Artillery and Sappers had sword-bayonets. The pattern for the Brunswick rifle had a blade with a slightly leaf-shaped tip, with a brass hilt shaped rather like a Roman sword.

The advent of the Minié and, later, Enfield rifles brought no major change; the bayonet was still a seventeen-inch long socket-type, the only difference being the addition of a ring on the socket which could be turned to lock the blade in place on the muzzle. Sergeants, Rifles and Royal Artillery field batteries had a 23-inch (0.58 m) sword-bayonet with a steel grip and either a straight or slightly curved blade. The bayonet for the Martini-Henry followed the same patterns, but the socket version for ORs was longer at 22 ins (0.56 m). The socket bayonet remained in service with the various conversions of the Martini, but the sockets were 'bushed' to fit the reduced Metford or Enfield barrel.

The Martini-Henry bayonet gave the soldier a formidable reach in hand-to-hand fighting, and was popularly known as 'the lunger'. Hand-to-hand combat in most battles was a rare and usually brief business, but the Zulu and Sudan campaigns both produced examples of protracted or particularly fierce fighting which stressed the bayonet to an unusual degree. After Rorke's Drift Private Hook of the 24th Regiment commented that 'they were very fine weapons too, but some were very poor in quality, and either twisted or bent badly. Several were like that after the fight; but some terrible

thrusts were given, and I saw dead Zulus who had been pinned to the ground by the bayonets going through them'. Similar comments were made after some of the 1885 Sudan battles, where bayonets had apparently bent under the weight of the bodies of charging Mahdists, and reports of these incidents created something of a scandal. The blame was placed on shoddy workmanship, on government parsimony, and even, in some extreme arguments, on a plot by foreign manufacturers to undermine the British army by supplying deliberately faulty steel! In the event a committee appointed to look into the matter found that the Martini-Henry socket bayonet stood up well to all the tests applied to it.

With the advent of the Lee-Enfield and Lee-Metford .303 rifle a plain 12-inch (0.31 m) sword-bayonet was adopted by all ranks except the Royal Artillery, who retained their Martini-Enfields and from 1888 took the old infantry sword-bayonets. Although close-quarter bayonet fighting did occur on occasion in the Boer War, the advent of weapons accurate at longer ranges had made it highly unusual. The Boers generally disliked hand-to-hand fighting, and usually withdrew once it became clear that a British charge was about to strike home; the number of the enemy killed by the bayonet between 1899 and 1902 therefore represented only a tiny proportion of casualties.

## Infantry Swords and Revolvers

Until the aftermath of the Crimean War, infantry officers were required to arm themselves with nothing more than a sword, and that of a pattern adopted in 1822. This had a slightly curved steel blade with a 'pipe back' – that is, a strong spine extending the grip along most of the length of the back of the blade. The hilt was of a type known technically as 'half-basket', in other words protected across the knuckles by bars of flat steel which were shaped to include the Royal cypher. It was carried in a black leather scabbard with brass mountings by all Line, Guards and Rifles battalions, although the Rifles had a steel scabbard.

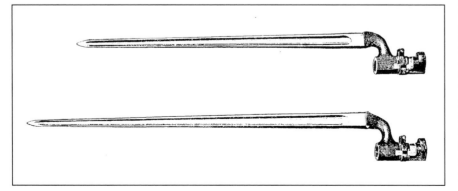

The 1822 pattern sword remained in service until 1891, although the design of the blade was modified in 1845 to reduce the 'pipe', which had interfered with its cutting power. Highland regiments carried the 1828 pattern broadsword, with steel basket grip, although some regiments also carried an undress version of the hilt, which had a plain cross-bar. From 1866 the black leather scabbards gave way to steel ones. The basic infantry pattern (ie, 1822 hilt with 1822 or 1845 blade) was carried by Artillery and Engineer officers, although in 1857 the latter received a brass honeysuckle-pattern hilt. In 1855 the Guards regiments received a slightly modified hilt in which a regimental device replaced the Royal cypher.

In 1891 a new sword was introduced, modified in 1895. The 1895 version had a sheet steel guard with a pierced design including the Royal cypher. Guards and Rifles retained their old 1822-pattern swords throughout, whilst Artillery and Engineer officers adopted the 1895 pattern only (not 1891). Broadswords were adopted in Lowland regiments from 1881, except amongst the Cameronians, who followed Rifle practice. General Officers carried a curved sword with Mameluke pattern hilt throughout the Victorian period.

Infantry sergeant-majors and staff sergeants carried brass-hilted versions of the officer pattern swords throughout. In Highland regiments these ranks' swords had iron hilts. In addition, Highland pipers, drummers and bandsmen carried a slightly shorter version of the same sword until 1871 when they were replaced with dirks. In Line regiments from 1856 drummers and buglers carried straight swords with a 19-inch (0.48 m) straight blade and a brass Roman-style guard. In 1891 the guards were made plainer and the length reduced by 6 inches (0.15 m).

The infantry sword was not an ideal weapon to fight with in colonial campaigning. It was cumbersome to carry in the field when moving through the bush, and had limited practical value. It was useful enough when encouraging the men, but was seldom strong enough to ward off the blow from a heavier Sikh talwar or a Mahdist straightsword. By the time of the Anglo-Boer War it was a positive disadvantage, since the Boers identified officers by their swords, and picked them off accordingly. This was not only unnecessarily dangerous for the individuals concerned, but it also meant that attacks might lose momentum through lack of direction, and within a few months of the start of the Boer War the use of swords amongst infantry officers was all but abandoned. As early as the China War of 1839–42 a Lieutenant Murray of the 18th Regiment had noted the sword's limitations, and was armed with a pistol as well as a sword when attacked by a Chinese swordsman: 'having no particular confidence in my regulation spit, or perhaps my skill as a swordsman, I stuck my sword in the mud beside me, took a steady aim, and shot him'.

Many officers had provided themselves with flintlock or percussion pistols since Napoleonic times, but the habit only became universal following the Great Exhibition of 1851, where the new revolvers of Messrs Adams and Colt were widely admired. The single-shot pistol had only been useful for close-quarter fighting as a last resort, but the revolver principal – in which a chamber containing several bullets revolved around a central axis, bringing each chamber in turn in line with the barrel – offered the prospect of a greatly increased rate of fire. Neither Adams nor Colt had invented the system, but both had independently developed production models which were fired by the percussion principal, but avoided the common problem of one discharge igniting all the rounds. Colt was an American but his factory had failed in his own country, and he set up business instead in London, provoking a fierce rivalry with British gunsmith Adams which intensified during the increased demand caused by the Crimean War and Indian Mutiny. Colt's revolver had six chambers and proved accurate at longer ranges than Adams' five-shot model, but whereas the Adams system was double action – one pull on the trigger cocked it and fired it – Colt's was single action, meaning that the hammer had to be cocked by hand for each round. Adams' revolver also fired a heavier bullet. The difference that this made – and the reason why Adams won the trade war, at least amongst British military customers – is ably demonstrated in an anecdote by Lieutenant-Colonel G.V. Fosbery, concerning the Mutiny:

An officer, who especially prided himself on his pistol-shooting, was attacked by a stalwart mutineer armed with a heavy sword. The officer, unfortunately for himself, carried a Colt's Navy pistol, which ... was of a small calibre and fired a sharp-pointed bullet of sixty to the pound and a heavy charge of powder, its range being at least 600 yards, as I have frequently proved. This he proceeded to empty into the sepoy as he advanced, but, having done so, he waited just one second too long to see the effect of his shooting, and was cloven to the teeth by his antagonist, who then dropped down dead beside him. My informant, who witnessed the affair, told me that five of the six bullets had struck the sepoy close together in the chest, and that all had passed through him and out of his back.

The Adams revolver had considerably more stopping power, and was quicker to use – exactly the requirements of British officers in colonial campaigning. Both systems, of course, took a long time to reload, as each chamber had to be filled with the charge, the bullet loaded, and the caps primed. The 1860s, however, saw marked improvements in revolver design, notably with the invention by Smith and Wesson of a hinged frame, that 'broke' to facilitate loading, and the development of an effective centre-fire cartridge. Although officers were still allowed to purchase whatever makes took

*Left: A typical revolver from the 1870s: the Webley Irish Constabulary model. This particular example belonged to Lieutenant John Chard, RE, and is thought to have been used by him at the battle of Rorke's Drift. (Royal Engineers Museum)*

their fancy, they were increasingly recommended to follow types which were compatible with the .45 ammunition issued by the government. Webley's 1867 Royal Irish Constabulary model proved very popular in the campaigns of the 1870s, as did the Mark II Adams, although few officers apparently bothered with much practice. During the Zulu War officers sent as reinforcements to South Africa indulged in target practice as the ship approached Durban, using a variety of targets, including passing sea-gulls and a shark; however, very little damage was inflicted all round, which perhaps explains the lack of respect felt by the Zulus for revolvers. In battle, during a melee, the revolver had a far more limited range than Lieutenant-Colonel Fosbery claimed – it was probably not accurate at much more than 25 yards (22.9 m), and even then it took a steady hand to place the shot well. Small wonder that, as one Zulu commander commented, the British at Isandlwana 'shot a great deal with "little guns", but they didn't shoot well. For every man they killed they fired a great many shots without hitting anybody'.

In 1880 the Board of Ordnance accepted the .477 Enfield revolver for use by senior sergeants in the Royal Artillery, but in 1887 switched to the

slightly lighter .455 Webley. The Webley proved to be strong, reliable and accurate, and in 1900 the army finally abandoned the policy of allowing officers to choose their own revolvers, and formally recommended that they used the Webley.

**Cavalry Weapons**

Throughout the Victorian period the British cavalry remained committed to the concept of the *arme blanche* – shock action with close-quarter weapons, chiefly the sword. Although, as the century wore on, the relevance of this concept in an age of accurate long-range firearms was increasingly challenged by radical cavalry theorists, the cavalry remained armed with swords, and only in the latter stages of the Boer War did they begin to fight increasingly as Mounted Infantry – on foot, with carbines.

The theoretical difference between Light and Heavy cavalry also became blurred during the Victorian period. In 1837, each had their own swords, both of patterns approved in the 1820s. The Lights were armed with a single-edged sword with a slightly curved blade and a three-bar hilt, whilst the Heavies also had a single-edged sword, slightly curved, but with a plain bowl guard for ORs and a scrolled hilt for officers. These

weapons were also issued to other units whose men performed mounted duties: the Royal Horse Artillery, for example, were generally issued with Light cavalry weapons, and the Royal Artillery with Heavy cavalry weapons, until the advent of universal pattern swords from the 1850s.

In 1853 a universal pattern sword was issued to both Light and Heavy cavalry troopers, which reflected the fact that in the field there was very little difference between their duties. The 1853-pattern sword was slightly curved, with a single edge, and had a three-bar guard. Only two regiments received this weapon before the Crimean War, and neither was particularly impressed with it. Officers continued to equip themselves with the older pattern weapons.

Up to the 1860s, swords were sheathed in plain steel scabbards. This had the effect of blunting the blades, and it was very difficult to maintain a keen edge, with the result that, in the heat of battle, cuts were often turned aside by the enemy's clothing or equipment. Similarly, any faults in the blade's construction became apparent when using the point, and it was not unusual for blades to buckle or snap rather than go through a human body. This accounts for the relatively light casualties inflicted during many cavalry actions. Properly used, however, a sharp sword could wreak carnage, but although there are many references to men receiving or inflicting wounds these were often essentially superficial. Indeed, both Heavy and Light cavalry were issued with gauntlets, with the specific intention of protecting the hands during sword fighting; of course, a strong blow with a sharp sword would hardly have been deflected by a gauntlet. At Balaclava the Heavy Brigade cut its way clean through a Russian cavalry force which considerably outnumbered it, yet eight minutes of fierce sword fighting only cost the Russians 270 casualties, and the Heavies seventy. This ineffectiveness of British swords contrasted notably with Indian regiments, where wooden scabbards were preferred and the common practice was to hone the blades to as sharp a point and edge as possible. Cavalry actions involving Indian troops therefore tended to be far more destructive, as an anecdote about Rumnaggar by Sergeant Forbes-Mitchell of the 93rd Highlanders suggests:

[The Sikhs] evidently knew that the British swords were blunt and useless, so they kept their horses still and met the British charge by laying flat on their horses' necks, with their heads protected by the thick turban and their backs by the shields; immediately the British soldiers passed through their ranks the Sikhs swooped round on them and struck them back-handed with their sharp, curved swords, in several instances cutting our cavalrymen in two. In one case a British officer was hewn in two by a back-handed stroke which cut right through an ammunition pouch, cleaving the pistol bullets right through the pouch and belt, severing the officer's backbone, and cutting his heart in two from behind.

At Tel-el-Kebir a trooper of the 7th Dragoons commented that 'the best fellows for fighting are the Indian troops. They cut heads off as if they were cabbages and the head fell in many cases eight foot away from the body'.

In 1864 some attempt was made to remedy the disadvantages of the scabbard design by issuing a new sword with a steel scabbard lined with wood. The 1864-pattern sword had the same blade as the 1853 pattern, but with a plain sheet metal guard pierced with the design of a Maltese cross. Officers continued with the older patterns until 1896, when they adopted the old Heavy Cavalry type with a scroll pattern guard. Household cavalry swords were slightly longer than the universal patterns, and in 1882 they adopted a straight blade, but in 1890 they were brought into line with the standard issue sword of that year. The 1864-pattern sword, carried in Zululand and Afghanistan, still had its problems. The sword rattled in the scabbard, making it difficult to achieve any degree of surprise, even when dismounted, and in the fighting around Kabul Roberts noted that the 9th Lancers frequently tripped over their swords when fighting on foot, and sometimes had difficulty in reaching their carbines, which were carried in buckets on their saddles. He solved this problem by the simple expedient of allowing them to strap their sabres to the saddle, and to carry their carbines on the back.

In 1882 the 1864 sword was further modified by turning in the edges of the guard, so that they didn't jar so much against the legs when the sword was sheathed, and a new scabbard was issued with fixed rings on either side, rather than the old hinged rings on the back alone. A scandal in 1884 – when it was discovered that up to 50% of the swords of the 2nd Dragoons, then in England but about to go overseas, bent or broke when tested – led to another refinement, the 1885 pattern, which broadly followed the design of the 1864 pattern but with a stronger 34½-inch (0.88 m) blade. This pattern was in turn issued with minor adaptations in 1890, and could be carried either on sword-slings or strapped to a leather frog on the saddle. A final variant, issued in 1899, was shorter and thinner than most previous types, and was generally disliked, but only troops reaching South Africa in the later stages of the Boer War carried it in the field.

Until 1868 the Lancers' principal weapon was a 9 ft (2.75 m) ash lance, with a steel point and a steel shoe which slotted into a cup on the off-side stirrup, to make the weapon easier to carry when not in action. It had a red-over-white pennon, and a buff leather wrist-strap. From 1868 ash was replaced with hard 'male' bamboo, but the dimensions remained the same. The lance was primarily intended to give the cavalryman extra reach in combat; on a number of occasions in almost all theatres it proved particularly useful in skewering an enemy who lay on the ground to escape the sword. In the Anglo-Boer War, following a successful charge by the 5th Lancers at Elandslaagte, the Boers declared that they would shoot any Lancer who fell into their hands; they hated the lance, which they considered an uncivilised weapon unfit for use against a Christian enemy. In a prolonged scrimmage, however, once the shock of impact had passed, many Lancers found the weapon impractical, and often resorted instead to their swords or carbines. At one point in the Eighth Cape Frontier War the 9th Lancers replaced their lances with double-barrelled carbines. Nonetheless, in 1892 it was decided to issue lances to the front rank of all Dragoon regiments, to enhance their shock-value in the charge.

Carbines, indeed, had always been regarded as the cavalry's secondary weapon. In 1837 both Heavy and Light regiments were armed with flintlock weapons, but these were replaced from 1839 with the single-shot, muzzle-loading Victoria percussion carbine, which was 3 ft 6 ins (1.07 m) long. Carbines were either carried strapped muzzle down on the saddle, or from a ring attached to the ammunition pouch-belt worn over the shoulder. Lancer regiments did not carry carbines at this period, but rather a pistol, carried in a wallet in front of the saddle. These became percussion models in 1842. These weapons were used in the campaigns of the 1840s and 1850s, including the Crimea, with minor local variations; at Zwartkopjes in 1845 the 7th Dragoons engaged the Boers with Brunswick rifles borrowed from the 60th, but these proved difficult to manage on horseback and by the time the War of the Axe broke out they had returned to the carbine.

From 1855 the Board of Ordnance began to experiment with various types of breech-loading carbines. Various makes were tested, but in 1866 it was decided to opt for the .45 Westley-Richards carbine, which was some 3 ft (0.92 m) long, weighed 6½ lbs (2.94 kg), and was sighted to 800 yards (732 m). Lancers lost their pistols in favour of carbines at about this time, which were increasingly carried in saddle-buckets. In 1877 the 3 ft Martini-Henry carbine, which was sighted up to 1000 yards (915 m), was taken into service; this was replaced with the Martini-Metford carbine, to bring it into line with the .303 cartridge, in 1892. In 1894 this was replaced in turn by the magazine-fed Lee-Metford, and in 1896 by the Lee-Enfield.

## Artillery

In 1837 the Royal Artillery was still largely trained, equipped and organised as it had been in the Napoleonic era. There was a fundamental distinction between the Royal Horse Artillery and the Royal (field) Artillery, which reflected the different role they had been created to perform. Horse artillery batteries were intended to act in close support of the cavalry; they were therefore required to be mobile; their guns were generally lighter than those of the Royal Artillery, and their gunners were mounted. The field batteries were expected to support the infantry, and mobility was not such a priority; their guns were heavier, and the gunners walked beside the limbers. The standard tactical unit for the Royal Horse Artillery was the troop, and for the Royal Artillery the battery, each commanded by a

Captain and consisting of four guns and two howitzers, with an ammunition wagon for each weapon. One gun, its limber and ammunition wagon made up a sub-division; two guns made a division, and there was a right, left, and centre division in each battery or troop.

Until the first faltering steps towards breech-loaders in the 1860s, all guns were smooth-bore muzzle-loaders. A Royal Horse Artillery troop usually consisted of four 6 pdr guns and two 12 pdr howitzers, whilst a Royal Artillery battery consisted of four 9pdr guns and two 24 pdr howitzers. The gun barrels were usually made of brass and the howitzers' of iron, and both were mounted on wooden carriages. The 6 pdr – probably the single most common gun used in action until the 1860s – was sighted up to 1200 yards (1098 m), and the 9 pdr to 1400 yards (1281 m). The working of all muzzle-loading guns was essentially unsophisticated: a standard pre-packed charge was rammed down the barrel, followed by a round projectile, often attached to a 'sabot', a round wooden plug at the base which prevented gasses from escaping around the edge of the projectile when it was fired. A gunner would use a small metal spike, a 'pricker', to clear the vent, and the piece would then be discharged, either by applying a slow-burning match to the vent or, from the middle of the century, using more sophisticated percussion and friction techniques. Between each shot the gun had to be sponged out, to prevent any burning embers in the barrel igniting the next round prematurely, whilst a gunner 'served the vent', covering it over with his thumb to stop a draft causing sparks. Each battery or troop had a mixture of ammunition types: solid shot, shrapnel, and case. Solid shot was simply a round iron cannon ball, used mainly for destroying walls or fortifications, or firing at heavy concentrations of enemy troops. It was particularly destructive against troops in column, or when used in enfilading fire from the flank, since a single round-shot would bowl over any troops in its line of flight like skittles, cutting men in half, or knocking off heads and limbs. Shrapnel, which had

been invented at the end of the eighteenth century by Lieutenant Henry Shrapnel, RA, was a round-shot fitted with a fuse and an explosive charge, and filled with lead balls; under ideal circumstances, a shrapnel shell was intended to burst over the heads of the enemy, showering them with the balls. Case shot, or canister, was a container of iron or lead balls which disintegrated as it left the muzzle, spraying its contents over a wide area like a giant shotgun. Howitzers also fired 'carcasses', incendiary shells which either burst on impact or exploded in the air and floated down supported by a parachute, lighting up the area below for several minutes. From 1878 star shells were available which exploded in air-bursts, releasing twenty-four magnesium stars which burned brightly for a few seconds, throwing an intense light on everything below. Under battlefield conditions rates of fire were two rounds per minute for round-shot and three for case, although considerably higher rates were possible in theory.

In addition to the 6, 9, 12 and 24 pdrs, there were a number of heavy guns, 18 pdrs and up, which were regarded as placement artillery – ie, to be deployed in fixed positions – or siege artillery, to be used to destroy enemy emplacements. These guns functioned as part of siege batteries, and were sometimes augmented by even heavier naval guns, supplied by Royal Navy landing parties. At Sebastopol, for example, the Navy supplied a number of 68 pdrs, whilst in the Indian Mutiny six 64 pdrs were used to devastating effect at Lucknow, and in New Zealand two enormous 110 pdr Armstrong breech-loaders were used – without great success – in an attempt to demolish Maori *pas*.

In the 1850s the Royal Artillery began to experiment with a number of rifled breech-loading weapons, chiefly of the Armstrong or Whitworth patterns. The rifle system had the same advantages for artillery as it did for small arms: the grooving in the barrel caused the shell to spin, and greatly improved range an accuracy. Rifled guns required elongated projectiles – there was nothing on round-shot to grip the grooves – and the new system therefore led to the development of improved fuses and shells, the phasing out of round-shot, and the increased importance of shrapnel. From the early 1860s Royal Horse Artillery batteries were equipped with 9 pdr Armstrongs, and Royal Artillery batteries with 12 pdr Armstrongs, both with steel barrels. This had a knock-on effect with regard to organisation, and both troops and batteries were increasingly armed with six guns, rather than four guns and two howitzers. Armstrong guns were used in China in 1860, and in the New Zealand Maori Wars, where they were found to be generally effective. Nonetheless, problems with breech-mechanisms, and the lessons of the American Civil War – where most of the fighting was carried out at close range, and powerful smooth-bores were more popular than more accurate breech-loaders – led to a triumph of conservatism, and a return to the muzzle-loading system in the 1870s, albeit with rifled barrels and using improved shells. In 1871 the standard field-pieces were the 9 pdr RML (Rifled Muzzle Loader) for RHA troops, which was sighted between

*Below: A battery of 5-inch howitzers in action during the Boer War. (Bryan Maggs Collection)*

2000 and 3300 yards (1830 and 3020 m), and the 16 pdr for RA batteries, sighted between 1800 and 4000 yards (1647 and 3660 m). Both guns were mounted on iron carriages, which were much stronger than the old wooden type, and this was changed in 1884 to steel; the carriage was painted grey and the barrel black. From 1880 a number of RHA troops were armed with a heavier 13 pdr RML; this proved a short-term measure, but two of the RHA troops sent to the Egyptian War were armed with these guns.

By the end of the 1870s, the British army was significantly out of step with its European rivals, who had long since adopted the breech-loading system. Indeed, by 1880 it was increasingly clear that the muzzle-loader was a dead-end, which allowed no further development or improvement, and in 1885 a new 12 pdr breech-loader sighted up to 5000 yards (4575 m) was issued to both RA batteries and RHA troops. With the introduction of cordite, which produced a greater detonation than black powder, it was possible to increase the calibre by adapting existing barrels, and the 12 pdr was converted to a 15 pdr amongst RA field batteries. In 1896 howitzers were reintroduced to provide a more effective arm to tackle an entrenched enemy, but, rather than return to the

old system of distributing different gun types within a battery, a number of batteries were created specially equipped with 5-inch breech-loading howitzers. The 12 pdr, 15 pdr and 5-inch howitzer were the principal weapons used throughout the Anglo-Boer War, the only significant change being the introduction of lyddite in 1898, a new high-explosive charge to replace cordite. In 1889 there was a change of organisation, with the old two-gun divisions now being styled sections.

One advantage of the introduction of breech-loading weapons, and the general improvements in design, was that guns became lighter. Until the 1850s it required twelve horses to draw the 18 pdr siege gun and limber, eight to draw the 9 pdr, 24 pdr and 32 pdr, and six to draw the 7 pdr and 12 pdr. The Armstrong breech-loaders of the 1860s needed only six horses to draw them, and by the 1870s most batteries used six-horse limbers. In India, bullocks were often used instead of horses, certainly until the 1860s, and the same expedient was also occasionally adopted in South Africa. Indeed, in India it was common for heavy artillery to be drawn or carried by elephants until right up to and even into the twentieth century.

In addition to the standard field pieces, a number of lighter weapons were employed where the situation called for them. In New Zealand, the Maori skill at constructing defensive earthworks led to the use of small 'coehorn' mortars, which were carried by hand, whilst light 'mountain' artillery was always popular on the North-West Frontier, where it was more suited to the rugged terrain. From the late 1860s the 7 pdr RML was the standard gun for mountain batteries, and it was also used in Abyssinia in 1868 and Asante in 1873. The 7 pdr was mounted on a small, light carriage, and could be dismantled and carried by mules. The same weapon was also used in South Africa in the 1870s, but the small carriage was found to be unsuitable in the hilly country of the Cape Frontier. Here it was mounted on slightly modified versions of the

9 pdr RML carriage instead; two such guns, belonging to N/5 battery, were over-run by the Zulus at Isandlwana. A 2.5-inch RML, the famous 'screw-gun', which could also be easily dismantled, carried on mules, and quickly re-assembled, remained in service on the frontier throughout the Victorian period.

Despite the improvements in weapon technology, and changes in tactical theory, the Royal Artillery still fought in 1899 in a way which the gunners of the Napoleonic Wars would have recognised. With no effective means of aiming indirect fire, firing was still carried out over open sights, against an enemy whose positions could be seen, and who, in turn, could see the guns. For more than half a century the Artillery had been used to fighting enemies who were armed with ineffective small arms, and who preferred to fight at close quarters, as the practice of arming gunners with swords, carbines and revolvers for personal protection bore witness. No attempt had been made to develop gun carriages with shields to protect the crews, because, on the whole, it had not been necessary. When the British army went into the Boer War, therefore, it was singularly unprepared to face an enemy who could pick off gunners at ranges which had hitherto been considered safe, and the disasters at Colenso and elsewhere were the result.

### Rockets

Although perhaps the least sophisticated aspect of the British army's firepower during the nineteenth century, rockets nonetheless played a

*Above: Royal Artillery battery in Abyssinia in 1868, with 7 pdr guns on mountain carriages. (Bryan Maggs Collection)*

*Below: A battery of 2.5 inch RML 'screw guns' on the North-West Frontier, 1897. Note the transport mules behind. (Bryan Maggs Collection)*

*Above: Naval Brigade rocket detachment with rocket-tubes, Abyssinia, 1868. (Bryan Maggs Collection)*

small but significant part, particularly during the colonial campaigns from 1868 to 1881.

The British military rocket had been designed by Sir William Congreve, and was first used during the Napoleonic Wars. It was, in effect, little more than a glorified firework; a metal tube containing a black-powder propellant, fired from a hardened leather trough, and stabilised in flight by a stick attached to the tail. Rockets had been used in colonial warfare from 1816, when the EIC established its first rocket battery, and were used in large numbers during the First Burma War of 1824-5. Here they had displayed all the abiding characteristics which were to dog their development for the next fifty years; although the rockets had a considerable psychological impact on the enemy, howling in flight and spewing out sparks and smoke, and had some success in setting fire to wooden Burmese stockades, they were almost impossible to direct with any accuracy. Although they tended to fly straight on leaving the tube, they could be easily deflected by sudden gusts of wind, and on striking any obstacle tended to bounce off at unpredictable angles – it was not unknown for them to come back towards their crews.

During the Crimean War, a number of artillery batteries were equipped with 6 pdr and 12 pdr Con-greve rockets, which had hollow heads which could be filled with a bursting charge and fuse. They were primarily intended as incendiary devices, and had a range of 600 and 1000 yards (549 and 915 m) respectively. They were used at all the principal battles, and a number were employed in the Indian Mutiny, but nevertheless, by the 1860s the Congreve system was largely discredited. Partly under pressure from the Duke of Cambridge, tests were undertaken to try to find a rocket system which was more accurate and reliable. The result was the Hale's rocket, which was approved in July 1867. Hale's system was similar to Congreve's, but instead of a stick for stability, the Hales's rocket had a number of flanges at the vent, which deflected the jet, and caused the rocket to spin in flight, giving it a more reliable trajectory. Hale's rockets consisted of a metal tube, which encased the propellant, and a domed cap, which contained no charge but was filled with oak. They were produced in two sizes, 9 lb and 24 lb (4.08 and 10.87 kg), the 9 pdr being just under 7 ins long, and the 24 pdr 23 ins. They had a burning time of eight and ten seconds respectively, and ranges of 500–600 yards (458–549 m) at 5° elevation, and over 1500 yards (1373 m) at 15° elevation. The Hale's rocket was first used during the Abyssinian War by a Royal Naval Rocket Brigade, where 9 pdr rockets were fired from tubes similar to the old Congreve apparatus. However, from June 1868 a new rocket trough was approved, first for the 9 pdr and later for the 24 pdr. This consisted of a 'V' shaped trough of metal, supported at the back by a tripod contraption; a movable arm connected to the longest supporting leg served to lower or elevate the trough. The rocket was placed at the back of the trough, and fired by a lanyard attached to a friction tube, which was screwed into the vent; the lanyard man was expected to lay the cord under his right foot, and give the other end a sharp tug with his left hand. Rockets were painted red and troughs black; in practice RA batteries tended to use the lighter 9 pdr rockets, whilst 24 pdrs were often supplied by Naval landing parties. Because of the particular conditions of ship-board service, the Navy continued to use a rocket tube which had a stanchion arrangement to clamp over the side of a ship; for land operations this was replaced with a tripod.

Although the Hale's rocket achieved some notable successes in Abyssinia, it was nonetheless as prone to error as the Congreve. For one thing, any degree of accuracy depended on the apparatus being set up on flat ground – not always easy to achieve on the battlefield. If the aim was not spoilt by the action of firing, the rocket could still be easily deflected. Furthermore, the propellant was unpredictable, particularly if badly stored or damp; it might explode almost immediately on launching, or it might fizzle out altogether. A Lieutenant T. Main of the Royal Engineers, who found himself temporarily in charge of a rocket battery during the Ninth

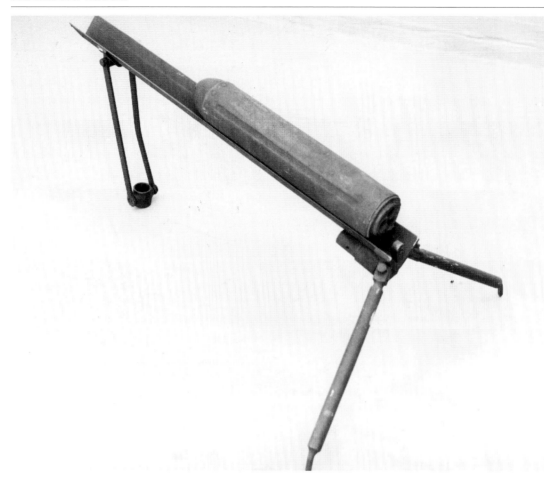

*Left: A 9 pdr rocket-tube which saw service in the Anglo-Zulu War; part of the supporting frame is missing. The rocket is of the heavier 24 pdr type. (Natal Museum, Pietermaritzburg)*

*Below: Rockets in action on the Frontier in the 1890s; their trail is sufficiently vivid for the camera to register. Two have struck the top of the hill, whilst a third falls off to the right. (Bryan Maggs Collection)*

Cape Frontier War, recalled that on one occasion a rocket exploded on leaving the trough, and a fragment severed the ear of the lanyard man. Rockets were primarily intended as psychological weapons, to overawe the enemy, but a detachment of two rocket troughs was overrun at Isandlwana after the Zulus singularly failed to throw down their arms in terror. Indeed, at the battle of Nyezane, which took place elsewhere in Zululand on the same day (22 January 1879), Lieutenant Lloyd RA, commanding a rocket battery, commented:

> The rockets, as I expected, proved of little value; so much has been said of their moral effect on savages, but, to my mind, the Zulus displayed the utmost contempt for them. The enormous 24-pounder Hale's war rocket fired by the Naval Brigade seemed to cause as much anxiety to our own men as to the enemy.

Nonetheless, several witnesses who examined the Zulu dead after the battle commented that 'some of [them] were terribly burned', and a number of travellers met Zulu survivors who displayed scars from horrific injuries caused by the burning propellant falling on their bodies.

The Zulu War was, perhaps, the rocket's finest hour. Rockets were used again in South Africa, at Laing's Nek in 1881, but to poor effect, and in small numbers in West Africa – Benin and Nigeria – in 1897, and even at the Atbara in the Sudan. Nevertheless, by the end of the century they were increasingly regarded as obsolete.

### Machine-Guns

If the war-rocket seems a curiously archaic contraption today, the machine-gun, which played an increasing role in Western warfare from the middle of the century, seems all too modern.

Although the concept of a machine-operated gun, firing rounds quicker and in greater quantity than a single rifleman was capable of, was almost as old as the invention of the firearm itself, the precursor of the modern machine-gun was invented by an American, Dr Richard Gatling,

in 1862. Gatling hoped that the Civil War, then raging between the States, would provide his market, but in fact the early 'Gatling gun' received only limited use towards the end of the war. Instead, Gatling turned his attention towards Europe, where political rivalries were intense, and here he found a number of customers, including the British government, who bought the weapon from 1871. It was manufactured under licence by the Armstrong company in Birmingham, and the Gatling became the first – and arguably the most famous – of a number of similar multi-barrelled guns used in colonial campaigns.

Gatling's system worked by rotating a number of barrels – ten, of .45 calibre, in the British version – around a fixed central axis. Cartridges were fed into the breach by gravity from a hopper which slotted into the top, and the gun was operated by turning a handle. At each

*Below: The Gatling gun; the first of the multi-barrelled machine-guns used by both the Army and Navy in the 1870s. (Author's collection)*

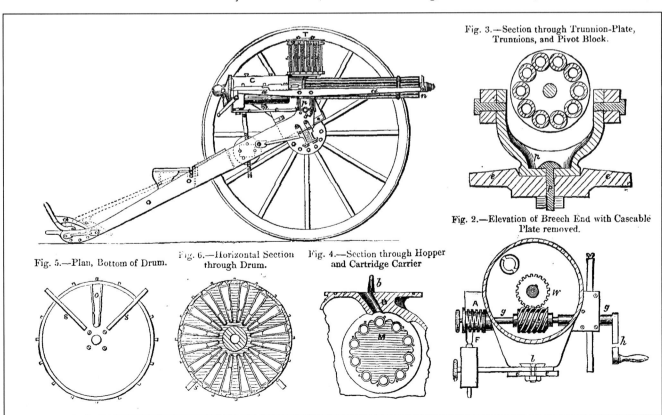

Fig. 3.—Section through Trunnion-Plate, Trunnions, and Pivot Block.

Fig. 2.—Elevation of Breech End with Cascable Plate removed.

Fig. 5.—Plan, Bottom of Drum.

Fig. 6.—Horizontal Section through Drum.

Fig. 4.—Section through Hopper and Cartridge Carrier

turn the barrels moved round in sequence, and individual bolts pushed the cartridge into them, fired them, and extracted them by turn. The rate of fire was 200 rounds per minute, and the gun was sighted up to 2000 yards (1830 m). In fact the Royal Navy appreciated the gun's potential before the army, since it was an ideal weapon to sweep the decks of an enemy ship at close range, or to counter the small, fast torpedo boat, which had just become a factor in marine warfare. Naval Gatlings could be adapted to fix on the side of ships or in platforms among the masts, and were equally useful as fire support for small landing parties. Thus, although the Gatling is widely associated with the campaigns of the 1870s and 1880s, it was usually operated by Naval – rather than army – crews.

Sir Garnet Wolseley took two Gatlings with him to Asante in 1873, mounted on light artillery-style carriages. Although they proved impractical for offensive operations – they were too wide for narrow forest tracks, and had to be manhandled into place because tsetse flies made it impossible to use horses – they were left along the river Pra, the border with Asante, to guard against Asante counter-attack. They were not used in action, but were fired into the river to impress a group of Asante envoys with British might. The first time that Gatlings were used with a British force was at Nyezane in the

Zulu War, where a Naval Brigade Gatling helped check a determined Zulu advance. Naval Gatlings were also used at Gingindlovu, where they were placed in the corner of a square – soon to become a common practice – and an RA half-battery of two guns saw action at the final battle of oNdini (Ulundi). When they worked, they were quite devastating, cutting clearly visible swathes through the enemy lines, and prompting one Zulu survivor to comment 'you stand still and only by turning something round make the bodies of our warriors fly to pieces; legs here, arms there, heads, everything. Whouw! What can we do against that?'. Lord Chelmsford was amongst the first to realise that the chief value of the machine-gun was as an infantry support weapon. They did, however, have their drawbacks, since after repeated use the retractor grip sometimes tore the base off the soft Boxer cartridges, leaving the rest in the breach, and causing jamming; at oNdini some of the bolts slipped out, causing delays as the crews searched for them in the long grass. Nevertheless, Naval Gatlings were used very successfully in Egypt, to clear the streets at Alexandria, and later to lay down a screen of fire on the Egyptian trenches at Tel-el-Kebir. They were also used, with rather less success, in the Suakin campaigns in 1884-5.

From the late 1870s the Navy began to replace its Gatlings with the five-barrelled Gardner gun.

Unlike the Gatling, the Gardner was a fixed barrel weapon. The ammunition was contained in parallel rows in a vertical magazine, and the rounds fell down into the breech of all five barrels more or less simultaneously. A turn of the handle moved the bolts forward, striking all five rounds within a split second of each other, so as to produce a cyclic burst of fire. The Gardner could fire 120 rounds a minute, and several were manned by Naval crews during the 1885 Sudan campaigns, around Suakin – both Gatlings and Gardners were used at El Teb – and on the Khartoum expedition. At Abu Klea, however, the Gardners jammed, contributing to the confusion which allowed the Mahdists to push into the square. The Gardner's service was short-lived, and from 1880 the Navy began to replace it with the four-barrelled Nordenfeldt. The Nordenfeldt was a comparatively simple and effective system which operated by moving a handle forward and backward, a movement which engaged the bolts, fired the rounds, and, on the backwards stroke, extracted the rounds.

For all the Navy's keenness to try new systems, however, multi-bar-

*Below: Maxim gun detachment in the field, Pathan Revolt, 1897. The guns are mounted on tripods and carried on mules; note the mule with ammunition boxes, right. (Bryan Maggs Collection)*

*Above: Maxim gun on horse-drawn carriage, 62nd (Wiltshire) Regiment, near Norval's Pont, Boer War. (National Army Museum)*

relled machine-guns were eclipsed at the end of the 1880s by a revolutionary new system, invented by another American, Hiram Maxim, and wholeheartedly embraced by the British army. The Maxim gun had just one barrel, and was trigger-operated; rather than depending on the sweat of the operator, it utilised the gun's own recoil to extract a spent cartridge, move another into the breach, and fire it. In theory, all the operator had to do was keep his finger on the trigger, and the Maxim would spray out bullets as long as his ammunition lasted. Overheating was an inherent risk in any such system, but Maxim countered this by surrounding the barrel with a cylinder full of water. The Maxim was sighted up to 2000 yards (1830 m), and could fire an astonishing 600 rounds per minute, fed by belts of 250 rounds apiece. The advantages of the Maxim were so obvious that from 1891 it was widely adopted as an infantry and cavalry support weapon. It could be mounted on a metal tripod, and carried by mule, or on a two-wheeled carriage. Rather than being distributed amongst battalions or squadrons, it was usually grouped into two-gun sections under brigade control. A cavalry section consisted of one officer and seventeen crew, with two four-horse ammunition carts, whilst an infantry section consisted of twelve NCOs and men and two two-horse carts.

Despite its obvious advantages, the Maxim generated no very new tactical theory, at least until the later stages of the Boer War. It was regarded simply as a support weapon, an addition to existing firepower, although its strengths in defensive positions were demonstrated several times on the North-West Frontier. It was used to good effect by both relief columns during the Chitral campaign, and at Omdurman Kitchener's Maxims were deployed at intervals along the line. Although they over-heated during the battle – an interesting comment on the extent to which they were used – they undoubtedly contributed in no small part to the mayhem wrought among the Mahdists, who literally ran into their path. A description of the Maxim in action at Omdurman leaves no doubt as to its destructive power, and foreshadows the yet more grim slaughter to come in the First World War:

The Maxim Det[achment] nearest to us Irish Fusiliers, I heard the Captain say steady now men, cease fire and wait till they come over the rise, pointing it out about 650 or 750 yards away. As they came over he said now, traversing fire commence and as the guns went from right to left they simply fell down in line, just the same as if they had been told to lie down. Some of the bodies they saw afterwards had been hit with bullets five and six times in a line across their bodies before they fell.

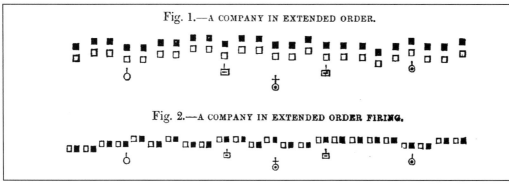

Fig. 1.—A COMPANY IN EXTENDED ORDER.

Fig. 2.—A COMPANY IN EXTENDED ORDER FIRING.

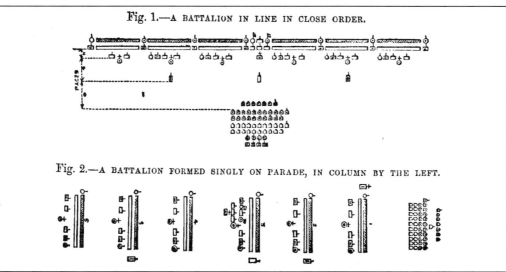

Fig. 1.—A BATTALION IN LINE IN CLOSE ORDER.

Fig. 2.—A BATTALION FORMED SINGLY ON PARADE, IN COLUMN BY THE LEFT.

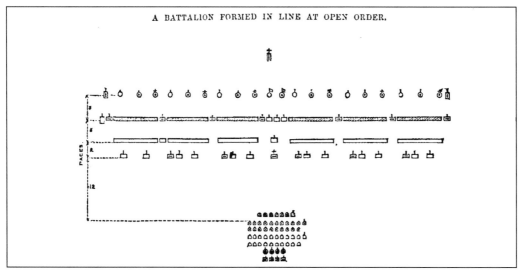

A BATTALION FORMED IN LINE AT OPEN ORDER.

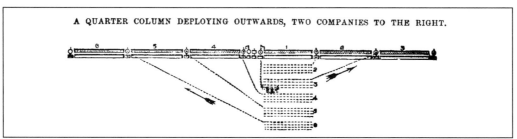

A QUARTER COLUMN DEPLOYING OUTWARDS, TWO COMPANIES TO THE RIGHT.

*Left: Diagrams from the 1877 edition of the* Field Exercises Manual, *showing the basic infantry tactical formations at a time when the emphasis was shifting from close-order to more open-order formations. Note that even at this date the formations called for the Colours to be carried in the centre of a battalion; this was the last edition which did so. (Author's collection)*

# 4

# THE VICTORIAN WAY OF WARFARE

'From the encounter with the Boers, the following would seem more particularly deduced... The necessity of practising the infantry soldier more frequently in the use of his musket with ball cartridge, more particularly in countries like the Cape, where he has so often to trust to his own individual correctness of aim and knowledge of his weapon, and has so little need of the ordinary evolutions en masse.'

Lieutenant Gibb, RE, commenting on the action at Port Natal, 1842.

In 1837, the basic tactical formations followed by the British army were those specified in the 1833 edition of the *Field Exercises and Evolutions* manual. These, in turn, were only marginally altered from the tactics which had defeated Napoleon. Thus, the lessons taught in the age of the smooth-bore, when men needed to be trained like automatons to carry out manoeuvres and fight within a hundred paces of the enemy, continued to shape British attitudes long after advances in weapon technology had rendered them redundant. Indeed, in some respects the British army never fully freed itself from them during the nineteenth century.

In tactical terms, the titanic contest of the Napoleonic Wars was between the French column system, and the British line. Napoleon himself was an advocate of the column, and used it to devastating effect in

*The final stage of Omdurman: British and Egyptian troops advancing in line to repel the last Mahdist attack.*

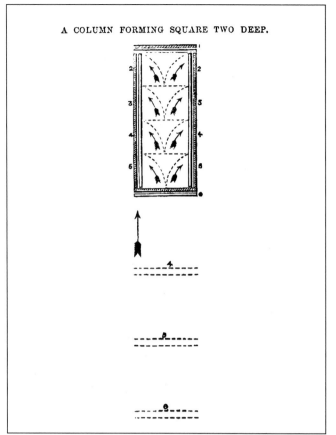

A COLUMN FORMING SQUARE TWO DEEP.

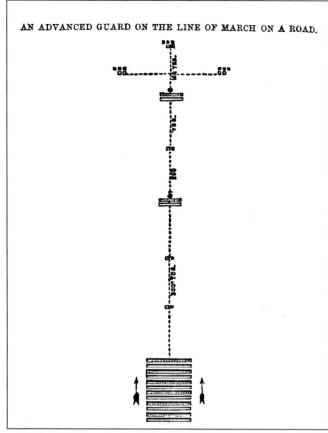

AN ADVANCED GUARD ON THE LINE OF MARCH ON A ROAD.

most of his classic victories. The column was a dense mass of men advancing on a narrow front, smashing through the enemy formations like a steamroller. As a formation it was acutely vulnerable to artillery fire, since a cannon-ball bowling down the length of a column would knock over entire files of men; but it was very difficult to stop by small arms' fire alone, since smooth-bore muskets lacked the range to inflict casualties on a column other than in the closing moments of its attack, by when there was normally insufficient time to halt it by musketry. Wellington, however, had proved that the column could be halted by formations drawn up in line. The line was a more cumbersome formation in attack, and it could not stand up to the column in melee, but it did maximise a unit's firepower, so that the greatest number of weapons could be brought to bear on the column at the critical moment. Time and again Wellington proved his theory in practice, and his example dominated tactical thinking well

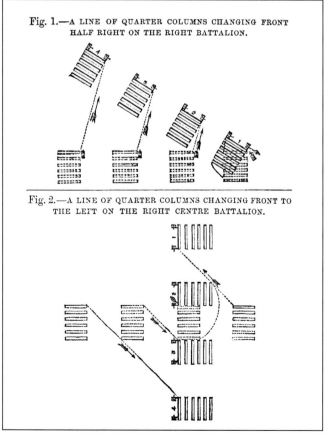

Fig. 1.—A LINE OF QUARTER COLUMNS CHANGING FRONT HALF RIGHT ON THE RIGHT BATTALION.

Fig. 2.—A LINE OF QUARTER COLUMNS CHANGING FRONT TO THE LEFT ON THE RIGHT CENTRE BATTALION.

*Diagrams from the 1877 edition of the* Field Exercises Manual, *showing the basic infantry formations. (Author's collection)*

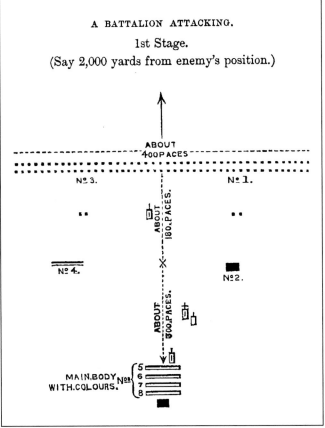

A BATTALION ATTACKING.

1st Stage.

(Say 2,000 yards from enemy's position.)

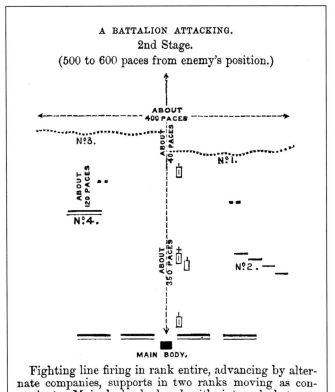

A BATTALION ATTACKING.

2nd Stage.

(500 to 600 paces from enemy's position.)

Fighting line firing in rank entire, advancing by alternate companies, supports in two ranks moving as convenient. Main body deployed with intervals between companies.

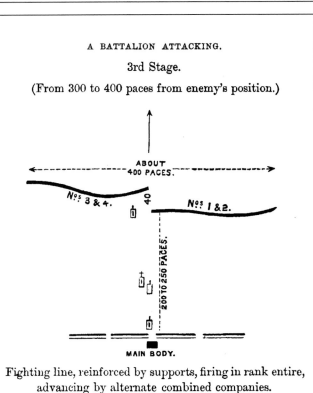

A BATTALION ATTACKING.

3rd Stage.

(From 300 to 400 paces from enemy's position.)

Fighting line, reinforced by supports, firing in rank entire, advancing by alternate combined companies.

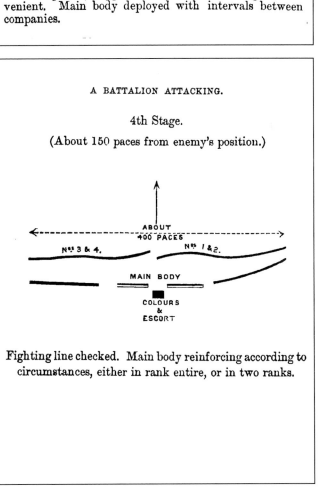

A BATTALION ATTACKING.

4th Stage.

(About 150 paces from enemy's position.)

Fighting line checked. Main body reinforcing according to circumstances, either in rank entire, or in two ranks.

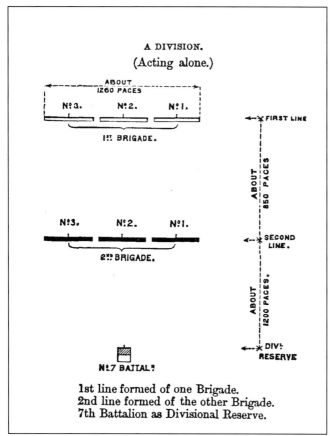

## A DIVISION.
### (Acting alone.)

1st line formed of one Brigade.
2nd line formed of the other Brigade.
7th Battalion as Divisional Reserve.

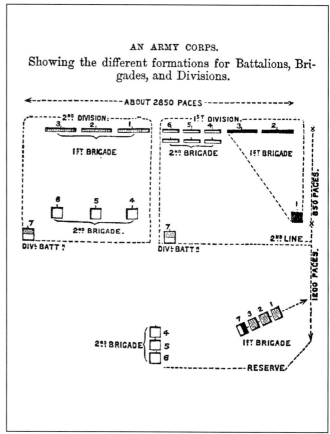

## AN ARMY CORPS.
### Showing the different formations for Battalions, Brigades, and Divisions.

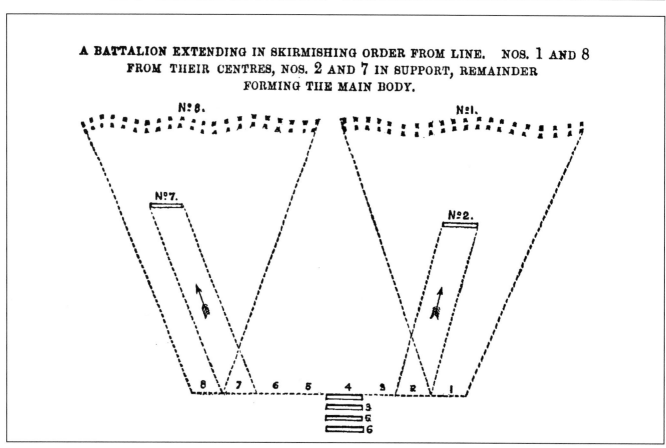

## A BATTALION EXTENDING IN SKIRMISHING ORDER FROM LINE. NOS. 1 AND 8 FROM THEIR CENTRES, NOS. 2 AND 7 IN SUPPORT, REMAINDER FORMING THE MAIN BODY.

into the Victorian era. Indeed, the British adopted the best of both worlds, advancing to the attack and manoeuvring in the more compact column, then deploying into line to fight. Normal movement was carried out in quick time – 108 paces per minute – but the advance was in double time, or 150 paces per minute. Against cavalry, the standard infantry response was the square, which presented a solid wall of fire on all sides, and countered the cavalry's manoeuvrability. The square was formed with the men either two deep – outer rank kneeling, inner standing – or four deep (two of each). With bayonets fixed, this presented a bristling hedge of steel which was usually enough in itself to frighten the horses and pre-

*Below: Although the attack in line owed much to the Napoleonic era, it still achieved successes well into the Victorian period, such as at Aliwal, in the Sikh Wars.*

vent the riders from closing in. Wellington himself placed no great trust in cavalry; he had too few of them to maximise their shock value, and he regarded them as undisciplined, liable to get carried away by the thrill of the chase.

And so it remained in the early part of Queen Victoria's reign. Infantry battalions – the basic battlefield tactical unit – advanced in column, then deployed in companies in close order, advanced, fired a volley, then charged with the bayonet. Volley firing, that great feature of the battlefield in the nineteenth century, was preferred because it was easier to teach recruits, and because in the age of the smooth-bore any sort of independent or aimed fire was largely pointless and wasteful of ammunition. Furthermore, the sudden noise and fury of a volley delivered at close range was undoubtedly unnerving to those on the receiving end. For the men in the ranks, firing was usually carried out in a standing position, if

only because it was difficult loading a muzzle-loader any other way. Although, by 1837, cavalry manuals specified that mounted men were expected to be adept at both Heavy and Light cavalry roles – shock charges and scouting and skirmishing respectively – the former was by far the more fashionable. The basic sub-unit of the cavalry regiment was the troop, and charges were carried out with each troop in a double line, the troops themselves either in line or behind one another in column. Cavalry officers had a rather chilling romantic attachment to the concept of attacking with the sword – the so-called *arme blanche* – and regarded all other duties as either subsidiary, or simply drudgery that was unworthy of them. In fact, as the century wore on the *arme blanche* became increasingly irrelevant, but the cavalry steadfastly refused to embrace the growing need for highly mobile riflemen.

The set-piece battles of the early Victorian period were fought almost entirely according to these principals. Indeed, the Sikh Wars were almost Napoleonic campaigns in an exotic setting; the Khalsa had been trained and equipped along French lines by veterans of Napoleon's armies, and the largely flat country of the Punjab – broken here and there by jungle and swamp – was otherwise ideal for extended battles in column and line. The British commander, Sir Hugh Gough, seemed unable to fight in anything but the most predictable way, and Chillianwallah was a classic example of an attack in line. The Sikh Wars also produced some rare successful examples of the *arme blanche*, notably in the charge of the 16th Lancers at Aliwal, and the 14th Light Dragoons at Rumnaggar. Generally, British artillery was somewhat neglected in the aftermath of the Napoleonic Wars, and no great tactical doctrine had therefore emerged, but the excellence of the Sikh artillery forced the EIC batteries to develop counter-tactics, in particular the use of the massed battery to suppress enemy fire. For the most part, however, the Royal Artillery – who

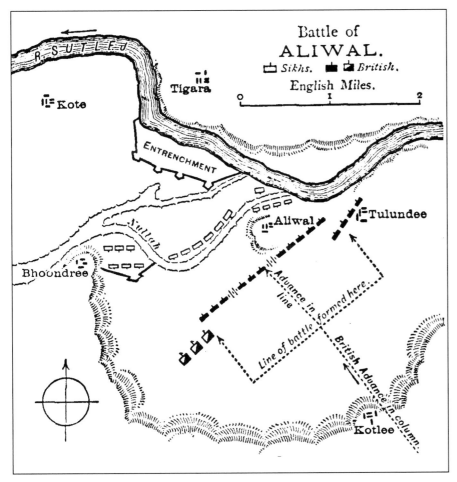

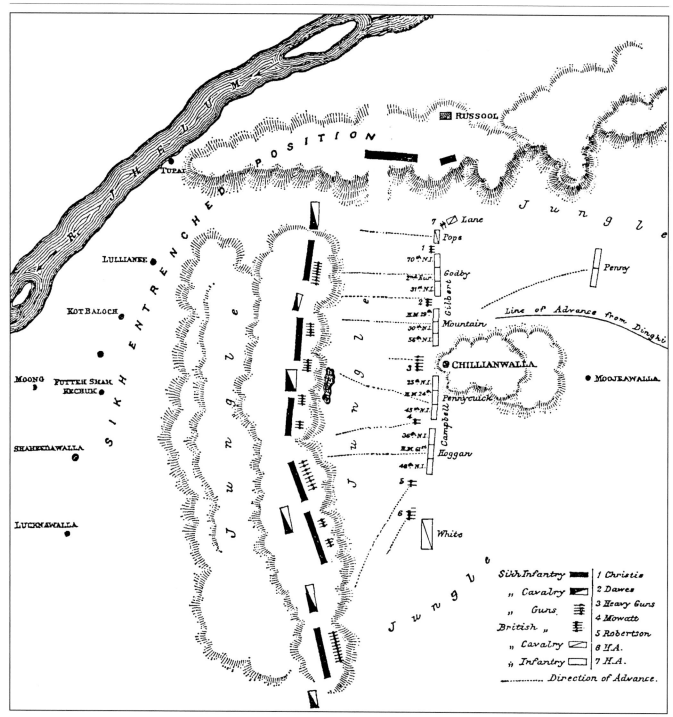

were not stationed in India at this time – was scattered throughout the Empire in small parcels, and was usually employed as an *ad hoc* infantry support weapon, often in two-gun divisions or single gun sub-divisions.

For all this, it was nevertheless the incessant colonial warfare of the 1840s and 1850s, rather than the anachronistic set-piece battles, which were the shape of things to come. Since the Napoleonic Wars, it had been recognised that skirmishers – men deployed in a light screen in front of the main body, thinking for themselves, making good use of cover, and harassing the enemy with aimed fire – had a valuable role to play in protecting the advance of close-order formations. The Rifle Regiment had been formed exactly for this purpose, and the Light Infantry, who were trained to manoeuvre at a faster pace than their Line counterparts, could fulfil much the same role. Indeed, every battalion had one Light company which could act as skirmishers if necessary. Since the army was scattered in small pockets about the Empire, however, there were seldom enough trained specialist troops to fulfil this function. In

*Left: Wellington's legacy: the old close-order line formation of the Napoleonic Wars was employed well into the nineteenth century. Whilst it was on occasion successful it was increasingly obsolete in the face of improved weapon technology, as the bloody frontal attack at Chillianwallah suggested. Nevertheless, it's ghost can still be discerned as late as the battle of Omdurman (below) in September 1898.*

fighting highly mobile enemies, like the Xhosa or the Maoris, who were themselves natural skirmishers adept at fieldcraft and at home in their own environment, it was impossible for infantry battalions to rely entirely on the old column and line formations. They needed a greater flexibility, for the men to work in a looser order, and make the most of the terrain. Thus, even before the Crimean War, most commanding officers who took a pride in their profession were beginning to see to it that all of their men understood the basic principals of skirmishing. For cavalry, too, there were few enough chances to use the *arme blanche*. True, the 7th Dragoons caught Chief Siyolo's Xhosa warriors in the open at Gwangqa river in June 1846, but this was largely a matter of luck; the cavalry had been pursuing the tracks of one band of Xhosa, and had ridden over a rise only to find another moving across their front in

the valley beyond. The Xhosa had stood up to the charge, and the Dragoons had cut their way through them several times with the sword, but the greater damage was actually caused by the locally-raised Cape Mounted Rifles, who followed behind with double-barrelled carbines. For the most part the Dragoons found that they were not merely ineffective in the face of warriors who habitually fought from the bush but, when they did attempt to confront them in such terrain, they were at a serious disadvantage.

The major campaigns of the 1850s, the Crimean War and the Indian Mutiny, were almost entirely conventional. The Russian army was trained, equipped and uniformed in a recognisably European fashion, and fought according to its own lessons from the Napoleonic Wars. At the Alma, the British attacked with two entire divisions in line

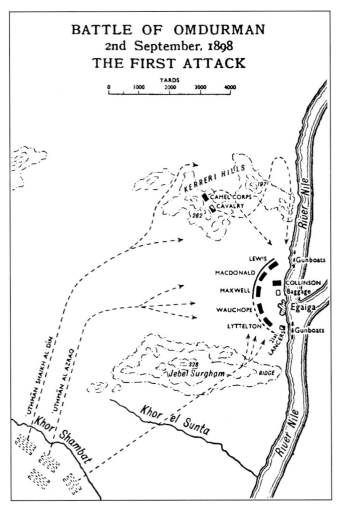

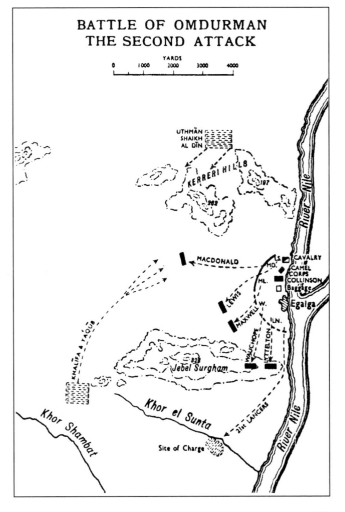

*Left: A drawing which illustrates the inappropriate nature of the conventional cavalry tactics in many colonial settings: Captain Bambrick of the 7th Dragoons is killed by Xhosa fighting from the bush in the Seventh Cape Frontier War. (Author's collection)*

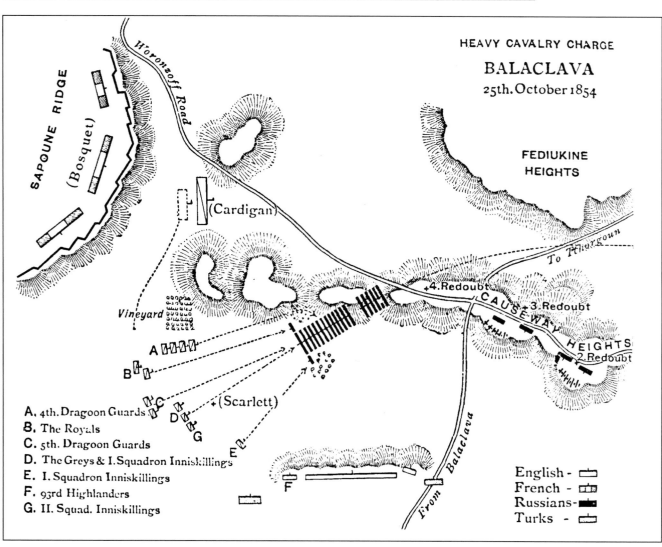

abreast, with two more in support. Each division had its battalions deployed side by side in two ranks, and screened by skirmishers. This approach was not without its difficulties, for neither the divisional commanders nor their subordinates were used to controlling such large numbers of men in action, and at one point the divisional flanks overlapped in the centre, causing some confusion. This was further complicated because the Russians had fired a village in the centre of the battlefield, and the smoke drifted across the British line of advance. Moreover, the terrain was broken by the River Alma, the vineyards on the flats, and the heights themselves. Nevertheless, on the whole the line carried everything before it although, interestingly enough, the Light Division's formations broke up as they struggled up the hills, and the men attacked instead like a swarm of skirmishers. Although one exposed battalion was not able to withstand a Russian counter-attack in column, the Russians in turn proved acutely vulnerable to the concentrated fire of the Minié rifle, proving once again the advantages of line over column. Indeed, the French had mounted their part of the attack in column, and, after a rapid start, had become bogged down and lost momentum in the face of heavy Russian fire. Balaclava was chiefly a cavalry action, and an untypical one at that; the 93rd had driven off the Russian attack in line, rather than square – in itself proof of the daunting effect of volley fire in line – whilst the Light Brigade's attack was against all principles of tactical theory, and recognised even

*Left: The Battle of Balaclava epitomised the nineteenth-century dilemma regarding cavalry theory; the charge of the Heavy Brigade succeeded through a vigorous use of the 'arme blanche', whilst the Light Brigade's charge down the valley between the Fediukine and Causeway Heights later in the day, against unbroken Russian artillery and cavalry, was recognised as a blunder even at the time.*

at the time as a mistake. Nevertheless, the Light Brigade had still managed to overrun an eight gun battery, despite being fired on from the front and flanks; the perfect example of the grandeur and folly of the *arme blanche*. Inkerman was an infantryman's action, and circumstances contrived to make it largely devoid of formal tactics; the Russian attack in columns was checked not by volley-fire but by determined hand-to-hand fighting amongst the broken terrain.

In the Indian Mutiny, British and loyal EIC troops were fighting an enemy whose core troops – the rebel sepoys – had been trained by the British, and therefore used exactly the same tactics. Although the sepoys were often augmented by large numbers of irregular or civilian forces, this did not significantly alter their tactics. In the open plains of northern India, battles again became a slogging match, in which the British, who were usually outnumbered, were nonetheless often victorious because the rebel armies – which had deliberately cut themselves adrift from their officer cadres by the very act of mutiny – lacked central direction and purpose. Furthermore, the British had better weapons, for the Enfield rifle easily outranged the old smooth-bores. The British began the war with a lack of regular cavalry, and so relied heavily on locally-raised irregulars. Even so, the absence of an effective means of pursuit often meant that early British victories were not always exploited as well as they might have been. This situation was to some extent rectified by the arrival of British reinforcements as the war progressed, and in the later stages, as the rebel forces began to disintegrate, both regular and irregular cavalry were particularly useful in harrying fugitive bands.

The 1859 edition of *Field Exercises and Evolutions* confirmed what had largely already become standard practice, namely that all troops within a battalion were to be trained in skirmishing techniques. If circumstances allowed, attacks were to be made with the main body – in col-

umn or line, whichever was considered more appropriate – screened by three lines, the skirmish line itself, a line of supports 200 yards (183 m) behind it, and a reserve 300 yards (275 m) behind that. In practice, in colonial warfare it was more common to fight with the entire force deployed as skirmishers, supports and a reserve, or, if there were sufficient troops to form a main body, to reduce the screen to two lines, skirmishers and supports. These techniques required a greater degree of decentralisation than had previously been the case; with troops scattered over a wide area, it became increasingly important that junior officers, NCOs, and even the men themselves be capable of taking the initiative. This was a radical departure from Napoleonic theory, where independent thought was considered a threat to the degree of discipline necessary to perform close-order manoeuvres. This shift towards independent action characterised the second half of the nineteenth century, but its principals were still only imperfectly understood by the time of the Boer War. Nevertheless, Wolseley had grasped the importance of an ability to act independently when planning for the Asante campaign, where the forest conditions were perhaps the ultimate example of difficult bush terrain:

When thus engaged in the bush, officers commanding battalions, and even officers commanding companies, will find it difficult to exercise much control over their men. For this reason it is essential that the tactical unit should be as small as possible. Every company will therefore be at once divided into four sections, and each section will be placed under the command of an officer or non-commissioned officer. These sections, once told off, are not on any account to be broken up during the war, nor are their commanders to be changed except under extraordinary circumstances, and then only by order of the officer commanding a battalion. All details

181

of duty will be performed by sections, or, when only very small guards or picquets are required, by half-sections...

Fighting in the bush is very much like fighting in the twilight; no-one can see further than a few files to his right or left. Great steadiness and self-confidence are therefore required from everyone engaged...

Nevertheless, the Asante campaign also highlighted the dichotomy which tormented tacticians in colonial warfare throughout the period: against the very real advantages of dispersal there was also an undeniable need to concentrate firepower, and present a solid line to a rapidly moving enemy. Wolseley had resolved this dilemma by deploying his skirmishing lines in a box formation, so as to be ready to fight on all fronts when the Asante switched the focus of their attacks to the flank or rear. As such he was simply adapting the old Napoleonic formation of the square to receive cavalry, and this became a standard tactic in the 1870s and 1880s, particularly when dealing with a rapidly moving enemy in open country.

The 1859 manual was, in any case, revised in the 1870s following the Franco-Prussian War, which British tacticians studied in great depth, though they did not always learn the appropriate lessons. Greater emphasis was now placed on attacking in depth, and the speed of movement was increased, quick time to 165 paces per minute and double time first to 116 paces, then to 120. The old line and column formations were effectively abolished. A battalion in attack deployed two companies as skirmishers, with two companies in line some distance behind them in support, and the remaining four companies in line behind them. The supports were supposed to be fed forward as the objective was reached, and by firing and advancing in rushes the attack was supposed to build up fire superiority over the enemy until the entire battalion could charge with the bayonet. The use of cover was accept-able, particularly by skirmishers, but it was not to be used to the detriment of cohesion.

At Tel-el-Kebir, essentially a conventional battle, Wolseley attacked in similar formations, with brigades supporting one another, and battalions in line. At Laing's Nek, however, the 58th manoeuvred into position in column, advancing towards Boer positions on a ridge using the dead ground at its base. They had not deployed, however, when they came under fire from the Boers at close range, and their attempt to do so was then shattered by the Boers' accurate marksmanship. Their officers tried to remedy the situation by ordering the men to charge, but many were winded after the stiff climb, and could achieve no momentum. Eventually the entire attack collapsed. If, however, the failure to disperse had been a major factor in the British defeat at Laing's Nek, open-order formations were themselves problematic on other occasions. At Nyamaga in the Ninth Cape Frontier War in 1878, Colonel Glyn of the 1/24th formed up with three companies in an extended line, with protected flanks, artillery in the centre, and a reserve line behind. The infantry firepower checked a Xhosa advance, and Glyn advanced in the same formation and drove the enemy from the field. When, however, the same battalion tried similar tactics against the Zulus at Isandlwana, where some 700 redcoats and several hundred auxiliaries tried to hold a line that stretched for nearly two miles against 20,000 Zulus, their firepower proved quite insufficient, and the line collapsed with disastrous consequences. Even when fighting the Boers, dispersal could be a problem; at Majuba, General Colley placed almost half the entire force at his disposal in reserve, leaving the remainder to hold the firing line with just one man defending each twelve yards – a screen which also proved quite incapable of holding the enemy back.

The emphasis on open-order tactics was made both necessary and possible by the improvement of weapon technology. The advent of breech-loaders – the Snider and Mar-tini-Henry – made it possible not only for men to fire more rapidly, but also to fire in positions which had been impractical before. It was quite possible to load a breech-loader whilst kneeling or even lying down, and the old practice of standing whilst firing became increasingly confined to close-order formations in defence. At ranges over 600 yards (549 m), volley-firing was still preferred, because it was much easier for the officers to control their men and prevent the waste of ammunition which resulted from jumpy independent firing. Volleys also had a tremendous psychological effect on the enemy, and it took a steady nerve to face them, even when the actual destruction they wrought was often limited. Volley-firing was usually carried out by company, or by sections, the firing starting at one end of a line with every section firing when it was ready thereafter. The main problem with volley-firing was that, until the widespread use of cordite, black-powder produced enormous quantities of smoke which tended to hang in the air on still days and obscure the target. This was not necessarily a problem in attack, when the troops were moving forward, but could cause difficulties in defensive formations like squares. Several times during Zulu War battles it was necessary to cease firing for a few moments to allow the smoke to clear. Volleying by section did at least break the regularity of the fire along a line, and offer some respite from smoke. At ranges closer than 600 yards, where it was necessary to pick off individual targets rather then fire into a dense body of the enemy, independent fire was used more frequently.

In defence, the square remained an important counter to fast moving and numerically superior enemies. In theory it provided an unassailable line of concentrated firepower on all fronts, but in fact it was by no means as invulnerable as its reputation suggests. For one thing it was very exposed to any type of return fire; the ranks of men packed densely together were almost as inviting a target as those in column. It was,

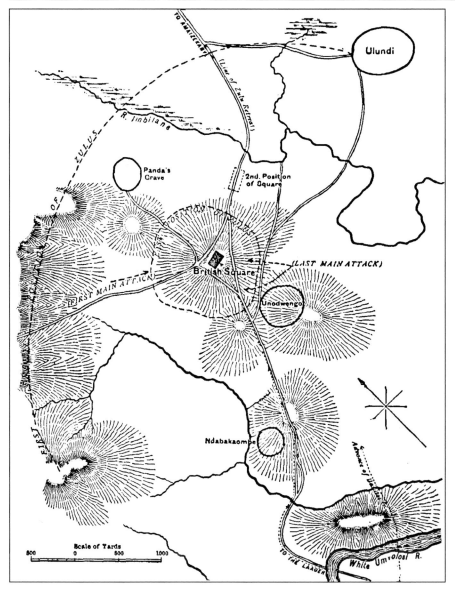

therefore, quite inappropriate against an enemy armed with firearms, and it is no coincidence that it was used to best effect in this period against enemies who did not rely primarily on firearms, such as the Zulus and Mahdists. Wolseley had used the square with some imagination against gun-wielding Asante, but the forest environment severely restricted the enemy's firepower. In an open battle, the square had two inherent weaknesses: firstly, the field of fire extended straight out from the sides, and there was a natural dead zone in front of the corners; and secondly, the square was a very difficult formation to manoeuvre. The solution to the first of these was to place guns or machine-guns in the corners, but most African enemies recognised that the corners nevertheless represented the formation's principal weakness and attacked them whenever possible. These assaults were often very determined; at both Gingindlovu and oNdini the Zulus came within an ace of charging right up to a corner of the squares, and only the timely reinforcement by troops taken from elsewhere within the formation saved the day. At Tamai and Abu Klea, in the Sudan, the squares were actually broken, principally because of the difficulties in keeping tight formation when on the move. At Abu Klea the large numbers of camels inside the formation, moving at a slower pace, caused the

*Above: The square – the Napoleonic defence against cavalry – proved a useful formation against large numbers of rapidly-moving enemy who were not armed with firearms. If the battle of Ulundi, or oNdini, demonstrated its strengths, however, Tamai (overleaf) in the Suakin showed it to be a difficult formation to maintain when manoeuvring with potentially disastrous consequences.*
*Right: The classic defence against cavalry or a highly mobile enemy: the 2nd Battalion of 'The Buffs' in square in Mullingar, Ireland, 1876, shortly before the battalion's departure for South Africa. (Bryan Maggs Collection)*

183

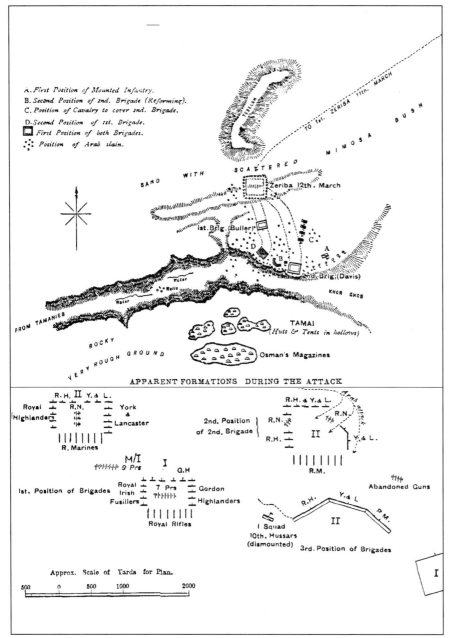

A. First Position of Mounted Infantry.
B. Second Position of 2nd. Brigade (Reforming).
C. Position of Cavalry to cover 2nd. Brigade.
D. Second Position of 1st. Brigade.
□ First Position of both Brigades.
∵ Position of Arab slain.

TO 1st. ZERIBA 11th. MARCH

MIMOSA BUSH

SAND WITH SCATTERED

Zeriba 12th. March

1st. Brig. (Buller)

D    C
     A
B
2nd. Brig. (Davis)

KHOR GHOB

Water    Wells
Water

FROM TAMANIEB

ROCKY

VERY ROUGH GROUND

TAMAI
(Huts & Tents in hollows)

Osman's Magazines

APPARENT FORMATIONS DURING THE ATTACK

R.H. II Y.& L.
Royal    R.N.    York
Highlanders        &
              Lancaster
|||||||
R. Marines

2nd. Position
of 2nd. Brigade

R.H. & Y.& L.
R.N.        R.N.
        II
R.H.            Y.& L.
|||||||
R.M.

M/I    I
|||||| 9 Prs    Q.H
1st. Position of Brigades    Royal    7 Prs    Gordon
              Irish        Highlanders
              Fusiliers
|||||||
Royal Rifles

Arab ravine
Abandoned Guns

R.H.    Y.& L
        R.M.
II
1 Squad
10th. Hussars
(dismounted)    3rd. Position of Brigades

I

Approx. Scale of Yards for Plan.
500    0    500    1000    2000

*Left: The battle of Tamai.*

rear face to bow outwards, leaving the square disconnected at one corner. The Mahdists immediately spotted this and poured into the gap. Ultimately, under such circumstances, the successful defence of a square depended on the willingness of soldiers in the ranks to stand their ground and fight it out, eyeball to eyeball with the enemy.

In the 1870s, artillery commanders were at last freed from the constraint of supporting the cavalry or infantry units to whom they were attached. Instead, they were told of the battle's objective, and allowed to decide the best way of using their resources to that end. The use of artillery therefore became increasingly flexible at a time when rifling allowed greater range and accuracy. Nevertheless, from a practical point of view most British armies in the field remained under-equipped with artillery, and batteries were still required to spread themselves thin on the ground. In South Africa, the two-gun division remained the most common form of deployment; thus although Lord Chelmsford had all six guns from N5 battery attached to his Centre Column in Zululand in January 1879, he typically chose to split them. Four guns accompanied his advance from Isandlwana, and two were left in camp – and were overrun with the rest of the garrison when the Zulus attacked.

By the 1880s, the trend towards flexible infantry attack formations had reached its logical conclusion.

*Left: The square in action: awaiting the Zulu approach, Gingindlovu, Zulu War 1879. (Killie Campbell Library)*

*Above: A square on the move, protected by skirmishers: Metemmeh, January 1885. (Rai England Collection)*

Attack was still in depth, with three lines advancing in open order; the first was supposed to dominate the enemy with its firepower, the second was to advance in support, then rush through the first to attack with the bayonet, whilst the third was either to pursue the defeated enemy in the event of victory, or cover the retreat of the first two if repulsed. As before, the use of cover was acceptable, but only if it did not disrupt the formations. Among the artillery, the trend was now towards concentrating guns, firstly in their constituted batteries, and secondly in larger divisions. In the Sudan, massed artillery fire proved particularly effective, notably at Atbara, where the devastated Mahdist camp after the battle looked as if a steam-roller had run over it. Even in the 1890s artillery manuals argued that small-arms fire from a distance greater than 1000 yards (915 m) could safely be ignored without danger to the enemy.

On the North-West Frontier, conventional infantry tactics had been

*Right: The debris of static warfare: the interior of the Russian defences of the Redan, photographed after the fall of Sebastopol. (Private collection)*

refined by constant experience. As early as the First Afghan War General Pollock's army had proved that the Afghans were highly vulnerable to attacks from ground which overlooked their positions, and threatened their flank or line of retreat. 'Taking the high ground' became a principal objective in all campaigning on the Frontier, as the fierce tussles for the Ambela picquets demonstrated. Given the Afghan's instinctive ability to spot errors, the speed with which he could move in his own landscape, and the ferocity of his attacks, it was particularly important on the Frontier that men learned to think for themselves, since one false move could cost them their lives. In retreat, a British force had to

take good care to cover its withdrawal, since the Afghans were quick at following up, and wounded could never be left to the enemy. In the 1880s and 1890s the North-West Frontier was the single greatest testing ground of the British army in battle, and the lessons learned there stood it in good stead. It is probably no coincidence that it was the contingent sent out from India which defeated the Boers in an almost textbook attack at Elandslaagte in the opening stages of the Boer War, whilst the Army Corps from Britain, by contrast, faltered at Colenso. At Colenso, the inexperience of brigade commanders in working together was all too apparent, whilst the artillery's refusal to consider the risks posed by Boer long-range fire had serious consequences.

The Victorian era produced only one full-scale siege where classic siege techniques were employed, that of Sebastopol. The Russians had fortified the port by building a chain of earthwork redoubts around it, linked with trenches. Since frontal assaults were clearly impractical, the Allies responded by digging lines of parallel trenches reinforced with gabions, large wicker containers full of earth. The Allied parallels were connected by zigzag trenches known as saps, which were built thus to deflect the blast of any shell falling into them. After a heavy preliminary bombardment, Allied infantry would rush across the open space between the

*Lieutenant Herbert Jenkins, 17th Lancers, who was wounded in the face during the regiment's charge at oNdini (Ulundi). (Royal Archives)*

*The ineffectiveness of regular cavalry in colonial skirmishing: the death of Lieutenant Frith at eZungeni, 1 June 1879. (Author's collection)*

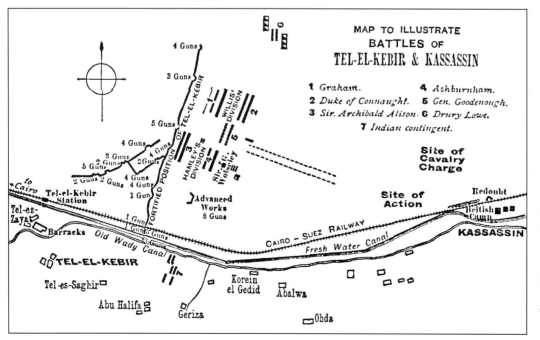

*Left: Night attacks were rare in Victorian warfare because of the difficulties of control. Wolseley's attack on Tel-el-Kebir was not a true night attack, but an approach under cover of darkness, followed by a dawn assault. It was mounted over largely featureless terrain against known Egyptian positions, and succeeded through careful preperation.*

*Right: 'After the Charge' by John Charlton. The 17th Lancers retrieved the reputation of the 'arme blanche' by their spectacular charge at oNdini. (Rai England Collection)*

lines of trenches and try to assault key Russian positions. In this respect the trench warfare of the Crimea was not fundamentally different from that of the First World War; the assaults could be terribly costly, and both sides mounted regular 'trench raids' to discourage the other's efforts. Ultimately, it was no more possible to break the deadlock of trench warfare around Sebastopol than it was on the Western front.

Few of the sieges in the Victorian period involved the same degree of sophisticated engineering skill. Although the British positions on the ridge above Delhi were protected by ramparts and gabions, the British for the most part had too few troops to engage in complex sapping operations, although at Lucknow the Mutineers did try to enter the British positions by tunnelling. In New Zealand, the complex earthworks built by the Maoris could not be taken by frontal assault without heavy artillery support, but digging offensive saps – cutting trenches towards the enemy to move assault columns as close as possible to the objective – were a successful if time consuming counter. At Eshowe during the Zulu War a complex earthwork was thrown up to protect the mission station; this was designed to be impregnable to an enemy lacking artillery, and indeed the Zulus never attempted to attack it, but merely kept the garrison bottled up by harassing all of their patrols. At Chitral the garrison defended an existing hill-fort; the Chitralis tried to undermine the walls with tunnels, and set fire to the wooden piles which supported them. In the absence of heavy Chitrali artillery, these attacks were only partly successful. During the

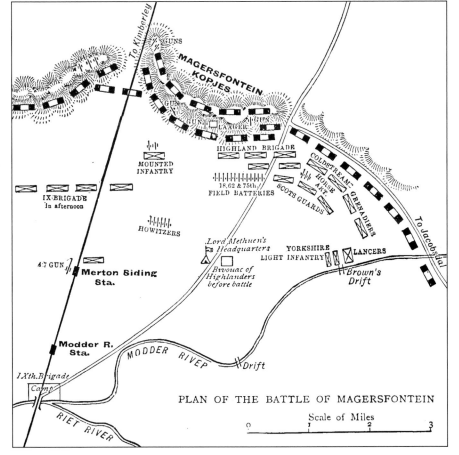

PLAN OF THE BATTLE OF MAGERSFONTEIN

Scale of Miles

*Left: At Magersfontein in the Boer War difficult terrain and confusion regarding Boer dispositions (exaggerated on this contemporary map) foiled a similar plan as that used at the Battle of Tel-el-Kebir, and led to the Highland Brigade advancing too close to the enemy positions in close formation, with fatal results.*

Boer War the fact that both sides during the three most famous sieges – Ladysmith, Kimberley and Mafikeng – were armed with long-range artillery and small arms, coupled with the Boer reluctance to mount open attacks on the defences, meant that the sieges were not closely prosecuted. The British defences were usually anchored on physical features, such as hills, reinforced by trenches and sangars.

For cavalry, there was little change in tactics from the 1870s through to the Boer War. Increasingly, cavalry were needed to provide competent long range scouting and picquet duties, although most cavalry officers resented the drudgery of such work and looked forward to the first chance for shock action. When opportunities to wield the *arme blanche* did arise, the results were often ambiguous; thus the 17th Lancers had proved disappointing as skirmishers in Zululand, but did pursue the broken Zulu army after oNdini to good effect. At both El Teb and later at Omdurman, cavalry got into trouble pursuing small groups of the enemy in broken ground, only to be drawn into unbroken enemy concentrations which had remained concealed. At Talana Hill, the first battle of the Boer War, a costly

British victory had been marred by a mounted pursuit which had gone too far, got lost in the mist, and was cut off and forced to surrender. Nevertheless, there were spectacular successes for the *arme blanche*, notably at Kassassin and Elandslaagte. On the whole, however, the experience of a squadron of the 17th Lancers at Modderfontein in the Cape Colony in September 1901 was probably more typical; sent to intercept a Boer commando led by Jan Smuts, they were cut off and pinned down by Boer rifle fire, and a gallant attempt to charge was shot to pieces.

**Mounted Infantry**
One lesson learned early in colonial warfare was the need to combine the cavalryman's speed and manoeuvrability with the infantryman's firepower. For much of the nineteenth century the British cavalry were reluctant to fulfil this role, feeling it deprived them of the true dash and élan which were their rightful inheritance. As a result, when the need arose the most imaginative commanders mounted able volunteers from the infantry battalions on horse or camel-back, and formed temporary units whose chief duties were scouting, picqueting, and, when necessary, fighting on foot with firearms.

As early as 1835, during the Sixth Cape Frontier War, the Light Company of the 75th Regiment were turned into mounted infantry and given double-barrelled smooth-bore carbines and cutlasses, after the manner of the local Cape Mounted Rifles, whose hard riding and ability to skirmish in the bush had earned them widespread respect. Indeed, the 'Mounted Infantry' experiment would prove particularly successful in southern Africa, although not without occasional equivalents elsewhere; during the pacification of Sind, for instance, Sir Charles Napier had mounted 350 men of the 22nd Regiment on camels. Back in South Africa, there was even an attempt to turn cavalry into Mounted Infantry when, during the Zwartkopjes campaign, the 7th Dragoons were issued with Brunswick rifles in place of their carbines in an attempt to match the range of the Boers.

During the Ninth Cape Frontier War two squadrons of Imperial Mounted Infantry were formally raised from among the infantry battalions serving there. The men wore their regimental frocks with dark buff corduroy trousers, giving them a motley appearance which earned them the nickname 'the bashi-bazooks'. They were armed with

*Right: Mounted Infantry in the Egyptian War of 1882; they are wearing the frocks from their parent units. A number of these men are wearing the medal ribbon for South Africa 1877–8–9. (Royal Archives)*

*Below: Mounted infantryman on the Suakin railway, Sudan, 1885. (Bryan Maggs Collection)*

Swinburne-Henry carbines, and carried ammunition in leather bandoliers over the shoulder. The same men also served in Zululand in 1879 – part of one squadron was present at Isandlwana – and the Sekhukhune campaign; although most of them were returned to their regiments when they were withdrawn from South Africa, some of those who remained in garrison duty also served as MI in the 1881 Transvaal War. In Egypt in 1882, an MI company was raised from amongst the

first infantry battalions to arrive; it included men from the South Staffordshire Regiment and 3/KRRC who had served in the same capacity in South Africa. A further company was later raised and served in the Tel-el-Kebir campaign. During the Gordon Relief Expedition in 1885 both infantrymen and cavalry were mounted on camels to form the famous Camel Corps. MI on both horses and camels were used in the operations around Suakin, and in the defence of the Egyptian frontier.

During the Third Burma War, and in particular the protracted operations against dacoit bands, infantrymen were mounted to good effect on small Burmese ponies.

The success of these *ad hoc* arrangements led to the creation of permanent Mounted Infantry schools in Britain in 1888. Men were drawn from ordinary infantry battalions and trained in MI techniques, before returning to their normal duties. The idea was to establish sufficient skilled men within each infantry battalion to form a Mounted Infantry detachment thirty-two strong. When operating in brigades, three such detachments could be combined to form a company. The new system first saw limited action in Zimbabwe (Rhodesia) in 1896, in a campaign which otherwise saw little involvement by Queen's troops. Here four companies were amalgamated to form an MI battalion. The system really came into its own in the Boer War, however, which was the mounted infantry war *par excellence*; the Boers themselves were, after all, nothing more than extremely effective mounted infantry. To counter them the British needed an equivalent force, and altogether twenty-eight MI battalions were raised, each of four companies. In addition, many Yeomanry and Colonial units adopted MI techniques.

## The Colours

The habit of carrying Colours – infantry flags – dated back to the English Civil War, when each regiment carried a number of large conspicuously coloured flags to mark the position of various officers within the regiment. By the time of the Napoleonic Wars, the number of Colours carried by each infantry battalion had been limited to two – the First or King's Colour, which was the Great Union, or national flag, and a Regimental Colour, which was largely the colour of the regiment's distinctive facings. Although the Victorian era saw several moves to make Colours smaller and more uniform in size, this general principal has survived among Line regiments until the present day. The practice of carrying Colours into action ceased in 1881, but they are still carried on ceremonial occasions. Cavalry flags, known as standards or guidons, were not carried in action throughout the Victorian era.

At the time of Queen Victoria's accession, the size of infantry

*Below: Officers of the 34th Regiment in India in the 1860s. Note the battle-torn Colours behind. (Bryan Maggs Collection)*

Colours was governed by a warrant dating from the eighteenth century. They were made of silk, 6 ft 6 ins (1.98 m) wide and 6 ft (0.92 m) deep, carried on a pike 9 ft 10 ins (3 m) from top to bottom, with a simple pike-head device on the top. The size was modified several times during the Queen's reign; in 1855 it was reduced to 6 ft (0.92 m) width and 5 ft 6 ins (1.68 m) depth, and three years later to 4 ft (1.22 m) width and 3 ft 6 ins (1.07 m) depth, when the pike-head was replaced with the royal crest (a lion on top of a crown). In 1859 the practice of decorating the edge of the Colour with a fringe, which had been common to cavalry regiments, was also authorised for infantry battalions. The size was changed again in 1868, to 3 ft 9 ins (1.14 m) wide and 3 ft (0.92 m) deep, exclusive of the fringe. Although the size of the Colours themselves remained constant for the remainder of the century, the pike was reduced to 8 ft 7 ins (2.62 m) in 1873 and increased to 8 ft 7½ ins (2.63 m) in 1898. Until 1855 the Colours were provided by the colonel of each battalion, but after that time they were provided by the Crown. The King's Colour was officially renamed the Royal Colour in 1844, but was generally referred to as the Queen's Colour. Colours were presented to a

battalion in pairs, and carried until they were worn out, when they were replaced, and the old Colours laid up in the regimental chapel in the home depot. New Colours were not issued when changes of size or pattern were authorised, and battalions often carried Colours of a pattern that had been superseded years before. Nevertheless, when Colours were replaced they were generally of the pattern then prevailing. Battle damage caused to Colours in action – the tears, rips and holes caused by shot and bullet – were not repaired, and were regarded as a proud badge of the battalion's service. As a result Colours which had been carried for a number of years looked, in Kipling's memorable phrase, like 'the lining of a brick-layer's hat on a chewed tooth-pick'. On the march Colours were usually carried furled, and wrapped in a black leather case with a brass cap, and were usually only unfurled on going into action.

Until the regulations published in 1844 it had been common for scroll devices bearing the names of officially authorised battle honours to be stitched to both Colours. From 1844, however, such honours were only added to the Regimental Colour among Line regiments, and the Queen's Colour remained a plain Union flag, with the regimental number in Roman numerals in the centre, surmounted by a crown. Those regiments which had two battalions had a small scroll bearing 'II Batt.' below the crown on the 2nd Battalion Colours. The Regimental Colour was of the facing colour of the regiment, with the Union flag in the upper canton. Those regiments which had historically been granted a particular device or badge bore this in the centre of the Colour on a crimson ground, whilst others bore their regimental number in Roman numerals instead. The central device was surrounded by a crimson garter bearing the regimental name or motto, and around that the Union wreath of entwined roses, shamrocks and thistles. Battle honours were borne on either side of the central motif and added as authorised, and it was not unusual for honours to be

*Right: A stirring representation of Colonel Wood rallying the 29th Regiment with their Colours at Sobraon, during the First Sikh War. (Author's collection)*

granted many years after the events themselves, and not necessarily in sequence, although they were usually displayed as such. The battle honour GIBRALTAR 1704–5, for example, was not awarded to the eight regiments present in that campaign until 1909, when many honours for intervening actions had long since been awarded. With the process of amalgamations of battalions which began in 1881, the design of new Regimental Colours was authorised, although many battalions stubbornly refused to give up their old Colours.

Among the Guards' battalions, which had their own proud and distinguished history, the system was rather different in that the First or Queen's Colour was crimson, with a Union flag in the first canton, whilst the Regimental Colour was the Union flag. In a further departure from Line regiments, battle honours were carried on both Colours; each company had a different device, and this was carried in the centre of the Regimental Colour in turn.

In a traditional fighting line, the Colours were usually carried in the centre of a battalion, and served to encourage the line forward in attack, or as a rallying point in defence. The Colours were carried by the junior officers of the battalion, with the rank of ensign or, later, second lieutenant, and the Colour party, or escort, was commanded by the colour-sergeant. In the conventional battles of the early Victorian period, the Colours were invariably carried into action, and to lose them to the enemy was a bitter disgrace. The 44th had their Colours with them during the disastrous retreat from Kabul in 1842; at Gandamak, rather than see the Afghans take them, Captain Souter tore them from their poles and wrapped them round his body, under his Afghan coat. Souter survived the massacre, because the Afghans thought his rich cummer-

bund denoted a man of wealth and importance, and kept him alive in the hope of a rich ransom. During the attack on the Sikh position at Chillianwallah, the 24th rallied on their Colours despite very rough ground, which was broken by jungle and swamp. The Colours presented the Sikhs with an obvious target, and both the officers carrying the Colours and the sergeants of the Colour party were shot down. According to one account, the Queen's Colour was rescued by a private, Martin Connolly, who wrapped it around his body; but Connolly was later killed, and the burial party failed to notice the Colour, which was apparently buried with him. The Regimental Colour was retrieved by another private, Richard Perry. At the Alma, most of the attacking battalions had their Colours flying, and Sergeant Luke O'Connor of the 23rd Royal Welsh Fusiliers won the VC for

taking the Queen's Colour of his battalion from a fallen ensign and carrying it into the Great Redoubt. During the confused melee at Inkerman, the Grenadier Guards used their Colours as a rallying point.

Colours were generally less appropriate to the small-scale colonial fighting of the 1860s and 1870s, particularly in the bush terrain of South Africa and New Zealand, and three serious reverses at the end of the decade finally led to a prohibition on their being carried in action. The first, and perhaps most famous, was the debacle at Isandlwana. The column overrun by the Zulus on 22 January 1879 had consisted of both battalions of the 24th regiment. Lord Chelmsford had left the camp at Isandlwana on the morning of the 22nd, before the Zulu attack, and had taken most of the 2/24th with him, but the battalion had left all its baggage and tents in the camp,

*Above: Isandlwana 1879: Lieutenant Melvill clings to a rock in the middle of the Mzinyathi river, holding the cased Queen's Colour of the 1/24th aloft; Lieutenant Coghill goes to his aid. The Colour was lost in the river immediately after this incident. (Author's collection)*

including both Colours. The 1/24th had been left to guard the camp, but only the Queen's Colour was present with the battalion, the Regimental Colour having been left with an outpost on the line of communication. None of the Colours were flying during the battle, but when the British position collapsed and the Zulus burst into the camp, the adjutant of the 1/24th, Lieutenant Melvill, secured the Queen's Colour of his battalion. Whether he intended to rally the men with it or simply to prevent it falling to the enemy remains unclear. In the event, there was no chance to organise a rally, and Melvill rode out of the camp with the Colour, still furled in its leather case, carried across his saddle. The Zulus were mopping up survivors of the massacre, and Melvill

had a difficult ride of three or four miles across very rugged country to reach the Mzinyathi river, the border with British Natal. Along the way he met up with Lieutenant Coghill, also of the 24th, and the two reached the river safely, only to find that it was in flood. The Zulus were slaughtering exhausted survivors along the banks, however, and both men plunged in; Coghill crossed safely, but Melvill came off his horse and, still holding the Colour, clung to a rock midstream. Coghill, seeing him under fire, turned back into the water and rescued him, but the Colour slipped away into the river. Unhorsed, both men struggled onto the Natal bank, but were overtaken and killed.

On 4 February, when the level of the river had dropped, a patrol from Rorke's Drift found the Colour lodged amongst the rocks. Although the silk was badly damaged, it was taken back to England, and presented to Queen Victoria at Osborne House. The Queen laid a wreath of immortelles – everlasting flowers – on the pole, and since that time the 24th and its successors have carried a silver wreath on their Colour poles in memory of the honour. There was

no provision for the award of the posthumous Victoria Cross in 1879, but Melvill and Coghill were amongst the first to be recognised when the rules were changed in 1904. The Colours of the 2/24th were never recovered, although one pole was found in a Zulu homestead towards the end of the war.

On 27 July 1880, during the Second Afghan War, the 66th Regiment suffered a disaster which was almost comparable to Isandlwana. They were part of a column which was attacked in overwhelming numbers near the village of Maiwand. The British line collapsed and the 66th retired in rallying squares. These were gradually broken up by the terrain and Afghan pressure, and the survivors tried to make a stand in a deep nullah, where the colonel, James Galbraith, seized the Queen's Colour to rally the men. Galbraith was killed and the Colour fell with him. The remainder of the battalion fell back on a village, where two second lieutenants were killed in turn holding up the Regimental Colour. This was taken up by Sergeant-Major Cuppage, who attempted to make a stand until he, too, was cut down. The survivors were driven back to Kandahar, with only a handful of the 66th among them. Neither Colour was recovered.

It was the experience of the 1881 Transvaal War, however, which finally forced the establishment to acknowledge that Colours had no place on a battlefield dominated by accurate long range rifle fire. Wolseley, indeed, is said to have remarked that any commander who ordered men to carry Colours under such circumstances 'should be tried for murder'. The three companies of the 94th Regiment, devastated at Bronkhorstspruit, included the headquarters, and the Colours were present at the action, though not flying. Once the firing had ceased, and the Boers rode up to seize ammunition and tend the wounded, the Colours were hidden under a wounded non-combatant, a Mrs Fox. Later, the Boers gave Conductor Ralph Egerton permission to walk to Pretoria to ask for ambulances and medical aid, and the men of the 94th secretly tore the Colours

*Right: The Colours of the 1/24th, presented to Queen Victoria at Osborne House in 1880, with the Queen's Colour, recovered from the Mzinyathi river, left. (RRW Museum, Brecon)*

*Right: The last Colours into action: the 58th's attack on the Boers at Laing's Nek, 1881. (Author's collection)*

from their poles, and wrapped them round Egerton's body under his tunic. By that time the Boers were searching for the Colours, but Egerton went on his way unmolested, and reached Pretoria, eleven miles away, after forty-two hours; he was later awarded a commission for his gallantry

At Laing's Nek the 58th attacked with both Colours flying. They were carried by Lieutenants Baillie and Peel, who both survived the actual attack, though Baillie, with the Regimental Colour, was wounded during the retreat. Peel went to help him, but Baillie replied: 'Never mind me, save the Colours'. Peel took both Colours but tripped and fell into an ant-bear hole. A Sergeant Bridgestock saw him fall and, thinking he was wounded, took both Colours, and carried them down the hill, where he handed them to the quartermaster, who took them out of action. Another lieutenant, Hill, tried to rescue Baillie, and when he couldn't lift him to his horse carried him off in his arms until Baillie was hit again and killed. Hill then rescued another man, and returned under fire to save a second. Hill was awarded the VC, but the devastation wrought amongst the Colour party was so obvious that in 1882 an order was published which finally banned Colours from the battlefield.

## Medical Services

At the beginning of the Victorian era medical facilities among the British army were minimal. Almost all medical services were dependant on the regimental medical officer, who was usually a civilian surgeon paid out of regimental funds, and perhaps one or two assistants. Though it was one of the duties of bandsmen to help the wounded from the field, there were no proper stretcher bearers, nor were there any ambulance facilities. Even in the most professional and conscientious units it was taken for granted that civilian transport would have to be hired in the field.

The shortcomings of this approach were made all too painfully obvious in the Crimea, where there was scarcely any civilian transport to be had, and where army administration broke down almost completely. A stretcher company, the Hospital Conveyance Corps, had been hastily raised from army pensioners, but soon proved completely inadequate to the task. Although some regimental medical facilities were available in the trenches outside Sebastopol, for the most part the wounded faced an agonising journey to Balaclava – on foot if they could walk, or thrown in a springless bullock wagon if they were lucky – where, amidst scenes of indescribable squalor, they were loaded on board ship and taken to the nearest base hospital, 300 miles away at Scutari on the Turkish Bosphorus. Conditions at Scutari were appalling; the hospital had

been built for 1000 men, but was soon overcrowded, and was completely overwhelmed when floods of casualties reached it after each battle. There were no beds, no furniture, no blankets, too few supplies and medicines, and the men often lay naked on the floor. Amputations were carried out in crowded wards in front of the men, the latrines soon became clogged, and urine tubs overflowed. Small wonder that of 2350 patients in the hospital at Scutari in January 1855, 2315 died.

The conditions at Scutari, made worse by lack of funds and squabbles between the authorities, were widely reported at home, and provoked Florence Nightingale's famous mission to the hospital in November 1854, accompanied by thirty-eight volunteer nurses. Nightingale was a strong and domineering woman, but her attempts to improve conditions were carried out in the face of bitter local resistance. The nurses were only allowed to fulfil menial duties until the influx of wounded from Inkerman and Balaclava, when the situation became so desperate they were at last allowed to help. Nightingale introduced a basic standard of care and hygiene, and improved the supply of food, often at her own expense; as a result the death rate at Scutari dropped from 44% on her arrival to 2.2% six months later.

Despite Nightingale's campaigning, the improvement to medical facilities in the aftermath of the Crimea remained gradual. In 1860

the Army Medical School was created, and the Royal Military Hospital built at Netley, at Queen Victoria's request. In the 1860s two further convalescent hospitals were built, at Woolwich and Cambridge. In 1857 the Army Hospital Corps was created to provide orderlies and bearers, but until 1873 it remained a Corps without officers, since all doctors remained on the regimental strength. In 1873, however, this system finally came to an end, and doctors were transferred to the Army Medical Department. This led to a significant improvement in medical care in the campaigns of the 1870s and 1880s, and a number of individual personnel distinguished themselves in combat conditions. At Rorke's Drift Surgeon Reynolds continued to treat the wounded under fire throughout the entire battle, whilst at Majuba Lance-Corporal J.J. Farmer was shot through the arm tending the wounded. He held up a white handkerchief in his uninjured hand, crying 'I have another' – and was promptly shot through that as well. Both Farmer and Reynolds were awarded the VC. At Ginniss a bearer company found themselves fighting in the front line. In Egypt in 1882 some 163 medical officers and 820 AHC were sent to the front, prompting Wolseley to comment: 'I never saw men better cared for, and the removal of the wounded was very well done'.

In the aftermath of the Egyptian campaign a Parliamentary commis-

*Left: The miseries of the Crimea: wounded men waiting to be taken on board ship at Balaclava. (Private collection)*

sion suggested that the AMD and AHC should be combined into one Corps; there was some resistance to this idea, however, which was not finally adopted until June 1898, when the Royal Army Medical Corps was finally approved by Royal Warrant. The Corps underwent its baptism of fire during Kitchener's reconquest of the Sudan, and provided the vast majority of medical care in the Anglo-Boer War. Initially some 850 officers, forty Warrant Officers, 240 Sergeants, and 2000 ORs were despatched for South Africa, although these soon proved insufficient to meet the needs of the widespread fighting. Some 700 civilian surgeons were employed as consultants by the army, and before the end of the war a total of 8500 men of all ranks had served in the field with the RAMC, in addition to 800 volunteer nurses. All in all the RAMC was able to mobilise 151 staff and regimental units, nineteen bearer companies, twenty-eight field hospitals, five stationary hospitals, sixteen general hospitals, three hospital trains, two hospital ships, and five store depots. These were further augmented by locally raised South African volunteer units.

## Transport and Supply

The task of keeping troops fed and supplied in the field is immensely important in any war – military success depends upon it just as much as on brilliant generalship – and this was doubly true in colonial campaigning, where the army habitually operated many miles from established bases and supply routes, often in harsh terrain with little water, minimal food resources, and often without roads. Indeed, many campaigns of the Victorian era were entirely shaped by the need to maintain viable lines of supply. Yet for much of the period the duties of commissariat and supply fell under different authorities, and the results were often chaotic. Although a number of attempts had been made since the end of the eighteenth century to establish some sort of formal authority to organise transport and supply, notably the Royal Wagoners and the

Royal Wagon Train of the Napoleonic era, these had been largely inadequate and had been disbanded in peace-time to save the expense of maintaining them. When the Victorian era began in 1837, the responsibility of organising provisions for troops in the field fell to the Commissariat Department, which was a civilian body, whilst no formal establishment existed at all to supervise the transport of such provisions. In the Napoleonic Wars the usual custom had been to hire transport equipment – wagons, mules and their civilian drivers – as and when they were needed. A similar system prevailed in India throughout the nineteenth century, where first the EIC and then the Queen's Indian Army were accustomed to hiring huge trains of ox-wagons and pack-camels, which were readily and cheaply available. The disadvantages of such *ad hoc* arrangements, however, were that the drivers were not subject to military organisation, and there was no guarantee of availability; civilian transport, in fact, was inherently unreliable. The implications of such an approach became all too obvious in the Crimea.

When the British expeditionary force landed at Calamita Bay, the men were ordered to take three days' rations with them. Although pack-animals and ambulances had been assembled at Varna, they were left there because there was no forage available in the Crimea, and the only horses landed belonged to the cavalry, artillery and officers. There proved to be almost no transport available in the Crimea itself, and the first wagons made available to the Commissariat were a handful captured from the Russians. The occupation of Balaclava at least afforded a landing site, but there were almost no means of moving provisions the eight miles to the lines in front of Sebastopol. Tons of supplies were left out in the open to spoil, and the situation deteriorated still further as the heavy rain of November 1854 heralded the onset of winter. The roads disintegrated into a quagmire, making it impossible to use even the few carts which

were available. Regimental officers were reduced to collecting supplies on horseback, but their horses began to die from the effects of exposure and lack of forage. Men making the journey on foot had to wade through knee-deep mud. Under such circumstances it was impossible to maintain an effective level of supply and in the trenches the men faced the onset of the bitter winter hungry.

The collapse of the Commissariat in late 1854 led to a Royal Warrant in January 1855 which created a new transport body, the Land Transport Corps. This was part of a concerted effort to reorganise the Commissariat in the spring of 1855, but it was not entirely successful. The Land Transport Corps eventually totalled over 8000 men organised into fourteen battalions, augmented by several thousand civilians of varied origins and precious little discipline. Indeed, most of the British element were unsuitable, being recruited from the urban poor, few of whom had any experience of horses or mules. Indeed, many were not used to the rigours of outdoor life, and the LTC had one of the highest mortality rates from disease and exposure in the field. Vehicles and carts were also brought from far and wide, and dumped unceremoniously amidst the squalor of Balaclava. Inevitably, the early efforts of the LTC were chaotic, and apart from a few experienced Commissariat officers it had to learn its duties as it went along. By the end of the war LTC units were attached to each front-line division, and were responsible for transporting its supplies and provisions along the lines of communication. Although this was a major improvement on the situation that had prevailed during the previous winter, the LTC never fully overcame its chaotic reputation, and its performance was generally considered disappointing.

Partly as a result of the publicity which surrounded the Crimean debacle, the Commissariat and supply services were reorganised in 1856. A new body, the Military Train, was formed to provide transport services, whilst the essentially

*Left: Piles of stores and forage landed at Zula for Sir Robert Napier's Abyssinian campaign, 1868. Note the tracks of the railway, built by Napier's Engineers. (Bryan Maggs Collection)*

civilian Commissariat Staff Corps was created to secure provisions. Although there were a number of advantages in the establishment of a proper supply corps, a new problem immediately arose. Many of the Military Train had formerly been members of cavalry regiments, and hard-pressed commanders in the field soon came to regard them as a substitutes to offset a chronic shortage of cavalry. The 2nd Battalion, for example, was en route to China when the Indian Mutiny broke out, and was immediately diverted. Its members proved capable of fulfilling most mounted duties, and were promptly divorced from their official duties and put into the field as cavalry. In that capacity they took part in a number of actions around Lucknow, and even earned two VCs. Similarly, the 4th Battalion found themselves cast in a similar role in New Zealand between 1861 and 1865. This created something of a cavalry spirit amongst officers of the Military Train, who rather resented the routine supply work for which they had been raised, and the fact that they were largely subordinate to the civilian Commissariat Staff Corps. Some attempt to resolve this was made by placing the Commissariat on a semi-military basis from 1858.

The Abyssinian campaign of 1867 foreshadowed a cluster of campaigns in the 1870s when success was largely dependant on the establishment of an effective system of supply. Zula on the Red Sea coast was selected as the landing place, despite the fact that it was 200 miles from Magdala and had inadequate landing jetties. Local labour had to be employed to build landing stages, erect huts for the stores, and dig wells. All of this work was still in progress when the first troops arrived, with predictably chaotic results. Because of the shortage of water, troops were ordered to camp near wells or water-holes, but these usually proved to be in areas where no fodder was available, and as many as a third of the available transport animals had to be employed to carry their own food. The situation was somewhat improved by the arrival of a more organised mule and elephant train from India, but Napier was still faced with a daunting task, made all the more urgent by the need to return to Zula before the onset of seasonal rains made the inland heights impassable. Napier organised his transport into two divisions, one ferrying supplies forward from Zula to the foothills, the other taking them to the advancing troops. The Royal Engineers built a railway to conduct supplies part of the way to the hills. The system almost ground to a halt, however, and food ran short when Napier was within a few days' march of Magdala, but the sit-

uation was saved in the nick of time by buying supplies from local civilians. In the event, the Abyssinians were quickly defeated, and Napier was able to begin the return march without the need for protracted campaigning; he reached Zula at the end of May just as the rains broke. Wastage amongst transport animals had been characteristically high: some 37,000 animals had been landed at Zula, of which as many as 7000 had died.

Shortly after the Abyssinian campaign, the Commissariat Staff Corps and Military Train were reorganised in an attempt to integrate their duties more fully. At the end of 1869 the CSC became the Control Department, which provided an officer establishment, whilst the Army Service Corps, formed shortly afterwards, provided NCOs and other ranks. As usual the Commissariat was responsible for providing supplies and the ASC for transporting them, but under the new system the two units were required to work much closer together. In many ways the ASC of the 1870s became the first true ancestor of the modern Royal Logistic Corps. The fledgling Corps was immediately put to the test when a small unit was attached to Sir Garnet Wolseley's Red River expedition in Canada in 1870. Wolseley was faced with the task of confronting a coalition of French

Canadian and Native Canadian separatists who had set up a government at Fort Garry, on the shores of Lake Winnipeg. To reach Fort Garry Wolseley first had to move his force 600 miles from Lake Superior. Roads were practically non-existent, and waterways served as transport arteries instead. Wolseley employed local boatmen, *voyageurs*, to supply the boats and pilot them. On no less than forty-seven occasions the boats had to be lifted out of the river and carried, but Wolseley, typically, had anticipated this, and all supplies were packed in small enough quantities to be carried manually. The Red River expedition proved demanding but entirely successful, as the rebel force was taken aback by Wolseley's rapid advance and dispersed without a fight.

A similarly thorough approach marked Wolseley's 1873–4 Asante campaign in West Africa. Animal transport was out of the question, because tsetse fly would have devastated it within days. Instead, Wolseley depended on a local system of transport by porters, and over 8000 local Africans were hired to ferry supplies in the army's wake. Control of the line of communication fell to Colonel George Colley – later to command in the 1881 Transvaal War

– and Colley tackled the task with flair and energy, organising the porters into tribal groups, who carried their loads to specified staging posts along the way. The system was fraught with difficulty, as the porters were often reluctant to work, especially close to the front, and on several occasions important loads were simply dumped in the bush, but it survived to the end of a mercifully quick campaign.

In South Africa, the chief problem was not the climate but the vast distances involved. The army was faced by no less than four different campaigns – the Ninth Cape Frontier War, the Zulu War, the Sekhukhune expedition and Transvaal War – which ran into one another over a period of five years, and at times involved lines of communication which stretched for over 1000 miles. The transport and supply resources were minimal: on the eve of the Zulu War, the Commissary-General in South Africa, Edward Strickland, had at his disposal just nineteen officers (the Commissariat and Transport Department had been formed from the Control Department in 1875) and twenty-nine men. The ASC was equipped with a number of light mule-drawn general service wagons, but these had been designed for European roads, and proved unsuit-

able in South Africa. Instead, Strickland had to hire or buy local ox-wagons, which were heavy, cumbersome, and needed an average of eighteen oxen to drag them. Managing oxen was itself an art; they had to be regularly fed and rested or they collapsed with exhaustion or succumbed to any number of contagious diseases. They were slow too, and even on a good day could only cover fifteen miles, or less if the track lay across rough country or was bisected by dongas or rivers, which might rise or fall at an alarming rate. Mules were hardier and therefore preferable, but they wouldn't eat local grasses, and so had to carry their fodder with them. So difficult did the supply situation become in the Ninth Cape Frontier War that it provoked a bitter dispute between General Cunynghame and the Cape government, which only ended when Cunynghame was replaced by Lieutenant-General Thesiger (later Lord Chelmsford).

Chelmsford's invasion of Zululand was entirely dictated by transport concerns. He had originally intended to invade Zululand with five separate columns, but since each infantry battalion needed a minimum of eighteen wagons to convey its tents, ammunition and supplies it proved quite impossible to find the necessary

*Right: The sprawling train of transport wagons with Lord Chelmsford's Eshowe Relief Column in Zululand in 1879 suggests something of the difficulties of keeping an army supplied in the field. (Author's collection)*

transport, and the invading force was reduced to three columns, with two in defence on the border. Even so, Chelmsford accumulated 10,000 oxen, 400 mules, fifty-six carts and 977 wagons by the time hostilities began in 1879. Many of these were purchased or hired from local settlers by inexperienced transport officers who paid considerably over the odds. Two of his columns were supplied along lines which stretched back to Durban, and the third from the Transvaal.

The war began disastrously, with the defeat at Isandlwana, although the Commissariat department distinguished itself when the border depot at Rorke's Drift was attacked, and two of its members were decorated. The arrival of reinforcements from Britain created a new logistical nightmare, despite the inclusion of three companies of the ASC and five Commissariat officers; not only had the loss of equipment at Isandlwana to be made good, but new wagons had to be found for the influx. This was exacerbated by the local climate, which swung from severe drought – which withered wayside forage – to heavy rain, which flooded the roads. To replenish losses mules were shipped to South Africa from as far afield as South America, and when the second invasion began at the end of May the line of one column was marked by the corpses of dead oxen which had collapsed every few yards along the way. The war ended with Chelmsford bitterly disputing the cost of the war with the Colonial authorities, much as his predecessor had done. Chelmsford's replacement, Wolseley, tried to repeat his Asante experiment by landing supplies on the Zululand coast and organising a Zulu Carrier Corps to transport them, but it was no more than a limited success. Wolseley had to undertake a campaign against Sekhukhune in a remote corner of the country in which horse-sickness was endemic, with a transport system which had largely collapsed under the strain of the Zulu War. That he was successful says much for the resourcefulness of his Commis-

sariat officers. The situation had not significantly improved in 1881 when Colley had to purchase local transport to supply his troops in northern Natal, although his inability to force the Laing's Nek pass at least meant that he had a static base to work from. Individual Commissariat personnel again distinguished themselves throughout, notably Conductor Egerton, who rescued the 94th's Colours at Bronkhorstspruit. ('Conductor' had been introduced in 1879 as the highest rank of NCO amongst the ASC; it was changed to warrant officer when that rank was introduced in 1881.)

Perhaps partly as a result of the problems in South Africa, the Commissariat department was overhauled yet again in 1880-1, the Commissariat and Transport Department being redesignated the Commissariat and Transport Staff, and the ASC the Commissariat and Transport Corps. The new formations were severely tested in North Africa between 1882 and 1885, but generally rose to the challenge. Wolseley, during the Nile operations, tackled the supply question thoroughly, and supplies of food and fodder were leap-frogged by boat, railway and overland, and stockpiled along the line of communication. When the Desert Column finally advanced on Khartoum, food and water were transported on

*Above: 'The rush for water': an incident after the battle of Kassassin, 1882. (Rai England Collection)*

camels, each carrying up to thirteen days' rations for eight men. Although this was largely successful from the supply point of view, the camels were difficult to control, especially when the column moved in square formation, and this contributed to the difficulties in the action at Abu Klea. Water remained in short supply, and the men suffered accordingly, while as much as 30% of the column's supply of biscuit was unfit to eat owing to faulty packaging. Around Suakin food was less of a problem, because the troops were operating from a fixed base which could be resupplied by sea. Dry stores could be left unprotected on the docks for weeks at a time, whilst live cattle were imported to provide a meat ration and bread was bought locally. Tinned 'bully beef' was less successful, however, as it turned to liquid jelly in the heat, and usually made the men thirsty. Water was again the major problem, since Suakin had poor supplies at the best of times, and water had to be distilled in ships anchored off-shore. It was stored in water-towers and transported by a variety of ingenious means, including by camel and water-cart, in canvas tanks, rubber cisterns, barrels and tins.

*Right: Stores accumulated at Datta Khel camp, Pathan Revolt, 1897. The blocks in the centre are of chopped and pressed forage for the horses; men are queuing in the foreground for their daily dose of quinine. (Bryan Maggs Collection)*

In December 1888 the Commissariat Transport Staff and Commissariat Transport Corps were finally reorganised into a new and fully integrated Army Service Corps. The reorganisation was carried out under the watchful eye of General Sir Redvers Buller, a Wolseley protégé who had served in the Red River, Asante and Sudan campaigns. Buller shared Wolseley's appreciation of the importance of transport and supply, so that by the time the system was fully put to the test – with the outbreak of the Boer War in 1899 – plans for supplying an Army Corps in the field had already been laid. The ASC detachments were sent out to South Africa ahead of the expeditionary force, and organised the purchase of local transport wagons and mules, so that as each fighting unit arrived it was issued a full compliment of battalion or regimental transport. If the difficulties were just as great in 1899 as they had been in 1877 – vast distances, poor roads, natural obstacles – at least the army went to the front with a functioning supply infrastructure already in place. Buller, when he took to the field himself, was renowned for the care he took to ensure his men were fed. Buller enjoyed a good meal, but would not eat until his men had

*Centre right: Transport in India: troops helping a bullock cart across a river. (Bryan Maggs Collection)*

*Right: A transport train at Ambigole Wells, Sudan, 1898. Note the men mounted on camels. (Bryan Maggs Collection)*

*Left: Stacks of military stores at Spearman's camp, during Buller's Spioenkop campaign, Boer War 1899. (S.B. Bourquin)*

received their rations, and Buller's hunger was a powerful stimulus to his supply officers. Nevertheless, the cumbersome supply trains which dogged the army in the field continued to hamper British movement, and during the Spioenkop campaign it is said that the Boers were first alerted to Buller's plans by the sight of his huge supply columns on the move.

Nevertheless, the system of established battalion transport worked well, and proved far safer than the system instituted by Roberts and Kitchener on their arrival in South Africa. Roberts, who had been schooled in India, which had a different tradition of supplying troops in the field, considered the system established by Buller wasteful and unnecessary. He planned to relieve Kimberley by moving across country, taking the Boers by surprise by abandoning the railway line which formed his principal supply route, and outflanking the Boer positions at Magersfontein. To that end he took all transport away from battalion commanders, and organised it into a central pool. The disadvantages of this system were perfectly demonstrated when De Wet caught one of these supply columns at Riet Drift on 15 February 1900, capturing or destroying nearly 2000 oxen and 170 wagons. Roberts was forced to abandon four days' rations for his entire force, together with a large quantity of medical supplies. This might have had serious consequences during the attack on Paardeberg had not French's cavalry – who had retained

their own transport – come to the rescue. Even so, Roberts' force was largely disabled by the incident, and the transport system ground to a halt. As a result his next move, towards Pretoria, was compromised, and the shortage of fresh food and medicines exacerbated the outbreak of typhus. Even Kitchener was forced to admit that, whatever Buller's failings as a commander, he had kept his army supplied when others had ground to a halt. Throughout the war the ASC performed its duties well, often under difficult circumstances, particularly during the fast-moving guerrilla war when supply trains inevitably delayed columns pursuing Boer commandos, or were themselves targets. Nevertheless, the fact that the British were able to take the war into all parts of southern Africa, without the serious danger that their troops would starve, was a testimony to the extent to which things had changed for the better since the days of the Crimea.

## Ammunition

Throughout the Victorian period, no proper system existed for the systematic supply of ammunition to troops at the front, with occasionally spectacular results. The issue of ammunition was the responsibility of the Ordnance department – whose name was changed several times across the period, but whose basic functions did not – but this took place at the principal supply depot in the rear. The responsibility of transporting that ammunition to the front fell to the senior Artillery officer, since

until 1914 the Artillery were charged with transporting not only their own ammunition, but small arms ammunition for infantry and cavalry units as well. The Royal Artillery had a number of ammunition trains for this purpose, although in practice these were only available in major campaigns, and the ammunition was usually transported in the same way as the rest of the baggage. In Asante, for example, it was transported in hand-carts, whilst in the Sudan it was carried on camels, and elsewhere frequently on mules. In the first phase of the Zulu War it was transported in local wagons, although an ammunition train was sent out to South Africa as part of the reinforcements after Isandlwana and served during the later stages of the war. In the field, each battalion was required to carry two reserves, one of which was issued to the men and carried in their pouches, whilst the other was under the care of the battalion quartermasters and issued as necessary. In the Zulu War, for example, the infantry carried seventy rounds per man in their pouches, whilst a further 200 rounds per man were carried in the battalion reserve. No system existed for distributing ammunition from the reserve to companies in action; it was left either for company officers to send back runners, or for the quartermasters to co-opt bandsmen or others not already employed.

Much has been said about ammunition failure as a contributory factor to the disaster at Isandlwana, which is often blamed on obdurate quartermasters refusing to issue ammunition without a requisition order, and faulty ammunition boxes which could only be opened with the correct screwdrivers. This is a distortion all the more curious for the lack of evidence that the infantry companies in the firing line – chiefly the 1/24th – experienced any shortage of ammunition during the crucial stages of the battle. Nor was the design of ammunition box particularly significant; the same box had been used throughout the Cape Frontier War and in other Zulu War battles without any notable difficulties. It does seem clear, however, that the haphazard means of distributing ammunition in action was imperfect, and vulnerable to confusion in the stress of a particularly intense battle like Isandlwana.

## The Royal Engineers

Whereas most regiments in the British army receive battle honours according to battles or campaigns in which they fought, the Royal Artillery and Royal Engineers are proud possessors of just one honour: *Ubique* – 'Everywhere'. It reflects the fact that detachments from these Corps have fought in almost every British campaign, and in the case of the Engineers it could not be more appropriate, since without their contribution many an army in the field would have ceased to function. The Royal Engineers were responsible for a formidable array of engineering duties, not merely constructing or destroying forts and earthworks, but surveying, building bridges, cutting roads, building railways, establishing and operating telegraph lines, searchlights and balloons, providing water supplies, and submarine mining. On top of all that, they were trained to fight as infantry, and more than once found themselves operating as front-line troops.

In 1837 the Engineers were divided into the Royal Engineers – who provided the officers – and the Royal Sappers and Miners, who provided the NCOs and other ranks. Officers had been trained at the Royal Military Academy at Woolwich, in a highly professional course which included not only the scientific aspects of engineering and gunnery, but also maths, astronomy, mineralogy, metallurgy, geometry, languages and landscape drawing, as well as the soldierly arts of fencing, horse-riding and foot drill. The RE were not a purchase corps, and took a pride in their professionalism, which tended to distance them from the more fashionable purchase regiments. In October 1856, after the Crimean War, the Royal Engineers and Sappers and Miners were amalgamated to form the Corps of Royal Engineers, and in 1862 took over the former EIC Engineer corps, the RE thereafter providing officers for the Indian Corps of Sappers and Miners.

The Engineers' record in the Victorian period was exemplary. It was a party of Bengal and Bombay Sappers and Miners who blew the Kabul gate at Ghazni in July 1839, during the First Afghan War. In the Crimea, RE and Sappers and Miners supervised the construction of the siege works around Sebastopol, the roads to the front from Balaclava, and the building of landing jetties in the port itself. The telegraph had been invented by Morse in 1832, and the first field telegraph was laid in the Crimea, twenty-five miles of it, connected to a submarine cable across the Black Sea. During the Indian Mutiny, the storming of Delhi would have been impossible but for the success of a party of Bengal Sappers and Miners blowing the Kashmir Gate whilst under a heavy fire which killed several of their number. In Abyssinia the 10th Company RE not only turned Zula into a viable port, but also built a railway across twelve miles of the coastal flats, and provided a photographic team to record the campaign. In 1871, the first submarine mining company was established, made necessary by the

*Below: First in, last out: Royal Engineer officers during the Second Afghan War. (Bryan Maggs Collection)*

gradual change in shipping to steam power; hitherto harbours had been protected by chains and booms, but the Engineers now had to perfect the new art of underwater explosives. In Asante, the RE erected miles of telegraph line in the jungle, whilst Kitchener's reconquest of the Sudan would have been impossible without the building of the Sudan Military railway, which crossed 370 miles from Wadi Halfa to Atbara. Not least of the RE's achievements in the Boer War was the cordon of barbed wire and blockhouses built across the country, which eventually deprived the Boer commandos of room to manoeuvre.

A surprising number of individuals who distinguished themselves during the Victorian period were Engineers. Robert Napier was a colonel in the Bengal Engineers before being given command of the Abyssinian expedition – the first time command of an army in the field was given to an Engineer. Charles Gordon was an Engineer, and enjoyed a remarkably varied career, which took him from the Crimea to Shanghai, where he was seconded to the service of the Imperial Chinese government in its struggle against the Taiping rebels, and to Khedival Egypt. It was Gordon's success as governor of the province of Equatorial Sudan, where he distinguished himself by his vigorous crusade against the slave trade, which led the British government to send him to Khartoum in the wake of the Mahdist revolt, and it was his background as an Engineer which enabled him to defend the city for so long. In the Zulu War, Colonel Anthony Durnford, the senior officer killed at Isandlwana, was an Engineer, and so was Lieutenant John Chard, who was supervising a ferry at Rorke's Drift when the Zulus attacked, and earned himself the VC. In Afghanistan, at about the same time, two Engineer officers, Captain Leach and Lieutenant Hart, also received the same distinction, whilst Lieutenant Henn died at the head of a party of Bombay Sappers and Miners at Maiwand. Herbert Kitchener – later Lord Kitchener of Khartoum, the hero of Omdurman and the Boer

War – was an Engineer, and so was Sir Charles Warren. Warren's career was no less exotic in its way than Gordon's, for he snatched Bechuanaland from under the noses of the Boers in 1885, and later served as Commissioner for Police in London – during which time he had failed to catch Jack the Ripper – before commanding a division in the Spioenkop debacle. Bindon Blood, a colourful Irishman whose ancestor had tried to steal the Crown Jewels, was commissioned in 1860 and joined the Bengal Sappers and Miners, but served in Zululand and Egypt, then returned to India to command the Malakand Field Force – Churchill was attached to his staff – and later held a lieutenant-general's command in the Eastern Transvaal during the Boer War. Small wonder that the Royal Engineers prided themselves on being able to turn their hands to anything.

In the field the usual RE unit was the company. A field company was 203 strong, and attached to a division, with another company as corps troops. Some companies were specialists in designated fields, such as telegraphy, railways or balloons – a balloon section was deployed at Suakin in 1885, and four more in the Boer War. In 1899, the regular establishment of the Royal Engineers, excluding the Militia, was a Mounted Detachment (the Field Troop), two Pontoon Troops (forming the Bridging Battalion), eight Field Companies, a Balloon Section, a Telegraph Battalion, eighteen Fortress Companies (excluding the West India Fortress Company), eight Depot Companies, twelve Submarine Mining Companies and a Coastal Defence Battalion (excluding five overseas Submarine Mining Companies in Ceylon, Hong Kong, Mauritius, Singapore and the West Indies), two Railway Companies, and four Survey Companies.

## Blockhouses

The blockhouse is, perhaps, one of the enduring images of the Anglo-Boer War – the physical symbol of the British army's inability to match the Boers in a war of manoeuvre, but

proof of the infinitely greater resources of the Empire which ultimately brought them to heel. Yet the blockhouse was by no means unique to the Boer War, even in South Africa. As early as 1799, during the first British occupation of the Cape, a stone blockhouse was built to protect the naval base at Simon's Town, and three more were built around Table mountain. At the same time another, called Fort Frederick, had been built to guard Algoa Bay, which was then the furthest point of British influence on the border with Xhosa country. All of these blockhouses were of a similar design, being two storeys high, with stone walls at the base and wood for the second storey. The upper level was loopholed, and projecting bastions were built to provide fire to enfilade anyone attacking close to the walls. In this respect they were similar in concept to the first stone blockhouses built during the Boer War. In 1838 the first garrison to occupy Port Natal built Fort Victoria, apparently a prefabricated wooden blockhouse, to guard the bay. Over the next fifty years a rash of forts were erected on the Cape frontier, including a chain of them, built during the last stages of the Sixth Cape Frontier War, intended to surround the Xhosa stronghold in the Amatola mountains. The basic principal which underlay their construction was the need to separate settlers and Xhosa, to protect the one and contain the other, and much the same applied in New Zealand, where settler encroachment on Maori land was a perennial source of conflict. At the very beginning of the First Maori War, in 1845, when the chief Hone Heke repeatedly cut down the flagstaff outside Kororareka, the army attempted to protect it by building a blockhouse. Hone Heke responded by attacking it, provoking the first serious military action in New Zealand. Later, during the campaigns of the 1860s, chains of forts were built to separate Maori and settler land. Most of these forts started out as simple earthworks consisting of ramparts of sods, often bound together with fern, and surrounded by a deep ditch, but as it became clear

*Right: 'Right Water Fort', a blockhouse on the outskirts of Suakin, Sudan, 1885. (Bryan Maggs Collection)*

*Below: Corrugated iron blockhouse and its garrison, Boer War, 1901. (National Army Museum)*

that they were likely to be occupied for some time they were either replaced by wooden blockhouses, or these were built within the ramparts. These blockhouses were different in concept to the forts built in Zululand and elsewhere, which were intended to guard lines of communication rather than contain the enemy, and were essentially temporary.

The first blockhouses of the Boer War were built at Roberts' direction in March 1900, following the capture of Bloemfontein. They were built along the line of the Cape Town–Bloemfontein railway, Roberts' principal line of supply, to protect points of obvious vulnerability from the Boers. They were solid affairs built largely of stone, and were two storeys high with a projecting bastion in one corner of the upper floor to house a machine-gun. The roof was usually of corrugated iron, and access was via a ladder to the second floor. The walls were properly loopholed, and the corners of the ground floor had small projecting bastions to enable the defenders to enfilade any attacker approaching the outside walls. They were very expensive, costing between £800 and £1000 apiece, and took three months to build. They were, however, very effective, and not one of the stretches of track they protected was successfully attacked by the Boers. In the eastern Transvaal a few less sturdy blockhouses were built, single-storey buildings made of two layers of corrugated iron, the gap between being filled with earth. When the guerrilla war began it was suggested that blockhouses should be built not merely to protect the railway, but across the veld to try to control Boer movements. It was clearly impractical to build large numbers of the stone type, so Kitchener, who had replaced Roberts, ordered an Engineer officer, Major Rice, to come up with a design based on the corrugated iron type.

Rice's blockhouse retained the concept of the double corrugated iron wall but was round, not rectangular. These blockhouses proved cheap and effective; when they were mass-produced they cost as little as £16 and could be erected in six hours by six trained men. They were further protected by trenches and walls of sandbags and a web of wire entanglements. By the end of the war over 8000 blockhouses had been built, covering a total of 3,700 miles, an average of one blockhouse for every half mile. In some places blockhouses were built just 1000 yards apart, and connected with wire entanglements which were hung with tin cans so as to make a noise and attract the garrison if anyone tried to cross them.

A typical blockhouse was garrisoned by a junior NCO and six men, a small enough number which nonetheless required the commitment of over 50,000 men at the guerrilla war's height. The men were generally safe from attack by Boers lacking artillery – as most were at this stage – but garrison duty was immensely tedious. The possibility of a Boer attack could never be entirely discounted, yet such excitement was rare enough, and for most men blockhouse duty meant weeks or even months of unremitting boredom, waiting and watching. Nevertheless, the system undoubtedly contributed to the British success in the war of attrition which ultimately defeated their will o' the wisp enemy.

## Communication and Control

In 1879, General Lord Chelmsford went to war in Zululand with no effective means of long-range communication. In that regard, his experience was typical of most colonial campaigns up to that time; he was faced with co-ordinating and controlling three separate columns operating many miles apart in a difficult environment which was, moreover, enemy territory. The only means available of communicating with his column commanders was the traditional one of riders carrying written messages. This system was not ideal, since riders were obviously fallible and vulnerable, and the dangers of Chelmsford's position became all too apparent when he was thrown onto the defensive by the Zulu victory at Isandlwana. His supporting columns were left high and dry, and when the Right Flank Column was besieged for three months at Eshowe, Chelmsford simply could not get messages through. African volunteers tried to run the Zulu gauntlet carrying orders and letters, but most were either killed or had to turn back. Signalling by flags was a common enough practice at the time, but although Eshowe was situated on a hill-top with a clear line of sight to Chelmsford's forts thirty-five miles away, it was impossible to distinguish figures at that distance. The garrison tried various ingenious means of communication, including a paper hot-air balloon, and a large screen erected on the hill-side, both of which were thwarted by heavy gales which destroyed them. Finally, Chelmsford's men found a mirror belonging to a local settler, and improvised a means of sending messages by reflecting the suns rays, and after various mishaps the Eshowe garrison found a way of flashing replies back.

There was nothing unique about this experience, for the technology necessary to send messages over long distances was in its infancy in the 1870s, and was seldom available to commanders embarking on small punitive campaigns. Although Samuel Morse had invented his famous code in the 1830s – the basis of all transmitted communication

until the advent of the field telephone – and the first military telegraph line had been laid in the Crimea, such sophisticated methods languished in the 1860s, largely due to government parsimony. It was not until the 1870s that the Royal Engineers received their first effective Field Telegraph companies, and these could not meet all the demands of an almost constant round of minor campaigning. A Telegraph Company was sent out to Zululand as part of the reinforcement after Isandlwana, but some idea of its state of readiness is suggested by the fact that the officer in charge protested that he was being despatched with only his peace-time allocation of just twenty miles of telegraph wire. Although this was in the end increased, the Engineers still had to fall back on their traditional ingenuity by extending the line with uninsulated fencing wire.

In India the situation was marginally better. In 1869 Henry Mance of the Government Persian Gulf Telegraph Department had invented a means of communicating by mounting a fixed mirror on the end of a tripod, and controlling the reflection of the sun's rays by means of a shutter. The apparatus was called the heliostat, and after extensive trials it was approved for use by the Indian Army in 1873. An improved version of the heliostat, the heliograph, which used a flexible rather than fixed mirror, was introduced in the late 1870s. On a clear day the heliograph could send a message which could be spotted at distances up to fifty miles, although the apparatus was entirely dependant on good weather and was useless on a cloudy day. Nevertheless both the field telegraph and the heliograph were extensively used in the Second Afghan War. The heliograph was not widely used elsewhere, however, and indeed the first heliographs sent out to Zululand were despatched from the workshops of the Bengal Sappers and Miners in Roorkee in India, after the relief of Eshowe. Perhaps because of the Eshowe experience, however, heliographs soon became indispensable in the field.

*Right: A field telegraph in action in Afghanistan, 1879. (Bryan Maggs Collection)*

*Right: A Royal Engineers field telegraph section on manoeuvres in England, 1880s. (Ian Castle Collection)*

*Right: The Headquarters' signalling staff, Kabul 1879; note the heliograph, right centre. (Bryan Maggs Collection)*

During the 1881 Transvaal War, messages could be relayed via a chain of heliograph stations from Colley's camp at Fort Prospect to the provincial capital, Pietermaritzburg, 250 miles away, in about three hours; this compared favourably to the three or four days it took to receive messages sent by rider from Lord Chelmsford's columns in Zululand, a comparable distance.

Heliographs, field telegraphs, and signalling by flag and by lantern at night were all used extensively in the Sudan, North-West Frontier and Boer campaigns, although they never entirely replaced the mounted rider.

The importance of effective communication as a means of controlling battles continued to be demonstrated as late as 1900 in actions such as Spioenkop. Here, on the Boer side, a courageous signaller, Louis Bothma, climbed almost to the summit and was able to direct the Boer artillery fire from a sheltered position only a few yards away from the British lines, with devastating effect. On the other side, however, the British divisional commander, Warren, was in a depression at the foot of the hill, with no line of sight to a British heliograph position on the rear slope of the summit. Messages

had to be carried to Warren by runner, whilst Buller – on a ridge to the rear – could see the heliograph messages from the summit, and was prompted to intervene, often issuing orders which contradicted Warren's. This undoubtedly contributed to the confusion over command, which was made worse when at least one runner was killed within a few yards of the officer to whom he was taking a message. At night, attempts to consult with Warren about the proposed withdrawal from the Kop were thwarted when it was discovered that no oil had been brought up the hill for the signal lamps.

# 5

# VOICES FROM THE RANKS
## Life on Campaign

'We're the Soldiers of the Queen,
  my lads,
who've been, my lads, who've seen,
  my lads...'
Contemporary song.

'I can assure you that the hardships I came through before I got this situation – were they told to me a year ago – I would have positively said that it was a matter of impossibility for me to come through them – but once you get used to them you think little or nothing of them...'

Lance-Corporal Donald MacDonald,<br>2/21st, Upoko River, Zululand,<br>14 June 1879.

For the Victorian soldier, active service overseas was often the start of a journey which took him to strange and exotic places, to live among alien peoples whose language and culture he did not understand, and from whose strangeness he shielded himself with a sense of inbred superiority. Furthermore, sooner or later that journey would bring him face to face with the harsher realities of his profession. Occasionally, it began on a high note. When troops were despatched from home postings on a particular expedition, crowds of patriotic or curious sightseers often gathered to cheer them through the streets on their way to embarkation, as Private Macaulay of the Scots Guards discovered, when his regiment was sent to Egypt with Sir Garnet Wolseley:

*The aftermath of Tel-el-Kebir, showing abandoned Egyptian artillery behind the rampart. (Private collection)*

207

About July 1882 ... we were warned for active service in Egypt. The order came so suddenly that no furlough was granted to enable us to bid our friends goodbye.

In consequence of this, thousands of people assembled in front of the barracks by three o'clock in the morning of the 29th July, the day on which we were to embark. There were among them, wives, mothers, sisters, brothers, fathers, friends, children, and relations belonging to the officers and men, all anxious to see us off. Amidst the greatest excitement and enthusiasm, we were marched to Westminster Bridge Pier, where there were, I think, four steamers waiting to take us down the river. Such crowds of people I had never seen before; they lined the streets as we passed along, and increased in numbers every moment. They flocked with us to the embankment and the Bridge, and watched our embarkation with much interest.

When at last we began to move off, the cheering was deafening, and, as we passed down the river, we noticed that the Embankment from Westminster Bridge to Blackfriars was packed with sightseers. Every bridge under which we passed was crowded to watch our progress, and when at last we had left London behind us, many people took the train for Gravesend, and, by the time we came in sight of the town, they were out on the river in small boats to see the last of us. We embarked on the Oriental Steam Navigation Company's steamship *Orient*, which was in the river waiting our arrival. There were upwards of seven hundred men in our battalion, which was under the command of Colonel Knox. The Duke of Connaught also embarked at the same time, and several members of the Royal Family came on board to bid him good-bye...

For most soldiers, however, there were no Royal goodbyes when they were sent overseas on routine postings, whether or not these might lead to fighting in their turn. Compare the pomp and circumstance of the Guards' departure for Egypt in 1882 to Private Hinton's description of the 58th's departure for the Australian garrison in 1844:

We embarked on the *Sir Robert Peel*, and went up to Deptford; where we took on board two hundred and fifty convicts, who came to the ship's side in small boats, under the charge of warders, while we formed a guard, each man with his firelock, or 'Brown Bess', loaded, to prevent any attempt at escape. The convicts were all handcuffed, and were conducted down to the hold, which had been fitted up with berths for their accommodation. They were afterwards brought on deck singly, and one of our men, who had been a blacksmith, had to rivet an iron ring upon each ankle. A long chain, fastened to a belt round the man's waist, was fixed to each ring, and these were not taken off till we landed the convicts at Hobart's Town, in Tasmania, except in cases of good conduct, when the men were allowed to work on board.

Our time was taken up in watching the prisoners, and we were glad to reach the end of our journey, which occupied five months and a half...

The long haul to Australia was, of course, unusual, even in the days of sail. It took over five months to reach Australia, allowing for stops along the way, and three to India. With the advent of steam such journeys were reduced to a more acceptable length. It took about a fortnight, for example, for the Russian Expeditionary Force to reach Varna in 1854, and rather less for the second stage of the journey to the Crimea. Wolseley's Asante expedition was at sea for just over three weeks before landing at Cape Coast Castle in West Africa in 1873, whilst Private Macaulay reached Alexandria, on the Egyptian coast, in just twelve days. In 1879 transports taking reinforcements to the Zulu War took just under a month to reach Cape Town – trimmed to three weeks by 1900 – and a further three or four days to Durban on the east coast. Nevertheless, despite Britain's reputation as a maritime nation the government did not maintain any naval transports of its own, and ships usually had to be hired for the purpose from civilian lines. Life on board a transport was uncomfortable and cramped; the officers were generally allocated the best cabins, whilst the men, who were issued with plain canvas smocks to prevent their uniforms from being dirtied, slept in hammocks in the hold. Food consisted of salt meat and biscuit – not much different from the daily ration on land – although the men were issued a daily allowance of lime juice, to ward off scurvy in the absence of fresh vegetables. Boredom was the greatest problem of shipboard life, and the men played cards, smoked, and occasionally organised concerts to pass the time. Sometimes last-minute target practice was organised, and the men fired over the rail at a target towed in the sea behind. Many probably fired as many rounds on these occasions as they had during several years of peace-time soldiering, whilst the officers took sporting pot-shots at passing birds. Harry O'Clery, who enlisted under a false name in the Buffs, describes another favourite method of letting off steam aboard ship during the passage to Zululand:

We embarked on the ship ... in company with a detachment of the 87th Regiment, known as 'The Old Fogs', or the 'Faugh-a-Ballagh Boys', from the war-cry of the corps, 'Fag-an-Bealoch', meaning 'Clear the way'. During the voyage to the Cape we heard this war-cry on several occasions, and the monotony of the voyage was varied by occasional fights between men of the two regiments, who

*Right: The troop-ship* Jumna *in dry dock in Malta in 1872. (Keith Reeves Collection)*

probably considered that, as they were going out to fight, there could be no objection to a little practise before-hand; and I can speak from my experience in saying that most of my countrymen enjoy nothing better than a lively argument, and a free fight to wind up with.

Bad weather could be an unpleasant experience for those used to a life ashore, but the first suggestion of land brought an air of excitement, an expectation of the journey's end, and of impending action. Second Lieutenant Arthur Mynors of the 3/60th Rifles, also en route for Zululand, took the hazards of shipboard life in his stride:

Friday night everybody was ill, as the sea was rough. Saturday in the Bay of Biscay it was awful, the waves were mountains high – a grand sight – so much so that the upper decks were washed over all day. I was awfully ill, in fact so was everybody. Our cabin, which is on deck, was turned upside down,

portmanteaus and everything flying about, we had to hold tight to stay in bed at all ... Saturday night the storm continued, the hatches were battened down to prevent the water going down on the lower decks. You know the boats slung up by the side of the ship, actually touched the sea when we rolled; also the sea broke over into the engines. On Saturday morning at four a.m., I was on watch, luckily for me it was much calmer, I found two of the horses had died in the night, and that several hammocks, and other things had been washed overboard ... We consigned the poor horses to the deep ... The men have an awfully bad time of it, packed so close they can hardly breathe ...

Some of the sun-rises are perfectly lovely, and when going at night the phosphorus is a magnificent sight. Have seen no end of different kinds of fish, such as flying fish and sharks, porpoises, and some sword fish,

about as big as the boat on the Railsyatt Pond, and other curious beasts. The number of shoals of porpoises that pass us is wonderful, they jump out three or four feet in the air. We have seen several birds, which is curious so many miles from shore, among them a stormy petrel ... We had some pistol practising yesterday, which was great fun. I spend the day mostly in reading, but it is awfully slow, nothing to do.

Shipwreck was, of course, an ever-present hazard, a risk the soldier had to run long before he ever set foot in enemy territory. The gales, reefs and shoals around the coast of southern Africa were notoriously treacherous, and were responsible for the wreck of many thousands of tons of civilian shipping across the nineteenth century. No less than two of the transports sent out with reinforcements for the Zulu War ran into difficulties. On 23 March 1879 the *City of Paris* ran aground in Simon's Bay, north of Cape Town, and the troops on board had to be transferred to

*Left: The SS Birkenhead, wrecked off 'Danger Point', South Africa. (Author's collection)*

HMS *Tamar*. Our friend Private MacDonald was among their number, but he made little of the incident in his letters home – 'some excitement prevailed on board for about half an hour or so – rockets went up in the air, but to no purpose, although we could easily see lights all along the coast. Fortunately, however, she veered off the rock and we came safely to anchor in the bay'. On 3 April there was a more serious incident when the *Clyde* ran aground off Dyer's Island. The *Clyde* was carrying drafts for the 24th Regiment, to replace those lost at Isandlwana, and the troops had to be ferried to the shore, about three miles away, by the ship's boats. Fortunately the weather was calm, and all were got off safely before the *Clyde* finally sank; the men were rescued by HMS *Tamar* the next morning after an uncomfortable night on shore. In November 1857 the *Sarah Sands*, carrying 368 men of the 54th Regiment to the Indian Mutiny, caught fire not long after rounding the Cape. For nearly eighteen hours the fire raged unchecked – at one point volunteers from the regiment braved the flames to rescue the 54th's Colours, stored below deck – and powder stored in the magazine exploded, but, remarkably, the *Sarah Sands* stayed afloat, and limped into

Mauritius without the loss of a single life. Not all were so lucky, however, and the most famous story of disaster to befall a troopship concerns the fate of the SS *Birkenhead*.

The *Birkenhead* was an iron paddle-steamer of about 2000 tons, which set sail from Queenstown in Ireland in January 1852, destined for the Cape. On board were drafts from nine regiments – the 12th Lancers, 6th, 12th, 43rd, 45th, 60th, 73rd, 74th and 91st – intended as reinforcements for the Eighth Cape Frontier campaign. There were about 500 troops on board altogether, with fifty-six women and children, and 138 officers and crew. The *Birkenhead* reached Simon's Town after a passage of forty-five days, and stopped to take on food, water and coal. She set sail again late on the afternoon of 25 February, heading for Algoa Bay and East London. At 2 am on the morning of the 26th, during calm weather, the *Birkenhead* struck a submerged rock off Danger Point, two miles off-shore near Cape Agulhas, the southernmost point of the African continent. A huge hole was immediately ripped in the ship's bow, and thousands of tons of water poured in, drowning many of the troops in their hammocks. The survivors rushed up on deck and attempts were made to work the

pumps, but in little more than twenty minutes the *Birkenhead* broke up completely. The bow fell into deeper water, the funnel collapsed, and the waves carried away one of the paddle-houses. There were six lifeboats on board the *Birkenhead*, but three were either damaged in the wreck, or rusted into place. Once the initial panic subsided, the officers helped the women and children to the lifeboats with, as one survivor, Corporal Smith of the 12th, recalled, 'a politeness and attention which is so wonderful that, sore as my own strait is, I cannot help smiling'. Once the boats had pushed away from the wreck, the *Birkenhead*'s master urged the troops to take to the water, but the officers, fearing they would swamp the boats, ordered them to form up on deck. Corporal Smith recalled the scene:

The old King of Prussia commanded that the story of the *Birkenhead* drill and fortitude should be read to every regiment in his army; artists have painted pictures of the troops drawn up in steady ranks on deck, and poets have sung of the way the bugles rang and the drums beat; but there was no sound of bugle and no role of drum; there was none of the

*Right: The 'Birkenhead Drill': troops line up on the deck, waiting for the women and children to go first into the boats. In fact, after a hot night below decks, most of the men were in their shirtsleeves or naked. (Private collection)*

*Right: Life aboard a troop transport: the 1st (King's) Dragoon Guards disembarking at Durban for the Zulu War. (Author's collection)*

stiffness of parade which pictures show – and yet there was a falling-in, a last muster, a standing shoulder to shoulder as the end came, and many a handshake and many a sobbed farewell...

The remainder of the *Birkenhead* broke up, and the men standing on deck were swept into the sea. Although the shore was only two miles away, there was a strong swell, seaweed clogged the approaches to the beach and, worst of all, the sea was infested with sharks. A few men managed to cling to wreckage and were carried ashore; the *Birkenhead* came to rest on the bottom with her main mast sticking up out of the water, and a handful of survivors managed to cling to it until rescued the next morning. But nearly 450 were drowned or taken by the sharks, and the reinforcement for Sir Harry Smith's army on the frontier was wiped out at a stroke. Yet not one of the women and children were lost, and the '*Birkenhead* Drill', the tradition of maintaining discipline, of obeying orders to the end, passed into the folklore of the Victorian army.

If the average soldier survived the voyage out without mishap – and the vast majority, of course, did – there were often fresh discomforts to be endured when they arrived at their destination. Such was the swell off the coast of West Africa that transports arriving with troops for the Asante wars had to lie off the open beach and unload the men into surf-boats, which local Africans paddled through the crashing breakers to the shore. For most of the nineteenth century, troops landing off Durban were at the mercy of the unpredictable sand-bar which blocked the entrance to the harbour. After a heavy rain, when there was a lot of water flowing out to sea, it was possible to sail across, but the rest of the time ships were compelled to anchor off the bar and transfer their passengers to smaller boats with a shallower draft for the final run ashore. In 1879 both men and horses were taken off the transports in large baskets, and lowered by pulleys into the boats; small wonder that both men and horses needed time ashore to recover from the voyage. Gunner Cox, RA, recalled that a particularly grim sight, a foretaste of the horrors to come, greeted him as the British fleet anchored of Eupatoria at the start of the Crimean War:

> I shaln't forget noticing several bodies of persons who had died, and had been sewn up in blankets and launched over-board, floating about round the sides of the vessels, as the shots put in to sink them were not sufficient for the purpose; and this was the beginning of the shocking scenes with which we were soon acquainted. I remember a poor chap dying on our ship, and I had to go with others in a boat and drop him overboard beyond the outer row of ships. There was no sort of funeral service about that time, and we soon got used to the terrors of death...

It was, nonetheless, unusual for troops to make a landing under threat of a potential attack. In all the wars in South Africa and India, the British commanded secure bases on the coast where they could land troops and supplies freely; during that first landing at the Crimea, the Allies had no such secure base, and might have been attacked at any time. As a result the troops were landed ready for action, in all the splendid finery of the 1850s, and left to fend for themselves in front-line conditions. Evelyn Wood, then a midshipman in the Royal Navy, described the extraordinary spectacle of the landing:

> The officers landed in full dress, carrying sword, revolver, with greatcoat rolled horseshoe fashion over the shoulder, some spirits in the wooden water-bottle, then called a canteen, three days' boiled salt pork, and three days' biscuit. The Rank and File being weak, many still suffering from intestinal complaints, it was decided to leave their knap-

sacks on board, and they were sent to Scutari. Each soldier carried fifty rounds of ammunition, three days' rations, greatcoat and blanket in which was rolled a pair of boots, socks and forage cap, of the curious pork-pie shape to which the Army clung until a few years ago. It was a useless article, but not so inconvenient as the handsome head-dress our Generals liked, but which the men discarded at the first opportunity. In the following winter I saw battalions throwing away their full head-dress as they left Balaclava.

> Some horses were hoisted out of ships into barges, others were lowered into the sea, and the supporting sling being detached by a tripping line, one or more horses were attached to the stern of a boat, which, being rowed to the shore, was followed by the other horses. All reached the land except three of Lord Raglan's, which on being lowered into the water swam out to sea, and were drowned. At sunset a heavy ground swell broke up the rafts, and obliged us to land articles by passing them from man to man standing in the water; but we continued to work till 11.30 pm, re-embarking in our boats on the Bluejackets' shoulders some sick soldiers. It rained dismally that night...

Sergeant-Major Richard Ellis of the Buffs recorded his impressions of that first night in the Crimea:

> I was with my company on the outlying picket, and I shall never forget my experience. We had no shelter from the storm but greatcoats and blankets. It was impossible to lie down, and the whole of the men kept moving about on that miserable beach to keep themselves alive and warm. No lights or watch-fires were possible. Officers and men alike shared the misery, which seemed unending...

Once ashore, the British soldier was exposed to an environment to which life in the villages of rural Britain or the narrow, dank claustrophobic alleys of the industrial slums had ill prepared him. Some theatres of war were not so different from home as to be positively disconcerting; many British troops found the scenery in Natal 'park-like', for example, although they were less impressed with the weather, which was alternately baking hot, or pouring with rain. Opinions about the open country of the Orange Free State and Transvaal were, on the whole, less flattering, and many a soldier on convoy duty in the Boer War complained of the endless monotony of the drab, featureless veld, whilst not everyone appreciated the harsh beauty of the arid Karoo. The bush country of the Eastern Cape, or the ferns and forests of New Zealand, were difficult to fight in, but they lacked the weirdness which many felt in the still rain-forests of Asante, as Evelyn Wood, again, describes:

> The country in which we were operating was a dense forest of gigantic trees, many 150 feet high, laced together with creepers supporting foliage so thick as to shut out the sun, which we never saw except in villages; indeed, the light was so dim that I could not read my English letters until we came to a clearing, and the dreary monotony of endless green was oppressive beyond description. There were scarcely any birds or animal life except small deer the size of a terrier, and rats and venomous insects; few flowers, except round the villages, where the undergrowth was not so thick as near the coast...

It was, perhaps, in India that most Victorian soldiers encountered life in all its most alien and incomprehensible forms. Sergeant-Major Ellis recalled some of the curiosities he witnessed in the 1850s, and his stories would have had a familiar ring to generations of British soldiers:

*Right: The discomforts of life in the tropics: an officer sleeping in a mosquito net, Asante, 1897. (Rai England Collection)*

During my eight years in India I saw many marvellous sights, so many, indeed, that I can scarcely set my mind on any particular one to begin with.

Here goes for the Fakirs. I remember once seeing one seated on his haunches by the roadside, in front of a charcoal fire, roasting his knees by way of penance. When I say roasting I mean actually burning – the flesh was peeling from his bones and frizzling, while the fat dropped on to the fire and added to the intense heat. All the while the man sat without moving a muscle, as though he were at his ease. Our Colonel remarked, as we passed, 'What a foolish man!', but he took no heed of us.

Once, at Arnee, I was out for a walk with a comrade, when presently we noticed a large toad blown out to an enormous size, and getting a little nearer to inspect it, found ourselves face to face with a cobra, which was just going to swallow the toad. On seeing us he raised himself about three feet, and in another moment would have darted upon us, but we beat a retreat...

I remember, when at Burdwan, visiting the King's Menagerie, by permission of His Majesty, who sent his bodyguard to escort us round. Here we saw large numbers of alligators kept in tanks, besides large numbers of animals of every description...

A gigantic idol, carved in stone, was placed upon the river bank, and painted with red ochre, and this the natives worshipped. At Cawnpore I witnessed a native festival called Ramma Luchman, where an enormous figure of this god with seven heads – who is believed by the Hindoos to drink up the Ganges – was filled with combustibles, and the fire flamed from his seven mouths, to impress the populace...

Nautch girls I have seen in plenty, dancing to the music of the tom-tom, played by men who go about the country with them and act as their protectors and keepers ... Snake charming never had much interest for me, and I seldom took the trouble to look on a performance. Juggling was more to my fancy, and I have seen some very wonderful performances...

For the most part the men in the ranks – and most of the officers, come to that – did not trouble themselves too much about the causes of the war they were embarking upon, or the enemy's way of life. They went where they were sent and did what they were told; for most of them it was enough to trust to duty. They believed in the essential righteousness of the British Empire, and that by spreading its boundaries they were championing the cause of Christian enlightenment and justice. 'You would have been astonished', wrote the Reverend Robertson, a missionary who was caught up with events in Zululand in 1879, 'to find how little all of them [*ie* the troops] knew of the people against whom they were fighting, or why they were fighting'. 'I knew absolutely nothing of the war except what came under my own notice', wrote Lance-Corporal George Masters of the City Imperial Volunteers, talking of the Anglo-Boer War. 'A soldier asks no questions, and has very little information given to him. He does what he is ordered, goes where he is sent, takes what is given to him, loses his individuality, and soon becomes a part of a machine'. The

213

*Above: Work: Seaforth Highlanders in camp, Pathan Revolt, 1897. (Bryan Maggs Collection)*

majority took it for granted that their white skins and technological advancement made them better men than the 'lesser breeds' whom they were called upon to fight. Such an attitude was not one of overt racial hostility, but rather of a patronising superiority which could be benevolent, paternalistic and, when thwarted, bitterly savage. Wolseley perhaps embodied this attitude in the notes he published for the guidance of the men under his command in Asante:

It must never be forgotten by our soldiers that providence has implanted in the heart of every native of Africa a superstitious awe and dread of the white man that prevents the Negro from daring to face us in combat. A steady advance or charge, no matter how partial, if made with determination, always means the retreat of the enemy. Although when at a distance, even though when under heavy fire, the Ashantis seem brave enough, from their practise of yelling, singing, and beating drums in order to frighten enemies of their own colour, with whom they are accustomed to make war, they will not stand against the advance of white men.

Perhaps the survivors of Isandlwana or Maiwand might have lived long enough to disagree with him.

For most troops in the field, of course, active service meant prolonged periods of boredom, drudgery and discomfort which the occasional bursts of violent action – providing they were successful – merely served to alleviate. Colonial battles were seldom protracted affairs, and even in the Boer War it was unusual for any battle to spill over onto a second day, and for every hour of fighting there were weeks of marching and picqueting, of escorting convoys and sentry-go, of living under canvas, often in appalling weather conditions, and of eating poor food. Lieutenant

William Weallens of the 2/24th gave a good account of his daily routine on the march in Zululand in 1879, which perhaps typified soldiering in South Africa from the War of the Axe to the Boer War:

I will now give you some idea of what our day's work would be. About four thirty a.m. reveille sounded, when all the troops would stand to their arms on their respective alarm posts until daylight, when the Disperse would sound. The camp would then be struck, waggons packed and moved out of the laager, and breakfast served; it would then perhaps be six-thirty or seven o'clock. If our regiment formed part of the advance guard we would start early, if rearguard perhaps not until two or three hours later, as the column was always from three to five miles long. We would then escort the waggons, the men aiding in every way with drag-ropes and by cutting roads where there were hills or difficult rivers to cross. Sometimes we would be nearly all day in getting the waggons over a hill and the men would be working hard the whole time. On reaching camp the waggons would be laagered, i.e. formed into one or more hollow squares or ovals, inside which the bullocks and horses were kept during the night. We would then have to pitch the camp, and entrench the laager, this always being followed by a laager parade when we manned the alarm posts. If it was our turn we would then have to go out on night picquet, which is anything but cheerful after a long day's

*Right: The bell-tent, home for generations of soldiers in the field; Boer War, 1900. (Bryan Maggs Collection)*

march. Sometimes we did not reach camp until late, and we ate our meals when and best we could...

Lance-Corporal Masters of the CIVs would have recognised much of that account, although of course he was a cavalryman rather than a foot-slogger. Indeed, his catalogue of discomforts might serve as a check-list of the miseries of life on campaign for almost any Victorian soldier, except, perhaps, for the last line, which is resonant of more modern horrors:

Looking through my little pocket-diary I find a great similarity in the entries day after day, for life was very monotonous sometimes, although each day brought its own excitement. Rough country to traverse, steep hills to climb, deep valleys to cross, small rivers to wade, rough weather, rain, sand, dust, wind storms, cold and heat, long rides, orderly duties, fatigue duties, forced

marches, plagues of vermin, locusts, flies, ants, and scorpions; rides in railway trucks, journeys in search of water and firewood, and stampeding, lame and dying horses; night alarms, veldt fires; sleeping in the open, frosty nights with only a blanket for additional warmth, wet nights with no shelter; hunger and thirst, drinking sometimes from stagnant and loathsome ponds as at Omdraai Vlie; lost tracks, nasty falls, and barbed wire entanglements...

All of this marching naturally took its toll on the men's appearance. Queen's Regulations specified that all those who were able, officers and men, should wear moustaches, and in the field it was generally considered acceptable for the men to grow beards, since it protected the face from the elements, and saved water. Uniforms were not only modified to make them practical in the field, but items were lost or damaged, and for troops in remote areas replacement

might take a good deal longer than the specified twelve months. As a result the army on campaign had little in common with the pristine look so favoured by contemporary artists, or familiar on the parade-grounds of home; indeed, for much of the time the men looked like scarecrows, and were dressed literally in rags. 'Boots and clothing were worn out,' recalled Sergeant-Major Ellis of the Crimea, 'and there were none to replace them'. Conditions in the Crimea were particularly harsh; rather than suffer frost-bite in the trenches, many men took the boots from dead Russians, or snatched them from their own dead comrades before they were buried. In South Africa, soldiers who went through the Ninth Cape Frontier War marched into Zululand with their clothes already patched; sun helmets became battered and shapeless or were lost and replaced by civilian hats, and boots wore out – by the time the 21st Regiment marched out of Zululand for the Transvaal, many went barefoot or had their feet wrapped in rags. After Isandlwana, where the camp for an entire column had been ransacked by the Zulus, the survivors were reduced to wearing mealie sacks as greatcoats, with a hole cut through the bottom, and the head pushed through. By the end of the Gordon Relief Expedition, Private Etherington recalled that 'our boots were worn out and our clothes were in rags, and it was no joke to toil across one hundred and seventy-five miles of yielding sand, under a blazing African sun'. Even the most prestigious of regiments were not immune; in the Boer War Lance-Corporal Masters of the CIVs 'saw some of the Coldstream Guards with their regimentals patched with sackcloth, portions of which bore various lettering, as 'A.S.C. Supplies', 'For use on board Ship', 'Sugar', etc, chosen, doubtless, to add to the absurdity of this grotesque clothing'.

Often camp itself was hardly a cheery home from home at the end of a hard day's work. For most of the Victorian period soldiers slept in circular 'bell' tents which had a circumference of forty feet and, with the pole and guy ropes, weighed 160 lbs, so that each battalion required a good deal of transport just to carry its own tents. The usual distribution of tents was on the ratio of two tents for every field officer, one for each other officer, one for two staff sergeants, and one per twelve NCOs and men. In fact the number varied according to the number of tents available and whether a battalion was up to strength or not; although it was not unknown for as few as eight men to have the luxury of a tent to themselves, it was far more common for one to be shared between 15 NCOs and men. Officers were generally able to equip themselves with some sort of collapsible bed, but the men slept on a waterproof sheet if they were lucky, or on the ground if they were not. The tents themselves were made of canvas, and provided only basic protection against the elements. In the bitter Crimean winter the wind cut through the canvas like a knife, and the men slept on frozen mud. In the heavy rains of Asia or even South Africa they might leak, and it was common for streams of water, rushing across the ground, to pour right through them under the guy-ropes, carrying off the contents. 'The men have been wet through every night', commented Major Thornhill of the garrison in the newly-annexed Transvaal, 'there are about 14 in each tent'. Charles Norris-Newman, a journalist covering the Anglo-Zulu War for the London Standard, has left a vivid description of just how unpleasant life could be under canvas in the unpredictable weather conditions of South Africa:

The members of the mess had intended having a great feed that evening, having been successful in getting a buck and other niceties; but just as the cook was preparing the savoury viands down came such a storm of wind, followed immediately by heavy rain, as not only to put out the fires, but even to blow over some tents, and quickly flood us all out. The Commandant and myself bore it patiently for some time, but when things began to float about and small streams to flow through out tent, we thought the time for action had commenced; so divesting ourselves of some of our clothing, we put on our waterproofs, made a rush to the nearest tent for spades, came back and commenced to dig a good-sized trench outside the tent, so as to direct the water into some other channel. In this we succeeded, after everything was wet through, and then, as our misery was at its height, we made a journey through the camp to see how others had fared. The result proved that there were many worse off than even we were...

One tent, in particular, had been erected over a pathway, and it was really a sight worth seeing to witness how – not withstanding that the occupants had dug a deep trench around it – the stream, unchecked almost, poured through the tent and over its contents. A small stream, percolating through the sand, close by one side of the camp, soon became a roaring torrent, and not only carried away our barrel (sunk to get decent water) but also upset the whole engineering scheme of one of the Captains, who had sunk several wells close to the stream in order to get water. These were now entirely filled up with soil, sand and gravel. The last seen of the unfortunate barrel was a few of its staves floating down the stream some miles off...

Of course, even the slender comforts of the bell-tent were luxuries to be dispensed with on some campaigns. Even in Zululand, to lighten the baggage load during the Eshowe Relief Expedition the men were ordered to take no tents, and had to sleep out in the open veld, lying down in their greatcoats with a blanket over them; this might have

*Right: Making the most of whatever comfort is available: Oxfordshire Yeomanry bivouacking in the field, Boer War, 1901. (Bryan Maggs Collection)*

been cosy enough in warm balmy conditions, but not in the heavy rains which greeted the expedition almost every night, and the men simply slept in mud and water. During the Boer War many of the mounted columns pursuing the Boers could not take tents with them, and faced similar conditions. Driver Wickenden, RHA, described life in the Egyptian desert during the Tel-el-Kebir campaign:

We had no overcoats, and the cold at night was intense, and we felt it terribly. I shall not forget my first night ashore, for we had to get into the water to land our horses, and had to wear our clothes until they dried, and they were still wet when the cold night air came on us. We made capital beds by scraping holes in the sand, rolling ourselves in our blankets, with our helmets for pillows, and then raking the sand over us, so that we were almost buried...

I never saw so many flies in all my life; they would settle on our eyes and lips, as it was too hot to wear our veils, and while standing talking to a comrade we had to keep our hands mov-

ing before our faces to drive them off. I used to wonder what on earth the place was like when the plague was on...

In the Chitral campaign, Colonel Kelly's relief column had to camp out on high mountain passes covered in snow, whilst in the Indian Mutiny men lived and fought in the stultifying heat of the plains. Living so close to the ground, of course, exposed the men to the full range of interesting insect life to be found in tropical climates, as Private George Pridmore of the Bedfordshire Regiment recalled of the Chitral campaign:

As we carried no tents on this expedition (in order to reduce the baggage as much as possible), we had again to bivouac for the night. This is unpleasant at the best of times in a tropical country. Not only are the nights very chilly, but the creeping things are simply legion. First there are the ants, which march over you in armies, and often get inside your clothes and bite desperately. Some species in particular seem to bite you with red-hot teeth. Then there are scorpions

and centipedes, which sting and bite in a far worse fashion. I have known men suffer very severely for hours after being attacked by them. Of course, when you are lying out in the open ground at night, you are in constant danger from these creatures.

Wild beasts never come near the camp, except the jackals, which are not at all dangerous, though they are most shocking thieves. The man who has drawn his rations over night will probably find nothing but the smell left in the morning...

He might have added that snakes, too, were a constant danger; although most species avoid obvious human contact, there was always a danger of disturbing a dozing snake when clambering across a rocky hillside or marching through thick bush. Lieutenant-Colonel. Scott, RAMC, described the grim consequences which followed an encounter between a mamba and Lieutenant-Colonel Montgomery, who was commanding a garrison of the Welsh Regiment on the Natal/Zulu border in September 1883:

We had crossed the Tugela river to the Zululand side. After luncheon Colonel Montgomery and his adjutant ... went out to shoot quail. When they were some distance from the camp they dismounted, and threw the saddles over the ponies' heads, as is the custom in South Africa, and then went into some long grass. Soon after Colonel Montgomery felt something prick his leg, which he took to be a thorn, but in a few seconds he felt a great shock to his system, and called out to his adjutant that he had been bitten by a snake and that he was to ride into camp [to fetch] me ... in a few minutes I saw Colonel Montgomery riding towards camp at a canter. He at the time looked like a drunken man on a horse, as he was swaying from side to side to such an extent I momentarily thought he would fall off. When I got to him, I and others helped him to dismount. His legs immediately collapsed (the result of paralysis), by which it may be seen that he rode in by balance only. The injury was sustained at 4

pm, and we helped him off his horse at 4.10 pm. On admission he was pale, nervous, very sick (vomited profusely), had cramps, and a feeling that he was going to die. The wound, which was in the inner and upper third of the leg, had the appearance of being pricked by something sharp. A very tight ligature was put around the leg above the wound, which latter was encouraged to bleed by incisions, sucking, etc. Stimulants were abundantly given by mouth and subcutaneously. Permanganate of potash was used locally. The restlessness somewhat abated, but now and then he would start up in bed and say, 'It's no use; I'm done'. For some time he began to improve and to become more hopeful, but at about 9 pm his sight began to fail, and he was unable to recognise articles in his tent. There was at the same time difficulty of breathing and of swallowing, and paralysis of the tongue and soft palate. Chronic convulsions of the upper extremities were frequent. Towards the end he got

more quiet, and death ended this trying scene ... ten hours after the accident.

If the soldier survived the more dramatic assaults on his health mounted by the environment and its fauna, he was still faced with the daily struggle to remain healthy, since food and water were almost always in short supply, and seldom of the best quality. The daily ration remained largely constant across the nineteenth century, whether in peace or at war, although on campaign it was difficult to guarantee either a steady supply of food or its quality. In India and South Africa, tinned meat was augmented by that purchased 'on the hoof' by the commissariat and slaughtered as necessary, which did at least ensure it was fresh; in North Africa, where cattle were scarcer, meat was usually supplied as 'bully beef'. Driver Wickenden recalled of the Egyptian campaign that:

...we were only ever allowed a pint and a half of water each day, and that seemed to disappear by magic. Now and then we had some tinned meat and a

*Left: Issuing rations during the siege of Mafikeng. (Bryan Maggs Collection)*

few potatoes, but I don't believe I had a hatful of these delicacies all the time. It seemed to me that the Commissariat Department was always behind for whenever we halted, the provisions were miles away, and had to be waited for.

Some enterprising commanders were able to establish mobile field bakeries, though the quality of the produce varied according to the availability of ingredients, and generally the men had to make do with hard army biscuits. Even meat from slaughtered beeves could be decidedly unappetising, especially if it had come from one of the tough, rangy transport oxen, and was issued on the bone. Even seventy-eight years later Trooper Bowers of the Imperial Yeomanry could still recall details of his diet in the Boer War:

Four biscuits a day was a full ration, but if you were short of rations you'd only get three and if you were very short you'd live on two a day. For your main meal when you were on trek, I think the cook would put some water on in a dixie a third full,

boil it up, chuck a handful of salt in it if he happened to have some – and don't forget the cook's hands were never washed from day to day – and they'd slice chunks off a dead bullock and chuck them in, chunks cut off like rough cricket balls. What else did we have? Tinned potatoes, not whole potatoes but chopped up potatoes ... I rather fancy mealie tops, you know with all the maize still on the cob, we used to have some of those chucked in – that was called stew...

Even these basic rations would have seemed like luxury to Sergeant-Major Ellis, who experienced the misery of the winter of 1854-5 in the trenches before Sebastopol:

The only thing that kept life in us was the drop of rum which was issued to us night and morning. The coffee was served out in green beans, and we had to attempt to roast it in the small fires which we could get now and then. The War-Office sent out coffee-mills, which were useless under the circum-

stances, and made us laugh. There seemed to be bad luck upon us the whole time. The meat was served out to us raw and salt, and we had no wood to light fires wherewith to cook it. Of bread and flour we had none, and biscuits were in many cases nothing but bags of dust and mildew. Water was scarce and often we had to use the melted snow.

Where possible soldiers augmented their diet with provisions bought from local civilians, or by foraging, if it was permitted. Occasionally, however, as every old sweat admitted, providence would come to the aid of the hungry. Ellis again:

[We] were not allowed to forage. A fine field of onions tempted us sorely. We dared not disobey the standing order of the army, although the French cleared the country for miles around of sheep, cows, bullocks, and everything eatable we could find.

They had to bring their spoil past our lines, and the sheep becoming wild at the sight of

*Right: Cookhouse in the veld, Boer War. (Bryan Maggs Collection)*

*Our best drinking water!*

*Well seasoned material
A pair of old Colony bush fighters!*

*Above: 'Our best drinking water':
fouled water supplies were the principal cause of disease, which killed
more soldiers than enemy action.
(Author's collection)*

the tents which we had been
able to pitch, ran in all directions. One accidentally got into
my tent, where my store-man
and his brother were busy
cleaning up, and that lost sheep
never went out again, for, having killed it, we dug a hole
inside the tent and buried the
offal, and covered the place
with a blanket. We divided the
carcass amongst the company;
and presently a Frenchman
complained to Lord Raglan,
who sent one of his staff with
an interpreter to make
inquiries. But as we were unable
to give him any information on
the subject, the matter

dropped, and we enjoyed our
supper.

Such incidents were rare enough,
however, and a poor diet and bad
water were the norm on most campaigns. Bad water was, indeed, a
greater killer than the enemy, since
contagious diseases such as cholera
and typhoid were far more destructive than enemy fire. In the Crimea
3845 men died in action, whilst
15,724 succumbed to disease; in
Asante in 1873–4 the sickness rate
was as high as 71%, whilst even in
the Anglo-Boer War, when over 7500
men were killed in action, 13,000
died of disease. Although medical
science understood that there was a
general correlation between good
drinking water, hygiene, and the
health of the men, the exact links
were not properly understood until
almost the end of the century. In
1853, on the eve of the Crimean
War, the *Lancet* had complained that

'all is darkness and confusion, vague
theory and speculation. What is
cholera? Is it a fungus, an insect, a
miasm, an electric disturbance, a
deficiency of ozone, a morbid off-
scouring of the intestinal canal? We
know nothing; we are at sea in a
whirlpool of conjecture.'

As late as 1879 Fleet Surgeon Nor-
bury, the senior medical officer during the siege of Eshowe, put the
decline in health of the garrison
down to unhealthy emanations from
the soil; nearer the mark, he also
tried to dissuade men from filling
their water-bottles from a stream
which drained off a slope where the
dead had been buried. In that
respect, too, the problems he experienced in finding a suitable water-
supply were typical of campaign life
in the nineteenth century. It was
always difficult to find a supply that
had not been contaminated, since
the very presence of troops, and of
the dead animals and waste which

accompanied them, ran an inevitable risk of polluting all supplies within reach. A description of the line of march of the 1st Division in the closing stages of the Zulu War illustrates the point:

There are eight hundred men hors de combat from the First Division. This is a big number, out of a total force of less than six thousand. If the present rate of sickness continues there will be no field officers left at the disposal of the General. Brigadier Clarke is now laid up with fever. Yellow jaundice has lately appeared among the troops. A great deal of the sickness may be ascribed to the effluvia which arises from the carcasses of oxen in different stages of decomposition. These lie on the road where the troopers have to escort the convoys, and at every hundred yards this horrible atmosphere has to be breathed.

The situation was worse when there had been any fighting – veterans of the western front in the Boer War dubbed the contents of their water bottles 'Chateau Modder', and likened it to a local wine that was 'full of body' – or where large numbers of troops were concentrated for any length of time. Although proper latrine trenches were recognised as a necessity by the second half of the century, it was not always possible to persuade all the troops to use them – in the Zulu War, black auxiliaries showed a distinct reluctance to do so – and in any case they soon became fouled. As a result, any camp that was not moved frequently became a health-hazard, especially in hot weather, or when a sudden downpour might sweep the contents of the latrines into a nearby water-supply. 'We had to ... shift our position every now and then,' wrote Wickenden of the Egyptian War, 'which is called cholera dodging; and I would rather be in action than at that game'. Nor were the methods of transporting water helpful; wooden water carts and wooden canteens in one form or another remained standard until the end of the century, and the germs from any infected water lingered in the fibre of the wood, spreading the contamination every time the container was filled. Even when troops were aware of the dangers, there was often little enough choice; with several thousand thirsty soldiers all keen to take advantage of an opportunity to fill their bottles, it was often bad water or none at all. The debilitating effects of dysentery and typhoid – or 'enteric', as it was generally known in the nineteenth century – are vividly described, again in a report from the Zulu War

The camp was pitched on a hill distant three miles from any actual flowing water, and had to get its supply from a stagnant puddle at its base formed by the drainage of the hill on which it stood, caused such an outbreak of illness, that I found on my arrival there ninety-three serious cases on the sick list, and four hundred on the visiting list, nearly all be cases of dysentery, colic, and diarrhoea. As for the officers, a more woe-begone lot it has never been my fortune to see ... Private supplies of food had been forwarded to [one battalion], and they had not been

*Right: Wooden water carts of a type used throughout the 1870s and 1880s, Suakin, 1885. (Bryan Maggs Collection)*

obliged to live on that utter abomination in the way of food, 'Chicago tinned beef'. They therefore looked better, though of course far from well. When, however, I came on the 60th Rifles, and saw them, so cadaverous were their looks, so utterly changed and wasted down from what I had left them but ten short days before, I felt quite dazed when they surrounded me. The colonel was sick and unable to move; the senior captain was doubled up, and a whole row of fine young fellows were lying for shelter from the burning sun under waggons, eking out there shade with an old tarpaulin – shaking with low fever, and exhausted by continuous dysentery – nine hundred men in the ranks, and only three officers fit to take charge of them, though others were manfully struggling against their sickness and holding the field.

Although the standard of medical knowledge improved over the Victorian period, the basic unsanitary nature of life in the field remained unchanged. Lacking modern chemical means of purifying water, the troops could only boil it if they could be bothered, and it is significant that Roberts' occupation of Bloemfontein was marred by an outbreak of typhoid which was the most severe since the Crimea, nearly fifty years before.

If life in the field, then, was characterised by extremes of weather, drudgery, curious foreigners, bad food and water, creepy-crawlies, and the ever-present threat of disease what, if anything, did the troops find to do, to make it at all bearable?

The possibility or otherwise of sex was always a distraction. The Victorians were notoriously reticent about recording their sexual habits, but there is nothing to suggest that the British army in the nineteenth century was any different from any other army over the years. It was, after all, an entirely male institution; only a small proportion of officers and men

were married, and even if wives accompanied them on overseas service, only the most adventurous ventured out to frontier garrisons, let alone war zones. The British army was composed of young men, who were probably fitter than their civilian counterparts, and whose needs were certainly no different. For some, indeed, the prospect of service overseas offered the possibility of adventuring of a different kind, and one or two secret diaries have survived which suggest that some individuals, at least, enjoyed a remarkably varied and inventive sex life away from the constraints of home society. Most, no doubt, took advantage of whatever opportunities were available to them, and officers, as in all other aspects of army life, were far better provided for than the other ranks. In India, where officers' wives spent much of their time separated from their husbands, who were soldiering in the plains or on the frontier, there was always the possibility of a dalliance with a bored and frustrated member of the same class, although the risks of social disgrace were severe. In colonies with a strong white settler community – South Africa, Canada, New Zealand – a pretty settler girl's head could often be turned by a smart turn-out and the twirl of a military moustache. Nevertheless, although officers general enjoyed the best of settler society, they usually considered themselves socially superior to it, and indeed the contrast between the officers of a fashionable cavalry regiment and the inhabitants of a small frontier town in, say, South Africa must have been quite marked. Wolseley apparently disapproved of several officers on his staff who formed liaisons with local settler girls at the end of the Zulu War, which is interesting, both because it confirms that such romances did occur, and because it reveals the social taboos which they transgressed.

If settler women were generally beyond the pale, relationships with women of a different colour and race were scarcely ever acknowledged. In the eighteenth century it was common for EIC officers to take Indian wives and mistresses, but the growing feelings of racial superiority, and

the sexual prudery which became more prevalent with the accession of Victoria herself, meant that such relationships were anathema to polite society at home. With improvements in transport from the 1850s – and particularly the opening of the Suez canal twenty years later – foreign postings were no longer out of reach for married couples; wives might visit their husbands overseas, and officers on leave were expected to return home more frequently. Semi-permanent liaisons with local women could no longer, therefore, be kept at a safe distance. Yet they undoubtedly did take place; in the First Afghan War, one of the principal causes of Afghan resentment towards the occupying Army of the Indus was said to be the outrage to Islamic morals felt by cuckolded husbands whose wives attended wild parties in the lodgings of British officers. In the Zulu War, British officers were intrigued by the figure of John Dunn, a colonist who had adopted the lifestyle of a Zulu chief, and who married more than forty local women; Dunn was not welcome even in colonial society, yet officers were happy to accept his invitations to dine or to shoot, and were clearly titillated by his matrimonial arrangements. Bindon Blood, an Irish Engineer officer whose twinkle in the eye is evident from his memoirs, flirted with both settler and Zulu girls, and hints at much more:

One day I was at Dunn's kraal talking to one of his married ladies who knew some English, and remarked to her that a girl of about fifteen – her daughter, as it turned out – was nice looking. So she said, 'Yes – very good figure – you can crack a flea on her – ,' not mentioning anything hard, like the thumbnail, as might have been expected! I was informed afterwards that the expression used by the lady was quite usual among the Zulus, and I must say I thought it to the point.

Another day I was riding towards Dunn's kraal with a large escort behind me, when

*Right: The unexpected delights of campaign life. (Author's collection)*

we met a party of Zulu women and girls carrying milk to a depot where we had arranged for it, and among them was the young lady I have mentioned above. I had turned my escort off the road, and halted a moment to talk to the women, who were full of remarks, complimentary and otherwise, of which we understood some! Presently I noticed that the young lady had on a very smart waist-belt, and I offered to swop my sword-belt – an old gold-laced one with a silver-mounted clasp – for her belt. To my surprise she jumped at the deal – so I took off my belt (my sword was on my saddle) and gave it to her, when she slipped behind a bush, made the change, and came back with her belt in her hand ready for me. As she had nothing on her besides the belt and some bracelets with a piece of muslin like a sash round her neck, one did not see the necessity for the retirement behind the bush – however, custom ordered it, so there was no more to be said. The girl was wonderfully

pleased with my belt; especially the 'slings', swinging against her legs, seemed to delight her. I still have her belt...

An interesting Zulu custom came to light in some of the more out-of-the-way villages. This was that whenever specially eligible-looking travellers came to them, they sought to improve the breed in the villages by arranging for the production of children by visitors. In this connection overtures were frequently made to my Pioneer friend and to me, as we were evidently thought likely individuals. I had come across similar ways in India, among the Hindus in the Himalayas, and among some of the more primitive Afghan and frontier Mohammedans in the early days of my service in the East.

Blood seems to have interpreted local custom rather liberally, and does not say whether he availed himself of these apparently frequent offers.

For homosexuals, service overseas was even more ambivalent. Homosexual activity was not merely

socially unacceptable in Victorian Britain, it was illegal; indeed, buggery was a military crime in itself, on the grounds that, amongst other things, it was prejudicial to discipline. Homosexual activity in the colonies was no less clandestine than at home, but for those who wished to indulge, the indigenous cultures of some eastern colonies took a rather more relaxed attitude than the mother country. Indeed, in some countries, including Afghanistan, relationships between older men and young boys were quite common, and the Frontier garrisons therefore afforded interesting opportunities to those so inclined. For at least one high ranking officer, discovery spelt downfall; in 1903 Sir Hector Macdonald, the crofter's son who rose through the ranks to become a General, the hero of Majuba and Omdurman, was caught *in flagrante* with four boys in a railway carriage in Ceylon. Macdonald was called to London to answer to Lord Roberts for his indiscretion; Roberts threatened him with a court martial and apparently told him the best thing he could do was go away and shoot himself, which Macdonald duly did. It is difficult to avoid the feeling, however, that Macdonald's fate owed much to his social origins, since on other occasions the officer class was prepared to close ranks and hide its peccadilloes behind shuttered doors.

For the men in the ranks, there was little chance of a romantic interlude, since they spent most of their time in barracks or camps, cut off from civilian society. The only opportunity afforded the other ranks for a lasting relationship with a local girl was to desert, and that was common enough. On campaign there was always the chance of a casual sexual encounter, however; Private Adams of the 7th Dragoons recorded that in September 1844 he was part of a group of about twenty soldiers sent out from a garrison on the Eastern Cape Frontier to collect wood. A Xhosa woman approached the party, selling milk, and allowed herself to be seduced by one of the soldiers. On this occasion, the story had a grim sequel, as tension between the British and the Xhosa was running high, and the local Xhosa were so infuriated with the woman for consorting with a soldier that a crowd gathered and she was put to death. The incident was particularly shocking, because such contact was clearly not unique, and usually aroused little protest. Such accounts are rare enough, but they do suggest that clandestine sexual contact between the British troops and local women – even when the troops were effectively an occupying force – was not infrequent. Although Bindon Blood's memoir is almost the only source which hints at sexual activity in the extensive literature of the Zulu War, a series of engravings, apparently scratched into cow-horns by a contemporary African artist and depicting scenes from the campaign, includes a representation of a soldier and Zulu girl making love. Clearly such contact left an impression on the African mind, at least.

For the rest, the only sexual contact was with prostitutes. Most garrisons around the Empire inevitably supported brothels which catered for the troops, but those stationed in India were lucky enough to have access to officially sanctioned brothels, which until about 1890 were built within regimental cantonments. The regimental brothel system recognised the inevitable fact that by maintaining a large army in India, with regiments often stationed in the country for years at a time, the British had imported a tremendous desire for sexual services which had to be satisfied. Visits to unauthorised brothels exposed the British soldier to a wide range of other vices, and, worst of all, threatened his military efficiency through the risk of venereal disease. Authorised brothels, first built in the years after the Mutiny, were regularly checked by regimental medical officers, to ensure that the prostitutes were healthy. The girls were, furthermore, supposed to be reserved for the use of white soldiers, although in practice it was common for Indian clients to be admitted whilst the soldiers were distracted by parades or other duties. Regimental brothels were cheap – the price was usually about one rupee – and undoubtedly helped relieve the tension of thousands of men for whom service life had little more to offer than mind-numbing routine in the suffocating heat of a confined cantonment. Curiously enough, however, the system didn't seem to reduce the risk of venereal disease; in the 1880s and 1890s as many as half the British troops in India were treated for it at some stage.

In South Africa brothels had long existed in towns that supported a large garrison, and others had flourished in the rowdy boom-town atmosphere of Johannesburg. During the Boer War the military authorities, influenced by Lord Roberts, whose background was in the Indian army, made some attempt to inspect and license some of these premises. As a result, commented a Trooper Perham, they 'were not considered to be places of ill-fame'. Trooper Perham has left a rare glimpse of the inside of a military brothel, though he clearly thought better of his own visit:

They took me to a place clean and well kept by appearances.

From the street we entered a cloak room and from there entered a large reception room with quite a number of chairs and couches. Also quite a number of girls, white, yellow and black. Leading from the reception room were a number of doors, presumably to small rooms designed for two. Anyway, to finish a tale, I sat on a chair and immediately a buxom black lass perched herself on my knees, put her arms around my neck, and commenced whispering in my ears in broken English.

Doing a bit of quick thinking I said to myself, 'This is no place for you, Frank!' Sliding gently from under, I said, 'Excuse me, Girlie, while I go into the cloak room.' I walked sedately into the room, grabbed my coat and hat, stepped through the door into the street and made tracks back to camp...

Drunkenness was just as much of a potential problem on campaign as it was in peace-time garrisons. Soldiers returning from an area of active service to a settlement behind the lines could generally be relied upon to make for the nearest pub, get drunk, and begin brawling. Generally, however, this risk was reduced when actually in the field, since the remoteness of many theatres of operation meant that the troops simply could not get access to supplies of liquor. In areas with a significant settler population, there was always the risk that civilian traders would supply the troops with booze; during the Zulu War several British column commanders refused to allow such traders access to camps. Evelyn Wood went even further:

[a trader] was selling trade gin at 1s. a glass to the soldiers, some of whom were already drunk. Campbell had the man seized, and sent for me. There was a full moon, and I executed summary justice by its light: ordering the man to be tied to the wheel of his own waggon, I sent for two buglers, and gave him two dozen lashes on the spot, upset the whole of his liquor (which must have been a considerable loss, for he had a large quantity under the groceries), and informed him that unless he trekked at daylight, I would impound his waggons and oxen for the rest of the campaign...

Nevertheless, the troops showed a habitual ingenuity in obtaining illicit supplies, as the following story told by H.L. Hall, a civilian wagon-driver in the Zulu War, shows:

One day a squad from an Irish regiment was on fatigue duty rolling large barrels of rum from the pont up to the store. The sergeant in charge was surprised at the number of his men who asked for a few minutes off and did not return, and at the number of men passing down to the river. On going to see what was up, he found a lot of his regiment sampling the rum. They had rolled some barrels down the bank and were quenching their Irish thirst. The Sergeant sent word to his O.C., and the Colonel turned out with his officers and all the sober men in camp and started out to collect his troopers. All that were able, however, fancying a change of liquor, took possession of the pont and crossed over to interview the hotel proprietor in his bar. In the meantime the Colonel had advised Colonel Pearson of the state of affairs, and asked him to get all the other troops into camp and leave him to fix up his own regiment. If the other troops interfered, he said, there was sure to be a devil of a fight. Colonel Pearson complied and ordered the troops into camp.

The Colonel of the Irish regiment was an Irishman and popular with his men. The drinking squad, who were still active sampling the hotel liquor, on seeing their chief approach, rushed through the hotel to escape, but were captured and taken to camp under arrest. Then a fatigue party was sent to bring in the incapables, and so ended this little spree. Their punishment was guarding the lines of communication for the duration of the war – a severe lesson, for they were keen fighters.

Nor was drunkenness confined to the men in the ranks, for the officers had no such prohibition on supplies. Evelyn Wood again:

I was strolling ... when I received a vigorous slap on the back, and, turning round, was greeted effusively by an Officer with the exclamation 'How are you, old boy?' He was not able to stand steady, and I sent him away under arrest ... Next day, when he was brought before me I asked: 'What have you got to say?' Now, I have had to deal with many similar offenders, but never before had such an honest answer; most men attribute the inebriety to an incongruous mixture with salad, or to the effects of a very small amount of alcohol on an empty stomach under a hot sun, but my officer replied: 'Drunk, sir, drunk; nothing but drunk.' 'This is very serious, and I should like some hours to think over your case.' 'Quite simple, sir; you must either let me off, or try me by Court Martial.' When I saw him again I said: 'It is not the question of our safety only, but also of our honour as soldiers; if you are in charge of the picquets when this happens again, you might cause a great disaster.' 'In the language of soldiers, sir', he replied, 'if you give me a chance I shall never be drunk again whilst under your command'. He kept his promise...

Such leniency was probably quite common between officers, but any transgressions by the men in the ranks were severely punished. Trial was by court martial, and flogging remained the most common punishment. For extreme cases, however – attacking an officer, mutiny, or sleeping on sentry duty – the penalty was death. Two accounts from the 1850s suggest the grim ritual with which these punishments were carried out; the flogging took place in the field in the Crimea, the execution at the Malta garrison:

[the prisoner, convicted of drunkenness] was again marched out to receive his sentence, which was fifty lashes. This was the second time he had been flogged, and to show his bravery he took off his clothes unaided. His coat was laid over the wheel of a gun carriage, and he was lashed to the wheel, with his chin resting on his coat. The man who was to give him the first twenty-five lashes was, at the tenth stroke, sent to the guard tent by the commanding officer, for not doing his duty properly, but was let off further punishment...

The Burial Service was read by the chaplain, and the prisoner blindfolded by the provost-marshal and conducted to the spot on which he was to suffer, which was strewn with sawdust, the coffin being placed by the man's side. A party of twelve men were served out with rifles, six only being loaded, so that the men could not tell which of them caused the death. The provost-marshal was a gunner, and a friend of the prisoner, and had, by the prisoner's request, been appointed to the post for the day only. He bound the hands of the condemned man behind his back, and placed him in position, with his face to the firing party, and the sea behind him. The man went down on one knee, and the sergeant in command of the firing party gave in an undertone the words, Ready! Present! Fire!!

*Left: Flogging in the field, Zulu War 1879. It was partly as a result of the high incidence of flogging in this campaign that the punishment was finally abolished in 1881. (Rai England Collection)*

The poor fellow fell to the ground riddled with shots, and the troops were ordered to march past, with the command to each company 'Eyes right!' and after that we saw no more of him...

Although the number of men executed by the army was small – thirty-seven between 1865 and 1898, with rather more at the beginning and end of the period due to the Crimea, Mutiny and Boer War – many men were flogged. More than 500 men were flogged in Zululand alone, a staggering total reflecting a need to ensure discipline in the light of a growing fear of the Zulu menace, spread by disasters such as Isandl-wana. This high incidence of corporal punishment caused something of an outcry, and flogging was finally abolished for men on active service in 1881.

If sex and alcohol were unavailable or too dangerous, the soldier on campaign had to resort to more mundane pursuits. Once again, the officers fared considerably better than the ORs. 'I am rather ashamed to own it, but I like this life', wrote Captain Hutton of the 3/60th of the Zulu War, 'and am as happy as the day is long. It is to me like a shooting expedition, with just a spice of danger thrown in to make it really interesting'. Drawn from the same class whose civilian counterparts enjoyed field sports as a matter of course, the officer on campaign had every opportunity to indulge in hunting, shooting and fishing. Colonial garrisons offered an exciting round of polo, cricket and hunting with hounds (in the absence of foxes, jackals served as the quarry in both India and the Cape). In India pig-sticking – hunting wild boar on horseback with the lance – was particularly popular because it depended on good horsemanship and skill with the lance, both essentially military skills. Wherever they went around the world, officers attacked the local wildlife with an even greater enthusiasm than that reserved for the enemy. Lieutenant-Colonel. Anstruther of the 94th recalled that in one's day's shooting in the eastern Transvaal, on the eve of the First Boer War, 'we got 14 bles-buck and 2 wildebeest. The latter beasts are very rare and I was certainly very lucky getting one.' And this was in a country which, by that time, had already suffered enormous losses in the game population due to professional hunting. Nor was Anstruther's experience unusual; almost every officer's diary of service in South Africa, up to and including the Boer War, contains similar cata-logues of a wholesale destruction of animal and bird life. 'Two rhinoc-eroses have been seen near here', wrote Second Lieutenant Mynors of the 3/60th at the end of the Zulu War, even as he was languishing from the enteric which would finally kill him, 'I wish I could get a shot at them, but can't get leave to go out'. In India, the army had the opportunity to indulge in the extermination of even more exotic creatures, and officers on leave regularly went on expeditions to hunt bears in the Himalayas, or to shoot tigers from the back of an elephant. Such hunting was not confined to peace-time garrison duty, for although most wildlife made itself scarce when large numbers of men approached, game was all the more appreciated on campaign as an addi-tion to the cooking pot.

For the men, there was little to do beyond improvising sports – cricket and races were always popular – or passing the time by smoking and

*Above: Officers and players; the 2nd South Lancashires polo team, Eshowe garrison, Zululand, 1885. (Bryan Maggs Collection)*

*Right: Other ranks' cricket team, 2nd South Lancashires, Helpmekaar, Natal, 1885. (Bryan Maggs Collection)*

playing cards. Tobacco was a great palliative – in pipes, rather than cigarettes – and the want of it, particularly in isolated garrisons, was always keenly felt. During the siege of Eshowe in the Zulu War, the troops were reduced to smoking home-made concoctions made from dried tea-leaves, whilst a few ounces of the real thing commanded prices way above its usual value. Private Fred Mason of the Warwickshire Regiment considered himself lucky to have found some Boer tobacco in a

coat he found discarded on the battlefield of Paardeberg, although he paid for it with an unsettling experience: 'We were both congratulating ourselves on our good fortune, when I happened to glance aside and saw the face of a dead Boer washed out from his shallow grave: his tongue protruded and his eyes were wide open and staring at me. It startled me pretty badly.'

For those troops unlucky enough to be on active service over Christmas, the army made some attempts

to enter into the festive spirit, though often in the most incongruous circumstances. If extra or particularly varied rations were available, these might be distributed by way of a Christmas dinner, and certainly in South Africa attempts were made to supply some units with Christmas puddings. In December 1878, however, on the eve of the Zulu War, a wagon full of Christmas puddings was swept away crossing a river and, although the supplies were salvaged, they did not reach their destination until 8 January! Private Mason of the Warwickshire Regiment described his Christmas dinner in 1899:

Our Christmas dinner was an eventful one. The regimental cooks made every effort to give the troops roast beef and plum-pudding, but the cooking was anything but satisfactory, until, as luck would have it, just as we had filled our canteen, the sky suddenly darkened, and in a moment, before we could seek the shelter of our tents, down came a dust storm, which lasted two hours and a half. It filled our eyes and ears, drove into the tents, and into our tin canteens, and rendered eating almost impossible. When we had cleared our canteens we partook of the Christmas pudding, which was at the time termed 'concrete', and then cleaning out the tin with the aid of dry sand, which was the usual method, we indulged in a pint of ale. Those who partook of this last-named luxury were charged fivepence.

There was so much to be done that even Christmas Day had to be a working day, and we laboured the usual number of hours. The day was fearfully hot, and at night we were allowed another pint of beer, and our accounts were each debited with another fivepence.

Christmas was also the traditional time for sending comforts from home for the troops. These were often of a purely private nature – gifts of food or clothing from an individual's family – and they were often shared out amongst a man's comrades. Charitable institutions and, during major campaigns like the Boer War, well-known manufacturers sometimes sent presents or gifts of their products to the front. The most famous example of such generosity, however, is undoubtedly the Queen's chocolate box, sent to South Africa as a new year's present in 1900. Queen Victoria had, apparently, first planned to send chocolate to the front during the Crimean War but, although a number of gift sets were produced, they did not reach their destination. In 1899, however, the three major chocolate manufacturers of the day, Frys, Rowntrees and Cadburys – all of whom, incidentally, were leading members of the Quaker movement, and thereby philosophically opposed to war – were asked to supply half-pound blocks of chocolate in specially impressed boxes. Initially some 90,000 boxes were ordered, but since this proved insufficient to cover all troops at the front, this was increased to 120,000. The boxes were shipped out to South Africa in wooden crates, and distributed to each battalion, reaching most areas by February 1900. Despite occasional quibbles about eligibility and distribution problems, it seems that each soldier, officer or private, received their tin of 'the Queen's chocolate'. The gesture was, apparently, much appreciated, so much so that many men refused to eat the chocolate, and kept the entire gift as a treasured souvenir. Others enjoyed the contents, which was undoubtedly a luxury, but tucked away the empty tins in haversacks, or posted them home to their families. Because of this, a surprising number have survived into modern times, some still with their contents intact, though rather less appetising now than in January 1900.

Amongst men on the more remote fringes of Empire, news from home was always in demand, and letters and papers from home were avidly

*Left: Comfort for the troops: the Queen's chocolate boxes supplied by Messrs Fry, Rowntree and Cadbury, January 1900. (Keith Reeves Collection)*

*Right: 'Don', one of the survivors of Isandlwana. (Author's collection)*

read, even if they were months out of date, and the news they contained passed on amongst the illiterate by word of mouth. 'You can't understand', grumbled Donald MacDonald, reproaching his brother for being slow to reply to his letters, 'the joy it gives a fellow when he gets a letter from home in this country'. Pets were another source of diversion; whilst officers sometimes brought out their favourite hounds on campaign, the men happily encouraged any strays which came their way. Of the 1850s, Gunner Cox, RA, recalled:

Our doctor, whose name was Barker, gave B Battery a lamb as a pet; he had purchased it in Balaklava, or it had been given to him, I suppose. It grew to a great size, and we made it a pewter medal, and taught it lots of tricks. It's usual food was tea-leaves, tobacco, potato-parings and porter! When we left England for India, Billy was handed over to our Quartermaster-Sergeant's father, with instructions as to his food. The Y Battery brought home a dromedary, which had been captured during the war; and the P Bat-

tery brought home a boar from Kenlow. The men always have a liking for a pet of some sort.

Dogs were a firm favourite, and every battalion had scores of dogs which it had collected along the way. These animals shared the hardships which sometimes befell their masters; when the Zulus overran the camp at Isandlwana, for example, many of the 24th's dogs were killed in the frenzied fighting, and others limped back to the camp at Rorke's Drift bearing fearful spear-wounds. Indeed, so many dogs escaped the slaughter that a pack of them, maddened by hunger, attacked British patrols in the vicinity of the camp for weeks after; a few were lured back into captivity, but most had to be shot. A few individual dogs achieved considerable fame in the army – Surgeon Reynolds's terrier, Dick, for example, which stood by him throughout the defence of Rorke's Drift, or Bobby, who belonged to Sergeant Kelly of the 66th, and survived Maiwand. Bobby was taken back to England and awarded the Afghan War medal by Queen Victoria herself at Osborne House; sadly, he was run over by a hansom cab in Gosport eighteen months later.

Despite such amusements, camp life in the field was inevitably hard and dull. General Fuller wrote an account of the monotony and frustration of life amongst the garrisons of the blockhouses in the Boer War which in many ways typifies the routine of life on campaign:

Apart from sentry duty and minor fatigue work there was absolutely nothing to do except talk, smoke and gamble. Frequently no signs of civilisation, or even of life, except for the two neighbouring blockhouses, could be seen for miles around ... almost unceasing sentry go, lack of natural exercise and monotony told on the nerves. Though they were in complete safety men would become jumpy and bad-tempered ... Directly one blockhouse fired, the chances were that a veritable *feu de terreur* would run down the line. On one occasion fire was actually carried ... down a line of some 120 blockhouses.

As this account suggests, the strain of life in the field would occasionally find expression in sudden false alarms, particularly at night, when it was easy enough to imagine that an alien and terrifying enemy was lurking in the darkness. The panic which seized the troops under these circumstances was tangible and quite irrational, and men who could be relied upon in other circumstances to go bravely into the cannon's mouth would suddenly be reduced to hysteria. Sergeant-Major Ellis recalled an incident in the Crimea:

We proceeded to bivouac in a small wood near here, and guards, outlying pickets, and sentries were posted, arms piled, and most of the men asleep in the open air under their blankets and greatcoats, when a barrage mule broke loose, and, taking fright, ran helter-skelter through the wood. Many men started to their feet, crying out, 'The

*Above: Maiwand Distinguished Conduct Medal group photographed after receiving medals from Queen Victoria in 1881: left to right, Private Clayton and Private Battle (2nd Berkshires), Colour-Sergeant Woods (Northumberland Fusiliers), Bobby the dog, and Corporal Lovell, Sergeant Williams and Lance-Corporal Martin (2nd Berkshires).*

enemy is on us!' and in a moment the whole of the division was rushing about in the darkness, groping for their arms; such a panic I had never before seen. By the time the mistake was found out, and everything got into proper order again, it was nearly time to march.

Private Etherington of the Royal Sussex Regiment described something similar on the Nile, during the advance to relieve Gordon at Khartoum:

One of the soldiers, who had been drinking hard, suddenly started up in a dream and threw himself overboard. The confusion which followed was indescribable. No sooner was the splash heard and an alarm given than our men sprang up, thinking that the enemy was boarding us under cover of darkness. We were moored on the bank, and the native soldiers bolted as soon as the alarm was given.

For the next few minutes a very dangerous state of things prevailed. To put it plainly, we were uncommonly frightened. Every man seized his bayonet, and as in the darkness we could not tell friend from foe, and the men at each end of the boat thought that the enemy was at the other, it is a great wonder that we did not kill one another by mistake. But happily Captain Harding appeared on the scene with a revolver, and soon restored order. The man who jumped overboard was soon rescued by one of his comrades.

Night alarms were particularly frequent in the Zulu War. In the aftermath of Isandlwana, the Zulu warrior achieved all the mythic status of a bogeyman as reinforcements arriving in the country were regaled with stories of his exceptional courage, ferocity, field-craft and marching skill. The Zulus were thought to lurk everywhere, waiting in the bush to rip up unsuspecting redcoats with their spears, and as a final confrontation with their army drew imminent, nerves became more than a little frayed. One scare, near the end of the war, very nearly finished the career of Lieutenant Chard, the hero of Rorke's Drift:

At nine p.m. we heard three single shots from the 58th sentries, on east of camp, the alarm sounded and musketry began all around the laager, and just as we all ran out buckling our swords, and filling our pockets with cartridges, we heard a 9 pounder at the N.W. angle. I went off to the Lancer lines, and then got on a wagon, at the corner of the laager, a regular blaze of rifles now going on round the laager, and men firing wildly, under and on the wagon. I felt sure then that it was all humbug, and I managed to make the men on my right cease firing, a bullet from somewhere inside the camp whizzing over my head as I was talking to them. Never saw anything so dangerous, and it was from beginning to end a false alarm ... we then walked outside, the firing at last having ceased, and we found the Engineers, Chard with them, in the little stone Fort Newdigate, had had a poorish time, crouching behind a little wall, with a storm of bullets over them, and a Sergeant wounded and two horses killed, in all, seven men were wounded, and three or four horses killed, why there weren't more I can't make out. Some of the men actually mistook the traverse for the outside of the laager. Many amusing incidents. Great waste of ammunition. One regiment alone fired 1,200 rounds...

Given the generally brutal nature of the fighting the Victorian soldier could expect to experience – with the possible exception of the Boer War – it is scarcely surprising that the anticipation of combat could tell on the nerves. Between 1837 and 1899 the British soldier experienced almost a full range of conflict, from the conventional slogging matches of the Crimea to the ferocious close-quarter

fighting of the Sudan. The experiences of individual soldiers was, therefore, often very different; the soldier in the Crimea was expected to hold his place unflinchingly in the line whilst shot and shell played havoc all around him; hand-to-hand conflict, that bitter contest of bayonets, clubbed rifles and boots, was brutal, but rare. By contrast, the soldier of the 1870s and 1880s seldom had to face efficient artillery, but was regularly exposed to the terrifying spectacle of the shock-charge, carried out by an athletic and determined enemy, who could be expected to fight with an extraordinary ferocity if they struck home. Both types of fighting required a mixture of raw courage and discipline which characterised the fighting qualities of the British soldier in the nineteenth century. Sergeant-Major Ellis left a vivid account of the first terrible moments when a battle began, when the men were exposed to fire in their formations, but could not yet find an outlet for their tension in attack. He is talking of the Alma:

On the following day we came in sight of the barricades erected by the Russians, on the hills overlooking the plain, across which our troops were advancing. About midday bang! went the first gun. 'Hullo boys!' I cried, 'now we are at it, it won't be long before we are into it.' Then came more heavy firing, ploughing up the ground around us, scattering dust all over us, and sweeping many of our men down like ninepins.

Lord Cathcart, one of the finest officers I have ever seen, called out, 'Be cool, men, in your formations'; and after a while the whole of the regiments were formed in fighting line, some of them going into action while others were forming up.

It was terrible work this forming up under fire; many of our men were spattered with the blood of their comrades, to whom they had been speaking but a short time before. Every

man who fell had to be left on the ground until assistance came to him; no man was allowed to assist a wounded comrade, his own services being required at the front. As the gaps occurred, the men closed up, and with as little delay as possible the order was given to charge.

'Every soldier will tell you that there is nothing more demoralising than to be inactive under fire. It is more than human flesh can endure, to remain a mere target, getting all the fire and giving none', agreed Sergeant-Major Parkinson of the 11th Hussars, a veteran of the charge at Balaclava. In the terrible tension of that moment, the repetitive training to obey orders like an automaton, so despised by later generations, at least stood the soldier in good stead. According to Private Howton of the 50th Regiment, the response to orders under fire was instinctive. He was in the thick of a charge on the Sikh guns at Ferozeshah:

How was it, I wondered, that, although we were so near to the batteries, there was no one to give us the magic word to rush them? Almost as soon as the thought flashed through my mind there was a wild, mad shout of 'Charge!' followed by 'Hurrah!' as madly. Then it was a dash and a rush again, and at a bound we were in amongst the guns, and they were ours.

Now, the curious thing is that no one knew who had given the order to charge – all we could find out was that in the intense excitement somebody had rapped the word out – and we had obeyed...

It was not the habit of most Victorian commanders to give their men any very clear idea of their objectives. For the most part they were brought close to the scene of the action, often without even knowing a battle was imminent, and were lucky if they were given a few cheering words before being launched into action.

The grand set-piece battles like the Alma, where the lie of the land afforded a reasonable view of events, at least allowed the soldier some sense of the wider picture, but once battle commenced the intense emotions of the fight – anger, excitement, fear, pain – narrowed his perception to his immediate vicinity. Big battles were, in any case, utterly confusing places to be, a nightmare universe of noise, smoke and confusion. At Inkerman the poor weather added to the chaotic nature of the fighting, as Private Hyde of the 49th recalled:

They came on like ants; no sooner was one knocked backwards than another clambered over the dead bodies to take his place, all of them yelling and shouting. We in the battery were not quiet, you may be sure, and what with the cheering and shouting, the thud of blows, the clash of bayonets and swords, the ping of the bullets, the whistling of shells, the foggy atmosphere, and the smell of the powder and blood, the scene inside the battery where we were was beyond the power of man to imagine or describe.

Accounts of battles often have a dream-like quality, a weirdness produced by the overwhelming assault on the senses produced by combat, and by the heightened emotional state. Private Macaulay's account of the opening stages of Tel-el-Kebir has an almost macabre beauty to it:

The forced march was something to be remembered. The darkness was intense, and we couldn't see where we were putting our feet, but marched over the yielding sand, many of us worn out and half asleep. When the final halt was called, we lay down where we were, and myself any many others fell asleep. But we were soon awakened by a shot on the extreme right of Arabi's position, then one in the centre, followed by another on his left, and then suddenly the whole line opened fire; and there we stood in the darkness, awaiting orders, while the Highland Brigade, after firing several volleys, charged the position, and carried it at the point of the bayonet.

In the grey light of morning, I saw what was to me the strangest sight my eyes ever rested on, for the sand in front of us looked as though a hailstorm was in progress, and the men marvelled at what appeared to be every foot of ground struck, except the spot on which we stood. I looked around in amazement, wondering why we did not fall, but saw only two or three go down...

A similar, almost hallucinogenic quality, like a slow-motion sequence in a modern movie, pervades an account of a mounted attack on retreating Xhosa warriors during the Eighth Cape Frontier War:

[The Xhosa] rose and letting their cloaks fall to the ground, started off at a gentle run towards some thick bush about a mile distant. They made no stand and offered no resistance, neither did they beg for mercy or show any fear, but kept on at a steady pace while our people rode up to them and shot them down.

Sergeant-Major Parkinson was of the opinion that 'those were hard days, remember, when troops went forth to kill more deliberately than now, I think, because they were not so highly educated; for education, let people say what they will against it, is a great humaniser'. It is perhaps difficult to argue that the early Victorian soldier, ill-educated and brutalised by his own experiences in the ranks, was not tougher because of it, yet many accounts from the period do not lack compassion and humanity. For most soldiers this was the testing time of their profession, and they had to face its horrors without betraying their country, Colours, officers and themselves. For many, the excitement of the moment was enough to see them through when opposing sides confronted each other man to man, and hand-to-hand fighting raged. Sustained bouts of hand-to-hand fighting, such as Inkerman, were in any case rare; more typical was the brief shock of impact and quick exposure to the horror of killing at close-quarters, as described by Private Grigg of the 4th Light Dragoons, recalling the Light Brigade's charge at Balaclava:

The first man I noticed was a mounted driver. He cut me across the eyes with his whip, which almost blinded me, but as my horse flew past him, I made a cut at him and caught him in the mouth, so that his teeth all rattled together as he fell from his horse. I can fancy I hear the horrible sound now. As he fell I cut at him again; and then I made for another driver, and cut him across the back of his neck, and gave him a second cut as he fell...

The full horror of battle usually struck in the aftermath, when passions cooled, and men were curious enough to wander over the battlefield. Sergeant-Major Ellis recalled the aftermath of the Alma:

When the sun rose the next morning, we were allowed to wander for a short time about the battlefield, but the strongest heart was soon affected by the awful scenes. Our own men were lying mingled with the enemy one on top of another, many of them clutching at each other in their death agony. As they had fallen, so they lay; many had writhed about during the night in terrible suffering, and we saw such sights that several of the men in my company fainted with sheer horror and repulsion...

The Alma was perhaps unique in Victorian experience, in that it left so many corpses concentrated in a small area. The sheer volume of the dead and dying was overpowering. Nevertheless, although most colonial battles were on a smaller scale, the feelings they evoked afterwards were much the same, as is made plain in an account of the aftermath of Gingindlovu by Captain Hutton:

I got the loan of a horse and rode round the laager and the position lately occupied by the enemy. The Martini-Henry bullets had indeed committed frightful havoc – every man struck, almost without exception – was stone dead – not so much, I conclude, by the deadliness of the wound as by the combined shock to the system of impact, and the short range. In the afternoon I was repaid for my curiosity by being told off to superintend the burial of the dead in our front, a most unpleasant task...

Tidying up after a battle was, of course, a very grim necessity, particularly if troops expected to remain on any part of the battlefield. Ellis again, on the Alma:

The pioneers of all regiments were set to work to dig long trenches about seven feet wide for the internment of the dead. Men were sent out in all directions to collect the bodies, which were brought up on stretchers, and laid, like sardines in a box, in about three layers, as near as I can remember, and then the earth was filled in and a large mound made over them. Our dead were buried by themselves, but no volleys were fired over them; and I saw no chaplain in the Crimea till near the close of the war, although several were there.

  The work of burying the dead, and collecting the arms, occupied two days. Every man who was not wanted for other duty was ordered to assist; and they made a good collection of money from the dead, for it did no one good to bury it. I saw

several cases of mutilation of the dead, particularly of a colour-sergeant of the 57th, whose finger was cut off for the sake of his ring.

The British were always careful to bury their own dead if they could – though the dead at Isandlwana had to wait four months before Lord Chelmsford risked sending a burial party into Zulu territory – and generally extended the same courtesy to their enemy, if it were practical. Often, however, the need to continue an advance, or simply the difficult nature of the ground, meant that the task was completed in a cursory manner. The result could be unpleasant, as Private Macaulay recalled of Tamai, in the eastern Sudan, and Private Mason of the Warwickshires described at Paardeberg, a few days after the fight:

The following days were very trying, for we had to pass to and from the zereba every day, marching over shifting sands which scarcely covered the recently slain enemy, whose legs and arms could be seen sticking out in all directions, with here and there a vulture tearing off the putrefying flesh...

Some of the sights we saw were frightful. Dead oxen, mules, and horses, of course, were not buried, and the stench was bad enough; but the worst sight of all was the many dead Boers who had been hastily buried, some of them not 18 inches under ground, and the heavy rain had washed the earth away, so that legs and arms and, in some cases, whole bodies were exposed to the burning sun.

Like many soldiers, Driver Wickenden, RHA, managed to find a certain grim humour in his experience of the lingering dead:

I was groom to Lieutenant Sir Godfrey Thomas ... One evening

he said to me, 'I think I'll sleep here to-night, Wickenden; down by this gun.' I answered 'Very good, sir'; and scraped a hole in the sand and laid his blanket in it. As a rule we could always sleep directly we lay down, but in a few moments he said, 'I can't sleep here, Wickenden.' 'Can't you, sir?' I asked; 'what's wrong, sir?' 'Why there's such an abominable smell just here.' 'Oh, that comes from over the hill yonder, sir, where there are a few dead horses,' I replied. However, I scraped a hole for him somewhere else, and while I was moving the blanket I discovered the body of a black, buried just below the surface, which my master had exposed by twisting and turning about in his restlessness. It gave me a bit of a shock, but I called out to one of my comrades to come and look, and we had a good laugh about it...

In the trenches before Sebastopol, the troops had to learn to live with the grisly reality of death on a daily basis, and in a way which would have been familiar to veterans of the First World War, more than half a century later. Sergeant-Major Ellis:

The enemy often kept up continual showers of balls, shells, and bullets into our trenches. Larger shells made a peculiar noise and the sailors who were with us called them 'Whistling Dicks'.

  When the firing slackened, we used to get on with the work of digging, leaving one man to watch the puffs of smoke at the enemy's batteries. He used to call out 'Down!' every time he saw one, and we would then crouch down till the shot had passed over us; but very often men were hit, and so the work of death went on. Officers going the round would often find sentries dead at their posts. Sometimes a shell would burst in a trench, knocking out the brains of one, smashing the face of another, cutting off the arm of a third, breaking the back of a fourth, splintering the leg of a fifth, and spreading dismay among us. Then we would take up the dead men, who a moment before had been cheerfully talking to us, and lay them together to await the time when we went off duty.

Sergeant Palmer of the 20th recalled that many preferred to risk injury, and the horrors of the field hospitals, rather than live under the continual strain of shellfire:

The misery of those days in the trenches will never be forgotten by those who had to endure them. I have seen men hold their hands above the parapet, hoping to have a shot through them so as to be invalided home rather than endure such wretchedness. I had to check several for so doing; they would pretend to be asleep, with an arm stretched out above their heads, so that if a shot came it might appear accidental. I can't call to mind all the hardships we endured, but I remember once, while eating a biscuit and piece of salt pork, a man lying next to me was struck in the head with a piece of shell, and his brains were splashed on to my biscuit. I thought so little of it at the time that I wiped the biscuit and finished my meal...

The colonial battles of the last half of the century were rather different from the conventional warfare of the Crimea. For one thing, the armies involved were much smaller; the British were usually outnumbered, but this was more than compensated for by their vastly superior weapons. Furthermore, whilst the Russian had been a recognisably European enemy, a man who, for all his alien language and habits, had white skin and fought in a uniform with a firearm, the majority of the enemies in the period 1860-98 were very different, and the British had a decidedly ambivalent attitude towards them. Feelings of racial superiority became increasingly popular as the century wore on, and many soldiers found a practical expression of this in their Christian beliefs, white skins and superior weapons. Thus even men like 'Chinese' Gordon or Colonel Durnford (who died at Isandlwana), who found much to admire in their enemies, never doubted that it was their Christian duty to bring them under British domination, by force if necessary. British soldiers were quite prepared to admire courage in an enemy, to romanticise him as a 'noble savage', but at the same time projected on to him all the negative associations of savagery – treachery, cunning, and cowardice. On the whole, the British liked their enemies brave but dead and defeated; it was quite possible to admire the courage of a Zulu or a Mahdist once they had been put in their place, and were no longer a threat, but it was a rather different matter when they might pop up out of the ground at any moment and wreak unspeakable havoc with their broad-bladed spears. As the civilian wagon conductor H.L. Hall wrote of the Zulu War, this engendered an inevitable double-standard:

I was rather amused when reading the English newspapers' reports of these two battles. At Isandhlwana, we were massacred by the Zulus; but at Ulundi, where we had literally mowed them down with our up-to-date firearms and they had not been able to get near enough to us to use their assegais, it was a glorious victory. But such is war.

In this attitude lay the origin of many of the instances of indiscipline amongst British troops after a battle. Generally British soldiers could be relied upon to treat any individual enemy they came across after a fight with kindness, particularly if he were wounded. Once the heat of the moment had passed, the ordinary soldier felt compassion for a fellow soldier in difficult circumstances. However, such humanity often went by the board if the enemy had been victorious on a previous occasion. Although Isandlwana was an entirely fair fight – the Zulus were defending their country against unwarranted aggression, and defeated the British in open battle, on their own soil – it was generally seen by the British as an example of the natural cruelty to which the African was believed to be prey, and for which they were to be justly punished. A desire for revenge was no doubt natural enough, but Isandlwana transformed the Zulus at a stroke from 'noble savages' to a sub-human species, to 'curs', who had forfeited all rights to humane treatment. Compare, for example, the treatment meted out to wounded Zulus at the battle of Nyezane, which took place before Isandlwana, and that during the pursuit in the closing stages of Khambula, which took place after it. The witnesses are two Volunteer officers, Lieutenant Robarts, VMR, and Commandant Schermbrucker:

Very pitiful it was to see the poor fellows lying with fearful wounds. They were very quiet, and seemed to bear pain well, no groaning or crying out. We could not do anything for them except give them water to drink ... It is a frightful thing to see a wounded man uncared for ... The excitement is all right enough while it is on – but I do not like to think of those poor fellows left.

They fairly ran like bucks, but I was after them like a whirlwind and shooting incessantly into the thick column, which could not have been less than 5000 strong. They became exhausted, and shooting them down would have taken too much time; so we took the assegais from the dead men, and rushed among the living ones, stabbing them right and left with fearful revenge ... No quarter was given.

In the Sudan there was an added complication, in that many wounded Mahdists remained

*Above: 'Why some wounded Dervishes were killed': the habit of wounded Mahdists attacking troops giving them succour enraged the British. (Rai England Collection)*

extremely dangerous. Most were, after all, committed to the cause of the *jihad*, or holy war; for them death in battle offered the prospect of eternal paradise, and many wounded undoubtedly clung to the last of their strength in the hope of delivering a final blow to the infidel. Soldiers attempting to help them or give them water were particularly vulnerable, and the sight of men attacked whilst offering succour was usually enough to drive their comrades into an indignant fury. As early

as El Teb, Captain Marling of the 3/60th, serving with the Mounted Infantry, observed, 'we shot or bayoneted all wounded men because it wasn't safe to leave them, as they speared or knifed everyone they could reach.' Guy Dawnay had a lucky escape after Tofrek:

I went out to get, or try to get, a sword for Parry, who lost his trophy of the day before, and nearly got more sword than I wanted, as an Arab who was seeming dead, sprang up as far as his wound would let him and made a cut at me after I had just passed – the old trick – he was short and was instantly shot by a Marine, who was also looking for loot.

By the time of Omdurman, Kitchener issued orders that 'all wounded Dervishes passed over had to be bayoneted, and it was absolutely necessary to do this, as if one was passed over alive he would turn round and shoot you, which event often happened.'

For the most part, such ruthlessness was temporary, but there is no doubt that humanity was steadily eroded by prolonged warfare, and in particular by the sight of British dead. Given that most enemies in colonial wars were armed with close-quarter weapons – spears, swords, knives, tomahawks – the dead often presented a terrible spectacle, which provoked a bitter reaction only rarely seen in conventional warfare like the Crimea. Private Hinton of the 58th described the grim aftermath of a successful Maori attack in New Zealand in the 1840s:

Poor Corporal Dockrill, in charge of the tent, had the top of his head cut off, and it was hanging down the back of his neck. Private Brett was also very much knocked about; and the bugler had three cuts on his right arm, four on his left, three gashes on his forehead, and his mouth cut from ear to ear, and, what's more, they stole his bugle, and we afterwards heard them sounding it in the woods.

During the Indian Mutiny this bitterness encouraged a ferocity that was unequalled in any subsequent campaign. Although it is stating the obvious to suggest that in most colonial wars the enemy were of a different race and creed to the British, this fact was usually incidental; in the Mutiny, however, it undoubtedly became part of the motivation which drove the troops to fight. For the rebels, the British had mounted an attack on their religious beliefs by trying to break their cast with contaminated cartridges, and many Mutineers therefore regarded all Christians as legitimate targets. The British, on the other hand, were worked up into a cold hatred by Mutineer attacks on white women

and children. Victorian society idealised women and motherhood; the slaughter of innocents unleashed all the dark subconscious fears of the colonial elite. By such acts the Mutineers had confirmed all the treacherous and murderous characteristics by which the British had damned them, and the result was an orgy of retribution which spared no-one:

> After a severe struggle, in which we lost a good many men, we succeeded in driving the rebels from their position, capturing their guns, and taking one hundred and forty prisoners. The next day every one of them was hung on trees surrounding the camp, simply hauled off the

ground by ropes around their necks, and left to die and be devoured by the birds...

> The slaughter was tremendous. We took, I should say, three hundred prisoners, and then came that horrible butchery which Englishmen practised then for the first and last time – and then, I suppose, only as a necessity; for the mutiny had to be stamped out, and I am sure we all expected to loose our lives in trying to regain possession of the country. Our prisoners had no fear of death, and were marvellous in their immovability. We took them out into an open space and tied

*Above: Total war: the remains of rebel troops slaughtered during the capture of the Sikander Bagh, Lucknow, in the Indian Mutiny. (Private collection)*

them together six at a time, placing them with their backs turned towards half a dozen guns, and at a little distance from them. As we placed them in position they never moved a muscle, but some of them spat at us and called us dogs. Every time the word was given to fire, thirty-six of them were blown to pieces. This was repeated over and over again, and as the heaps accumulated, we drew the guns back, and continued

*Right: Hanging captured Mutineers, India, 1857. (Private collection)*

*Below: 'Thomas Ray': an officer in the Indian Mutiny, with grim accessory.*

the slaughter till the men were all destroyed...

When we began to storm the town, an old Hindoo, who stood on top of one of the flat-roofed houses, bowed to us most ceremoniously, I suppose to show us he was friendly; but our orders were to fire, and fire we did, our Captain saying, with a laugh, 'I can't help it, old chap,' and down he went into the ruins ... A young officer, whom I did not know, drew his sword and went forward to enter the building, but a wretched Sepoy, who was hiding behind the door, fired and killed him. I shall never forget the rage the men were in, and the punishment they meted out to the fellow...

Such ferocity was unusual in colonial warfare, but not exceptional. In the last stages of the Eighth Cape Frontier War the British, exasperated by protracted Xhosa resistance, and enraged by the Xhosa custom of disembowelling enemy dead, increasingly resorted to a war of extermination. In the last sweeps through the Xhosa strongholds, men, women and children were all killed out of hand, in an attempt to reduce the will to resist.

On the whole such conduct differed considerably from the Anglo-Boer War. Although essentially a colonial war, the enemy here were white men, and Christians. They may have seemed uncouth, particularly to the fashionable young cavalry officers fresh from London society, but the Boers were at least civilised. British soldiers at first despised them, and later came to respect their field-craft and humanity. They did not generally hate or fear the Boers in the same way that they hated and feared many of their black enemies. Now and then stories of Boers firing under cover of a flag of truce, or killing wounded men on the battlefield, would provoke retribution, but these were aberrations. Whilst troops seldom had any qualms in destroying Zulu or Maori homes, for example, or blowing up Pathan villages during punitive expeditions on the Frontier, many soldiers felt deeply uncomfortable about the policy of forcibly removing Boer civilians to concentration camps and burning their farms. This mutual respect manifested itself in a number of ways, including the care afforded by each side for the other's wounded.

This last aspect also led to a marked difference of attitude when British troops found themselves in a tight corner in action. In colonial warfare, the British generally regarded surrender as anathema; not only was it dishonourable for a soldier as such, it was also disgraceful for a white man to give in to a racially inferior enemy. In any case, surrender was often impractical; although the Afghans occasionally took prisoners, largely with a view to ransom, they were equally capable of torturing them to death, and few soldiers voluntarily surrendered. As the poem from which the title of this book is taken suggests, some even preferred suicide to the tender mercies of the Afghans. Nor did the Zulus take prisoners; in the heat of battle, they killed everything they came across, soldiers, non-combatants and animals alike. Herein lies the grim truth which underpins the heroic last-stands so beloved by the British public at home;

many troops fought to the last simply because they had to, because it was better to die in a fighting rage than to beg for mercy which was unlikely to be forthcoming.

In the Boer War, however, there was less shame in surrendering to a white enemy, and a far greater chance of being well treated. This is not to say that soldiers did not fight bravely in the Boer War; of course they did. When desperately pressed, however, they were at least able to weigh up the chances, and make a choice between surrender and death which was otherwise lacking in so many colonial fights.

In many other respects, too, the battles of the Boer War were not like other colonial fights. Occasionally, as at Spioenkop, British troops found themselves huddled together in inadequate trenches, under pitiless shell-fire, now and then attacked by small groups of the enemy who had to be driven off with the bayonet. For the most part, however, Boer War battles were widespread affairs, and there was none of the fierce enemy rush which was so characteristic of the Zulu, Sudan, or even Afghan wars. Although large numbers of troops were often employed, they were spread out in extended order, often over many miles, so that it was usually quite impossible for the average soldier to have any very clear idea of what was happening across the whole battlefield. Although many late Victorian soldiers experienced heavy shell-fire for the first time in the Boer War – though the Mahdists possessed artillery, it was generally very poor, and the last time British soldiers had been on the receiving end of a serious cannonade was at Tel-el-Kebir seventeen years earlier – there was none of the close-order manoeuvring which characterised the Crimea. With a few notable exceptions, Boer War battles did not seem particularly brutal or destructive to those participating in them, whilst the enemy, firing from concealed positions at a distance, remained a largely unseen menace. It has been said that the vast majority of British troops who were under fire at Colenso never saw

a Boer all day. Lance-Corporal Mason of the CIVs gave a good description of a typical battle in the middle period of the war:

Toiling along over the uneven ground on the following day, a puff of smoke appeared upon a kopje about five miles to the right of us. A few seconds afterwards came a hiss and a roar, and looking round, I saw a shell burst right under one of the guns, and raise such a cloud of dust that for a little while we could not see the result; but, after all, there was no damage done, and we changed our direction to the left, while a section of our guns replied.

The Boer shells fell round us until we were out of range, doing but little harm. To our left rose a big kopje, upon which the enemy were well posted, and our Infantry attacked in open order. These attacks in open order, although dangerous, are tame affairs either to witness or to take part in. There is often a feeling of contempt for the slow rate of progress, and a desire to get from behind your cover and rush with a yell towards the hill from whence death is dropping upon you. Patience, however, is a very necessary quality in modern warfare.

Those unfortunate enough to be wounded in action experienced very different treatment across the Victorian period. Medical advances in the 1870s and 1880s, coupled with the reorganisation of army medical facilities, meant that by the time of the Boer War a wounded man could expect prompt and sophisticated treatment, and stood a very high chance of surviving it. Until the 1860s, however, there was no organised system of casualty evacuation, and front line hospitals were little more than butchers' yards.

This was not entirely the fault of medical personnel. In major battles, such as those in the Crimea, it was a tactical imperative that attacks should be allowed to develop their own momentum, and men were therefore ordered on no account to stop and tend to the wounded, in case the assault bogged down. This in effect condemned the wounded to lie untended on the field until the battle was over, when non-combatant personnel – and the task traditionally fell to bandsmen – had the chance to pick over the battlefield and sort the living from the dead. The bandsmen had no medical training themselves, and simply carried the injured to the regimental hospital tent in the rear. Many men had, of course, already died by that time, whom prompt first aid would otherwise have saved, and many more were suffering from infection. Front-line medical facilities were in any case minimal; until the 1860s there were no readily available anaesthetics, and the best the victim could hope for was a slug of rum or whiskey to dull his pain. If there was none, he simply had a rag or pad thrust in his mouth to stop him screaming. Although many medical officers were conscientious and humanitarian men, others were brutalised by years of exposure to floggings and suffering; few, in any case, had the skills, instruments or medicines to offer sophisticated care even if they wanted to. Bullet injuries were probed with a metal tool, and the bullet extracted if possible; wounds from slashing weapons were sewn up; and any major damage to limbs was treated by amputation. The surgeons had little choice but to act quickly – any delay carried with it the threat of gangrene – and many were renowned for their willingness to amputate.

The situation was exacerbated after major battles such as the Alma, when regimental medical officers were overwhelmed by the flood of casualties carried down from the field. The surgeon's tent was marked by a grisly pile of severed limbs outside – the task of burying the limbs fell to fatigue parties, and was particularly hated – and many soldiers preferred to try to heal themselves rather than risk a visit to the surgeon. Sergeant-Major Ellis of the Buffs was wounded at Inkerman, and left an account of his experiences:

When I recovered consciousness I found that I had also received a bullet through the muscle of my right arm, and another embedded in my left leg between the calf and bone. A bandsman of my company, whom I discovered lying near me slightly wounded in the side, assisted me to the hospital tent, where I found the doctors all busy and the place almost afloat with blood. I was temporarily attended to, and the bullet being extracted from my leg, I was carried to my own tent, where I lay for seven days, getting worse ... [later] I was placed in the regimental hospital.

Here it was considered necessary to amputate both my leg and arm, but I strongly protested; and as one of the doctors said that he had treated a similar case without amputation, I was allowed to retain those useful appendages, and gradually became convalescent...

The process of amputation was quick and unpleasant. If some form of anaesthetic was available, the patient was put out; if not, he was held down, and the surgeon cut through tissue with a knife, then severed the bone with a saw. Many surgeons prided themselves on the speed with which they could carry out such an operation, whilst many troops reacted to the experience with a stoicism which seems shocking to modern sensibilities. Private Hinton of the 58th witnessed an amputation in the Maori Wars in 1845: 'I remember, after the skirmish, seeing one of the artillery propped up on a table having his leg amputated. He had a rum-bottle by his side to give him courage, and during the whole operation he did not say so much as "Oh".'

To prevent haemorrhaging, the open arteries were either tied up or cauterised – sealed by burning, either with hot instruments, or with carbolic acid. Some injuries were just too terrible to cope with, particularly the blast injuries from shell-fire, which smashed limbs and carried away tissue at random. Gunner Cox recalled one terrible incident in the trenches before Sebastopol:

A chum of mine ... was stooping down to pick up something, when a shell burst close to him and blew off both his arms and legs. I was just going to fire when they told me I was wanted, and I found the poor fellow had just been put on a stretcher. He could not speak, but I shall never forget the expression of his eyes when I put my flask to his lips. I covered him over with a bit of old blanket, and returned to my duty; and when I was relieved, about two hours afterwards, the poor fellow was still alive. The doctors could do nothing for him but to tie his veins up...

Such initial treatment was not, however, always the worst of it. Having been patched up by the regimental surgeon, the injured man then faced a gruelling journey back down the lines of communication to the nearest convalescent hospital. If the fighting had taken place in a particularly remote or inaccessible location, this experience could be worse than the initial injury. In the Seventh Cape Frontier War, wounded men were loaded into springless wagons, and faced journeys of several days over rutted tracks and through rivers; by the time they arrived at their destination, the interior of the wagon smelled foul, the men were tormented by flies, and their wounds were festering with maggots. In the Crimea, injured troops were first carried from the Uplands to Balaclava hospital, then taken on board ship – where rotting severed limbs floated in the water – and to Scutari. In the aftermath of each major battle the numbers of injured far outstripped the hospital's capacity to deal with them. Conditions here before the arrival of Florence Nightingale deserved their appalling reputation, as Sergeant Taffs of the 4th Regiment recalled:

To give an idea of the discomforts of the place, I may mention that the floor boards in the upper rooms formed the ceilings for the lower ones, and when they were scrubbed the water came down upon us as we were lying in our beds below. Some of the men's wounds were left so long unattended to, that those men who were able would do a good turn by picking the maggots from them. This fact is almost too bad to print, but I mention it as one of the horrors of war.

Medical knowledge in the 1860s and 1870s improved dramatically, but the problem of casualty evacuation remained. In almost all colonial warfare it was quite impossible to leave wounded on the field, since Zulus, Afghans and Mahdists could be expected to kill them immediately. In Zululand, once a battle was over and the initial treatment given, the wounded man could at least expect to be sent down the line with a degree of safety, but on the North-West Frontier, where wounded men were carried away in *dhoolies* – covered hammocks slung from a pole – the wounded continued to be vulnerable. The Afghans knew that the British would always protect their wounded, and that by picking off *dhoolie*-bearers they could be provoked to exposing themselves in rescue attempts. On the Frontier,

*Above: The Royal Army Hospital Corps: Sergeant-Major Wilson and Sergeants Escott, Johnston and Edwards, Egypt, 1882. (Royal Archives)*

however, the existence of permanent garrisons at least meant that the casualties were afforded some degree of comfort once they reached them, but in Zululand, as they were passed down the line, the injured were often housed in makeshift temporary hospitals, with mattresses laid on piles of mouldering supplies and foul-smelling straw. None-the-less, accounts from surgeons in Zululand suggest that the standard of care was far higher than it had been twenty years before. Crude antiseptics and

Above: Field hospital, Pathan Revolt, 1897. Note the covered dhoolies, foreground. (Bryan Maggs Collection)

Below: Giving first aid to the wounded, Tirah, 1897. (Rai England Collection)

241

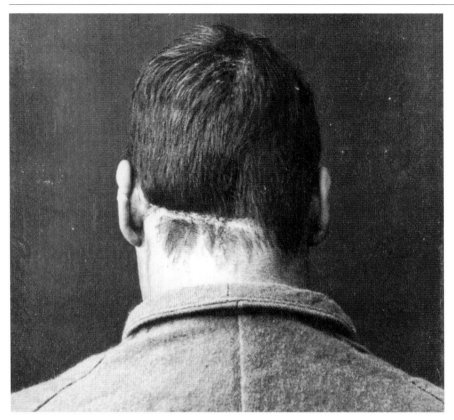

anaesthetics were generally available, and surgeons had a far greater understanding of the need to 'debride' injuries – to cut away damaged tissue and splintered bone to prevent infection. Attempts were made to repair damaged limbs with splints, although amputation was still a regular occurrence. Head, chest and abdominal injuries were still largely impossible to treat when major organs had been damaged.

Colonial warfare, in any case, provided a different range of injuries to the Napoleonic-style battles of the Crimea. Injuries from shell-fire, for instance, were rare until the advent of the Boer War, whilst the almost mediaeval range of wounds inflicted by opponents such as the Mahdists and Zulus – slash wounds from swords, stab wounds from spears – could generally be treated if the wound was clean, and no major organs damaged. The most dangerous wounds were those inflicted by poor-quality firearms, such as those

*Above: Men wounded in the Sudan campaigns could expect to suffer an almost mediaeval range of injuries: Private J. Steele, 4th Dragoon Guards, wounded by a sword-cut at Abu Klea, January 1885. (Royal Archives)*

*Right: Men of the 1st Berkshires, wounded at Tofrek, photographed at Netley in May 1885: left to right, Privates Foley, Powell and Murgatroyd, Corporal Fugwell (seated), Private Jeffries and Drummer King. (Royal Archives)*

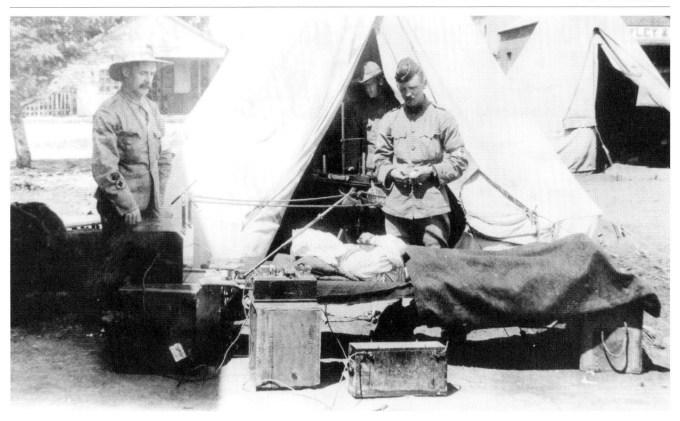

*Above: A mobile X-ray unit at Ladysmith during the siege, tangible proof of the enormous advances in medical care since Queen Victoria's accession in 1837. (Bryan Maggs Collection)*

*Below: A field dressing station, Klipdrift, Boer War. (National Army Museum)*

used in large quantities by the Chinese, Asante, Maoris, Zulus and to some extent Mahdists. These were usually obsolete patterns, firing irregularly shaped, home-made projectiles, which had very little velocity due to poor-quality powder. They would often penetrate the flesh, but then bounce off from bone, and take bizarre courses through the body. Private Gilham of the Rifle Brigade recalled that during the Asante War 'an old chum of mine was shot just by the side of his right eye, the bullet passing round the side of his head under the skin, and coming out the back'. Generally, such projectiles lacked the power to cause major injuries to bone and internal organs, and their chief danger lay in the fact that it was difficult to find and extract them; if they were missed they would often cause infection.

The improvements in weapon technology curiously matched the developing skills of the surgeons. In the 1881 Transvaal War British surgeons noted the effects of the sophisticated high-powered but heavy calibre rifles of the time, which tended to clip neatly through muscle and sinew, leaving wounds which could be easily sewn up, but which had sufficient weight to cause nasty injuries to bones by splintering them lengthways. This was, of course, giving the British quite literally a taste of their own medicine, since the Boers were armed with weapons like the Westley-Richards and the Martini-Henry, which the British were at that time using against their enemies. By 1899, however, gunshot injuries were, on the whole, less dangerous; both the British and the Boers were using small-calibre, high-velocity bullets with metal jackets, which were designed to inflict relatively humane injuries. They produced small entrance wounds, generally took a regular course through the body, and did not create the massive exit wounds characteristic of the Snider and Martini-Henry. Of course, they could just as easily cause instant death if they hit the head or the heart, but a remarkable number of men survived wounds which would have undoubtedly been fatal a gener-

ation before. Indeed, the sensation of being hit by a Mauser bullet was, apparently, quite painless; many who experienced it said that they merely felt a light blow or a push, and some even carried on fighting for some time without realising they had been hit. Pain came later when sensation returned to the wounded area.

By 1899 medical facilities had, in any case, improved beyond all recognition from the Crimean War period. Army medical services had benefited immensely from the reorganisations of the 1860s and 1870s and the creation of the Royal Army Medical Corps. No longer were injured troops carried to the rear by untrained bandsmen; they were carried away by RAMC bearers, who were themselves able to apply first aid. Even for those who were wounded in inaccessible places, and whom the stretcher-bearers could not reach, help was at hand in the form of a field dressing – a wad of sterilised gauze and a bandage – issued to each soldier. This had first been introduced in the Prussian army in the 1880s, and was adopted amongst the British a few years later. Casualties were taken first to field dressing stations where they were assessed under a recognisably modern system of triage – divided up into those who were slightly wounded, and who needed no immediate treatment other than pain relief; those who were so badly wounded that nothing could be done for them beyond pain relief; and those who were desperately injured, but could still be saved, those under most risk being given emergency treatment. This system benefited greatly from the fact that no Boer War battles produced a desperate flood of casualties like those in the Crimea, and the surgeons were never overwhelmed. The wounded were then sent down to mobile field hospitals, and ultimately to stationary hospitals which were established on the line of communication of each division. Technological advances like mobile X-ray machines were used to examine injuries, and the use of sterilised instruments, antiseptics and anaesthetics – chloroform, ether, nitrous oxide – were by now standard. Indeed, a number of highly

skilled civilian surgeons were hired as consultants by the British government, and spent time at the front advising on the treatment of the injured. Volunteer nurses came out from Britain to tend the wounded in the stationary hospitals, whilst a number of volunteer stretcher-bearer companies were formed; in Natal the local Indian community provided one, which included no less a personage than Mohandas Gandhi, then a young lawyer living in Natal.

In some areas, however, results remained poor. Both head and abdominal injuries remained dangerous, whilst no system of blood transfusion existed until the First World War. Nevertheless, the fatality rate amongst the 22,000 soldiers treated for wounds during the Boer War was just 2% – a figure that would have staggered the regimental surgeons who plied their trade in the 1850s.

If the Victorian soldier managed to survive the hardships of campaign life, the exhausting marching, poor food, bad water, poisonous wildlife, horrible diseases and occasional bouts of action, what rewards might he have accumulated along the way? Precious few; a campaign medal, perhaps, and a pension, which was small enough. In a number of campaigns – India, China, Asante – British troops were exposed to a good deal of tangible wealth, belonging to local citizens, ripe for the taking. Yet looting was generally strictly forbidden, and often it was seized by officially appointed prize agents. Taken back to Britain, its value was assessed, and it was distributed proportionately, the bulk of it going to the Crown, but some of it being shared amongst the officers and men who took part. Gunner MaCallam of the Royal Artillery recalled some of the treasures he encountered during the Mutiny, and what became of most of them:

I believe the sergeant who had charge of the hanging party obtained possession of the diamond from [a victim's] turban, and other jewels, I suppose, were not left for the birds. But we had nothing like the loot that one would expect, seeing the vast riches that were strewn about. We were unable to carry much about with us, and in consequence had to leave it for the natives who were under the command of the prize agents. Many kind promises were made by the generals, so that we all expected to live in plenty to the end of our days...

The value of the riches found in Kirwee was beyond the power of man to imagine. Heaps of jewels and gold were found stowed away, and the gold bricks were so numerous that it took thirty bullock-waggons to remove the treasure, an Englishman and a Sepoy being placed to guard each waggon.

At a parade about this time the General said that every man who heard him, if he were spared to return to England, would be worth £500. Alas! the most fortunate of us only received £75, and that after considerable delay...

If the average soldier received nothing of any real value from his active service, he might at least return with an interesting selection of souvenirs, to impress his family at home. The British soldier was an inveterate souvenir-taker, and regiments returned from active service laden down with Russian helmets, Afghan Khyber knives, Zulu shields and spears, Mahdist patched coats and swords. Generally, officers were better placed to procure souvenirs than the men, since they were allowed more baggage in which to transport them; indeed, so great was the rush to King Cetshwayo's royal homestead at oNdini after the final battle of the Zulu War that a number of officers grumbled in letters home that by the time they arrived all the best souvenirs had gone. In one particular respect this fascination for souvenirs carried with it a touch of the macabre: a combination of half-baked ideas of racial superiority, a genuine thirst for medical knowledge, and the inevitable sense of triumph which followed victory meant

that many officers were quite happy to collect human remains as souvenirs, without any appreciable sense of guilt. Skulls were particularly desirable, since experts claimed to be able to see in them the marks of inferior development to that which characterised the European type. Usually they were taken from old battlefields, when the dead had already decomposed; one of Lord Chelmsford's staff recalled visiting the battlefield of oNdini some months after the event, and seeking out the remains of a Zulu commander he had seen shot down. When he found his skeleton lying in the grass he brought away the skull. Occasionally, however, there were grislier stories to tell, like this one, which concerns the final brutal stages of the Eighth Frontier War:

Doctor A– of the 60th had asked my men to procure for him a few native skulls of both sexes. This was a task easily accomplished. One morning they brought back to camp about two dozen heads of various ages. As these were not supposed to be in a presentable state for the doctor's acceptance, the next night they turned my vat into a cauldron for the removal of superfluous flesh. And there these men sat, gravely smoking their pipes during the live-long night, and stirring round and round the heads in that seething boiler, as though they were cooking black-apple dumplings.

The habit had not entirely died out as late as 1898, when Kitchener apparently toyed with the idea of sending the Mahdi's skull home to England, after his artillery had desecrated his tomb. The idea was abandoned when Queen Victoria let it be known that she was not amused.

For most, retirement from the army meant the end to a hard but adventurous life, with little more than a few medals and a small pension to show for it. Private Edward Hyde of the 49th concluded his account of his Crimean experiences with some observations which prob-

ably summed up the lot of most Victorian soldiers:

I took my discharge, having served for twenty-one years and two hundred days. My pension was eightpence a day, and would have been eightpence halfpenny if I had completed my twenty-second year. I had received the Crimean medal with three bars, the Turkish medal, and a Good Conduct medal, which last carried with it a gratuity of five pounds. For sixteen years I had been clear of regimental entry, and this good conduct entitled me to four stripes on my right arm, and thus increased my pension by fourpence a day.

And finally, what of Donald MacDonald of the 21st Royal Scots Fusiliers, with whom we began our look at the life and times of the Victorian soldier? Having survived the grounding of the *City of Paris*, he went through the Zulu War without incident. He was promoted to Corporal, and served as a clerk for a while to the Headquarters Staff. At the end of the war he returned to his regimental duties, and marched with his battalion to Wakkerstroom in the Transvaal. He realised that trouble was brewing with the Boers, and fully expected to take his part, but instead fell victim to jaundice. He was invalided home on the SS *Ontario* in February 1880. He was shortly thereafter reunited with his family, and his correspondence ceased, but his last letter suggests something of the exhausting effects of Victorian colonial campaigning on an ordinary infantry battalion: 'We have', he wrote, 'over 200 invalids and time expired men, and I expect we shall all go after our arrival to the Royal Victoria Hospital, where we shall likely stay for 2 or 3 weeks'...

The soldiers of the Queen had, indeed, been, to places that their civilian counterparts could scarcely dream of, and seen sights that would haunt many of them for the rest of their lives, and they knew the price of Empire better than most.

*The price of Empire: the full horror of early Victorian warfare is demonstrated by this poignant group of wounded men, photographed at Chatham after their return from the Crimea. (Royal Archives)*

**Contemporary key to the photograph:**
1. Cpl David Williams, 23rd Foot, grapeshot wound left arm, Alma. 2. Pte James Alexander, 30th Foot, gunshot wound left leg, Inkerman. 3. Pte James Doolan, 19th Foot, impaired health, Crimea. 4. Pte James Higgins, 7th Foot, amputation left leg after Alma. 5. Pte George Cope, 95th Foot, gunshot wound right leg, Sebastopol. 6. Pte Henry Pye, 7th Foot, cannon shot wound of both legs, Alma. 7. Pte John Smith, 21st Foot, gunshot wound left leg, Inkerman. 8. Pte John O'Shaughuissy, 41st Foot, gunshot wound right arm, Inkerman. 9. Pte William Frevillier, 8th Hussars, impaired health, Crimea. 10. Pte Thomas Drew, 93rd Foot, wound right leg by a fall, Crimea. 11. Pte Henry Cushla, 57th Foot, frostbite right foot and both hands, trenches. 12. Cpl Patrick O'Callaghan, 30th Foot, injuries of both sides by a fall, Crimea. 13. Pte Alfred Gibbs, RB, frostbite both feet, trenches. 14. Pte James Clarke, 88th Foot, frostbite right foot, trenches. 15. Pte James Guest, 7th Foot, frostbite right foot, trenches. 16. Pte Francis Ormond, 20th Foot, impaired health, Crimea. 17. Pte Charles Cardwell, 47th Foot, impaired health, Crimea. 18. Pte John Storey, RB, impaired health, Crimea. 19. Pte Henry Minchin, 10th Hussars, impaired health, India. 20. Pte Benjamin Hall, 4th Foot, impaired health, Crimea. 21. Pte Mark Pierei, 97th Foot, impaired health, Crimea. 22. Pte Robert Smith, 34th Foot, impaired health, Crimea. 23. Pte Edmund Glendon, 14th Foot, impaired health, Malta. 24. Pte Patrick McCarthy, 34th Foot, impaired health, Crimea. 25. Pte Daniel Grey, 6th Dragoons, impaired health, Crimea.

# APPENDIX 1
# Notes on Infantry, Cavalry and Artillery
# Organisation in the Victorian Period

## Infantry

Throughout the Victorian period, the standard infantry tactical unit remained the battalion.

In 1837 there were 99 numbered line infantry regiments, each consisting of a single battalion.* Accross the period, in one form or another, each battalion consisted of a service element and a depot element; the former was employed in active campaigning, whilst the latter remained at home to raise recruits, who were sent out in drafts in due course to top up the service companies. In 1837 the typical battalion consisted of six service companies and four depot companies. Of these, one was designated the grenadier company, which formed the right flank company when the battalion was formed in line, and another was the light company, which formed the left. Each company was numbered consecutively after its position in the line, counting from the right. Grenadiers had not, in fact, carried grenades since the eighteenth century, but were considered the elite company of the battalion. Light companies were trained in skirmishing techniques, a speciality which became redundant early in the period as more and more battalion commanders trained all of their men as skirmishers.

Each service battalion consisted of a headquarters – a lieutenant-colonel and a major – and six companies, each under the command of a captain. There were in total eight lieutenants, four ensigns (later second lieutenants), a surgeon and his assistant, four staff sergeants, thirty-six colour-sergeants and sergeants, twenty-four corporals, twelve drum-

mers and 516 privates. This gave an average of eighty-six privates per company. One corporal and ten privates were designated pioneers, and one sergeant and twenty privates were trained as bandsmen, whose duties in battle included stretcher-bearing. The depot companies were significantly smaller than their service counterparts.

By 1840 the number of privates in each company had risen to ninety-one, but this system remained largely unchanged during the great wars of the middle of the century, the Crimea and Indian Mutiny. In the Crimea, the service element consisted of eight companies, whilst the number of depot companies fluctuated; eight were initially authorised, but when this proved impractical the number was reduced to four, only to rise to eight again as the war dragged on. A typical service battalion then consisted of a colonel or lieutenant-colonel, assisted by two field officers (either a lieutenant-colonel and a major, or two majors), with one adjutant, one quartermaster, one paymaster, one surgeon, one assistant surgeon, two staff sergeants (sergeant-major and quartermaster-sergeant) and five sergeants (paymaster, armourer, schoolmaster, hospital and orderly room clerk) attached to the headquarters. Each company was commanded by a captain, assisted by two subalterns (lieutenants or second lieutenants), and consisted of one colour-sergeant, three or four sergeants, four or five corporals, and between eighty-six and ninety-five privates. There were two drummers or buglers per company, and the usual complement of pioneers and bandsmen.

In the aftermath of the Crimea, battalion strength was standardised as eight service companies – frequently to be found fielded as two

wings on campaign – and four depot companies, with a strength of 952 privates. This period saw the first break with the tradition of single battalion regiments. Third battalions were raised for the Rifle Regiments – the 60th Rifles and the Rifle Brigade – in 1855, and fourth battalions in 1857. In 1858 the 2nd to 25th Regiments all received second battalions, and in 1861 nine European regiments of the East India Company army were taken onto the Queen's strength as the 101st to 109th Regiments.

In 1860, the distinction between grenadier, light and centre companies was abolished, reflecting the fact that all had been doing much the same job for at least the previous decade. Companies were still usually numbered consecutively from the right, although a few battalions chose to refer to their companies by letter. In the 1860s the typical strength of a battalion was ten service companies and two depot, but this changed significantly with the Cardwell reforms, which, from 1872, linked single battalions in pairs and tied regiments to particular locations within the United Kingdom. From this point – more or less until the end of the Victorian period – an infantry regiment consisted of a depot detachment (usually four understrength companies, commanded by a major, a captain, and two subalterns) and, in the case of two-battalion regiments, one home battalion and one overseas battalion.

In 1881 this system reached its logical conclusion in that all regiments (except Rifles, which already had three) were given two battalions. The first twenty-five regiments remained as they were, whilst the remainder were amalgamated in pairs, to form the first and second battalions of new regiments. The

* The 1st and 60th Rifles each had two, as did the Rifle Brigade (formerly the 95th, but taken out of the Line in 1816) and the three regiments of Foot Guards.

number of battalions therefore remained basically the same, but the old numbering system was abolished in favour of new territorial titles. In addition, each regiment had two attached militia battalions – numbered three and four – and a volunteer battalion. Each service battalion consisted of a headquarters and eight companies of roughly 100 NCOs and men, although troops stationed in India generally maintained a higher overall establishment of 1000 NCOs and men. Each company was commanded by a captain, and divided into two half-companies (commanded by subalterns), each of two sections. This system remained in service with only minor modification until the end of the Victorian period, so that in 1899 a service battalion nominally consisted of headquarters and eight companies, each of three officers and 110 other ranks. In 1896 the Coldstream and Scots Guards acquired a third service battalion. Some Line regiments which recruited in large industrial conurbations, received third and fourth battalions. The Cameron Highlanders, which hitherto consisted of just one regular battalion, received a second.

It should be noted, however, that battalions were rarely up to strength on active service. Sickness, disease and desertion thinned the ranks before ever a shot was fired in anger, and battalions often went into battle minus several companies which had been detached for other duties. In the early days of the Cardwell system the demands of the Empire meant that battalions supposedly appointed to home service often had to be sent overseas, although it was unusual for both battalions to serve side by side in the same campaign – as the 1/24th and 2/24th nonetheless did in the Anglo-Zulu War, for example. Battalions remained largely self-contained institutions throughout the Victorian era, and usually functioned as separate units on the battlefield. In the Crimea battalions were formed into brigades (three to a brigade), whilst two brigades constituted a division, but these were essentially temporary formations. The officers commanding battalions had no experience – initially, at least – of fighting alongside the other battalions within their brigades, and this ad hoc approach to larger formations continued throughout the period. Although this was recognised as a failing, the realities of colonial warfare, where troops were inevitably spread thinly on the ground, mitigated against fundamental change; even in 1899, when the 1st Army Corps was despatched from England, the officers commanding brigades had little experience of working together. Only after several months of campaigning in South Africa did brigades and divisions learn by experience how best to work together.

## Cavalry

At the beginning of the Victorian period, a cavalry regiment consisted of a headquarters (ten officers and five NCOs) and six troops, each troop consisting of one captain, one lieutenant, one cornet, one troop sergeant-major, two sergeants, three corporals, one trumpeter, one farrier and forty-seven privates, giving a total of 363 altogether. This was a low establishment based on peace-time soldiering at home and was likely to be higher in India or in the field. Like infantry battalions, cavalry regiments remained largely self-contained, with the troop as the standard tactical unit. In the Crimea and Indian Mutiny the number of troops was raised to eight, but troop strengths varied between forty and seventy men according to circumstances. Eight troops remained largely the norm across the Victorian period, and from about 1870 it was common to group two troops to form a squadron. Establishments continued to fluctuate, according to home or overseas service, and service in India. In the late 1870s the establishment of a cavalry regiment in the field consisted of thirty-one officers, including headquarters (one lieutenant-colonel, one major, eight captains, sixteen subalterns, one adjutant, one paymaster, one quartermaster, one medical officer, and one veterinary surgeon), eleven staff sergeants and sergeants, eight troop sergeant-majors, 24 sergeants, 22 artificers (farriers, saddlers etc), and 549 rank and file, including eight trumpeters, thirty-two corporals, fifteen bandsmen, 480 privates and twenty-two drivers, giving a grand total of 653 of all ranks. Each squadron therefore consisted of 150 all ranks, and each troop of seventy-five. In 1897 three squadrons within each regiment were designated for active service, each with a nominal strength of six officers and 128 in the ranks, and the fourth for depot duties. The depot squadron included such personnel as bandsmen and clerks, and it was to this squadron that the Maxim gun was attached. In India, however, all four squadrons were designated for active service.

In larger formations, two or more regiments constituted a brigade, and two brigades a division. With the total regular cavalry establishment standing at just twenty-eight regiments (excluding three regiments of Household cavalry), however, which were required for home service and garrison duties in India* as well as periodic campaigning, large formations were unusual, and most campaigns from the 1860s onwards were characterised by a chronic shortage of cavalry.

## Artillery

In the early Victorian period, the Artillery was divided into Horse Artillery troops and Foot Artillery batteries. Each of these consisted of four lighter and two heavier guns: RHA troops were equipped with lighter guns, usually four 6 pdrs and two 12 pdr howitzers, rather than the RFA's four 9 pdrs and two 24 pdr howitzers. Each gun was drawn by a limber with three or more pairs of horses, according to weight. A pair of guns and their limbers constituted a division – three to a troop or battery, right left and centre – and each gun and limber a sub-division. The establishment of a troop or battery varied slightly according to the calibre of its guns, but an average battery in 1854 consisted of one captain, one second captain, three lieu-

*There were 39 regiments of Indian cavalry.

tenants, one assistant surgeon, six bombardiers, two staff sergeants, four corporals, one farrier, six shoeing-smiths, three collar-makers, two wheelers, ninety-seven gunners and 123 drivers, with a total of ninety-two riding horses and 180 draft. In the aftermath of the Crimea and Indian Mutiny, Artillery organisation was standardised. The term troop was abandoned in favour of battery for both RHA and RFA units, and in 1889 section and sub-section substituted for the old divisions and sub-divisions. Each battery was commanded by a major and a captain, with one lieutenant to each sub-section, and a surgeon and a veterinary surgeon. NCOs consisted of one sergeant-major and one quartermaster-sergeant, six sergeants, six corporals, six bombardiers, seventy-two gunners (seventy for RHA), sixty-

four drivers (seventy-two for RHA), two trumpeters, one farrier, four shoeing-smiths (five for RHA), two collar-makers and two wheelers, giving a total of 174 personnel per RFA battery and 184 for RHA batteries. RFA batteries included thirty riding and 132 draft horses, and RHA seventy-seven and 183 respectively. In addition to the six guns, each battery included six gun-carriages, six ammunition wagons and a forge. In action, a gun was manned by three crew, with a sergeant in command, whilst an NCO was in charge of the ammunition wagon, two men acted as ammunition numbers, two were in reserve, and six served as drivers (with three horse-holders in RHA batteries). Mountain batteries – light guns which could be broken down and carried on mules – first appeared in the 1860s. Mountain batteries

equipped with 7pdr RML guns were used in the Abyssinian and Asante campaigns, but the more effective 2.5 inch RML 'screw gun' began to replace them during the later stages of the 2nd Afghan War, and this remained the standard weapon of both RA and Indian Army mountain batteries to the end of the period.

This basic organisation remained largely unchanged until the end of the period. Batteries were self-contained tactical units, although when artillery was in short supply it was not unusual for guns to be deployed in sections of two pieces. Although, by the 1890s, tactical theory allowed for massed fire, and guns were more frequently employed in complete batteries, there were seldom sufficient available in any single action to be combined together in larger formations, such as divisions.

# APPENDIX 2
## Infantry Titles before and after 1881,
## with pre-1881 Facing Colours

| Pre-1881 number | Post-1881 title | Pre-1881 facing colour | Pre-1881 number | Post-1881 title | Pre-1881 facing colour |
|---|---|---|---|---|---|
| 1st | Royal Scots | Blue | 43rd | 1st Bn Oxfordshire Light Infantry | White |
| 2nd | Queen's Royal West Surrey Regiment | Blue | 44th | 1st Bn Essex Regiment | Yellow |
| 3rd | East Kent Regiment | Buff | 45th | 1st Bn Derbyshire Regiment | Lincoln green |
| 4th | King's Royal Lancaster Regiment | Blue | 46th | 2nd Bn Duke of Cornwall's Light Infantry | Yellow |
| 5th | Northumberland Fusiliers | Bright green | | | |
| 6th | Royal Warwickshire Regiment | Blue | 47th | 1st Bn North Lancashire Regiment | White |
| 7th | Royal Fusiliers | Blue | 48th | 1st Bn Northamptonshire Regiment | Buff |
| 8th | King's Liverpool Regiment | Blue | | | |
| 9th | Norfolk Regiment | Yellow | 49th | 1st Bn Royal Berkshire Regiment | Lincoln green |
| 10th | Lincolnshire Regiment | Yellow | 50th | 1st Bn Royal West Kent Regiment | Blue |
| 11th | Devonshire Regiment | Lincoln green | | | |
| 12th | Suffolk Regiment | Yellow | 51st | 1st Bn Yorkshire Light Infantry | Blue |
| 13th | Somersetshire Light Infantry | Blue | 52nd | 2nd Bn Oxfordshire Light Infantry | Buff |
| 14th | West Yorkshire Regiment | Buff | | | |
| 15th | East Yorkshire Regiment | Yellow | 53rd | 1st Bn Shropshire Light Infantry | Scarlet |
| 16th | Bedfordshire Regiment | Yellow | 54th | 2nd Bn Dorsetshire Regiment | Grass green |
| 17th | Leicestershire Regiment | White | 55th | 2nd Bn Border Regiment | Lincoln green |
| 18th | Royal Irish Regiment | Blue | 56th | 2nd Bn Essex Regiment | Purple |
| 19th | Yorkshire Regiment | Grass green | 57th | 1st Bn Middlesex Regiment | Yellow |
| 20th | Lancashire Fusiliers | Yellow | 58th | 2nd Bn Northamptonshire Regiment | Black |
| 21st | Royal Scots Fusiliers | Blue | | | |
| 22nd | Cheshire Regiment | Buff | 59th | 2nd Bn East Lancashire Regiment | White |
| 23rd | Royal Welsh Fusiliers | Blue | 60th | King's Royal Rifle Corps | Scarlet |
| 24th | South Wales Borderers | Grass green | 61st | 2nd Bn Gloucestershire Regiment | Buff |
| 25th | King's Own Scottish Borderers | Blue | 62nd | 1st Bn Wiltshire Regiment | Buff |
| 26th | 1st Bn Scottish Rifles | Yellow | 63rd | 1st Bn Manchester Regiment | Lincoln green |
| 27th | 1st Bn Inniskilling Fusiliers | Buff | 64th | 1st Bn North Staffordshire Regiment | Black |
| 28th | 1st Bn Gloucestershire Regiment | Yellow | | | |
| 29th | 1st Bn Worcestershire Regiment | Yellow | 65th | 1st Bn Yorkshire & Lancashire Regiment | White |
| 30th | 1st Bn East Lancashire Regiment | Yellow | | | |
| 31st | 1st Bn East Surrey Regiment | Buff | 66th | 2nd Bn Royal Berkshire Regiment | Grass green |
| 32nd | 1st Bn Duke of Cornwall's Light Infantry | White | | | |
| 33rd | 1st Bn West Riding Regiment | Scarlet | 67th | 2nd Bn Hampshire Regiment | Yellow |
| 34th | 1st Bn Border Regiment | Yellow | 68th | 1st Bn Durham Light Infantry | Dark green |
| 35th | 1st Bn Royal Sussex Regiment | Blue | 69th | 2nd Bn Welsh Regiment | Lincoln green |
| 36th | 2nd Bn Worcestershire Regiment | Grass green | 70th | 2nd Bn East Surrey Regiment | Black |
| 37th | 1st Bn Hampshire Regiment | Yellow | 71st | 1st Bn Highland Light Infantry | Buff |
| 38th | 1st Bn South Staffordshire Regiment | Yellow | 72nd | 1st Bn Seaforth Highlanders | Yellow |
| | | | 73rd | 2nd Bn Royal Highlanders | Dark green |
| 39th | 1st Bn Dorsetshire Regiment | Grass green | 74th | 2nd Bn Highland Light Infantry | White |
| 40th | 1st Bn South Lancashire Regiment | Buff | 75th | 1st Bn Gordon Highlanders | Yellow |
| | | | 76th | 2nd Bn West Riding Regiment | Scarlet |
| 41st | 1st Bn Welsh Regiment | White | 77th | 2nd Bn Middlesex Regiment | Yellow |
| 42nd | 1st Bn Royal Highlanders | Blue | 78th | 2nd Bn Seaforth Highlanders | Buff |

| Pre-1881 number | Post-1881 title | Pre-1881 facing colour | Pre-1881 number | Post-1881 title | Pre-1881 facing colour |
|---|---|---|---|---|---|
| 79th | The Cameron Highlanders | Blue | 94th | 2nd Bn Connaught Rangers | Lincoln green |
| 80th | 2nd Bn South Staffordshire Regiment | Yellow | 95th | 2nd Bn Derbyshire Regiment | Yellow |
| 81st | 2nd Bn North Lancashire Regiment | Buff | 96th | 2nd Bn Manchester Regiment | Yellow |
| 82nd | 2nd Bn South Lancashire Regiment | Yellow | 97th | 2nd Bn Royal West Kent Regiment | Sky blue |
| 83rd | 1st Bn Royal Irish Rifles | Yellow | 98th | 2nd Bn North Staffordshire Regiment | White |
| 84th | 2nd Bn Yorkshire & Lancashire Regiment | Yellow | 99th | 2nd Bn Wiltshire Regiment | Yellow |
| 85th | 2nd Bn Shropshire Light Infantry | Blue | 100th | 1st Bn Leinster Regiment | Blue |
| 86th | 2nd Bn Royal Irish Rifles | Blue | 101st | 1st Bn Royal Munster Fusiliers | Blue |
| 87th | 1st Bn Royal Irish Fusiliers | Blue | 102nd | 1st Bn Royal Dublin Fusiliers | Blue |
| 88th | 1st Bn Connaught Rangers | Yellow | 103rd | 2nd Bn Royal Dublin Fusiliers | Blue |
| 89th | 2nd Bn Royal Irish Fusiliers | Black | 104th | 2nd Bn Royal Munster Fusiliers | Dark blue |
| 90th | 2nd Bn Scottish Rifles | Buff | 105th | 2nd Bn Yorkshire Light Infantry | Buff |
| 91st | 1st Bn Argyll & Sutherland Highlanders | Yellow | 106th | 2nd Bn Durham Light Infantry | White |
| 92nd | 2nd Bn Gordon Highlanders | Yellow | 107th | 2nd Bn Royal Sussex Regiment | White |
| 93rd | 2nd Bn Argyll & Sutherland Highlanders | Yellow | 108th | 2nd Bn Royal Inniskilling Fusiliers | Pale yellow |
| | | | 109th | 2nd Bn Leinster Regiment | White |
| | | | Rifle Bde | Rifle Bde | Black |

# FURTHER READING

The literature of the Victorian army, its personalities and its campaigns, is so large that to list it critically would take several volumes. It ranges from contemporary training manuals, official and semi-official accounts of campaigns, and regimental histories, through endless memoirs, collected letters, biographies and autobiographies, to modern popular histories and stringent academic re-assessments. All of this material is valuable to a greater or lesser degree: accounts by participants are usually framed by the author's contemporary perspective and attitudes, are seldom critical of Imperial objectives, usually have little understanding of the enemy, and are occasionally economic with the truth when the author has an axe to grind; they are, nonetheless, the very stuff of history, a glimpse of events and times as they seemed to those who witnessed them. Many modern works, on the other hand, fall either into the trap of recycling a *Boy's Own Paper* blood-and-thunder mythology for the modern armchair adventurer, or are so deeply analytical as to be as dull as proverbial ditch-water; the best of them, however, succeed in balancing modern research techniques – including sources from 'the other side', unavailable to contemporary commentators – to produce history which is not only richly observed and rounded, but riveting to read. Some of the books listed here are not entirely free of the faults outlined above, but they have been selected to introduce new readers to some of the themes touched upon in *Go To Your God Like A Soldier*, and most of them include excellent bibliographies of their own; they represent no more than the surface of a well from which those interested are invited to drink much deeper.

The Victorian army has been the subject of a number of recent sociological studies, of which the best are two works by Edward Spiers, *The Army and Society 1815–1914* (London, 1980) and *The Late Victorian Army 1868–1902* (Manchester, 1992), which, together with Alan Ramsay Skelley's *The Victorian Army At Home* (London, 1977), contain a thorough analysis and a wealth of statistics on such aspects as recruitment, pay, health and living conditions, and crime and punishment, as well as some insight into the gulf between the officer class and the other ranks. For a fascinating glimpse into an area which the Victorians preferred to shut away behind closed doors, there is Ronald Hyam's *Empire and Sexuality: The British Experience* (Manchester, 1990).

With regard to individual campaigns, the Crimean War has produced a great many studies – as befits its status as the most significant of the early Victorian wars – although many are rather too coloured by the popular image of the war as one of unmitigated ineptitude and blundering. L.V. ffrench Blake's *The Crimean War* (London, 1971) is an excellent introduction, which includes a concise history of the war as a whole – not merely the land operations in the Crimea – and a useful critical summary of contemporary literature. Andrew Lambert's *The Crimean War: British Grand Strategy 1853–56* (Manchester, 1990) is a modern analysis of broader British strategic aims and options, whilst Christopher Hibbert's *The Destruction of Lord Raglan* (London, 1961) presents a sympathetic portrait of its subject. W. Baring Pemberton's *Battles of the Crimea* (London, 1962) gives good, crisp descriptions of the major battles in which the British were involved. John Mollo's *The Valley of Death* (London, 1991) is an exhaustive and beautifully illustrated study of the Light Brigade's action at Balaclava. The two best contemporary histories – although both are flawed – are A.W. Kinglake's *The Invasion of the Crimea* (eight volumes, London, 1863–87) and E.H. Nolan's *The History of the War against Russia* (two volumes, London, 1857). For an overview of colonial campaigning – a rather different type of warfare – Philip Haythornthwaite's *The Colonial Wars Source Book* (London, 1995) includes a résumé of all major campaigns, with a thorough bibliography for each, as well as a useful assessment of contemporary documentation, both written and pictorial. Similarly, *Victorian Military Campaigns*, edited by Brian Bond (London, 1967) includes a number of essays on various campaigns, whilst the Journal of the Victorian Military Society, *Soldiers of the Queen*, has, over twenty years, produced an extraordinary range of articles, many of which have greatly influenced the present work.

To the Victorians themselves, it seemed self-evident that India was the most important of their Imperial possessions, and the literature describing their campaigns to conquer and keep the sub-continent secure far outweighed that of any other military adventure. Curiously enough, the emphasis has shifted in recent times, with more attention being given to Africa. T.A. Heathcote's *The Military in British India: The Development of British land forces in South Asia, 1600–1947* (Manchester, 1995) provides a necessary overview, setting the Raj in the context of broader Indian military tradition. The rise of British power in India falls largely outside this review, but *Six Battles for India: The Anglo-Sikh Wars 1845–6, 1848–9* (London,

1969) by G. Bruce, and *The Sikh Wars: The British Army in the Punjab 1845–1849* by Colonel H.C.B. Cook (London, 1975) provide an introduction to the campaigns against the Kingdom of Lahore. Christopher Hibbert's *The Great Mutiny: India 1857* (London, 1978) is a good place to start when unravelling the events of 1857–59, whilst Michael Edwardes provided vivid accounts of not only the Mutiny as a whole but the siege of Lucknow and some of the principal battles in *Red Year: The Indian Rebellion of 1857* (London, 1973), *A Season in Hell* (London, 1973), and *Battles of the Indian Mutiny* (London, 1963) respectively. Probably the most complete contemporary history was Sir John Kaye's multi-volume *History of the Sepoy War in India of 1857–8* (London, 1864–7; final volume, completed by Colonel G.B. Malleson, published 1897); for an Indian view of events see P.C. Gupta's *Nana Sahib and the Rising at Cawnpore* (Oxford, 1963), whilst Eric Stokes' *The Peasant Armed: The Indian Revolt of 1857* (Oxford, 1986) successfully unravels the tangled question of who exactly the British were fighting. Two modern histories provide a good general view of the Afghan Wars and North-West Frontier campaigns, Michael Barthorp's *The North-West Frontier: British India and Afghanistan, a Pictorial History 1839–1947* (Poole, 1982), and T.A. Heathcote's *The Afghan Wars 1839–1919* (London, 1980). For the First Afghan War see P. Macrory's *Signal Catastrophe: The Story of the Disastrous Retreat from Kabul 1842* (London, 1966), and J.A. Norris' *The First Afghan War* (Cambridge, 1967). Indispensable as eyewitness accounts are Lieutenant Vincent Eyre's *The Military Operations at Cabul* (London, 1843), and *A Journal of the Disasters in Affghanistan 1841–2* by the feisty Lady Sale (London, 1843; reprinted as *Lady Sale: The First Afghan War*, London, 1969). Brian Robson's *The Road to Kabul: The Second Afghan War 1878–1881* (London, 1986) is arguably one of the best modern studies of a British campaign on the Indian borders, whilst Colonel Leigh Maxwell's *My God! – Maiwand: Oper-*

*ations of the South Afghanistan Field Force 1878–80* (London, 1979) is the definitive study of a battle which stands comparison with Isandlwana as a downright disaster. Captain H.L. Nevill's *North-West Frontier* (London, 1912, reprinted 1992) includes many military details of the Frontier campaigns, whilst Sir Olaf Caroe's *The Pathans, 550BC–AD 1957* (London 1958) is still a valuable study of one of the most intractable enemies faced by the British army in the Victorian era. For the campaigns in Burma, see G. Bruce, *The Burma Wars 1824–1886* (London, 1973), and A.T.Q. Stewart's *The Pagoda War: Lord Dufferin and the Fall of the Kingdom of Ava 1885–86* (London 1972).

British campaigns in southern Africa during the nineteenth century have recently attracted a good deal of attention, and this is likely to continue as the centenary of the Boer War approaches. Michael Barthorp's *The Anglo-Boer Wars: The British and the Afrikaners 1815–1902* (Poole, 1987) is one of the few works which places the 1899–1902 campaign in the context of the earlier fights with the Voortrekkers and the 1881 Transvaal War, although the early material is inevitably covered in brief. For the most part, accounts of the fight for Port Natal, and of the battles of Zwartkopjes and Boomplaats, can only be found in more general histories, such as Oliver Ransford's *The Great Trek* (London, 1972). Joseph Lehman's *The First Boer War, 1881* (London, 1972) is the most recent history of that fiasco, although perhaps in need of some revision. Contemporary accounts of the 1881 campaign include Lady Bellairs' *The Transvaal War 1880–81* (Edinburgh, 1885, reprinted Cape Town, 1972), T.F.A. Carter's *Narrative of the Boer War: Its Causes and Results* (London, 1896), and Charles Norris-Newman's *With the Boers in the Transvaal and Orange Free State 1880–1* (London, 1882, reprinted Johannesburg, 1976). Ian Castle's *Majuba: Hill of Destiny* (London, 1996) presents a fresh and lively analysis of the campaign's most famous battle. The literature of the Second Anglo-Boer War is, of course, immense; G. Hackett's *South*

*African War Books* (London, 1994) is an indispensable guide to books published on the subject before 1920. Thomas Pakenham's *The Boer War* (London, 1979) is justifiably regarded as the best modern single-volume history of the war, although sometimes a little weak on military matters (the same author's *The Scramble for Africa* [London, 1991] provides a perceptive study of the European rush to colonise Africa as a whole, but is marred by lapses of detail). The most detailed contemporary study is the seven-volume *The Times History of the War in South Africa* (London 1900–9), edited by L.S. Amery, which covers the fighting in exhaustive detail, but which, being written partly as a critique of Buller and the army's early failings, has a definite bias. W. Baring Pemberton's *Battles of the Boer War* (London, 1964) provides a crisp study of the major battles, whilst Emanoel Lee's *To the Bitter End: A Photographic History of the Boer War* (London, 1985) sheds light on areas of the conflict often overlooked in more conventional accounts, such as the guerrilla struggle and medical aspects of the war. W.H. Wilson's jingoistic *With The Flag To Pretoria* (London, 1900–1) and *After Pretoria, the Guerrilla War* (1902) are still important, if only for the extraordinary wealth of illustrations they contain, whilst modern academic approaches to the war are outlined in Peter Warwick (ed), *The South African War: The Anglo-Boer War 1899–1902* (London, 1980). Boer perspectives of the conflict can be found in Christiaan De Wet's *Three Years War 1899–1902* (London, 1902) and Denys Reitz's *Commando: A Boer Journal of the Boer War* (London, 1933, reprinted many times).

The campaigns against black Africans south of the Limpopo are in urgent need of a modern reappraisal. This process has already begun with the Cape Frontier Wars with Noel Mostert's mammoth yet enthralling and moving *Frontiers: The Epic of South Africa's Creation and the Tragedy of the Xhosa People* (London, 1992), the first complete history of a century of conflict which sympathetically examines the plight of the

Xhosa. John Milton's *The Edges of War* (Cape Town, 1983) covers the same ground in less depth, but with a greater military emphasis and more illustrations. The campaigns against the BaSotho have not been satisfactorily covered, but are outlined in Peter Sanders' *Moshoeshoe, Chief of the Sotho* (London, 1975). Peter Delius' *The Land Belongs To Us* (Johannesburg, 1983) provides an analytical study of the Pedi kingdom, but is rather better on the causes of conflict with the British in the 1870s than on military detail. Ian Knight's *Warrior Chiefs of Southern Africa* (Poole, 1994) includes introductory biographies of black leaders who resisted colonial expansion, including Moshoeshoe and Maqoma of the Xhosa.

By contrast, the literature on the Anglo-Zulu War is immense; Ian Knight's *Brave Men's Blood: The Epic of the Zulu War* (London, 1990) is an illustrated account of the war from British and Zulu perspectives, whilst the same author's *Zulu: The Battles of Rorke's Drift and Isandlwana* (London, 1992) is a detailed study of Isandlwana, as *Nothing Remains But To Fight* (London, 1993) is of Rorke's Drift. *Fearful Hard Times*, by Ian Castle and Ian Knight (London, 1994), is the first detailed study of the neglected Eshowe campaign. *Kingdom and Colony at War*, by John Laband and Paul Thompson (Cape Town and Pietermaritzburg, 1990), consists of a number of essays examining less well-documented aspects of the war. John Laband's *Kingdom in Crisis: The Zulu Response to the British Invasion of 1879* (Manchester, 1992) is the definitive study of the war from the Zulu perspective, whilst the same author's *Rope of Sand: The Zulu Kingdom in the Nineteenth Century* (Cape Town, 1995) is the best and most comprehensive modern history of the Zulu Kingdom. *The Anatomy of the Zulu Army: From Shaka to Cetshwayo 1818–1879* by Ian Knight (London, 1994) is a detailed description of the military machine the British strove so hard to break up.

For the campaigns in northern Africa, the Abyssinian expedition of 1868 is discussed in Sir Darrell Bates' *The Abyssinian Difficulty: The Emperor Theodorus and the Magdala Campaign 1867–68* (London, 1979) and Frederick Myatt's *The March to Magdala: The Abyssinian War of 1868* (London, 1970). Michael Barthorp's *War on the Nile: Britain, Egypt and the Sudan 1882–1898* provides a good illustrated overview of the Egyptian entanglement and subsequent campaigns in the Sudan, whilst a detailed military account of the 1882 expedition can be found in Colonel J.F. Maurice's semi-official *Military History of the Campaign of 1882 in Egypt* (London, 1887). Most accounts of the Sudan campaigns concentrate on the Gordon Relief Expedition, such as Julian Symons' *England's Pride: The Story of the Gordon Relief Expedition* (London, 1965). Contemporary biographies of Gordon encouraged his image as a Christian martyr and are often poorly researched and openly eulogistic, but Gordon's own journal of the siege of Khartoum has been published as *General Gordon's Khartoum Journal,* edited by Lord Elton (London, 1961), whilst C. Chevenix Trench's *The Road To Khartoum: A Life of General Gordon* (London, 1972) attempted a clear and unbiased portrait of a complex personality. Brian Robson's *Fuzzy-Wuzzy: The Campaigns in the Eastern Sudan* (Tunbridge Wells, 1990) is an excellent modern account of the fighting around Suakin. For histories of the Mahdist state, see *The Mahdiya: A History of the Anglo-Egyptian Sudan 1881–1899* by A.B. Theobald (London, 1957) and *The Mahdist State in the Sudan 1881–1898* by P.M. Holt (Oxford 1958). 'Ismat Hasan Zulfo's *Karari: The Sudanese Account of the Battle of Omdurman* (translated by Peter Clark; London, 1980) is an invaluable account based on Sudanese sources.

For campaigning in West Africa, Alan Lloyd's *The Drums of Kumasi: The Story of the Ashanti Wars* (London, 1964) is a good introduction to a century of conflict on the Gold Coast, whilst Captain Henry Brakenbury – Wolseley's military secretary – described the 1873–4 campaign in semi-official detail in *The Ashanti War: A Narrative prepared from Official Documents* (London, 1874). Robert Baden-Powell's *The Downfall of Prempeh: A Diary of Life with the Native Levy in Ashanti 1895–96* (London, 1896) is an account of the 'bloodless' 1895 campaign by a participant, whilst I. McInnes and M. Fraser's *Ashanti 1896* (Chippenham, 1987) provides an exhaustive study of the troops eligible for the 'Ashanti Star' medal. The 1900 campaign is described in Major Frederick Myatt's *The Golden Stool: An Account of the Ashanti War of 1900* (London, 1966). H. Bacon's *Benin, the City of Blood* (London, 1898) provides an account of the 1897 expedition – though, as the title suggests, it is hardly even-handed – whilst Lieutenant Seymour Vandeleur's *Campaigning on the Upper Nile and Niger* (London, 1898) describes the little-known British campaigns against the Moslem Caliphates of Northern Nigeria. Douglas Jardine's *The Mad Mullah of Somaliland* (London, 1923) is the standard work on the Somali campaigns.

Surprisingly, in recent times the British campaigns in China during the 1830s–40s and 1850s–60s have attracted rather more attention than the later Boxer Rebellion. J. Beeching's *The Chinese Opium Wars* (London, 1975), E. Holt's *The Opium Wars in China* (London, 1962), Douglas Hurd's *The Arrow War: An Anglo-Chinese Confusion 1856–60* (London, 1967) and Michael Mann's *China 1860* (Salisbury, 1989) all consider the early entanglements. Much of the literature in English on the Boxer Rebellion tends to concentrate on the siege of the foreign legations, such as P. Fleming's *The Siege at Peking* (London, 1959), but Major E.W.M. Norrie's official history, *Military Operations in China 1900–1901* (London, 1903, reprinted 1995), includes in addition the activities of the China Field Force. Similarly, the Anglo-Maori Wars have traditionally excited little interest outside New Zealand, despite the extraordinary nature of Maori resistance. A superb modern study, which includes a brief outline of operations, an analysis of both British and Maori fighting techniques, and a stunning collection of illustrations, is Tim Ryan and Bill Parham's *The Colonial New Zealand Wars* (Wellington, 1986). J. Belich's *The New Zealand Wars and the Victorian Interpretation of Racial Conflict* (London, 1986) is highly regarded as a modern analytical appraisal. T. Gibson's *The Maori Wars: The British Army in New Zealand 1840–1872* (London, 1974) provides a useful overview. For the Canadian campaigns, see Michael Mann's *A Particular Duty: The Canadian Rebellions 1837–38* (Salisbury, 1986), Captain J.A. Macdonald's *Troublous Times in Canada: A History of the Fenian Raids of 1866 and 1870* (reprinted London, 1985), and D. Ross and C. Tyler's *Canadian Campaigns 1860–70* (London, 1992).

There have been a number of studies of the evolution of British battle techniques over the Victorian period – notably Hugh Strachan's *From Waterloo to Balaclava: Tactics, Technology and the British Army 1815–1854* (Cambridge, 1985) and Frederick Myatt's *The Soldier's Trade* (London, 1974) – but for a concise introduction one need look no further than Michael Barthorp's series of four monographs, *The British Army on Campaign 1816–1902* (London, 1987–8). These also include by far the best résumé of campaign uniform details and weapons, although the same author's *British Cavalry Uniforms since 1660* (Poole, 1984) and *British Infantry Uniforms since 1660* (Poole, 1982) are also worth consulting. Ian Knight's *Queen Victoria's Enemies* (four volumes, London, 1989–90) are intended to provide a counterpart to *The British Army on Campaign*, and therefore cover the armies of the various opposition groups, from Afghans to Zulus. C. Callwell's *Small Wars: Their Principles and Practice* (London, 1906) is a classic text-book on colonial campaigning, drawing lessons from across the Victorian period, yet, ironically, published when such campaigning was largely a thing of the past. For a detailed study of the British cavalry, which includes not only history, but analysis of tactical theory and way of life, see the Marquess of Anglesey's *A History of the British Cavalry* *1816–1919* (four volumes, London, 1973–86). A useful summary of the mechanics of colonial warfare in Africa can be found in Howard Whitehouse's *Battle in Africa 1879–1914* (Nottinghamshire, 1987).

It was almost *de rigeur* for Victorian officers to spend their retirement writing their memoirs; it would be impossible to list them all here, though almost all are worth reading in direct proportion to the role played by their author. Almost all of the principal commanders of the period either wrote an autobiography or have been the subject of a biography. To mention but a few, Sir Garnet Wolseley's *The Story of a Soldier's Life* (London, 1903) is primarily concerned with his early career and the influential Asante campaign, whilst Evelyn Wood's autobiography covers a remarkable career which took him *From Midshipman to Field Marshal* (London, 1905), via most of the campaigns from the Crimea to Egypt. Redvers Buller, whose outstanding career in the 1870s and 1880s was plunged into controversy by his handling of the Natal campaign in 1899–1900, was the subject of C.H. Melville's *The Life of General Rt. Hon. Sir Redvers Buller* (London, 1923), which made extensive use of his papers, and, more recently, Geoffrey Powell's reappraisal, *Buller, a Scapegoat? The Life of General Sir Redvers Buller VC* (London, 1994). The eccentric Sir Harry Smith's autobiography was edited by G.C. Moore-Smith as *The Autobiography of Sir Harry Smith* (London, 1902). Lord Chelmsford never wrote an autobiography, but his papers form the basis of the supportive *Lord Chelmsford and the Zulu War*, by Major G. French (London, 1939), and the rather more critical *Lord Chelmsford's Zulu Campaign 1878–1879*, edited by John Laband (Manchester, 1994). Some accounts are interesting for the staggering amount of service they describe; Sir Horace Smith-Dorrien's *Memoirs of Forty-Eight Years Service* (London, 1925) see him make an extraordinary journey from survivor of Isandlwana to a Divisional commander in the First World War, whilst Sir Bindon Blood's *Four Score Years and Ten: The Reminiscences of Sir Bindon Blood* (London, 1933) cover similar ground and reveal a delightful *joie de vie*. Field Marshal Sir William Robertson's *From Private To Field Marshal* gives a vivid insight into that rare breed, the officer who rose through the ranks, chiefly through Indian service, whilst Winston Churchill – whose own rise was by no means insignificant – described his early Frontier, Sudan and Boer War adventures in *The Story of the Malakand Field Force* (London, 1898), *The River War: An Account of the Reconquest of the Sudan* (London, 1899), *London to Ladysmith via Pretoria* (London, 1900), and elsewhere.

Accounts by men in the ranks are, of course, much thinner on the ground, if only because many remained illiterate throughout the period; they are, therefore, all the more interesting where they do survive. Sergeant Major Tim Gowing's *Voice From The Ranks; A Personal Narrative of the Crimean Campaign by a Sergeant of the Royal Fusiliers* (London edition, 1954, edited by Kenneth Fenwick), *Sergeant Pearman's Memoirs* (edited by the Marquess of Anglesey, London, 1968), F. Richard's *Old Soldier Sahib* (London, 1936; reprinted 1983), and Private Tucker's *Boer War Diary* (edited by P. Todd and D. Fordham, London, 1980) between them straddle the period. Michael Barthorp's *To Face the Daring Maoris: Soldiers' Impressions of the First Maori War 1845–47* (London, 1979) presents the early New Zealand conflicts through the eyes of soldiers of the 58th Regiment, whilst Frank Emery's masterly anthologies, *The Red Soldier* (London, 1978) and *Marching Over Africa* (London, 1986) bring vividly to life the realities of campaigning in the Zulu War and Asante, Egyptian and Sudanese campaigns respectively. *The Royal Magazine* published a number of eyewitness accounts of great battles in a series entitled *Survivors' Tales of Great Events* in 1905, and finally a number of accounts quoted in the present work first appeared in a little-known but vivid anthology, *Told from the Ranks* (London, 1897).

# INDEX